Ways of Reading

Ways of Reading is a best-selling core textbook for undergraduate students of English Language and English Literature, providing readers with the tools to analyse and interpret the meanings of literary and non-literary texts.

Six sections, comprising twenty-five self-contained units, cover:

- techniques of analysis and problem-solving
- language variation
- attributing meaning
- poetic uses of language
- narrative
- drama and performance texts.

The book combines the linguistic and literary background to each topic with discussion of examples from books, poems, magazines and online sources, and links those examples to follow-up practical activities and a list of titles for further reading.

This fourth edition has been redesigned and updated throughout, with many fresh examples and exercises. Further reading suggestions have been brought up to date and new material on electronic sources and the internet has been integrated. *Ways of Reading* continues to be the core resource for students of English Language and Literature.

Martin Montgomery is Head of the Department of English at the University of Macau, China. He is the author of *The Discourse of Broadcast News: A Linguistic Approach* (2007) and *An Introduction to Language and Society* (1995), both published by Routledge, and a contributor to several books and journals.

Alan Durant is Professor of Communication at Middlesex University, UK. His books include *Meaning in the Media: Discourse, Controversy and Debate* (2010), *Language and Media* (co-written with Marina Lambrou; Routledge, 2009) and *How to Write Essays and Dissertations: A Guide for English Literature Students* (co-written with Nigel Fabb, 2006).

Tom Furniss is Senior Lecturer in English Studies at the University of Strathclyde, UK. His books include *Reading Poetry: An Introduction*, 2nd edition (co-written with Michael Bath, 2007).

Sara Mills is Professor in the Department of English Studies at Sheffield Hallam University, UK. Her books include *Language, Gender and Feminism* (2011), *Feminist Stylistics* (1995) and *Discourse* (1997), all published by Routledge.

Ways of Reading

Advanced reading skills for students of English Literature

Fourth Edition

Martin Montgomery, Alan Durant, Tom Furniss and Sara Mills

Routledge
Taylor & Francis Group

LONDON AND NEW YORK

Fourth edition published 2013
by Routledge
2 Park Square, Milton Park, Abingdon, Oxon OX14 4RN

Simultaneously published in the USA and Canada
by Routledge
711 Third Avenue, New York, NY 10017

Routledge is an imprint of the Taylor & Francis Group, an informa business

First edition published 1992 by Routledge
Second edition published 2000 by Routledge
Third edition published 2007 by Routledge

British Library Cataloguing in Publication Data
A catalogue record for this book is available from the British Library

Library of Congress Cataloging in Publication Data
Ways of reading: advanced reading skills for students of English
   literature/Martin Montgomery . . . [et al.]. – 4th ed.
   p. cm.
   Includes bibliographical references and index.
   1. English literature – History and criticism – Theory, etc. 2. English
   literature – Problems, exercises, etc. 3. Reading (Higher education)
   4. Reading comprehension. 5. Books and reading. 6. College readers.
   I. Montgomery, Martin. II. Title.
   PR21.W39 2012
   808′.0427 – dc23   2012009855

ISBN: 978–0–415–67748–6 (hbk)
ISBN: 978–0–415–67747–9 (pbk)

Typeset in Times Ten Roman and Stone Sans
by Florence Production Ltd, Stoodleigh, Devon

Printed and bound by CPI Group (UK) Ltd, Croydon, CR0 4YY

Contents

Acknowledgements

Many people besides the authors have contributed in different ways to earlier editions of this book, including editors at Routledge and teachers, students and other readers who have offered feedback on the text and activities. With this fourth edition, the authors would like to thank Sophie Jaques at Routledge and especially Jack Howells at Florence Production for his detailed work on the manuscript.

The publishers and the authors would like to thank the following for permission to reproduce copyright material:

1.1 Ee Tiang Hong for kind permission to reprint 'Tranquerah Road', *Ee Tiang Hong Selected Poems*.

3.1 Credit line: The lines from 'anyone lived in a pretty how town'. Copyright 1940, © 1968, 1991 by the Trustees for the e.e. cummings Trust. From *Complete Poems: 1904–1962* by e.e. cummings, edited by George J. Firmage. Used by permission of Liveright Publishing Corporation.

4.2 Random House Inc. for kind permission to reprint extract from Ralph Ellison, *Invisible Man* (Penguin, 1965 – first published by Gollancz, 1953).

5.1 Rogers, Coleridge & White Ltd for permission to reprint extracts from A.S. Byatt, The Children's Book (Chatto and Windus). Copyright © 2009 A.S. Byatt. Reproduced by permission of the author c/o Rogers, Coleridge & White Ltd, 20 Powis Mews, London W11 1JN.

7.1 Faber & Faber for permission to reprint T.S. Eliot, 'The Love Song of J. Alfred Prufrock' (1915).

7.1 Houghton Mifflin Harcourt for kind permission to reprint Excerpt from 'The Love Song of J. Alfred Prufrock' from *Collected Poems 1909–1962* by T.S. Eliot (Orlando: Harcourt, 1991).

7.2 'Vlamertinghe: Passing the Chateau, July 1917', by Edmund Blunden, is reproduced by permission of PFD (www.pfd.co.uk) on behalf of the estate of Mrs Claire Blunden.

8.1 *Hotel du Lac* by Anita Brookner (Copyright © Anita Brookner, 1984) reprinted by permission of A.M. Heath & Co. Ltd Authors' Agents.

8.2 Penguin for kind permission to reprint *Under the Volcano* by Malcom Lowry (Jonathan Cape 1947, Penguin Books 1962). Copyright © The Estate of

Malcolm Lowry, 1947. Introduction copyright © Michael Schmidt, 2000. From *Under the Volcano* by Malcolm Lowry, published by Jonathan Cape. Reprinted by permission of The Random House Group Ltd.

8.3 *The Keys to the Street* by Ruth Rendell, published by Arrow Books. Reprinted by permission of The Random House Group Ltd.

8.3 Extract from *The Keys to the Street* by Ruth Rendell (© Ruth Rendell, 1997) is printed by permission of United Agents (www.unitedagents.co.uk) on behalf of Ruth Rendell.

12.2 'L'art, 1910' by Ezra Pound, from *Personae*, copyright © 1926 by Ezra Pound. Reprinted by permission of New Directions Publishing Corp.

12.2 Faber & Faber for permission to reprint 'L'art, 1910' by Ezra Pound, from *Personae*, copyright © 1926 by Ezra Pound. Reprinted by permission of New Directions Publishing Corps and Faber & Faber.

12.3 Alan Spence. '2 Haikus' from *Intimate Expanses*. Reproduced with permission of Curtis Brown Ltd London on behalf of Alan Spence. Copyright © Alan Spence, 1986.

12.4 'You Fit into Me' from *Power Politics* by Margaret Atwood. Copyright © 1971, 1996 by Margaret Atwood. Reprinted by permission of House of Anansi Press, Toronto.

12.5 Rogers, Coleridge & White Ltd for permission to reprint material from Adrian Henri's 'On the Late Late Massachers Stillbirths and Deformed Children a Smoother Lovelier Skin Job'. Copyright © 1986 Adrian Henri. Reproduced by permission of the Estate of Adrian Henri c/o Rogers, Coleridge & White Ltd, 20 Powis Mews, London W11 1JN.

12.6 René Magritte, Belgian, 1898–1967, *Time Transfixed*, 1938, oil on canvas, 147 × 98.7 cm, Joseph Winterbotham Collection, 1970. 426, The Art Institute of Chicago. Copyright © ADAGP, Paris and DACS, London 2011.

13.1 Bloodaxe Books for permission to reprint extract from Sonnet III from 'Fifty Sonnets', Eleanor Brown's *Maiden Speech* (Bloodaxe books, 1996).

13.2 'We talk of taxes, and I call you friend', copyright © 1921, 1948, by Edna St. Vincent Millay. Reprinted by permission of Holly Peppe, Literary Executor, The Millay Society.

14.3 Poem written anonymously in France during the thirteenth century and trans. by Carol Cosman, 'I am a young girl', *The Penguin Book of Women Poets*. Penguin.

15.5 Horoscope for Libra and Aquarius from the *Observer* magazine (2005). Reproduced by kind permission of Neil Spencer.

18.2 Curtis Brown for permission to reprint extract from Winston Churchill's speech: reproduced with permission of Curtis Brown, London, on behalf of the Estate of Sir Winston Churchill. Copyright © Winston S. Churchill.

19.1 'Message Clear', by Edwin Morgan, reproduced by kind permission of Carcanet Press Ltd.

19.2 'The Paschal Moon', by E.J. Scovell, from *Selected Poems, 1991*, Carcanet Press Ltd. Reproduced with permission.

19.4 *A Hanging* by George Orwell (Copyright © George Orwell, 1931); *Nine-teen Eighty Four* by George Orwell (Copyright © George Orwell, 1949). Reprinted by permission of Bill Hamilton as the Literary Executor of the Estate of the Late Sonia Brownell Orwell and Secker & Warburg Ltd.

19.4 Houghton Mifflin Harcourt Publishing Company for kind permission to reprint extracts from *Nineteen Eighty Four* and *Shooting an Elephant* by George Orwell.

21.1 Reprinted with the permission of Scribner, a division of Simon & Schuster, Inc., from *The Great Gatsby* by F. Scott Fitzgerald. Copyright © 1925 by Charles Scribner's Sons. Copyright renewed © 1953 by Frances Scott Fitzgerald Lanahan. All rights reserved.

21.2 Faber & Faber for permission to reprint William Golding, *Lord of the Flies* (1954).

21.2 Penguin Group US, Inc., for kind permission to reprint extracts from William Golding, *Lord of the Flies* (1954).

21.4 The Society of Authors as agent for the Estate of Rosamond Lehmann for kind permission to reprint an extract from Rosamund Lehmann, *The Weather in the Streets* (1936).

22.3 Rogers, Coleridge & White Ltd for permission to reprint material from Nancy Mitford, *The Pursuit of Love*. Copyright © 1945 Nancy Mitford. Reproduced by permission of the Estate of Nancy Mitford c/o Rogers, Coleridge & White Ltd, 20 Powis Mews, London W11 1JN.

23.1 *The Well of Loneliness* by Radclyffe Hall (copyright © Radclyffe Hall, 1928). Reprinted by permission of A.M. Heath & Co. Ltd Authors' Agents.

23.2 Aitken Alexander Associates Ltd for permission to reprint extract from Mark Haddon, *The Curious Incident of the Dog in the Night-Time*, p. 7. Copyright © Mark Haddon, 2003.

23.2 Random House Inc. for kind permission to reprint extract from Mark Haddon, *The Curious Incident of the Dog in the Night-Time* (2003), p. 7.

24.1 *Cloud Nine* by Caryl Churchill, copyright © 1979, 1980, 1983, 1984, 1985 Caryl Churchill. Reprinted by permission of the publisher: www.nickhern books.co.uk.

25.1 Dylan Thomas's 'Under Milk Wood' (Orion) used with the permission of David Higham Associates.

Disclaimer

Introduction

This is the fourth edition of *Ways of Reading*, a textbook that has now been in use in universities and colleges for approximately twenty years and sold over 40,000 copies. Our overall aim in preparing this new edition remains the same as with earlier editions: we intend the book to provide you with a one-stop shop in developing the reading skills needed in any programme that requires you to combine observation, textual evidence and argument in your engagement with literary works. The skills we introduce will support and clarify your reading of literary texts, and help you articulate your response to what you read. They will also provide you with an informed route into more specialized literary–critical and literary–theoretical topics explored in more detail elsewhere in your programme.

To achieve this overall aim, the book is divided into a series of twenty-five units. Each unit is organized into sections dealing with particular areas of description and skills (asking questions; method of analysis; variation in language; narrative; drama; etc.). The units are presented in an order we consider coherent if the book is read straight through from beginning to end. *Ways of Reading*, we know from feedback on earlier editions, is commonly used in this linear way, as a prescribed textbook accompanying a course that takes place over somewhere between twenty and thirty sessions. In such courses, each unit typically represents a week's work, combining the following activities: reading the unit and looking closely at the examples it contains; carrying out the activity (usually in class, and often in groups); following up with further reading; and drawing comparisons with other similar or contrasting literary and non-literary examples.

But *Ways of Reading* can also be used in other ways. Each unit is designed to be self-contained. Any given unit can be read on its own to support work on a particular topic or project, in isolation from engaging with the rest of the book and independently of group work or course participation. Cross-references between units are given in boldface throughout, so that a reader who is unsure of some aspect of discussion, or who wishes to carve out a particular, developing thread of ideas for himself or herself, can quickly refer to relevant material elsewhere in the book (subject to the proviso that extensive cross-referencing in a book presents the same risk as links on the internet: displacement from one thing you are reading into browsing many related but different pages that can distract you from what you were originally thinking about). An extensive Glossary is also provided, to help readers who start on a particular topic from an unexpected direction or without sufficient familiarity with key terms and concepts explained elsewhere in the book.

Each unit in *Ways of Reading* contains exposition of the main terms, concepts and techniques associated with the topic it addresses. The units also illustrate those concepts and techniques with short extracts and commentary, and present an activity at the end for further self-study or group work, or for use as an assessed coursework task. Where there are specific answers to questions posed in the activities, or additional information that is needed to progress through the tasks we propose, further essential material is presented at the end of the book. Most of the activities, however, are more open-ended. They outline a framework for your discussion and analysis, usually in a series of steps that build cumulatively but that are not expected to lead to a fixed destination point. Carrying out the task successfully calls for engagement with the questions or problems posed, based on pre-reading of the exposition given in the unit.

The extracts we use to illustrate our discussion, and as the basis for the activities at the end of each unit, come from a wide range of literary works and related kinds of discourse. In some cases, we have chosen extracts from well-known literary works as illustrations and to provide material to work on in the activities. In other cases, we have chosen extracts from texts that we do not expect readers to have seen or even heard of. Indeed in some cases, the *point* of our use of a passage depends on, or is significantly strengthened by, its unfamiliarity. The result is that for any given reader some excerpts may appear highly familiar while other excerpts will almost certainly be completely new. This combination is not intended to feel unsettling or to imply a list of books that people studying literature courses should have read or which should be on a prescribed syllabus. We are not seeking to promote a particular corpus or canon of works in our selection of excerpts. The extracts are exactly *illustrative*: they show how a concept applies, or how a technique can be used. The texts to which they are applied in a given unit are chosen to be helpful, as well as to be suggestive of various kinds of historical and thematic significance. But the test of ways of reading is to carry over methods and insights into reading new texts: not always literary works, but also kinds of non-literary discourse such as newspaper or magazine articles, or adverts, as well as media discourse such as films, television or radio programmes, and websites. Such transfer of skill and approach should significantly sharpen your reading of all texts with new modes of observation, description and analysis.

In preparing the present edition, we have built on what was distinctive in our original concept for the book. But we have also taken the opportunity to make changes in a number of ways, beyond general updating. By reorganizing material, for example, we have emphasized how some topics and skills relate especially closely to the different established literary forms of novel, poem and play. We have also extended our range of literary examples, still combining canonical with new or unfamiliar extracts as before but seeking as far as the book's format permits to reflect more prominently the changing geography of literary writing in English.

Our discussion of using information sources in reading now focuses far more – as it should, given not only student readers' but everyone's rapidly changing habits in using information sources – on internet-based and other electronic resources.

Two main educational considerations distinguish the period in which the first edition was conceived (around 1990) and the present, and we have tried to respond to changing circumstances as we understand them.

First, in literary studies of that earlier period, it was far less common than it is now to draw attention to linguistic similarities between literary writing, non-literary print texts and creative semiotic work in other media (such as television and film). The first edition of *Ways of Reading* accordingly placed considerable emphasis on demonstrating such similarities. For example, we sought wherever possible to make connections between literary language, the language of news-papers and advertising, and the soundtracks of radio, television and film. We also worked to highlight the transfer of what (in the current era of digital convergence) is generally called 'content' between different media 'platforms', for example by means of script writing, storyboarding, and the creation of new versions of literary material in different formats. That overlap and interaction is now much more accepted than it was then, and has been extensively discussed in other works referred to in our Further Reading. It is still the case, of course, that literary works have a lot in common with other uses of language, and yet are distinctive in some significant respects. But the belief that it seemed important to challenge around 1990 (namely, that such distinctiveness amounted to a unique 'literary language', consisting of devices rarely encountered in other kinds of discourse) was already weakening then and is now largely discredited. What is specific in ways of reading *literary* texts needs now to be understood slightly differently: as a combination of language forms with particular interpretive approaches conditioned by social expectations as regards what literature is. Overlap of techniques and effects between ways of reading literary works and ways of reading other kinds of discourse is now something that can be built on, as much as something that needs to be demonstrated or campaigned for.

A second major difference between that earlier period and now concerns the perceived status of literary studies (as of humanities education more generally). A particularly vigorous period of linguistic and literary investigation during the two decades prior to 1990 had combined with fresh analyses of forms of culture in ways that suggested that literary linguistics and stylistics might provide an effective key to wider cultural understanding and change. Literary studies were commonly elevated within the wider field of cultural enquiry into a sort of 'master discipline': a source not only of insights into questions of aesthetic value and taste but also of insights into political concerns such as gender relations and interaction between different class and ethnic groups in contemporary societies. The importance of these topics has not diminished at all, either as regards the challenge they present to interdisciplinary understanding or in relation to social reform and innovation. But increased emphasis in recent years, internationally, on vocational education and training has shifted perceptions of what literary studies is and what it is for.

We have tried to reflect such changes where appropriate, in order to engage as fully as possible with the expectations of contemporary student readers. But we also question many current expectations. Developing advanced reading skills continues, we believe, to be a crucial process in questioning and affirming personal identity, as well as in developing cultural perspective and a sense of priorities, including but not only professional priorities. In a way more sharply delineated now than when *Ways of Reading* was first written, major challenges face literary studies in drawing attention to how reading skills and the critical reflection they make possible are empowering, both personally and in the wider social sphere.

It would be inappropriate not to include in the Introduction to a book called *Ways of Reading* at least some brief comment on 'reading'. In a familiar sense, reading is a developmental skill typically acquired in childhood with varying amounts of instruction and support, then built on throughout the rest of life; it offers an essential means of access to information, opinion and entertainment. But reading understood in this way involves a set of skills which remain unevenly socially distributed and developed to different extents in different people, partly depending on social and educational opportunity. Ways of reading are accordingly not only a resource that can take alternative forms but are generally available; they are individual and social assets that need to be actively cultivated, promoted and nurtured.

What seems important to keep in mind, in thinking about ways of reading in this context, is the idea of activity: especially activities of question-raising, observation, description, conjecture and evaluation. An emphasis on such activity is especially important in literary studies now because among the many materials easily available online are to be found very large numbers of whole student essays, scholarly articles of different kinds and quality, and other sources of ready-made interpretation, comment and opinion. Some readers, especially those feeling daunted by or pressurized in their studies, may be tempted to conclude that the best 'way of reading' is to copy and paste the expressed opinions of other people into their own outward presentation of reading.

If reading is merely to serve the purpose of passing an exam, in literary study or some other field, then it might be thought that passing off an approved reading produced by someone else, either by copying or looser imitation, is a sensible strategy. That strategy brings with it a practical problem, nevertheless, along with its more obvious ethical complications: that other people can search the internet equally easily, and can use specialized software to check (including quantify) how original or not any derivative reading actually is. But there is in any case a limitation to the strategy that is far more important than this, which this book seeks to tackle. We try to show that a passive or dependent approach to reading, as a circulation and exchange of ready-made products, is neither desirable nor necessary. Whereas copying someone else's reading is disempowering, the alternative of developing your own ways of reading is empowering both in personal development, in literary studies, and across many professional fields in which close reading, interpretation and an ability to be confident and articulate about discourse you have read serves to inform decisions, assist value judgements, and guide strategic action. Such professional fields include not only those with obvious connections to literary studies, such as literary composition itself, or teaching or journalism, but also management, public and charitable service of various kinds, law, public relations, politics at all levels, and many kinds of social activism.

When we started on the first edition of *Ways of Reading* around 1990, we had little idea that the book would be in widespread use nearly a quarter of a century later. In its beginnings, *Ways of Reading* was a local initiative, conceived as teaching materials the authors wanted to develop for a new undergraduate course we were going to teach together at the University of Strathclyde, Glasgow. Seven members of the course team were involved in initial planning. One of those original members (Gillian Skirrow) sadly did not live to see the completed book, but is fondly remembered in each new edition. Another (Derek Attridge) had moved to another university before teaching materials had translated into book. The five remaining authors saw *Ways of Reading* through three editions, alongside other individual and collaborative projects (some included as further reading in this edition). Other commitments have now prevented two more of the original co-authors (Nigel Fabb and Martin Montgomery) from playing an active role in revising and adding new material for this fourth edition. But their earlier contributions remain an important element of the book and its continuing evolution.

Alan Durant
Tom Furniss
Sara Mills
2012

Basic techniques and problem-solving

SECTION 1

UNIT 1

Asking questions as a way into reading

This unit:

- introduces the main challenges presented by reading literary texts;

- outlines different kinds of 'meaning' and 'effect' that texts can give rise to, as well as the relations that exist between different kinds of reading;

- offers guidance on how to get started with reading when faced with a new passage you are not familiar with;

- distinguishes between text-related questions that have specific answers (which you can discover); 'how' questions, which call for close analysis; and more open-ended 'why' questions, which require interpretive response and argument based on such analysis, not only specific facts or information.

UNIT 1

You open a book that begins:

PROLOGUE

The Storming of Seringapatam (1799)

Extracted from a Family Paper

I address these lines – written in India – to my relatives in England. My object is to explain the motive which has induced me to refuse the right hand of friendship to my cousin, John Herncastle. The reserve which I have hitherto maintained in this matter has been misinterpreted by members of my family whose good opinion I cannot consent to forfeit. I request them to suspend their decision until they have read my narrative. And I declare, on my word of honour, that what I am now about to write is, strictly and literally, the truth.

What happens next, in reading this passage? Clearly you try to comprehend, in the sense of identifying meanings for individual words and working out relationships between them, drawing on your implicit knowledge of English **grammar** (see **Unit 3, Analysing units of structure**). If you are unfamiliar with words or idioms, you guess at their meaning, using clues presented in the context (as possibly with 'the right hand of friendship'). On the assumption that they will become relevant later, you make a mental note of **discourse** entities, such as 'my relatives in England' and 'John Herncastle', as well as possible links between them. You begin to infer a context for the passage, for instance by making decisions about what kind of **speech event** is involved: *who* is making the utterance, to *whom*, *when* and *where*? (In this case, an unnamed writer in India is addressing relatives in England – relatives who are therefore presumably also related to a certain John Herncastle – and the purpose of writing appears to be in order to correct an impression we are invited to believe the writer feels they have formed of the writer's 'reserve' in a matter that has nevertheless not, at this stage, been explained.) A world created by the text begins to build up, even though you are obliged to leave gaps: who *is* the writer who remains for the time being just 'I'? Who *are* the relatives? And what has gone on before?

As you follow interpretive strategies of this kind, which apply to all discourse (not just literary works), you are likely to speculate about what kind of text this is: how it fits into a discourse-type, or **genre** (see **Unit 4, Recognizing genre**). As it happens, the author's Introduction at the beginning of this particular book opens with the words, 'In some of my former novels . . .'. So you may surmise that the text that follows is a novel, as its title also suggests: *The Moonstone: A Romance*, by Wilkie Collins, published in 1868. Your possible assumption that you are reading a slightly formal letter must now be embedded in a more complex model: that of a fictional letter within a **narrative**, functioning (so we are told by the subtitle) as the 'Prologue' to a story that will include 'the Storming of

Seringapatam' – about which you therefore expect at some stage to be informed. Because of the fictional context, you also have to adjust any straightforward reading you may have made of the assertion that what you will be told will be 'strictly and literally, the truth'. That assertion may apply within the fictional world, but is unlikely to hold beyond it.

1.1   Comprehension and interpretive variation

The ways of reading indicated here are all kinds of comprehension. But they show comprehension to be not just a matter of passive assimilation but rather of active engagement in **inference** and problem-solving. You infer information you feel the writer has invited you to grasp by presenting you with specific evidence and clues; and you make further inferences, for instance about how the text may be significant to you, or about its plausibility. Such inferences will form the basis of a personal response, for which the **author** is far less responsible.

Conceived in this way, comprehension will not follow the same track for each **reader**. What is in question is not the retrieval of a fixed or 'true' meaning that can be read off and checked for accuracy. Rather, we ascribe meanings to texts on the basis of interaction between what we might call textual and contextual material: between kinds of organization or patterning we perceive in a text's formal structures (so especially its language structures) and various kinds of background, social knowledge, belief and attitude that we bring to the text in a reading of it.

Such background material inevitably reflects who we are. Factors such as the place and period in which we are reading, our gender, ethnicity, age and social class will encourage us towards certain interpretations but at the same time obscure or even close off others. This doesn't, however, make interpretation merely relative. Precisely because readers from different historical periods, places and social experiences will tend to produce different readings of the same words on the page – including for texts that engage with fundamental human concerns – debates about texts play an important role in social discussion of experiences, beliefs and values.

How we read a given text also depends on our particular interest in reading it. Are we studying the text and trying to respond in a way that fulfils the requirement of a given course? Reading it for pleasure? Skimming it for information? Ways of reading we follow when on a train or propped up in bed are likely to differ considerably from reading in a seminar room. These aspects of reading suggest – as others introduced later in the book will also do – that we bring an implicit (often unacknowledged) agenda to any act of reading. It doesn't necessarily follow from this that one kind of reading is more advanced or more worthwhile than another. Different kinds of reading act as useful reference points for and counterbalances to one another in a larger picture of how we use texts in making sense of and responding to the world around us. Together, they make up the reading component of your overall literacy, or relationship to your textual environment.

1.2 Types of meaning

Faced with variability in reading of this kind, some people maintain that they would prefer a single model that all textual investigation could or should follow: a 'search for meaning' that would keep to a pre-given sequence of procedures or tests. The points made above, however, suggest that meaning cannot be made uniform or singular in this way. Looking for the meaning of a text involves exploring many different sorts of question. There is a positive way of looking at this inherent variability of meaning that doesn't see it as merely loss of truth or clarity. Variation in reading can be productive as a catalyst to reflecting on how language works, what meaning is, and how reading contributes to our development and negotiation of beliefs and social values.

Before moving on to consider specific questions that can kick-start your reading of any given text, we list here the main alternative kinds of general meaning that compete for attention as you read.

1.2.1 The intended meaning?

One of the commonest ways of looking for the meaning of a text is to wonder what the author meant by it. To speculate about authorial intention, such as Shakespeare's intention in writing *Hamlet*, involves trying to extrapolate from what the text says, second-guessing a set of social circumstances very different from your own. In effect, you try to reconstruct the likely meanings or effects that a given sentence, image or reference might have had when first communicated: such meanings might be the ones that the author intended. In trying to reconstruct in this way, you make a huge imaginative leap: you try to gauge an author's beliefs, emotions, knowledge and attitudes, and to guess what the author 'had in mind' at the time of writing.

There are obvious difficulties with deciding on a text's meaning like this. A **persona**, or invented voice, might have been adopted for example, separating what the speaker or **narrator** of the text says from the writer's own thoughts or feelings. In plays, novels and narrative poems, characters speak as constructs created by the author, not necessarily as mouthpieces for the author's own thoughts. Even the speaker of a first-person **lyric poem** (the poetic 'I') must be regarded as an invented speaker, not a clear window into the writer's self.

Besides, there is no infallible way in which an intention can be verified. That is largely why the critics W.K. Wimsatt and M.C. Beardsley (1946) dismissed the quest to discover what the author 'had in mind' as an **intentional fallacy**: an unwarranted shift from what the words of a text appear to mean to what we imagine the author meant by them. In addition to difficulties presented by reading a text created in a different place or period (and by 'voices' created by the author that may be deliberately different from his or her own usual voice), language can occasionally slip away from the speaker's intentions, producing meanings that were not anticipated and sometimes undermining any seemingly intended or coherent meaning completely (see **Unit 14, Authorship and intention**).

1.2.2 The text's own meaning?

If you look for this kind of meaning (which some critics have called 'objective' interpretation), then it will be specific features of the text that provide the key to your interpretation. How the text is organized (what words and structures it uses, how images and ideas are patterned) will direct you towards a specific interpretation. What is important in this framework is to observe details of language and **form**. You examine choices of expression and the use of stylistic devices, such as parallel structures or **figurative language**, and contrast the ways the text is presented with other, alternative ways it *might have been* presented (which would have produced different meanings).

If pursued in isolation, however, this search for a meaning that should be predictable simply from the text's own organization runs into difficulties. The fact that texts are interpreted differently in different historical periods, and by differing social groups or **readerships**, challenges the notion of an 'objective' meaning determined by the words and structures of the text alone – unless only you are right and all those other readers were somehow simply mistaken. Interpretive variation suggests that the expectations readers bring to a text, and the social circumstances in which the text was produced and is interpreted, can significantly affect what it is taken to mean.

1.2.3 An individual meaning?

Perhaps the meaning of a text is neither of the above, but whatever your personal response to it is: what the text means to you. Texts are suggestive, and they undoubtedly connect with individual experiences, memories and personal associations for words and images. What you might look for and value, therefore, is your own engagement with the text, reworking it into a mental and emotional construct linked to your own life experiences.

Many critics, however, including Wimsatt and Beardsley (1949), have argued that this sort of reading involves what they call an **affective fallacy**: an over-attention to personal response at the expense of what the words of the text actually say. Concern with personal resonances of a text can displace attention away from the text's own structures and rhetorical organization: what 'the text itself says'. It is also possible that many of the memories or associations triggered as you read may be either stock responses (reactions generated by the broad topic rather than by its specific treatment in the text), or idiosyncratic reactions that go off at purely personal tangents, which may be enjoyable and rewarding but have little to do with the text that prompted them.

1.2.4 General processes of making meaning?

Meanings are produced in acts of reading that you perform on a text. So perhaps, instead of investigating details of wording that guide a particular interpretation, emphasis should be placed on the processes or procedures by which texts come to have whatever meanings are attributed to them. If that aspect of interpretation is emphasized, then looking for meaning should involve exploring conventions involved in the active process of reading such as identifying and contrasting themes, or treating elements of a text as symbols, rather than reporting outcomes of particular acts of reading. 'Readings', as products, would be valuable to the extent that they illustrate general reading processes; and the meanings you articulate would be finally only as interesting as the processes through which they were arrived at.

Reading texts in this way, however, would quickly become repetitive. Almost any text would be equally interesting as an object to apply interpretive processes to; and, while reading clearly does involve general processes, readers bring different expectations to bear, with the result that readings cannot be fully understood in terms of general codes. Nor is 'interest' in reading texts reducible to *how* interpretation takes place. It is often prompted by concern with or enthusiasm for the particular experiences or topics being represented.

1.2.5 Meaning and a text's reception?

People don't all think as you do, and they certainly haven't always thought the same as you in the past. So perhaps what a text means (since readers bring their own beliefs, attitudes and expectations into how they read) is all the various things it has meant to different readerships in the past, along with the different meanings the text has for different communities of readers today.

Readings of texts are diverse, but they are not random; they fall into types or categories, with shared or overlapping meanings in each group of readings changing over time and differing between places in describable ways. Understanding the meaning of a text might therefore mean not only accounting for an individual person's response, but also charting such responses within larger, social and historical patterns of reception: looking at readings produced by given readerships.

In advertising and market research, readers (for instance, of newspapers or magazines) are classified on the basis of social characteristics, or demographic variables, including class, age, gender and income (as As, Bs, ABs, C1s, C2s, etc.); they are commonly also classified by characteristics of mental attitude, or psychographic variables (for example as initiative-takers, individualists, tradition-followers, etc.). More often in literary criticism readers are distinguished on the basis of their taste or preference in relation to other groups (as elite and mass audiences, or readers with highbrow or popular taste). Readerships can also be identified on the basis of other considerations, including the function that reading a given text serves for someone (e.g. as a marker of social accomplishment, for study, as distraction from pain or work, or out of cultural curiosity). What potentially makes patterning within the responses of actual readers interesting is how various groups of readers appropriate core features of or statements in a discourse into their own preoccupations and ways of thinking and living.

1.2.6 Critical social meanings?

Critical social meanings are found where there is a collision or contradiction between one reader's response and a meaning commonly accepted by another group of people. As an individual reader, you are always a specific social subject, with an age, gender, ethnicity, class and educational background. Your responses and interpretations are to some extent shaped by these aspects of your location. If you express a critical or polemical view of a given text's significance and influence, you are reading that text in an actively socially engaged, rather than detached, disinterested or simply curious way. A socially 'critical' meaning of a text, in this sense, consists of a combined form of analysis: analysis of a prevailing culture's established imagery and meanings (e.g. how particular topics such as race, sexuality, work, religious belief, social conflict or money are conventionally represented); and at the same time analysis of how the established images of a given topic relate to or clash with your own sense of how such topics should be represented.

1.3 How to get started in ways of reading

In practice, the different senses of the 'meaning' of a text described above are not always easily separable from one another. Historically, however, different aspects of a text's possible meanings have been emphasized by different schools of criticism and reflected in different kinds of reading strategy. Listing the principal directions of analysis here – whether they are viewed as alternatives, or combined in more complex reading strategies – is useful if it challenges a tendency to assume that finding one kind of meaning in a text exhausts that text's interpretive possibilities.

Often when you start reading, questions about a text and a sense of its potential for meaning will flood in. Your responses begin to form, and can be traced back – if you stop to do so – to particular textual features, echoes of other texts, and parallels and contrasts with your beliefs and experiences. But not always. Sometimes you may feel stuck or uncertain how to start, as if the text is somehow blocking your usual reading strategies and reflexes. When this happens, a checklist of conventional entry points into reading can be a welcome aid. So with such occasions in mind, we offer below a list of question prompts that can help to get a reading started. In the various units that make up the rest of the book we then investigate specific topics associated with these prompts in more detail. Each question below should lead you into a practical line of enquiry. Use the contents page and index of this book to find relevant units that explore each topic further.

1.3.1 Textual questions

- Is the piece of text you are looking at the whole of that text?
- Does the text exist in only one version, or in many different versions? If in many versions, are there likely to be significant differences between them (e.g. as regards spelling, layout, typeface or even **content**)?

- Has the text been cut, edited or expurgated?
- Has the text been annotated, possibly for a new readership or new market? If so, who added the annotations, and do those annotations direct you towards one particular way of looking at the text?

1.3.2 Contextual questions

- When, where and in what circumstances was the text written?
- Do aspects of the text (such as aspects of its narrative, setting or themes) have obvious connections, especially parallels or contrasts, with things going on in the society contemporaneous with the text being produced?
- Who was the text originally aimed at? Are you part of that anticipated readership or audience?
- Was the author or text-producer male or female? Professional or amateur? A native speaker of English or a non-native speaker?
- How old was he or she when the text was written?
- How does the particular text you are looking at fit into what you know of the rest of the text-producer's output (typical? exceptional? etc.)?

1.3.3 Questions regarding the 'speech situation'

- Who is supposed to be speaking the words of the text?
- From whose point of view is the text being told?
- Who does the text appear to be addressed to?

1.3.4 Referential questions

- Does the text contain quotations from other texts?
- Does the text contain references to other literary, media, mythological or religious texts, figures or events? If so, do you know – and how much is it likely to matter whether you know – what these references refer to?
- Does the text refer to particular social attitudes, facts or beliefs about the world, or to particular historical or geographical knowledge?

1.3.5 Language questions

- Is the text in its original language or is it a translation?
- Is it likely that all the words in the text, especially words used to describe key topics or narrate key moments, still have the same meaning that they did when the text was produced?
- Are the sentences generally of the same length and complexity? If not, are the differences between them patterned or distributed in any way that appears significant?

- What sort of vocabulary do the words of the text generally come from (elevated or colloquial; technical or non-technical; standard or regional; Latinate or Germanic; etc.)?
- Were all the words and structures still current at the time the text was written or is it possible that some (e.g. 'thou') are archaisms, or words that were no longer in use and which therefore suggest an earlier period or style?
- As regards all of the above, is the text consistent, or are there contrasts or shifts within it? (For example, do different characters or speakers use language in significantly different ways?)

1.3.6   Questions of convention

- Should the way you read the text be guided by specific conventions to do with what sort of text it is (e.g. spoof or satire, 'rom com', science fiction)?
- How realistic do you expect the text to be? How, for instance, does the text create an appearance of being real or true, if it does (e.g. by including well-known or checkable details; by seeking an underlying or deeper truthfulness, despite surface implausibility)?

1.3.7   Symbolic questions

- Do names in the text refer to particular, unique individuals or do they seem to be representative, standing for general characters or character-types?
- Is it likely that places (mountains, sea, rivers . . .), weather (storms, sunset . . .) or events (marriage, travel . . .) have extra, symbolic meanings in relation to what is going on in the text?
- Is the text concerned with a specific set of events or could it be representing one set of concerns in the form of a story about another set of concerns, as a kind of allegory?
- How far could the text's title be a key to its meaning?

1.3.8   Questions of emotional effect and identification

- Do you see significant aspects of yourself in any of the characters or events depicted?
- Do any of the problems, dilemmas or issues represented in the text resonate especially with your own experience, perhaps as a member of a given social group or class?
- Does the text present anything that you consider to be a conventional fantasy scenario or form of wish fulfilment?
- Do any sections or aspects of the text repel, offend or embarrass you?

1.3.9 Questions of representation

- Do you think the text is in some way typical of its time, place and context of presentation or publication, or in terms of the **representation** of its selected themes?
- Does the text present images of socially important 'topics' such as race, women, industry, money, crime, health, personal success or fulfilment? If so, do these images seem to you to be unfair, biased or problematic?
- Does the text omit any major aspects of the topics it deals with, in ways that may restrict or limit the viewpoint it is presenting?
- Does the text treat topics in ways that seem to you to be new and instructive?

1.4 Starting your reading with questions

If you spontaneously see interesting features or details when you first engage with a given text, and feel interpretive hunches to follow, then it is probably best not to interrupt your reading to work more mechanically through a checklist of questions of the kind given above. Better, in such circumstances, to refer to such a list after you have made notes or drafted an essay outline based on your own first insights. At that later stage in your thinking, you may be able to fill out your ideas (and build up evidence you can present to support them) by comparing the viewpoint you have developed with other perspectives implicit in the checklist.

The questions listed above are only starting points. They are intended to lead into active modes of enquiry rather than being taken as a ready-made agenda that consists of simply answering them. (This applies especially if you just pick out individual questions from the list and focus on those exclusively.) One practical way of using the questions is to skim quickly through them after reading the text, deciding without any further investigation of the text what you might say in response to each (in many cases this may quite reasonably be nothing at all). As you work through the questions, however, your attention is likely to be drawn to half-noticed details you may not have considered important in your initial reading; some of these may now seem relevant or interesting in ways that can stimulate further enquiry. Generally, asking questions in this way will show you that you have richer intuitions about a text than you thought at the outset, simply by being a language user and because you have been exposed to many texts previously.

Finally, how can you deal with having no information with which to answer a given question? First, you should not see this as a permanent setback; a question in need of an answer identifies something specific to look into, and there are many ways of finding things out (see **Unit 2, Using information sources**). Also, being aware of how an answer might – or would not – contribute to an interpretation can guide your reading even without ever finding a specific answer. For many questions we ask about texts no single, definitive answer could exist; only a range of answers put forward by other people who have asked and investigated the same question before. Such answers may be immensely informative and insightful. But reading for 'meaning', as we have seen above, is a matter of interpretation rather than tracking down a single correct answer. This is partly why it is empowering to develop ways of reading through which you become better at articulating your own analysis, opinion and evidence.

1 Make a list of questions you feel it would be useful to ask about the following text. Note what information it would be helpful to know beside each question.

2 Arrange your questions under the various headings listed above ('Textual questions', 'Contextual questions', etc.). Don't worry about answers to the questions, or even about where such answers might be found. Focus instead on what *kinds of question* are worth pursuing.

ACTIVITY 1

Tranquerah Road

1
Poor relative, yet well-connected,
same line, same age as Heeren Street
(more or less, who knows?),
the long road comes and goes –
dream, nightmare, retrospect –
through my former house,
self-conscious, nondescript.

2
There was a remnant of a Portuguese settlement,
Kampong Serani, near the market,
where Max Gomes lived, my classmate.
At the end of the road, near *Limbongan*,
the Tranquerah English School,
our *alma mater*, heart of oak.

By a backlane the Methodist Girls' School,
where my sister studied
See me, mother,
Can you see me?
The Lord's Prayer, Psalm 23

The Japanese came,
and we sang the *Kimigayo*,
learnt some *Nihon Seishin*.

continued

Till their *Greater East Asia Co-Prosperity Sphere*
collapsed, and we had to change
our tune again – God Save the King
Meliora hic sequamur

The King died when I was in school,
and then, of course, God Save the Queen

While *Merdeka* inspired –
for who are so free
as the sons of the brave? –
and so *Negara-ku*
at mammoth rallies
I salute them all
who made it possible,
for better, for worse.

3
A sudden trill,
mosquito whine
like enemy aeroplane
in a blanket stillness,
the heave and fall of snoring sea,
swish and rustle of coconut,
kapok, tamarind, fern-potted,
where *pontianak* perch
by the midnight road.

Wind lifts its haunches off the sea,
shakes dripping mane,
then gallops muffle-hoofed,
a flash of whiteness in sparse bamboo in
a Malay cemetery.

Yet I shall fear no evil
for Thou art with me
though the wind is a horse
is a *jinn* raving free
Thy rod and Thy staff
they comfort me
and fear is only in the mind
as Mother said
why want to be afraid
just say *Omitohood Omitohood Omitohood*
                                        Amen.

continued

3   When you have completed your list, read the information about the poem given on p. 335. This information is drawn from notes provided with the poem in the author's *Selected Poems*. Consider how far the information provided answers the questions you have asked.

4   How would having access to the information you have now been given, when you *start* reading, affect the kind of interpretation you would be likely to produce?

5   Now examine questions that remain *unanswered* by the information provided on p. 335. Some of these unanswered questions may just require pieces of information not provided in the notes. But many will involve the word 'why?'. Consider whether there is a difference between questions beginning with 'why?' and your other questions. If so, how would you describe that difference and what implications follow from it?

6   Finally, generalize from what you have done with this particular passage. Consider how far texts in general rely on background information that will be available to differing extents to readers with different cultural background knowledge and experience.

Reading

Fabb, N. and Durant, A. (2005) *How to Write Essays and Dissertations: A Guide for English Literature Students*, 2nd edn, Harlow: Pearson.

Furniss, T. and Bath, M. (2007) *Reading Poetry: An Introduction*, 2nd edn, London: Pearson Longman, Chapter 1.

Lodge, D. (1994) *The Art of Fiction*, Harmondsworth: Penguin, especially Chapter 1 ('Beginning').

Wimsatt, W.K. and Beardsley, M.C. (1946) 'The Intentional Fallacy', in D. Lodge (ed.) (2008) *20th Century Criticism*, 3rd edn, Harlow: Longman, pp. 334–44.

Wimsatt, W.K. and Beardsley, M.C. (1949) 'The Affective Fallacy', in D. Lodge (ed.) (2008) *20th Century Criticism*, 3rd edn, Harlow: Longman, pp. 345–58.

UNIT 2

Using information sources

UNIT 2

This unit:

- introduces different kinds of information resource you will find helpful in reading literary works, including dictionaries, encyclopaedias, biographies, dictionaries of quotations, annals of literature and other reference works, both in print and online;

- shows how referring to the *Oxford English Dictionary* (OED) can illuminate a number of different aspects of a text;

- advises on use of internet-based materials, and on conducting online searches;

- discusses the issue of the relative authority of different sources you may rely on and/or quote from in writing about a literary text.

When we read a literary text (and other kinds of text, too), a stream of questions typically comes to mind, at different levels of awareness. **Unit 1, Asking questions as a way into reading** showed how those questions are of different kinds. But raising questions also begs answers, or at least routes to further investigation, and such investigation also comes in different types or categories. In this unit, we distinguish different resources associated with those various types of question, and illustrate how using information sources can enrich readings you may be developing.

2.1   Using information sources to address questions *within* the text

Most approaches to engaging with questions you raise while reading involve examining some particular feature or aspect of the text more closely.

2.1.1   Looking up words you don't know

The vocabulary of English is somewhere approaching one million words (depending on how you count them and on the difficulty of defining what a 'word' is). But the active vocabulary of any individual language user varies. There are, for example, only between 20,000 and 25,000 words in the entire works of Shakespeare; by contrast, there are typically somewhere between 60,000 and 70,000 in an average modern speaker's repertoire. One consequence of the gap between any speaker's vocabulary and the number of words available in the language overall is that there will be many words an individual speaker never uses, including many that the speaker doesn't know at all – even if English is the speaker's first (or only) language. Looking up words is therefore not a sign of ignorance but of curiosity and interest in how language is used.

Some words that you look up (or combinations of words as distinctive idioms) will turn out to be technical, others archaic, others again specific to a particular region of use, and others again words borrowed from another language (see Units 5, 6 and 7 for discussion of these possibilities and their significance). You will be able to see which characteristics apply by checking abbreviations in the dictionary entry for the word (and possibly symbols that you may need to check in the dictionary's list of symbols).

Where should you look words up? A preliminary search might be made in any general dictionary, either in print or online. But you then need to decide whether the information you have gained is sufficient for your purposes, or whether to look for more detail. For instance, you might also look in the *Collins Online Birmingham University Corpus of English* (CO-BUILD), which lists commonest contemporary meanings first, followed by other meanings. Or you might look the word up in the *Oxford English Dictionary* (the **OED**), the largest dictionary of English vocabulary. The main advantage of the OED for literary study is that it sets out the changing meanings of words, linked to the periods in which those meanings were current. Quotations are also given to show the word in use, including its earliest known occurrence. The OED online also links meanings, by means of its related thesaurus, to clusters of other words used in a given period to denote the same semantic area.

2.1.2 Looking up words you *do* know

Sometimes a word you are already familiar with may be used in an unusual or complex way. 'Nature', in Shakespeare's play *King Lear*, is a famous example. The word is used frequently by different characters, but switches between (and may combine) senses, including the brute, physical environment; the given or legitimate order of things; innate character; and ungovernable human impulses. Many literary works explore their topics by playing on (and so investigating) different possible meanings of one or more key terms. You can begin to disentangle such senses by looking the word or words up in the OED, or, for many words, in Raymond Williams's *Keywords: a Vocabulary of Culture and Society* (1976/1983), which offers mini-essays on over 100 words that have proved significant in cultural debate over the last two centuries. An online update and extension of Williams's keywords studies can be found at: http://keywords.pitt.edu.

We can illustrate what can happen if you look individual words up by considering the first stanza of Percy Bysshe Shelley's 'To a Skylark' (1820):

> Hail to thee, blithe Spirit!
> Bird thou never wert,
> That from heaven, or near it,
> Pourest thy full heart
> In profuse strains of unpremeditated art.

If you look up 'blithe' in the OED, you will find two main relevant meanings in the numbered list:

> Meaning 2: exhibiting gladness . . . In ballads frequently coupled with 'gay'. Rare in modern English prose or speech; the last quotation with this meaning is 1807.

> Meaning 3: Of men, their heart, spirit etc.: joyous . . . Rare in English prose or colloquial use since 16th century but frequent in poetry.

The dictionary entry now acts as more than a definition. It provides interesting insights into the poem. First, the word 'blithe' is used primarily in *poetry*. In Shelley's poem, even so, it may already have seemed a little old-fashioned, since 1807 is the last citation date for meaning (2). Second, the word is typically used in **ballads**. This seems significant, if we consider that Romantic poets such as Shelley were influenced by folk poetry. Third, the word is explicitly associated with the word 'spirit' in the entry, under meaning (3).

Sometimes unexpected discoveries are made by such word checks. As a result, the OED, like other dictionaries, can be used as a 'brainstorming' aid when starting out on a study project. For example, if you were interested in the concept of 'spirit' in Romantic poetry, it would be a good way of starting to look up 'spirit' in the OED, in order to see who used the word, what its history had been up to that time, how religious or otherwise its meanings were, and so on. By using an information source in this way you are adapting the OED to a new goal: you are using it as an (admittedly partial) guide to culture, as embodied in language use.

2.1.3 Investigating words or expressions that seem significant

Investigating questions of meaning in a text by exploring one or more of its key terms is not confined to disentangling that word's meanings in the abstract. Investigations can also be advanced by listing instances of the word as they occur in the work. Listing instances ('tokens') of the word can be done long-hand, by careful re-reading, manually highlighting each instance of its use. Or the same task can be done electronically, using a searchable electronic text version. For non-copyright works, you can usually find full-version copies available online; these versions are convertible into a searchable text file. To follow up initial study, it is then better to copy an editorially more authoritative version, with permission, from a specialized academic corpus. You can easily, for example, download the whole of Jane Austen's novel *Persuasion* (1818) or John Milton's epic poem *Paradise Lost* (1667).

Once you have an electronic version of the text in question, you can use a word processor or text editor to search for all examples of a particular word, such as the word 'persuasion' in the novel *Persuasion*. This could be a good way of beginning to understand why the novel has that title (though in fact there turn out to be only six tokens of 'persuasion' in the novel, less than the eight of 'persuade' and fourteen of 'persuaded'). The search process can be developed beyond a simple 'find' command, by using concordancing software (a number of simple versions are legally downloadable free online). A concordancer will yield a KWIC (or 'Key Word in Context') listing, in which each instance of the word in the text is accompanied by a stipulated number of preceding and following words (and the line can usually be clicked through to its context in the text). It is now possible to see, for example, what words are the immediate **collocates** of (words next to) 'persuasion'. This material is potentially useful since, when examined, those collocations can be related to the word's distribution and different meanings in the text (e.g. use by a particular character; use mainly in dialogue rather than in the narrator's voice; used less frequently towards the end of the text, and so on).

Even the simple number of how many times a word is used may be illuminating. By comparing the number of instances of a particular word in a given text with figures derived from much larger 'reference' corpora (collections of whole classes of material), it is possible to calculate how the frequency of a word (in the case above, of 'persuasion', only six instances) relates to frequency (often stated as number of occurrences per million words of text) in a comparable amount of discourse in the same genre, or from the same period, or in printed material generally. Alternatively, by using Google's free Ngram Viewer, you could chart relative frequency throughout the history of printed books – as so far scanned by Google (roughly 4 per cent of all printed works, but less reliable for earlier periods) – in the form of a graph. The historical Ngram for 'persuasion', whether looking at the Google corpus of British English, American English, or more specifically of British fiction, shows by far its most significant spike between 1780 and 1840, the period during which Austen was writing (*Persuasion* was published posthumously, in 1818).

2.1.4 Investigating words or expressions that may be quotations

Literary texts commonly contain quotations from other works. But how is it possible to know if something is a quotation, if there are no obvious triggers to searching for the relevant source? Recognizing embedded quotations develops with familiarity with a **corpus** of work, or literary canon (hence the premium placed in literary culture on extensive reading in a given cultural tradition). But it can also be kick-started by a query or hunch. One section of text may have quotation marks round it, yet not be attributed to a speaker; a passage may be indented or presented in a different font, without explanation; or a stretch of text may stand out because its style doesn't fit with the language around it. Following up such an observation can be done in stages, and stopped if no rewarding connection is found. A preliminary look at the OED might be combined with a browser search and/or use of a **concordance** (either in print or online). Dictionaries of quotations (again either in print or online) can also be checked.

2.1.5 Investigating cultural references

Sometimes particular words or phrases seem to refer to, or name, something that requires knowledge you don't have, but that appears to exist beyond the text world rather than in it. The information is assumed, as if you should already know it. Passages of description in fiction are often full of such references: to streets and cities, clothing, types of furniture, makes of cars, contemporaneous or well-known historical events, and aspects of assumed cultural behaviour (and conventional attitudes to them). Such assumed knowledge, however, will differ, sometimes profoundly, between places and periods. An obviously important example of this, as regards English literature, is the major difference between knowledge and beliefs as represented in – and anticipated by – Renaissance literary works and the knowledge and beliefs of modern-day readers.

We can illustrate some aspects of how some cultural references – in this case, references to names – can be identified and interpreted by looking at the opening lines of *Paradise Lost*:

Of man's first disobedience, and the fruit
Of that forbidden tree, whose mortal taste
Brought death into the world, and all our woe,
With loss of Eden, till one greater Man
Restore us, and regain the blissful seat,   (5)
Sing heavenly Muse, that on the secret top
Of Oreb, or of Sinai, didst inspire
That shepherd, who first taught the chosen seed,
In the beginning how the heavens and earth
Rose out of chaos: or if Sion hill   (10)
Delight thee more, and Siloa's brook that flowed
Fast by the oracle of God; I thence
Invoke thy aid to my adventurous song,
That with no middle flight intends to soar
Above the Aonian mount, while it pursues   (15)
Things unattempted yet in prose or rhyme.

For most modern readers, regardless of religion, this passage presents a puzzling mix of references, some better known than others. The lines are also complicated by their grammatical structure: in line 6 of the quotation the poet invites a 'heavenly Muse' to help the poet narrate in poetry ('my adventurous song') the consequences 'of man's first disobedience' until 'one greater Man' saves humankind – topics that the passage has already stated (lines 1–5).

A preliminary sense of the likely domain of cultural references is given by the title, *Paradise Lost*, although use of the term 'paradise' is not confined to only one religion. Further information can be found in Milton's statement of 'The Argument' of the poem, given at the beginning of each of the poem's twelve books (ten, in the differently arranged first edition). In relation to this opening passage, Milton states, 'This first book proposes, first in brief, the whole subject, man's disobedience, and the loss thereupon of Paradise wherein he was placed: then touches the prime cause of his fall, the serpent, or rather Satan in the serpent...' This summary is reflected directly in a statement of purpose shortly after the passage quoted above, as the poet's proclaimed wish to 'assert eternal providence, / And justify the ways of God to men'. Usefully for most modern readers, in most editions of *Paradise Lost* footnotes by an editor provide an additional information source besides the poet's own statement of 'The Argument'. Such footnotes explain particular references (so that, for instance, 'that shepherd' will be glossed as Moses); collectively, such editorial notes help to bridge the gap between what Milton assumed his readers would be familiar with and the very different typical frame of reference of modern readers.

Even if footnotes are *not* provided for particular references, however, there are often still verbal clues as to which words are likely to be significant cultural references. Proper names, beginning with upper-case letters, invite attention: 'Eden', 'Oreb', 'Sinai', 'Siloa', and so on. They can be looked up. So do phrases (often beginning with 'the' or 'that') which suggest entities being presented as already known, even where they have not been introduced directly in the text itself: 'the fruit', 'that forbidden tree', 'one greater Man', 'that shepherd', 'the chosen seed'. Each has an assumed referent that can be traced. More difficult are references to ideas, rather than to entities that convey ideas in story form: for example, 'how the heavens and earth / Rose out of chaos'. Understanding a reference of this kind calls less for simply looking something up than for an effort to understand possibly very different ideas and beliefs from the reader's own, in this case beliefs certainly from another period and for many readers also from another religion (or from *any* religion, as compared with secular belief).

The references isolated in the opening lines of *Paradise Lost* are mostly traceable to the Bible, and can be researched with a concordance of the Bible and other reference resources related to the Genesis story. But some references in the passage point in a different direction. Consider 'heavenly Muse', for instance. If we look up 'Muse', our first information is likely to involve classical Greek and Latin, rather than Biblical, origins (i.e. goddesses who were daughters of Zeus/Jupiter and Mnemosyne and who presided over poetry, music and dancing; in some accounts, nine of them but sometimes only three). Another term in the passage quoted, 'the Aonian mount', also relates to this different, polytheistic body of cultural reference. (As with all searching, it is good to compare multiple sources. But a particularly detailed guide to Classical literary references and mythology is *Lemprière's Classical Dictionary of Proper Names in Ancient Authors*, which relates references back to the Greek and Latin texts in which they can be found.)

But does such searching, we should ask, add much to reading? It will seem mechanical unless we relate what we find to some observation about the text's meaning or significance. In this case, we might infer that the density of allusions is part of Milton's evocation of an epic style. Or we might note that, unlike the Biblical references, the Classical references relate to Milton's *composition* of the poem, rather than to details in the story being narrated. We might then suggest that Milton announces his Biblical story by drawing on a Classical frame of reference for epic poetry. This would not be a new or controversial insight into how Biblical and Classical cultures are brought together in Milton's *Paradise Lost*. But the inference is built here from evidence in the poem's pattern of references (which initially we may not have known or even noticed), rather than taken on trust from someone else's critical commentary.

2.1.6 Finding out more about themes, myths and symbols

In some texts, reference is made – by means of **motifs** and symbols – to a body of folklore, cultural tradition or myth. Such references can be difficult to see because the beliefs and stories referred to often occupy a peripheral position within contemporary culture, and may have been handed down as much in oral traditions as in texts you can easily refer to. A useful general source when dealing with such references is *Brewer's Dictionary of Phrase and Fable*. This work is an originally nineteenth-century reference source described by its author as a 'Treasury of Literary bric-a-brac', periodically updated with a wide range of idioms, allusions and symbols.

Consider an old English folk poem that begins, 'A frog he would a-wooing go'. One question you might ask is: why a frog? Brewer outlines the significance of 'frog' in Aesop's Fables and in Ovid. A more specialized reference book for these purposes is also de Vries' *Dictionary of Symbols and Imagery*, which gives the following meanings:

> a frog is amphibious and therefore often ambivalent in meaning; its natural enemy is the serpent; it has a number of favourable meanings – it symbolises fertility and lasciviousness, creation, the highest form of evolution (hence princes turn into frogs), wisdom, and poetic inspiration; it also has unfavourable meanings – in religious terms it is considered unclean, and it is said to have a powerful voice but no strength.

This dictionary also tells us that in myth, 'Frogs are great wooers': there are several songs about frogs who go 'a-wooing' a mouse (perhaps originally spinning songs, as the mouse is referred to as 'spinning' several times). So we have a possible answer to the question 'why a frog?' Frogs are symbols of fertility and lasciviousness, hence wooers. The other meanings of frog as a symbol do not seem relevant (e.g. creation, wisdom, uncleanness). We may achieve similar results by using an internet search engine, but in that case we will need to search for 'frog as symbol' (just searching for 'frog' or for 'frog wooing' is unlikely to be productive). We can then perform an equivalent search, if relevant, for 'mouse'.

Despite the risk of generating irrelevant, and at worst misleading, information, it is worth using dictionaries of symbolism to investigate conventional implications of natural things mentioned in texts in this way: body parts, animals and plants, planets and stars, weather, geographical phenomena, etc. Such investigation can be especially illuminating where the text appears to be part of, or to allude to, oral or folkloric traditions in which conventional symbolic meanings will tend to have special significance.

2.2 Using information sources to address questions *about* the text

So far, we have looked at references *made in the text* to a world of facts and beliefs outside or beyond a world that the text evokes. We now consider how information sources concerned with external circumstances such as a text's publication and circulation can throw light on what the text says.

Critics in different critical traditions disagree over the significance of such 'external' information. Some have urged readers to focus exclusively on the wording of 'the text itself', or at least on an experience of reading or engagement with that wording. Other critics have countered that understanding texts – especially texts written in earlier periods or in different societies – requires an engagement with the circumstances of the text's production, as well as with the likely motives of its author, with its publication and immediate reception, and with different ways in which it has been re-read subsequently.

2.2.1 The edition of the text

A small amount of work can often tell you whether the version of a text you are reading even contains the same words as the original published version (it may have been abridged; spellings and punctuation may have been modernized; parts of the original text may have been lost or incomplete, and so on).

Consider Thomas Hardy's *Tess of the D'Urbervilles* (1891). The textual history of this novel can seem complicated and merely distracting: a series of variant manuscripts and successive published editions. But this history reveals deep hesitancy on the part of the author as regards the controversial key element of the plot: Alec's first sexual encounter with Tess, which Hardy repeatedly adjusted in seeking to represent it as a borderline between rape and some other kind of exploitative seduction. The same textual history shows pressure on Hardy to make cuts required by others in order to conform to limits on what could be depicted in the period. In one version of an episode in the novel, one Sunday morning the character Angel Clare helps four young women to keep their church clothes clean and dry by pushing them through a puddle on a flooded track in a wheelbarrow. This contrived detail was adopted because Hardy was not able to show Clare carrying each of the young women in his arms (which is how modern editions depict the episode, reflecting Hardy's wishes).

Relevant and potentially illuminating information about 'the text' can be found in most editions. Often the final stages of an editorial introduction comment on a work's publication history; and further editorial notes may be provided in footnotes or at the end of the book. In some cases, as with Milton's *Paradise Lost* above, it may be important to distinguish material added by an editor from material considered desirable or necessary at the outset, by the author. Milton judged it appropriate to add his own prose summary of 'The Argument' to each book of *Paradise Lost*. T.S. Eliot added footnotes to his modernist epic of loss and breakdown, *The Waste Land*. Publication details about texts are only *un*-interesting if they remain unconnected to lines of enquiry about *why* the text is as it is.

2.2.2 The text's author

Sometimes information about the author of a text can seem irrelevant. It may even get in the way of reading, by distorting perceptions to make the work reflect some selected aspect of the life, minimizing the power of imagination and empathy that typically leads readers to literary works in the first place. In some circumstances, however, information about for example the sequence of works in a lifetime's writing, or the relation of a publication to major events in or simultaneous with some part of the writer's life, can illuminate insights that start on the page. Information about an author's life, accordingly, if used cautiously, can be worth gathering from dictionaries of biography such as the *Dictionary of National Biography* (DNB), or from more general encyclopaedic works about literature such as the *Oxford Companion to English Literature*. We consider how views of authorship, and the assumed intentions of an author, affect reading in **Unit 14, Authorship and intention**.

2.2.3   Wider aspects of social context

Possibly more difficult in using information sources to help with reading a text is looking at relations between the text and the wider social context in which the author produced it. It is easy to jump straight from words on the page into a history of kings and queens, famous dates and events, and generalized narratives of historical progress, decline or class war. Information required to build a view of the world in which the text was published has no obvious limits. It also serves no particular purpose unless linked to an interpretive problem or objectives.

Where the social context of the text is very different from the reader's own, then alongside works of reference and general histories a graphical timeline may be useful as a means of orientation. That timeline might be divided into different historical strands (e.g. political context and public affairs; technological inventions; significant dates in the history of communication; relevant publications; changes in the conditions of social life across different social groupings). Preparing or consulting such a timeline offers a tool to trigger thoughts and connections: it can help locate the text in long-term processes of social change, and clarify a cross-sectional view of social life that illuminates the environment in which the author was working and in which the text had its initial significance. To strengthen awareness of what was going on at the same time as the work being read, an *Annals of English Literature* is similarly useful.

If we locate John Milton's *Paradise Lost* in such a historical timeline, for example, even confining our attention to a time span of roughly one human generation we might note a number of suggestive details. The poem's publication in 1667 is preceded by religious and theological upheavals of the English civil wars of the 1640s; there had been recent scientific developments, including Harvey's discovery of the circulation of the blood (1628) and Galileo's promotion of the Copernican view that the Earth moves around the Sun rather than vice versa, for which Galileo had been condemned by the Inquisition during the 1630s. Any or all of these topics might be relevant to the poem, in that they relate to events that took place in the poet's lifetime and acted as background to his own thinking. From the *Annals*, we might note other works published in the same year as *Paradise Lost*: Dryden's *Annus Mirabilis*; works by Mary Cavendish and Andrew Marvell; and a revised edition of Thomas Sprat's influential *History of the Royal Society*.

Lists of this kind, of course, confirm that information sources are sources, but not more than sources. They provide raw materials that stimulate observations, inspire connections and support links between ideas and evidence that contribute to interpretation. The plausibility or interest of any given contextual link law inference depends on how the information is worked into an argument, not just on the quality of the sources from which it is taken (no matter how impeccable those are).

There is also another social context that is relevant, for which artificial lists seem less urgently needed: the context in which the text is now being read. This context, however, tends not to raise the same degree of difficulty as earlier historical contexts, partly because the reader generally (though not necessarily) knows more about their present social context without relying on extra inputs of information. The reader is likely to come to the text with a viewpoint and reading 'agenda' already formed or half formed in this social context. Such an agenda allows already acquired information to be selectively drawn on. In such circumstances, using further information sources deepens – but may also challenge – the assumed knowledge and beliefs we bring to a text.

2.3   Too much information?

For many readers, reading is most satisfying when it is a private and self-contained experience. Not interfering too much with that experience is therefore something to be taken account of in deciding how often to interrupt reading in order to look things up. Searches for information in re-reading open up aspects of the text possibly missed altogether in such spontaneous reading, but do not negate the first experience of the text. Indeed, comparing meanings derived in these two experimental conditions – with and without extra 'searched' information – adds an extra dimension to understanding.

With so many information sources available, however, which ones should be chosen? All information sources, we suggest, should be treated with caution. This is not only because information is always selective: brought together and filtered through a person's or organization's value judgements. It is also because the significance of information comes from what it adds to a point being developed with it. When using the internet in particular, it is sensible to use sites that are likely to be reliable, including (though not only, and possibly not in all cases) sites associated with government sources (often with .gov in the address), with universities (often with .edu or .ac in the address) and with public bodies and related organizations (often with .org in the address). Whichever sites are used, it is a good idea as far as possible to compare what is presented on different sites, testing what is said from different points of view or for different purposes.

Finally, using information sources should not be expected always to produce definitive answers; and the inconclusiveness of a particular search should not be simply regretted as a waste of time or effort. Information enriches a context within which relevant interpretations will be found. Searching starts with questions, as we saw in **Unit One, Asking questions as a way into reading**. The process develops in a series of steps: first into preliminary search or clarification, using easily accessed resources; then, if an interesting detail or pattern emerges, into more detailed analysis, using extended and more reliable sources. Finally, exploration of the initial question, along with others that have snowballed on the way, merges into fuller engagement with critical and theoretical discussion.

The two tasks that make up this activity tackle contrasting aspects of the use of information sources: first, searching and assessing evidence in response to a given query; second, weighing up the impact on the meaning and significance of texts that filling out readings with additional information can have.

1 John Keats's poem 'On first looking into Chapman's Homer' was written in 1816. But the poem refers in part to an earlier period. Among the discoveries mentioned in the poem is the discovery of a 'new planet':

> Then felt I like some watcher of the skies
> When a new planet swims into his ken.

Find out which planet is the most likely reference in these lines, by looking for information about the discovery of the various planets and relating that information to dates or periods associated with the poem. Write a brief statement marshalling evidence you can find for the view you arrive at. Is there any significance in which planet it was, or is Keats's emphasis on the experience of discovering something rather than on the particular planet?

2 Jonathan Swift's *Gulliver's Travels* (1726) and George Orwell's *Animal Farm* (1945) are two famous satirical prose works of English literature whose specific satire depends on close parallels with contemporaneous political events. Many readers become familiar with these two texts, however, without using editorial notes or other information sources to explicate the references. How would detailed mapping of the references in each text be likely to affect such readers' interest and pleasure? What is gained (and/or what is lost) in an 'information-source intensive' approach to reading?

ACTIVITY 2

Reading

Biber, D., Conrad S. and Reppen, R. (1998) *Corpus Linguistics: Investigating Language Structure and Use*, Cambridge: Cambridge University Press.

Feather, J. (1988) *A History of British Publishing*, London: Routledge.

Harner, J.L. (2008) *Literary Research Guide: An Annotated Listing of Reference Sources in English Literary Studies*, 5th edn, New York: MLA Publications.

Kirkham, S. (1990) *How to Find Information in the Humanities*, London: Library Association.

O'Keeffe, A. and McCarthy, M. (2010) *The Routledge Handbook of Corpus Linguistics*, Abingdon: Routledge.

Rivers, I. (1994) *Classical and Christian Ideas in English Renaissance Poetry: A Student's Guide*, 2nd edn, London: Routledge.

Williams, R. (1983) *Keywords: A Vocabulary of Culture and Society*, 2nd edn, London: Fontana.

UNIT 3

Analysing units of structure

This unit:

- describes the elements that give structure to literary works at different levels, from individual sounds and word choices up to larger compositional patterns including rhythm and text type;

- introduces the concept of a 'grammar' of such units;

- explores the relationship between literary conventions and two notions of regularity or 'rule': prescriptive (or 'regulative') rules, which must be followed; and 'constitutive' rules, which provide a framework governing how something such as a game, social institution or text is put together;

- shows how literary texts draw on, but can also exploit (and in doing so deviate from), such structures;

- illustrates how the idea of a linguistic grammar has been extended to other aspects of text organization, including in non-print media and multimodal texts.

U N I T 3

When we talk about texts, we use categories. It would be almost impossible not to. Such categories include not only text types, or genres, such as sonnet, thriller or tragedy, but also smaller-scale elements of composition that make up those text types: verse, rhyme, sentence, character, and so on. Is there a list of correct and incorrect categories that we should use? And are textual categories just part of a **metalanguage**, or how people *talk about* the language of texts, or do they actively guide understanding or even shape composition?

Texts, we might say, have a sort of 'mechanics'. They are constructed for a purpose, with anticipated meanings and effects likely to be prompted by the chosen combination of signs. Intuitive identification of elements that combine to form an overall text can be a starting point for interpretation, and so contribute to an active process of understanding as outlined in **Unit 1, Asking questions as a way into reading**. For example, an arrangement of textual components that shows interesting regularities, or forms a pattern, can point towards a text's meaning and significance. To understand how a text works, we may therefore be helped by finding out about its units of structure and how they combine. The field of **stylistics** – whether discourse stylistics generally, or literary stylistics – is based on this insight: that interpretations are guided to a significant extent by perceptions of structure that can be described, even if that sense of structure is not always immediately evident to the reader (for recent developments in stylistics, see Lambrou and Stockwell, 2007).

Consider the twelve-bar blues. The blues form consists, with some variation, of the following units (among others): three groupings of words, as lines, with the second line a repeat of the first, and with each line harmonically accompanied by particular chords in a given sequence of bars. In this description, lines, chords and bars are important units of structure for the twelve-bar blues. Here is a verse from a twelve-bar blues in the key of C:

chords:	C	/ F	/ C	/ C7 /
line 1:	Early one mornin',	/ on my way to the penal /	farm	
bars:	[1]	/ [2]	/ [3]	/ [4] /
chords:	F	/ F	/ C	/ C7 /
line 2:	Early one mornin',	/ on my way to the penal /	farm	
bars:	[5]	/ [6]	/ [7]	/ [8] /
chords:	G7	/ F7	/ C	/ G7 /
line 3:	Baby, all locked up	/ and ain't doin' nothin' /	wrong.	
bars:	[9]	/ [10]	/ [11]	/ [12] /

(Francis Blockwall, *c.* 1910–20)

We cannot, of course, be certain that the labelling offered here is a 'correct' description of the units. The original singer and subsequent performers, for example, may not use such terms; and many admirers of the blues form may not recognize them at all, or feel that these units are significant in their listening. Nor can we be certain that the list is exhaustive or comprehensive. How many times, for example, is the chord strummed in each bar and what is the unit for that? We cannot presume, either, that the grouping of the elements, as units, matches real distinctions. Perhaps it merely reflects categories we have chosen to impose. On the other hand, without some notion of units of structure (lines, chords, bars), it would be impossible to describe what distinguishes the blues from other forms that prompt fairly consistent judgements that, whatever they are, they are not blues.

3.1 'Form' and 'structure'

Units of structure are also called formal elements, and sometimes they are called formal properties. The terms 'structure' and 'form' – each of which has a long history and has given rise to critical movements (**formalism** and **structuralism**) – are used here simply to describe an arrangement of elements in a text. It should be noted, however, that these terms are used widely in discussion of **aesthetic** objects and texts with varying meanings and implications.

3.1.1 'Form' as coherence and unity

One sense of 'form', which has a long history in philosophy since Plato, considers it as an underlying essence or ideal of something that exists beyond, and separately from, its physical manifestation. 'Form' in this sense is something inherent, beyond analysis. The poet Samuel Taylor Coleridge (1772–1834) developed the term **organic form** to capture the idea that aesthetic form occurs or grows of itself, naturally, rather than being a human or social construct. In **New Criticism** (an originally American literary critical approach at its height between the 1930s and the 1960s), the idea of organic form in literature takes on an added dimension: poetic 'form' is said to involve a complex balancing of potentially conflicting elements (a view that leads to an emphasis placed in New Criticism on **irony**, **paradox** and **ambiguity**). What unites this later sense of form with the Platonic sense is that, in each case, while formal elements are seen as distinguishable from physical reality they are nevertheless in some sense inseparable from each other in the text as a whole. By contrast, when we refer to formal elements in this unit, we are working with a different assumption: that it is possible to isolate and examine individual formal elements.

3.1.2 'Structure'

The term 'structure' is also commonly used in discussion of how formal elements in a text are arranged. Structure refers to what might be called the 'insides' of a text: its network or system of underlying relations. That system of relations can be discovered by analysis. But here again it is worth remembering that there is another common use of the term 'structure', a use that refers to the text itself, rather than its configuration of elements of components (a use analogous to calling a house or a bridge a structure).

3.2 Grammars of language

The most basic way we can represent the structure of a written (or spoken) text is by means of a set of organizing principles called a grammar. To understand how units of structure function in a particular text we need first to consider the grammar of a language more generally.

3.2.1 The descriptive grammar of a language

The descriptive grammar of a language is a characterization of (a) how words can be thought of as different kinds of unit; (b) how those units fit together into larger units (called phrases); and (c) how these larger units combine into sentences. The grammar of English (like all other human languages) turns out to be highly complicated, and parts of it even now, despite generations of research, are not well understood. It is nevertheless possible, by looking at the most basic elements of the system – words and the different parts of speech they can be grouped into – to see the scope and power of even an incomplete grammatical description.

If we were to build a grammatical description of our own, we might begin with a basic rule, for example a rule that says that a sentence is made up of a sequence of units called 'words'. This seems adequate for the following sentence:

(1)   someone lived in a pretty little town

But if we reorder these words, our basic grammatical rule turns out to be only partly reliable:

(2)   someone pretty lived in a little town
(3)   someone lived a in pretty little town

We recognize that sentence (2) is an acceptable sentence, while sentence (3) is not. Our theory of units, as it stands, cannot explain why (3) is not an acceptable sentence. So, in order to understand why changing the order of words gives these different results, we need to distinguish between different *kinds* of words, on the basis of their different functions in sentences. In other words, we need to divide the basic unit 'word' into a number of sub-units, such as 'noun', **'verb'**, 'adjective', 'article', and so on. These different sub-units, or types of words, are called **parts of speech**.

Using available distinctions between parts of speech, we might now analyse our original sentence as follows:

(4)   someone   lived   in   a   pretty   little   town
       (noun)   (verb) (preposition) (article) (adjective)   (adjective)   (noun)

In sentence (3) above, the problem seems to be with the sequence 'a in pretty'. Using analysis by part of speech, this sequence takes the following form:

article–preposition–adjective

Since this sequence does not make sense in the above example, we might add a provisional descriptive rule to our grammar: that a preposition does not come between an article and an adjective.

Rules are only useful, however, if they apply in most cases. So we should now try out our rule using other words in the article–preposition–adjective positions. The sequence 'the of happy', for example, also turns out to be a combination that is never found in a normal-sounding English sentence. In fact, we have found a general grammatical rule in English, and we can safely predict that prepositions will never appear in between an article and an adjective.

Not all grammatical rules are as straightforward or as general in their application as this one. But the process of discovering them would be essentially the same. By analysing sequences, formulating provisional rules, testing them out with different combinations of words and modifying the rules where necessary, we could build up our own descriptive grammar of English. In doing so, we would learn important things about the structure and possibilities of the language.

The system of units called 'parts of speech' has been studied since classical times. Some fairly generally accepted names for different parts of speech, together with examples, are set out in Table 3.1 (note that this list of parts of speech is not exhaustive).

TABLE 3.1 Parts of speech

Name of unit	Examples
Verb	go, went, seemed, give, have, be, am, eat, broken
Noun	thing, book, theory, beauty, universe, destruction
Adjective	happy, destructive, beautiful, seeming, broken
Adverb	fast, quickly, seemingly, probably, unfortunately
Preposition	in, on, beside, up, after, towards, at, underneath
Article	the, a
Demonstrative	this, that, those, these
Modal	should, could, need, must, might, can, shall, would
Degree word	how, very, rather, quite
Quantifier	some, every, all

3.3   Literary applications of grammatical description

Analysing a text into **constituent elements** will be useful if it illuminates how that text is working. Rather like an action replay, descriptive analysis can examine in slow motion and close detail a process that in composition or in spontaneous reading occurs without conscious attention.

3.3.1   Descriptive analysis

Perhaps the most basic usefulness of analysis employing units of structure in literary texts is that it enables us to describe potentially significant patterns, such as repetition. Take the first stanza of William Blake's 'London' (1794), for example:

> I wander thro' each charter'd street,
> Near where the charter'd Thames does flow,
> And mark in every face I meet
> Marks of weakness, marks of woe.

This textual fragment could be described in terms of a range of different units: stanza, sentence, line, phrase, word, parts of speech, etc. The notion of repetition would almost certainly be involved in a description involving any of these units. Consider here, though, a description based simply on observed repetition and analysis by part of speech. An account of the poem might want to discuss not only the repetition of 'charter'd' in the first and second lines of the stanza, but also the repetition of 'mark' in the third and fourth lines. It is more accurate, however – and so potentially more useful – to note that 'mark' in line three is being used as a verb, meaning to see or to notice, while in line four it is used (in the plural) as a noun. We might then use that distinction to ask why these 'marks' in the fourth line are being linked, through the verbal echo in the preceding line, with the speaker's act of seeing, or 'marking', them.

3.3.2   Parallelism

By identifying units in a text that are repeated, or repeated with local variation, we can make visible the structure of certain kinds of **parallelism** (see **Unit 18, Parallelism**), for example the repetition of grammatical structures. Consider Blake's 'London' again. The whole of this poem is highly structured by verbal and grammatical parallelism, a characteristic illustrated in the fourth line of the verse quoted above: 'marks of weakness, marks of woe', which follows a formula we could describe precisely using parts of speech.

3.3.3   Descriptions of style

The example drawn from Blake focuses on specific, local effects. By analysing larger stretches of text (or a number of whole texts), it is possible to identify characteristic linguistic choices made, repeatedly, by individual writers. A writer, for example, may show a predisposition towards – or a reluctance to use – adverbs, complex sentences or relative **clauses**. By detailed analysis of recurrent structures (or noting structures that do not occur but that are known to occur frequently in the given type of discourse generally) it is possible for editors to ascribe a text of unknown origin to a particular author. This process of attribution of authorship is greatly helped by computer analysis of a large number of texts, or corpus (as discussed in **Unit 2, Using information sources**). It is also possible to begin to describe exactly why the **styles** of different authors can feel different when you read them, almost irrespective of what they are writing about. The perceptible differences between the writings of Ernest Hemingway, Virginia Woolf and Henry James, for example, can be accounted for in grammatical terms.

3.3.4 Deviation

A grammar of a language is the set of rules for combining units (parts of speech) into sequences. But it is always possible to break such rules, in order to achieve a specific effect (see **Unit 19, Deviation**). Rule-breaking texts can be analysed by looking at which rules have been broken and considering what effects are created by each transgression.

Consider, for example, the first line of a poem by e.e. cummings (1940):

anyone lived in a pretty how town

This line seems odd. But we can begin to explain its oddity by showing which grammatical rules it deviates from. The sequence 'a pretty how town' is odd because 'how' is a degree word (see Table 3.1 on p. 39) which appears in the line in a place where we would expect not a degree word but an adjective (e.g. nice, awful). In fact, the sequence article–adjective–degree word–noun is not a possible sequence in English. (A parallel example would be 'the stone very houses'.)

Another problem with the line is 'anyone'. 'Anyone' is an indefinite pronoun, and as such potentially fits into the place it appears in. The pronouns 'it' or 'someone', for example, would be perfectly acceptable before the verb 'lived'. But users of English instinctively realize that 'anyone' does not make sense in the sequence of words that cummings has used.

How can analysis in terms of units of structure help in this case? The reader might simply abandon the poem as nonsensical. Alternatively, however, he or she might try other ways of reading it. It might help, for example, to rearrange the words in order to 'make sense' of them, as if other, related strings of words are being echoed or evoked but not directly stated: 'how anyone lived in a pretty town'.

In this altered sequence, 'anyone' does make sense in the position preceding the verb 'lived'; and we seem to have the beginnings of an interpretation, which would go something like 'how anyone lived in a pretty town like that is a mystery to me'. Yet if we try to match this interpretation with the rest of the poem, we find it doesn't seem to work: nothing similar or evidently compatible seems to happen elsewhere. So this beginning of a reading, despite its apparent potential, probably needs to be abandoned. There is, however, another way we might use analysis of units of structure to deal with this grammatical problem. If we look at other uses of 'anyone' in the poem, we may discover a pattern. Consider:

> anyone's any was all to her (line 16)
> one day anyone died i guess (line 25)

Neither of these lines makes grammatical sense. But we can see that 'anyone' appears consistently in a position in sequences where we would normally expect expressions that refer to particular, definite entities (e.g. proper names; noun phrases, such as 'the woman'; or pronouns, such as 'he' or 'she'):

> one day (Bill/Alice/the woman/he/she) died i guess

Close reading of the poem following this insight suggests the possibility that 'anyone' could be a man who lived in a pretty town and married a woman referred to as 'no-one', and that they were eventually buried side by side. Whatever the merits of this reading, we have begun to make sense of an initially highly resistant poem by exploring how it may work through a kind of grammatical substitution: indefinite pronouns seem to be used in it as if they are definite pronouns referring to particular people.

The next step in reading the poem would be to ask *why* the poem would be written like that, and what effects it has as a result. The paraphrase given above suggests that, if we substitute definite nouns in place of 'anyone' and 'no-one', the poem becomes quite banal. One general effect of using 'anyone' and 'no-one', therefore, might be that of making the poem ambiguous or more thought-provoking. The two figures and their experience are made less banal and given more general significance (they stand for every man and every woman) by being kept anonymous and emptied of individual significance (they are both anyone and no one).

3.4 Extending the notion of grammar

So far, our main suggestion is that the grammar underlying a text governs how it is constructed. We have also suggested that a text's grammatical organization constrains and guides how it will be interpreted. If both these claims are sound, then notions of grammar are essential in bringing to conscious attention the organizing principles of texts that, in our everyday practice of reading, may be simply acted on spontaneously and taken for granted.

In addition to being useful in analysing written texts, a grammatical approach can also be applied to other systems of signs. Think of any grammatical sequence as a series of slots that can be filled by different items. We can then extend the notion of grammar to domains besides language. For instance, we may view how we dress as a matter of possible combinations involving what can be thought of as clothing units. If we extend the notion of grammar in this way, the body is divided into zones, each of which is thought of as a 'slot' within the clothing system: head, upper torso, legs, feet, etc. Each zone may be covered with an item of clothing, chosen from a set of available alternatives. The 'fillers' for the slots are individual items of clothing (e.g. for the feet: boots, shoes, nothing at all). Specific fillers can be used in some slots but not others; and predictable effects are generated by patterns of their combination. By examining combinations of selected items, specific styles can be described in terms of their consistency in selection. Deviations from conventional clothing 'statements' can also be described (e.g. wearing hiking boots and a baseball cap with an office suit), in ways that parallel the treatment of the e.e. cummings poem above.

Consider an equivalent general approach applied to narrative film. The film as a whole has a number of slots: its credit sequence (and possibly pre-credit sequence); the main body of its narrative (including sub-units such as establishing **shots**, dialogue, car chase sequence, special effects scenes, etc.); and end credits. Each of these slots can be handled in different ways by a director, by selecting different options or by omitting optional elements. Car chases, for instance (where they are included in a film 'statement'), can end in the death of the person chased, loss of the person being followed, collision involving the car chasing, etc. An overall filmic style is produced by manipulating possibilities within each slot – and so also implicitly calling to mind how slots are typically filled and combined in other film narratives (See **Unit 13, Allusion and intertextuality**).

Study of the units of structure (slots and fillers) of a wide range of cultural texts, institutions and ideas (from literature and photography through to what people eat) forms a central part of the theoretical movement known as **structuralism**, which developed in the late 1950s (see Culler, 2002). The grammar of narrative, which allows us to describe the range of possible slots and fillers for any narrative, has received particular attention (see **Unit 20, Narrative**).

3.5 Constitutive rather than regulatory rules

The rules of what might be called the 'cultural grammars' proposed by structuralism are often described as 'constitutive' rules. This means that, as grammatical rules, they are not regulating an already existing system (as rules do that tell you what you must and must not do while driving). Instead, they define what can count as an allowable move within a conventional system that only comes into being at all because of the existence of those rules. It is only by invoking particular conventions or rules of a game such as chess or football, or of social behaviour such as greeting or eating in a restaurant, that you are able to recognize the activity as whatever you know it to be. The same applies to social institutions such as weddings, birthday parties, money or law.

Structuralism's descriptions gained much of their power and interest from the possibility they offered of isolating and describing basic structures in how conventional social codes operate. That power of description was often linked to two further claims. The first is the suggestion, made by many thinkers, that the formulation of grammatical rules in terms of layers of often **binary oppositions** (or oppositions involving a contrast between only two alternative terms) has deep origins in human psychology. The second claim is that the means for describing such systems – considered to be available in linguistic techniques for analysing the grammar of language – would be similar across a very wide range of sign systems.

3.6 Possibilities for analysis

How useful, in our everyday practice of reading, is analysis in terms of units of structure likely to be? Arguably the value of such analysis ranges from better understanding of how a given form comes to have a particular meaning to general ideas about how people create new forms (whether in sentences, poems, new clothing styles or weddings) by adapting and extending existing ones.

In many areas of analysis, relatively little work has been done on naming and justifying the use of relevant units, or working out their possible combinations. It may often be the case, therefore, that when you analyse a text you will have to invent your own units and rules of combination, and justify them in terms of new ideas and insights they make possible. There are only the beginnings, for example, of a grammar of contemporary popular music, of video games and of a wide range of other online, multimedia and virtual reality forms. This unit has suggested that, even though such grammars might require new units and rules of combination, the procedure for developing them would follow broadly the same operations (including tests of replacement and movement to identify units and how they function) that have long been used in descriptions of English grammar.

ACTIVITY 3

The fifteen sentences below make up a plot summary of Charles Dickens's novel *Oliver Twist* (1837–8). But those fifteen sentences have been jumbled up to form a different order. Each sentence describes an event in the novel (so the unit of structure here is something like 'event description'). To contrast that level with a different level of analysis, the words of sentence (1) in the jumbled sequence of sentences have themselves been scrambled. (The original ordering is given on p. 336.) You have two tasks: one based exclusively on sentence (1); the other involving the sequence of all the sentences together, as an overall description of the plot of the novel.

continued

1 Construct a possible English sentence out of the jumbled words of sentence (a) below. Use all the words and do not use any word twice. Keep a note of how you go about rearranging the scrambled sentence. (Your note may show that you can do this on a more systematic basis than trial-and-error, and you may be able to carry over your method into working out structure in other sentences.)

   (a) escape and tries Nancy's cry to following hue the death
        Sikes

2 Now work out a plausible sequence for all fifteen jumbled event statements. Again, keep a note of the kinds of evidence – especially particular linking words or expressions, or possible and impossible/implausible sequences of events – that you use to help you decide in favour of one particular order rather than another. (It may help to photocopy the page and actually cut the copy into strips, with one event on each, so that you can physically reorder them.)

3 When you have found and noted down what you take to be the most plausible sequence, rearrange the fifteen events into a *new, different order*. This time, your order should tell the story in a different way, while using the same units. In carrying out this second reordering, only take into account what happens, not the particular wording of the description of each event. In your rewritten sequence, you can also refer to a single event more than once if you wish to (for example, if you want to insert events into the description of a particular event in order to create a flashback).

4 Finally, consider how different your new narrative structure is from the one in the summary you assembled earlier. What are the main differences at other levels of structure for which relevant units of analysis might also be developed: point of view; suspense; chronology; genre?

   (1) [*Write your rearranged version of sentence (1) here.*]

   (2) Keen to take advantage of these offers, the gang of thieves kidnap Oliver from Mr Brownlow.

   (3) The thieves try to convert Oliver into a thief.

   (4) Nancy discovers that Monks knows about Oliver's true parentage; having developed redeeming traits, she informs Rose of the danger Oliver is in.

   (5) With Sikes dead, the rest of the gang are captured; Fagin is executed.

   (6) Oliver accompanies Sikes on a burglary, but receives a gunshot wound.

   (7) Nancy's efforts are discovered by the gang, and she is brutally murdered by Bill Sikes.

continued

(8) Oliver runs away and is looked after by benevolent Mr Brownlow.

(9) The thieves become especially interested in Oliver, because they receive offers concerning him from a sinister person named Monks.

(10) Found and threatened with exposure, Monks confesses that he is Oliver's half-brother, and has pursued his ruin in order to acquire the whole of his father's property.

(11) Oliver falls into the hands of a gang of thieves, including Bill Sikes, Nancy and the Artful Dodger, and headed by a rogue called Fagin.

(12) Suffering pain from the gunshot wound, Oliver is captured by Mrs Maylie and her protégée Rose, who brings him up for a time.

(13) Monks emigrates and dies in prison; Oliver rejoins Mr Brownlow and is adopted by him.

(14) He accidentally hangs himself in the process.

(15) Oliver Twist, a pauper of unknown parentage, runs away to London.

Reading

Aitchison, J. (2004) *Teach Yourself Linguistics*, 6th edn, Teach Yourself Series, London: Hodder.

Culler, J. (2002) *Structuralist Poetics: Structuralism, Linguistics and the Study of Literature*, 2nd edn, London: Routledge, Chapter 1.

Fabb, N. (2005) *Sentence Structure*, 2nd edn, London: Routledge.

Lambrou, M. and Stockwell, P. (eds) (2007) *Contemporary Stylistics*, London: Continuum.

Leech, G. (1969) *A Linguistic Guide to English Poetry*, London: Longman.

Leech, G. and Short, M. (2007) *Style in Fiction: A Linguistic Introduction to English Fictional Prose*, 2nd edn, London: Longman, Chapter 1.

UNIT 4

Recognizing genre

This unit:

- examines how literary works are described in terms of their different text type, or genre;

- outlines the bases of classification used in creating genre categories, including subject matter, formal arrangement, mood or effect, occasion of performance, and use;

- discusses the functions served by genre, and for which groups of people (e.g. authors, readers, publishers and booksellers, reviewers);

- shows how genre can be used innovatively to create effects such as pastiche or parody, as well as to comment on genres that are imitated but combined in new and distinctive ways.

UNIT 4

In its most general sense, 'genre' simply means a sort, or type, of text: thriller, musical, autobiography, tragedy, etc. The word comes from the Latin word 'genus', meaning 'kind' or 'type' of anything, not just literary or artistic works. ('Genus', in fact, is still used to describe a technical sense of type, in the classification of species; and 'generic' is sometimes used to mean 'broad' or 'with the properties of a whole type or class'.) There is an obvious convenience in grouping texts together. We can fit any given text into a class, which offers a convenient way of describing what it is like: it resembles other texts that people already know. Such a notion is useful when applied not only to literary works but also to non-literary discourse: we can distinguish the typical features of, say, a shopping list from those of food labelling, a recipe or a menu (for detailed description, see Biber and Conrad, 2009).

For all its convenience, however, the notion of genre presents conceptual difficulties. Is there a fixed number of sorts of text? If so, when and how was this decided? And on what basis? Who will decide in the case of still evolving types, such as emergent styles in popular music or in digital media? A more theoretical question also arises: whether genre is a prescriptive category, grouping features on the basis of rules regarding what *should be* incorporated into writing or production of a given type; or whether it is a descriptive category, generalizing on the basis of *how things are in fact created* by language users.

4.1 Sorting texts into types

Each of the main criteria involved in distinguishing members of one genre from members of another has its own history and implications. Typically, different aspects work in combination with one another. It is nevertheless worth listing them separately before considering how they work together.

4.1.1 Classification on the basis of formal arrangement

One basis for classifying texts is their formal properties (see **Unit 3, Analysing units of structure**). Sonnets, for instance, have fourteen lines; they also follow distinctive stanzaic and rhyme patterns. At the same time, sonnets are a type of poetry, and poetry in turn exists within a conventional three-way distinction between poetry, drama and fiction. This general, three-way classification between poetry, drama and fiction is derived historically from Aristotle's distinction between lyric, epic or narrative, and drama.

Aristotle's distinctions were primarily, though not exclusively, based on formal properties. Poetry involves **rhythm** and other kinds of sound patterning. Fiction does not, at least not necessarily. But it does involve narrative. Drama involves characters speaking and acting in relation to each other. In *Poetics* (fourth century BC), Aristotle emphasized one further, distinguishing aspect of form: who speaks. Lyrics are uttered in the first person; in epic or narrative, the narrator speaks in the first person, but lets characters speak for themselves; in drama, the characters do all the talking.

Although common ever since Aristotle, any 'pure' genre classification based on formal differences can be difficult to sustain. What about verse drama? Or narrative poetry (as in ballads)? Or dramatic monologue (in which a single character or persona speaks, but without any given dramatic context or action)? Such difficulties multiply when multimodal kinds of discourse or other media are taken into account: such forms bring together conventions drawn from more than one **medium** (say written words, still images, speech, music and video).

4.1.2   Classification on the basis of theme or topic

Sometimes subject matter is the basis for genre classification. Texts show thematic affinities by treating the same or similar topics, often topics or subject matter that may be especially important for the society in which the texts circulate (e.g. war, love and marriage, religious festivity, royal succession, independence struggles).

The pastoral, for instance, is concerned with country life; crime fiction is about crime; biography relates events in a life; and science fiction explores possible future or alternative worlds. In principle, however, it is possible to treat any of these topics following formal conventions of any of the different kinds listed above, or in different moods that will lead to different kinds of effect on the reader or viewer.

4.1.3   Classification on the basis of mood or anticipated response

What a text is about can overlap with an attitude or emotion conventionally adopted towards its subject matter. **Pastoral** often implies not just a concern with country life, but also a reflective or nostalgic attitude towards this topic. **Elegies** – although first defined on the basis of the **metre** they used – came over time to be primarily concerned with lamenting deaths (and often take the form of pastoral elegies, delivered in the **persona** of a shepherd). War poetry has a complex history both of jingoistic and anti-war traditions, though both strands tend to explore ideas of patriotism, moral values and loyalty.

A more complex case is that of **tragedy**. Classical tragedy combines conventions about the **protagonist** (the 'tragic hero', who has a character with a crucial flaw) and conventions about the nature of the **plot** (in which the main character typically suffers and dies). At the same time, tragedy is also defined (at least in Aristotle's account in *Poetics*) by its characteristic mode of audience response. Aristotle called that response **catharsis**, or a purging or purification by means of feelings of pity and fear that are aroused in the audience by the dramatic spectacle. Later developments of tragedy – associated particularly with Seneca in classical Rome (first century AD), then during the European Renaissance and into the modern period – vary in each of these main respects, while retaining some quality that is still thought to be characteristic of tragedy (Williams, 1966). Whereas classical tragedy involved kings and princes, for instance, modern tragedy commonly involves relatively anonymous, often socially alienated main characters; and modern tragedies tend to involve little or no significant action, in contrast with the major political events and destinies of nations that formed the usual concern of classical tragedy. Given the scale of such changes within the genre, it is arguable that what most allows a modern audience to consider a new text to be a tragedy is less its formal properties or subject matter than the mood it creates or audience reaction it evokes.

4.1.4 Classification on the basis of occasion

Literary forms may now seem specialized kinds of discourse that are isolated from the rest of society and mainly discussed in literature classes. But for most of its history literature has not been marked off by social boundaries in this way. Rather, its involvement in public life, including in various kinds of social ritual, meant that many different texts had their origins in composition for or performance on some specific kind of social occasion.

Drama in classical times, for instance, was a ritual involving important cultural customs, and had social implications for members of its audience. Many later dramatic genres also developed in particular historical contexts and for specialized kinds of occasion. **Chronicle plays** dealing with English history, for example, flourished in the sixteenth century in a period of patriotic fervour following the defeat of the Spanish Armada in 1588. In the late sixteenth and early seventeenth centuries, **masques** were a form of court entertainment that combined poetic drama, music, dancing and elaborate costumes, and staging; they also involved participation by the aristocratic members of the audience in the performance (for further discussion, see **Unit 24, Ways of reading drama**).

Poetic genres have developed in analogous ways. An **epithalamium** is a poem written for – and proclaimed at – a public occasion, in celebration of a victorious person (e.g. an athlete or a general). The genre of **elegy** evolved during the seventeenth century into its modern role as a consolatory lament for the death of a particular person. **Ballads** began as poems to be danced to. But they gradually evolved in two divergent directions: continuing folk ballads in the oral tradition; and urban **broadside ballads** circulated as single sheets or chapbooks that typically contained popular songs, jests, romantic tales and sensational topical stories.

4.1.5 Classification on the basis of mode of address

Even when dissociated from specific social occasions or performance rituals, texts are still in some cases labelled on the basis of how they **address** their readers or anticipated audience. Some texts involve **direct address** (e.g. public speeches, letters and emails, news anchoring); others have a specific **addressee** named in the text but are written so as to be overheard (e.g. odes, dialogue in most stage drama). Sometimes within a single form there is variation between alternative **modes of address**. Essays addressed to 'Dear Reader' are interpolated into narratives in some eighteenth-century novels, stepping outside the frame of the imagined world and narrative style of the rest of the text.

Mode of address is not the same as who the text is actually addressed to (its anticipated audience). As the distinction above suggests, it is possible for a text to be addressed, in terms of the techniques it adopts, to one person or category of person but with the expectation that the resulting utterance will be 'overheard' by an actual audience with possibly very different characteristics, attitudes and values.

4.2   Deciding what genre a text is in

Criteria for distinguishing different genres tend to work together rather than independently of one another. This can make it difficult to judge whether a text fits a category simply by ticking off features in a list of required attributes.

Consider the **sonnet**, which is often viewed as the exemplary case of a highly codified form. Sonnets consist of fourteen lines, grouped as an octave (eight-line stanza) and a sestet (six-line stanza). There are typically ten **syllables** in each line, a prescribed **rhyme scheme**, and a change of direction or reversal in the poem's argument between the two stanzas at a point called the volta. This attractively simple picture nevertheless has to be refined, not least because of the existence of two main alternative traditions: the Italian (or Petrarchan) style, with its highly patterned, closed and interlaced rhyme scheme (ABBA, ABBA, CDE, CDE); and the English (or Shakespearean) style, with a different rhyme scheme (ABAB, CDCD, EFEF, GG) that reshapes the poem as a douzain (twelve lines, consisting of three open-rhyme quatrains) plus a final rhyming couplet that in effect shifts the volta to near the end (we discuss rhyme schemes generally in **Unit 16, Rhyme and sound patterning**). This still simplified account then needs to be refined further, to acknowledge that each of these traditions allows for variation. The description also needs to incorporate thematic criteria: specialized conventions relating to love, heroic and sacred sonnets, as well as (later in development of the form) related to the characteristics of nature sonnets and political and moral sonnets. And even this enriched account of rules governing the sonnet needs to be refined further, before it could serve as a comprehensive list of necessary and sufficient conditions of being a sonnet.

Refined, though, in what direction? What is missing from the account so far, focusing as it does on formal and thematic conventions, is relevant history. In this case, the composition of sonnets has a history almost continuously from the thirteenth century through to the twenty-first century, with complex interaction between sonnet traditions in different languages and different periods.

To view the sonnet form in a way that incorporates social dimensions of the genre involves thinking not only of formal rules but also about cultural interaction and influence. Forms evolve through innovations based on established conventions but that do not respect pre-set boundaries. When Milton writes broadly Petrarchan sonnets with the volta apparently out of place, or when Blake writes a sonnet that fails to rhyme, or when John Updike writes a sonnet in which none of the lines after the first even contains whole words, these authors are not so much failing to follow rules of the genre as pushing back the genre's boundaries (for discussion of these and other examples, see Fuller, 1972). It is readers of the genre, and subsequent writers in it, who decide whether such experiments still count as sonnets – or whether a borderline has been crossed into some new genre or sub-genre that merits a category of its own.

4.2.1 Genre as an expression of conventional agreement

An obvious alternative to thinking of genre as a list of essential properties is to start instead with the idea that genres may be grasped by means of especially influential texts that serve as exemplary cases. Sophocles' *Oedipus Rex* (*c.* 400 BC) is often appealed to as an exemplary tragedy, for example. The play provides a sort of benchmark, with other texts defined as tragedies to the extent that they resemble it. This view of genre, where a prototype is taken to exist and other texts are judged to be more or less close to that prototype, allows texts to be assigned to genres even when they do not have all the apparently necessary features. It is then possible for a text to be considered a novel even if it has no discernible narrative (as many experimental novels don't), so long as the text works with or exploits our *expectation* that it should have.

Even notions of the typical or 'prototypical' are not fixed, however. Generic conventions come to us as a historical legacy. They are shaped and reshaped by the changing production and circulation of texts, as well as by changing attitudes towards texts. What constitutes a typical novel in the early twenty-first century – even allowing for huge variation within the novel form – is not the same as what constituted a typical novel during the eighteenth or nineteenth centuries (see Watt, 2010). Such difference as regards the genre prototype makes possible a paradoxical observation: that some novelists may be writing highly successful nineteenth-century novels even now, at the beginning of the twenty-first century.

4.3 Functions of genre

So far, we have looked at different ways of understanding what genre is. But why should it matter whether we assign texts to types or classes? And who in fact does? To understand what functions genre serves, we need to explore how distinctions created by notions of genre fit into larger, aesthetic and social frameworks that govern how texts are created, how they circulate and how they are evaluated.

The various functions attributed to genre, as we will see even in the brief descriptions that follow, are problematic, resting on a major fault line within literary history: in some periods and places, it is thought a valuable achievement to produce a good 'generic text' (a pastoral ode that respects the conventions, a formulaic but clever detective thriller, or a good pop song recounting a failed relationship completely irrespective of the song-writer's actual circumstances); but in other periods and places, the aspiration to write within a genre is dismissed as vacuous and imitative, lacking in imagination and individual creativity. This unresolved issue of the nature and scope of literary creativity is reflected in the various functions that genre is thought to serve.

4.3.1 Genre as a framework for a text's intelligibility

The main psychological function of genre is to act as a sort of **schema**, or structured set of assumptions within our tacit knowledge, that we draw on to guide reading. Such schemas work rather like a series of signposts or instructions. Expectations in reading are structured at many different levels, from the sorts of local inference we make in order to fill in gaps between obviously related but not continuous details through to vague assumptions about overall point or significance. Genre dictates procedures for reading at each level, signalling the general trajectory that a text is likely to be following, the amount of detail we expect it to go into at any given stage or on any topic, topics it is unlikely to explore, and the degree of **realism** or truthfulness it is likely to show (Semino and Culpeper, 2002).

4.3.2 Genre as reflecting the nature of human experience

Relating the general, **cognitive** role of genre to speculation about basic human categories of thought, some critics have suggested connections between specific genres and what they take to be fundamental kinds of human experience. The distinction between tragedy and **comedy** is often made along these lines. One notable scheme in this area is that of **archetypal genres** developed by the literary critic Northrop Frye (1912–91). For Frye, four selected genres (comedy, romance, tragedy and satire) correspond emotionally to the four seasons, which are linked in turn to perceived stages of human life and a rich cultural reservoir of myth and symbolism.

One problem with such a view of genre, however – and with genre classifications that order genres in a hierarchy of seriousness, ambition and cultural worth – is that this approach is unlikely to have much to say about the emotional functions of less traditional or less high-cultural genres: the dance mix, the performance pop-video, the Bollywood masala movie or the tweet. Archetypal classifications take for granted a distinction – in itself 'generic' – between serious or profound forms that somehow correspond to essential human experience and other, non-serious forms that are presumably less worthwhile or significant.

4.3.3 Genre as a promotional device

By comparison with the previous two functions, most other functions suggested for genre are concerned more with the social circulation of texts than with cognitive processes involved in interpreting them. Sometimes the idea of genre is used to support classification systems that indicate a textual product range, or to locate texts in a given market. In this context, genre signals an appeal to specific audience tastes and wishes (for news, for the problem-solving pleasure of detective fiction, for a story to make you cry or feel better after a bad day, etc.). Genres allow audiences to predict and select kinds of experience, and to repeat with local variation (in the manner of a very loose sequel) particular kinds of pleasure or entertainment they have previously enjoyed. TV scheduling and online entertainment listings display precisely this type of thinking, by picking out a mixture of textual features to suggest continuity with variation. Genre categories understood in this way feed back into the production activity of 'content providers', who can work to genre expectations in order to fill a given market niche and respond to known audience tastes.

4.3.4 Genre as a way of controlling markets and audiences

This view of the usefulness of genre categories overlaps with the last. But it extends it into the idea that genres do not so much reflect audience wishes as create them. Genres in this view are seen as part of a process of controlling the production of entertainment and directing culture markets, by actively repeating the formula of whatever has already been successful. Saturating media space with texts created according to proven formulae allows confident investment in production. To some people, however, this use of genre as a set of planning categories represents a kind of conspiracy, bringing about a detrimental standardization of cultural products into predictable forms. (The financing of Hollywood films, with notable exceptions, is often argued to follow this pattern.)

4.4 Exploited genres

Once genres become established in our patterns of expectation, they lend themselves to quotation and creative adaptation; they can be mixed, merged and manipulated (see **Unit 13, Allusion and intertextuality**). Such secondary use of genre takes a number of forms, but the two most common are **collage** and **pastiche**.

4.4.1 Collage and pastiche

In **collage**, different genres (or features of different genres) are placed alongside one another and so implicitly joined together. Such collage can be used, as it commonly is in modernist texts, to set up a dialectic, or process of contrastive inter-action, that results from the juxtaposition of different voices or quoted texts (see **Unit 12, Juxtaposition**).

Pastiche (along with subgenres of pastiche, such as burlesque, mock-epic and mock-heroic) is similar. It undermines or offsets a text's seemingly authentic speaking voice by bringing different styles together. But it does so by clearly signalling the element of imitation – especially incongruous imitation – that it contains, generally by merging conventions from one genre with subject matter from another.

Both kinds of genre mixing or layering are common techniques in satire, whether in print, film, or radio and television comedy. In the case of collage, something in the text – or in our expectations – signals that we are to respond to one of the genres in the compound as more powerful or convincing than the other(s). That genre undermines or displaces those other genres or genre features, implying an often critical comparison anchored in the values carried by the genre which is presented as dominant. In pastiche, it is the tension between the subject matter and the generic conventions followed that indicates satire, which can be directed either towards the form adopted or towards the topic (for discussion of techniques in satire, see Simpson, 2003).

Kinds of **irony** created in this way are not always controllable, however. Genre combinations sometimes appear to overspill authorial control, and can turn the text into an open-ended dialogue between the different voices it has juxtaposed, with no stabilizing, dominant voice to confer a fixed point or meaning (see **Unit 11, Irony** and **Unit 14, Authorship and intention**).

4.4.2 Postmodernism and genre

When the kinds of generic compounding and formulaic imitation outlined above bring a text's genre into the foreground (making the issue of genre more prominent than whatever the text appears to be talking about), such techniques create one major dimension of **postmodernism**.

Roughly, postmodernism has been a response to a set of cultural conditions believed to characterize the contemporary period. As viewed in postmodernism, our exposure to language and media saturates social experience so thoroughly that any act of communication calls for a high degree of self-awareness regarding the genres in which communication is possible. In most situations, self-consciousness about the means rather than the content of communication – about the range of conventional forms available for representing things – is played down. What makes a text postmodern is that, rather than downplaying form and trying to com-municate some content to you, the text instead draws attention to the modes of writing and reading that are in play, often undermining them by doing so. This kind of postmodernist effect is mainly seen in texts that use collage and pastiche techniques. But such effects can also be found in texts written or produced before the rise of postmodernism, where traces of juxtaposed styles, moments of uncertain **register** or incongruities between topic and adopted form can be found. By searching out such traces, it is possible for a postmodernist reading concerned with the interrelationship between any given text and a history of other texts to be created for works written in earlier periods. A Romantic poem, for instance, might be approached not as an expression, in apparent good faith, of its author's spirit but as a text reflecting its own creation as an example of the Romantic poetic genre.

ACTIVITY 4

Describing a genre can be undertaken at a 'general' level and at a number of more 'specialized' levels. In this activity, we look at the genre of fictional autobiography, which we can initially locate as follows:

First-person
Prose writing → Fiction → First-person fiction → fictional life account
(= autobiography)

A genre can also be described in terms of typical properties that a text within that genre has at some given stage (e.g. as its introduction, in a series of narrative events, as a midway reversal or transformation of action or character, as a **dénouement**). In this activity, we look at what we will call 'autobiographical beginnings'.

1   Read the three extracts below (A–C). Describe what genre features they have in common that serve as 'autobiographical beginnings' in fiction. We have noted one characteristic above: first-person narration. Remember that the similarities need not be features of form; they could involve theme, setting, time sequence, etc.

2   A genre is a *type* of text; variation within the type is expected. Now describe the main differences you see between the three texts, considered as representatives of 'autobiographical beginnings' in fiction. Where you feel there is a difference, generalize from that difference to a *basis*, or criterion, of the difference (e.g. if you were comparing two people and one was tall and the other short, you would say they differ in height).

3   As well as conveying an autobiographical beginning, the passages draw attention to some kind of awkwardness in relation to a conventional autobiographical idiom. What aspects of the narration of a narrator's life do the narrators comment on or distance themselves from? (You may find

continued

it easiest to start by looking at references in text C to other types of text that the narrator sees as significantly different from the approach adopted in text C itself.)

4 One complication with 'fictional autobiography' is a tension between the two elements of the genre label: fictional (as something made-up or imagined) and autobiography, as the relation of a person's own experience (i.e. something the narrator might be presumed to know about and be able to relate truthfully). Are there indications, in these three self-introducing passages, of how close or distant the persona of the fictional narrator is in relation to an author behind the work?

Text A

In the beginnings of the last chapter, I informed you exactly *when* I was born; – but I did not inform you *how*. No; that particular was reserved entirely for a chapter by itself; – besides, Sir, as you and I are in a manner perfect strangers to each other, it would not have been proper to have let you into too many circumstances relating to myself all at once. – You must have a little patience. I have undertaken, you see, to write not only my life, but my opinions also; hoping and expecting that your knowledge of my character, and of what kind of a mortal I am, by the one, would give you a better relish for the other: As you proceed further with me, the slight acquaintance which is now beginning betwixt us, will grow into familiarity; and that, unless one of us is in fault, will terminate in friendship.

(Laurence Sterne, *The Life and Opinions of Tristram Shandy* (1759–67), Volume 1, Chapter 6)

Text B

Whether I shall turn out to be the hero of my own life, or whether that station will be held by anybody else, these pages must show. To begin my life with the beginning of my life, I record that I was born (as I have been informed and believe) on a Friday, at twelve o'clock at night. It was remarked that the clock began to strike, and I began to cry, simultaneously.

In consideration of the day and hour of my birth, it was declared by the nurse, and by some sage women in the neighbourhood who had taken a lively interest in me several months before there was any possibility of our becoming personally acquainted, first, that I was destined to be unlucky in life; and secondly, that I was privileged to see ghosts and spirits; both these gifts inevitably attaching, as they believed, to all unlucky infants of either gender, born towards the small hours on a Friday night.

continued

I need say nothing here, on the first head, because nothing can show better than my history whether that prediction was verified or falsified by the result. On the second branch of the question, I will only remark, that unless I ran through that part of my inheritance while I was still a baby, I have not come into it yet. But I do not at all complain of having been kept out of this property; and if anybody else should be in the present enjoyment of it, he is heartily welcome to keep it.

> (Charles Dickens, *The Personal History and Experience*
> *of David Copperfield the Younger* (1849–50),
> Chapter 1, 'I am Born')

Text C

I am an invisible man. No, I am not a spook like those who haunted Edgar Allan Poe; nor am I one of your Hollywood-movie ectoplasms, I am a man of substance, of flesh and bone, fibre and liquids – and I might even be said to possess a mind. I am invisible, understand, simply because people refuse to see me. Like the bodiless heads you see sometimes in circus side-shows, it is as though I have been surrounded by mirrors of hard, distorting glass. When they approach me they see only my surroundings, themselves, – or figments of their imagination – indeed, everything and anything except me.

Nor is my invisibility exactly a matter of bio-chemical accident to my epidermis. That invisibility to which I refer occurs because of a peculiar disposition of the eyes of those with whom I come in contact. A matter of the construction of their inner eyes, those eyes with which they look through their physical eyes upon reality.

> (Ralph Ellison, *Invisible Man* (1952), 'Prologue')

Reading

Aristotle (*c.* 400 BC) *On the Art of Poetry*, in T.S. Dorsh (ed.) *Aristotle, Horace, Longinus: Classical Literary Criticism*, Harmondsworth: Penguin.

Biber, D. and Conrad, S. (2009) *Register, Genre and Style*, Cambridge: Cambridge University Press.

Duff, D. (ed.) (2000) *Modern Genre Theory*, London: Longman.

Frye, N. (2007) *Anatomy of Criticism*, Princeton, NJ: Princeton University Press, especially pp. 158–239.

Fuller, J. (1979) *The Sonnet*, Critical Idiom Series, 2nd edn, London: Routledge.

Simpson, P. (2003) *On the Discourse of Satire: Towards a Stylistic Model of Satirical Humour*, Amsterdam: John Benjamins.

Spiller, M. (1992) *The Development of the Sonnet: An Introduction*, London: Routledge.

Watt, I. (2010) *The Rise of the Novel*, Harmondsworth: Penguin.

Williams, R. (2006) *Modern Tragedy*, 2nd edn, London: Chatto & Windus.

Language variation

UNIT 5

Language and time

This unit:

- describes how languages change over time and illustrates consequences of such change as regards the structure and meaning of literary texts;

- shows how language change affects different aspects of linguistic structure, including pronouns, vocabulary, and the arrangement and interrelationship of words (syntax);

- contrasts alternative theories of language change, especially formalist and functionalist accounts;

- assesses the impact of earlier styles of language use on contemporary readers, including contrived effects of literary archaism;

- discusses efforts to change language, including campaigns by feminists to contest the expression of traditional power relationships in discourse.

UNIT 5

All languages change over the course of time. Within a language group, these changes may develop to the extent that the language use of a particular community becomes significantly different from that of other users of the 'same language'. This language use may then be described as a **dialect** (if changes are at the level of small differences in grammar and vocabulary), and as a separate language (if grammatical and lexical differences are significant). Language change of this kind is relevant to the study of texts in several ways. A text may be a force *for* language change, or it may retain (and so associate itself with) older usages. A text may become difficult to understand because of language change, by containing words and phrases that are associated with earlier periods of the language's history: these words and phrases have become archaisms, and rely for their meaning on an understanding of what an earlier state of the language was at a given time. A modern text may deliberately use archaisms for particular effects.

5.1 Theories of language change

There are various different accounts of how and why language changes over time.

5.1.1 Formalist theories: change as an autonomous process

Many linguists have described language change as being caused by and working according to structural pressures that are internal to the language itself. For example, between 1500 and 1700 many of the vowel sounds of English changed into other vowel sounds, in a process called the **Great Vowel Shift**. The modern English word 'make', for example, was pronounced in the sixteenth century with a different vowel, a little like the one you get if you pronounce 'mack', stretching the vowel out. The tongue is higher and therefore nearer to the roof of the mouth in 'make' than it is in 'mack', so we can say that the vowel was 'raised' from its sixteenth-century pronunciation to its modern pronunciation. Many linguists, from nineteenth-century philologists to contemporary generative linguists, have investigated how these changes relate to each other and to the larger structures of the language. For example, it is possible to classify vowels as 'high', 'mid' and 'low' on the basis of the height of the tongue when it makes them, and we can then say that, in the above example, a low vowel becomes a mid vowel. This change seems to have 'pushed' the old mid vowel to become a modern high vowel (modern 'meat' changed from a sixteenth-century word sounding like 'mate') and pushed the older high vowel to become a modern low vowel (modern 'ride' was once pronounced like 'reed'). What interests linguists is that there seems to have been a system of interrelated changes that can be understood in relation to one another. Linguists interested in such phenomena give a **formalist** account of these changes in language: that is, an explanation in terms of the form or units of structure of the language (see **Unit 3, Analysing units of structure**).

5.1.2 Functionalist accounts: change as a socially motivated process

There is another view of language change and how to study and explain it that suggests that changes in language result from social activity, in particular from political struggle. Leith (1983) accounts for the Great Vowel Shift described above by suggesting that migration of workers into London during the period produced a clash of dialects that led Londoners to distinguish their speech from that of the immigrants by changing their vowel system. Culpeper (1997) suggests that the development of Standard English, through the use of the East Midlands dialect in the fifteenth century, can also be accounted for by examining social factors. It was the East Midlands dialect that was used by William Caxton when he set up his printing press in London in 1476, for example, and this dialect became a lingua franca among merchants and government officials in the London area. This kind of **functionalist theory** claims that language change is socially motivated, rather than being motivated primarily or exclusively by the formal system of the language itself. A functionalist way of looking at language analyses language change from the perspective of the social values carried by certain usages at specific points in time.

It is possible to combine functionalist and formalist accounts. For example, the Great Vowel Shift may have been triggered and supported in general terms by a struggle for linguistic identity; but the details of the shift – for example, which vowels changed and how they changed – might be best explained in formalist terms. Political, economic and social change can result in words being pronounced in new ways, and given new meanings, and can lead to new words being invented. In this context, it should also be remembered that words rarely, if ever, have one single fixed meaning or pronunciation. According to some Marxist accounts of language, the pronunciation and meaning of words is a potential 'site of struggle', where two or more social groups or interests have a political stake in enforcing one meaning of a word or phrase (see **Unit 9, Language and society**). For example, a local government tax levied on property in Britain during the 1980s was called 'the community charge' by the Conservative government that introduced it, but called 'the poll tax' by those opposed to its introduction. The latter term was coined because it has political implications in English history associated with who can vote and who cannot vote. The OED tells us that 'poll' used to mean 'head' (the current usage associated with voting comes from a poll as a counting of heads); one reason for reviving the archaism 'poll tax', among those who did so, was because while it can now refer to something levied on all 'heads' – i.e. on everyone of a voting age – the term also made a specific allusion to the Peasants' Revolt of 1381, which, *Brewer's Dictionary of Phrase and Fable* notes, was 'immediately occasioned by an unpopular poll-tax at a time when there was a growing spirit of social revolt' in England. Thus, revival of the term poll tax was a politically motivated gesture that, simply through choice of word, made an analogy between 1381 and the situation at the time of the introduction of the property tax. The success of opposition to that tax might be judged in part by how widely and by whom the alternative name 'poll tax' was used during the controversy. A less politically charged term was later introduced: the more neutral 'council tax'.

5.2   Change and linguistic media

The main linguistic mediums or media in which verbal language is used are speech and writing (see **Unit 22, Speech and narration**), together with various other technologically enabled forms (language can be broadcast, recorded, telephoned, emailed, texted, etc.).

5.2.1   Writing

Before the seventeenth century, written texts varied enormously in their spelling and punctuation. Such variation arose partly from lack of a central standardization of spelling, partly from variability and rapid changes in pronunciation and partly from typesetting practices such as the symbolic use of capital letters to indicate importance and the insertion of letters to fill out a line. From the seventeenth century onwards, however, printed texts began to look more like modern English texts, because standards were implemented that mostly still hold. One result is that, while spellings have stabilized but pronunciations have continued to change, spellings that once corresponded to pronunciation no longer do so. This is one of many reasons for the difficulties that all English speakers encounter when writing: when English spelling was formalized, it led to a rift between the way words were spelt and pronounced in the seventeenth century and the way that pronunciation of words has changed subsequently.

5.2.2   Speech

It has only recently become possible to record speech as sound. Our evidence for how English was spoken in the past therefore generally takes the form of: (a) reports made by contemporary linguists; (b) transcripts of speech, as in trial transcripts; (c) representations of speech in literature and drama; (d) indirect evidence from sound patterns in literature (e.g. rhymes); and (e) indirect evidence from informal writing, such as diaries and letters.

Speech seems to change more rapidly than writing, partly because it is not codified to the same extent, and partly because it is open to much wider cultural variation. Youth subcultures, for example, generate a large number of new terms and phrases to mark membership of social groups, and, as importantly, to mark non-membership of and resistance to membership of such groups. Such subcultural words and phrases occasionally filter into mainstream spoken English and into the written standard. Consider, for example, the word 'wicked' (as well as many more recent examples) as meaning something exceptionally good. This use appeared in mainstream pop music via African-American youth subcultures; today, the term rarely appears in the mainstream, except parodically. American Valley Girl expressions such as 'Whatever' (a response that displays a bored, cool indifference) were initially restricted to youth subcultures; but they are now used in the mainstream (though hardly any longer in youth subcultures). In 1960s' subcultures, a key distinction was made between 'heads' (those who took drugs and shared a set of radical beliefs about the world) and 'straights' (those who did neither of these). Today, these terms are archaic, with strong period connotations; and, indeed, 'straight' has changed its meaning to signify 'heterosexual'.

5.2.3   Twentieth-century technologies and linguistic change

New technologies have brought new ways of using English. Historically, this has been most obvious with specialized languages such as those used for short-wave radio or for telegrams. It is also true, however, of linguistic practices developed for talking on the telephone or on the radio: so-called 'BBC English' was for instance a pronunciation standard developed for radio and television.

Email and forms of instant messaging have resulted in a number of changes mainly centring on questions of register. Because email messages are generally short and sent immediately, the writing style they typically adopt is more informal than letters or memos and does not include formulae such as 'Dear Sir/Madam', 'Yours faithfully', and so on. Grammatical and typographical errors are often left uncorrected in email messages. Email style has more in common with informal notes left for friends or family, and this informality is widely used even where the person being addressed is not known to the message writer. This new informality follows a trend described by Norman Fairclough, who has argued that within British English in general the use of more informal and seemingly more personalized forms of expression is becoming more widespread across a range of situations of use (Fairclough, 1992). However, other commentators routinely complain about the supposedly detrimental effects on language usage of 'email English'.

5.3   Some types of language change

5.3.1   Sound

We have seen that many English vowel sounds (particularly long vowels) changed as a result of the Great Vowel Shift, but that the relics of older pronunciations are still preserved in the spellings of English words codified before the Shift was complete. For example, the spelling of the word 'knight' reflects a very different pronunciation from the current one. If we go back five hundred years, we can find evidence that the 'k' was pronounced, that the vowel was pronounced more like the vowel in 'neat' and that the 'gh' was pronounced like the 'ch' of 'Bach'.

5.3.2 The arrangement and interrelationships of words (syntax)

In the early form of English known as Anglo-Saxon or Old English (spoken in much of Britain, in various dialects, from about AD 400 into the early Middle Ages), word order was fairly flexible. Relations between words were signalled by word-endings rather than by sequence. Some aspects of the flexibility this allowed survived into the modern English of the seventeenth century, such as permitting particular parts of sentences (such as the verb or an object) to be moved to the front of sentences. But the fact that this flexibility seems to have survived more or less only in literary texts (it is difficult to find examples of such rearrangement of word order in non-literary documentary evidence, such as letters and diaries) provides one example of how literature uses archaism to create literary effects. Residual signs of this flexibility in word order can be found in Wordsworth's writing, in the late eighteenth century. The first stanza of 'The Last of the Flock' (1798), for example, is given an archaic feel by the placing of elements (italicized in the extract) before the verb, rather than (as normally) following it:

> *In distant countries* I have been,
> And yet I have not often seen
> A healthy man, a man full grown,
> Weep in the public roads alone.
> But such a one, *on English ground*,
> *And in the broad high-way*, I met;
> *Along the broad high-way* he came,
> His cheeks *with tears* were wet.

In the first line, for example, a more usual sequence in modern English would be:

I	have been	in distant countries
(subject)	(verb)	(adjunct)

Although adjuncts (in this case a prepositional phrase) are more movable than other elements, it is unusual for them to be consistently placed before the verb as they are here. Such rearrangement of word order can also be thought of as a kind of literary deviation from more usual syntactical sequences (see **Unit 19, Deviation**).

5.3.3 Pronouns

The history of the distinction between the second-person pronouns 'thou' and 'you' is a revealing example of how language change can relate to social change. The OED tells us that early forms both of 'thou' (plus 'thee', 'thine' and 'thy') and of 'you' (plus 'ye', 'your' and 'yours') were used in ordinary speech in Old English. The distinction between these forms was primarily a grammatical one. In Middle

English, 'you' began to be used as a mark of respect when addressing a superior and (later) an equal; 'thou', in contrast, was retained for addressing an inferior. This distinction between 'thou' and 'you' related to the relatively rigid stratification of society in the Middle Ages. It allowed an aristocratic speaker to distinguish between an equal (referred to as 'you') and someone inferior in social standing (referred to as 'thou'); the distinction could also be used to signal intimacy. The lower social orders, on the other hand, were required to address aristocrats as 'you' as a mark of deference. In the fifteenth century, the rising merchant classes began using 'thou' to the lower orders. Increasing social mobility and competition between this merchant class and the aristocracy meant that by the time of Shakespeare, in the late sixteenth and early seventeenth centuries, there was widespread confusion about who should use the term 'thou' to whom. The seventeenth-century radical Quaker, religious movement seized on the confusion between 'thou' and 'you' by using 'thou' to everyone, as a political act of levelling. The distinction eventually collapsed, and only 'you' survived. 'Thou' now only appears in archaizing registers, including those of poetry and religion. In these registers it functions, curiously enough, as a marker of respect rather than of inferiority. The *King James Authorized Version of the Bible* (1611) perhaps influenced the change in function of 'thou' by having biblical characters address God as 'thou', which is likely to have created a different stylistic effect in the seventeenth century than it does now.

The distinction between 'thou' and 'you' was partly, then, one of register (see **Unit 7, Language and context: register**), in that 'thou' was a familiar form of address whereas 'you' was more formal. Shakespeare's texts often seem to mix 'you' and 'thou' indiscriminately, but the distinction is occasionally important, as in the following exchange between Hamlet and his mother:

> *Queen.* Hamlet, thou hast thy father much offended.
> *Hamlet.* Mother, you have my father much offended.
> *Queen.* Come, come, you answer with an idle tongue.
> *Hamlet.* Go, go, you question with a wicked tongue.
>
> (*Hamlet, c.* 1600, III, iv, 10–13)

The queen's initial use of 'thou' to Hamlet and his 'you' in return are standard choices for parent-to-offspring and offspring-to-parent respectively. It is the queen's follow-up 'you' that is significant; annoyed by Hamlet's caustic rejoinder, she switches icily to a distancing 'you'.

5.3.4 Lexis: words and their meanings

The vocabulary of a language can change for different reasons. First, new terms may be introduced on the model of older forms (for example, 'personal stereo' described a new machine by using a combination of already existing words; and 'air rage' describes a form of violent behaviour on aeroplanes, based on the model of word-combinations such as 'road rage'). Alternatively, word forms may be adopted from other languages, such as 'pizza' or 'segue'. The reasons for such vocabulary changes include pressures of social change and the introduction of new technological inventions. In Britain during the current period, many American vocabulary items are being adopted, such as use of the verb 'to progress something' and of nouns such as 'ballpark figure' and 'raincheck', reflecting the social, economic and political influence of the United States on Britain. The vocabulary of computers has also been productive in introducing new terms into mainstream usage (e.g. 'log in/out', 'interface', 'to access').

5.4 Archaism

A linguistic **archaism** is the use of a particular pronunciation, word or way of combining words that is no longer in current usage. The term comes from the Latin word *archaismus*, meaning to model one's style on that of ancient writers. Thus, an archaism is an anachronistic use of a word or phrase. Certain registers are characterized in part by their use of archaism, particularly registers associated with institutions whose functioning and significance are based largely on tradition (such as the Church or the legal system).

The Bible, as the central document of Christianity, exists in a number of different English translations. Until recently, the *King James Authorized Version* (1611) was the most widely used translation. Many Christian groups and churches, however, have adopted more recent translations such as *The New English Bible* (1961), on the basis that it seems more 'up to date' and accessible. A measure of the difference between translations can be gained by comparing the language of equivalent passages (here, I Corinthians 15, 53):

King James Version:
For this corruptible must put on incorruption, and this mortall must put on immortalitie.

New English Bible:
This perishable being must be clothed with the imperishable, and what is mortal must be clothed with immortality.

Although the new version is easier to understand, for modern readers, the old version is preferred by some Christians because its archaic language seems more mysterious and evocative, and therefore somehow more appropriate to religious experience.

Many English legal texts are also characterized by archaism. Use of archaisms such as 'be it enacted', 'shall have effect' and (even in recent legislation) 'cinematograph film' arises partly because of history: law was the last social institution to stop using the French and Latin of the Norman occupation (French was still used in law in some circumstances into the eighteenth century). It is also, however, partly a result of function: legal language has to be seen as distinct from ordinary usage – more technically precise and less open to ambiguity, and yet at the same time continuous with the historical traditions, and so authority, of the common law (for more extended discussion of the legal register, see **Unit 7, Language and context: register**).

There is also a long tradition of archaism in poetic texts. Edmund Spenser, for example, writing in the late sixteenth century, developed a vocabulary for poems such as *The Faerie Queene* by copying words from Chaucer, who was writing 200 years earlier. Spenser's language was then imitated by later writers, especially by Romantic poets such as Keats in the early nineteenth century. As a result, most attempts to define a general 'poetic' register include archaism as a component feature. Here, for example, is a line from Walter Scott's 'The song of the Reim-kennar' (1822): 'Enough of woe hast thou wrought on the ocean'. Archaisms here include the syntax (word order) – a modern English word order would probably be 'You have brought enough' – and words such as 'thou', 'hast' and 'wrought'. A more recent poem that exploits archaism is W.H. Auden's 'The Wanderer' (1930), which is directly modelled on an Anglo-Saxon poem of the same name and uses Anglo-Saxon word-formation patterns, such as 'place-keepers' or 'stone-haunting', as well as alliterative patterns common in Anglo-Saxon poetry. The first line of the poem is: 'Doom is dark and deeper than any sea-dingle', which uses a repeated 'd' sound on stressed syllables (see **Unit 16, Rhyme and sound patterning**). In using such archaisms, the poem suggests meanings and values that create an impression of transcending time and place.

It should be noted, however, that problems can arise in identifying archaism, since 'archaisms' may sometimes not appear archaic in the register in which they are used. For example, 'thee' and 'thou' are not necessarily archaic forms in a certain type of poetic register; they are archaic only in relation to our contemporary day-to-day speech and related expectations. Use of an archaism can therefore be interpreted either as conforming to a register or as looking back to the past (or as both). One of the questions it is necessary to ask, therefore, in reading a text is whether apparent archaisms are archaic only relative to current usage, or whether they would also have been archaisms in literature written at the time the particular text was written. Only by using a historical dictionary such as the OED, which charts the meanings of words over time, is it possible to find out whether certain words were current or archaic at the time of composition.

5.5 Feminist changes to language

Some writers on the relation between language and political and social power, such as Michel Foucault (1978), have stressed how language is both an instrument of social constraint and at the same time a means of resisting that constraint. This is perhaps most clearly seen in feminist theory, where language is identified as one of the means through which patriarchal values are both maintained and resisted (see **Unit 8, Language and gender**). As a result of campaigns by feminists against sexist language, arguably sexism has changed and become more indirect. For example, on a mainstream pop radio station such as BBC Radio 1 DJ Chris Moyles has controversially used many phrases that are openly sexist to his female co-presenter and to female callers to the programme, referring to them as 'dippy'. But the BBC has argued in response that he is using these terms in a parodic and humorous way. Such masking of sexism by irony and humour, which is common in media controversies about language use, makes sexism more difficult to identify and take issue with.

Jane Mills's *Womanwords* (1989) is a dictionary that demonstrates how words associated with women often have a revealing history of meanings. The word 'glamour', for example, once meant 'magical strength' and was used to refer to both men and women; when the word began to be used for women alone, however, it took on sexual and trivializing connotations, as in 'glamour girl'. A similar trajectory can be noted for words like 'witch', which was once used for both men and women but began to acquire negative connotations when its reference became restricted to women. It would be hard to identify a particular individual or social group responsible for such changes. Rather, we tend to interpret such changes as occasioned by more general, ideological and discursive structures that make up what feminists call 'patriarchy' (i.e. economic, social and political norms within a society whose end result is that women are treated as if inferior to men).

To counter such verbal discrimination against women, some feminists have attempted to reform the language in a variety of ways. For example, they have argued that offensive or discriminatory terms should be replaced by more neutral terms: 'chairperson' instead of 'chairman'; 'humankind' instead of 'mankind'; 'staff' instead of 'manpower', and so on. Pauwels (1998) has demonstrated how successful this type of language reform has been by showing how many of the trivializing and discriminatory terms that feminists campaigned against in the 1980s now have an archaic feel to them, or are no longer used (consider, for example, words like 'usherette' and 'aviatrix'). However, as Cameron (1992) has noted, although it is possible to make changes in language on a small scale, getting the changes adopted more generally is less easy. Changes in language have to go through what she calls 'the gatekeepers of language', which are institutions such as the media, education, the government, lexicographers, and so on, that tend to be resistant to the type of changes feminists wish to see. Those changes may also be labelled mere 'political correctness' by their detractors (Dunant, 1994). However, as Cameron makes clear, one of the effects of this debate about negative connotations of gendered terms is that, within the public sphere at least, sexist terms are now largely unacceptable. In addition, those who wish to continue to use terms such as 'chairman' for women will be viewed as making clear statements about their beliefs.

A more general point that emerges from the foregrounding of a political dimension in language change is that, for the most part, changes in language occur beyond the conscious control of particular individuals or social groups. Even when 'gatekeepers of language' seek to resist or introduce change there is no guarantee that they will be successful. British and American history offers many examples of failed attempts to reform the language according to an imposed standard (see Cameron, 1992). By contrast, as Pauwels (1998) has shown, concerted efforts by anti-racist, feminist and gay and lesbian activists have shown how pressure groups can bring about change in language, despite such change often being resisted and derided by other groups in society.

A.S. Byatt's *The Children's Book* (2009) appears to simulate the style of a nineteenth-century novel. Analyse the elements in the following extract which signal to you that the passage is drawing on the style of a nineteenth-century novel in this way. Consider in particular: sentence length, subject matter, vocabulary, narrative point of view and assumed reader knowledge.

> Basil and Humphry Wellwood had begun to argue about Bimetallism and the Gold Standard. They came across the grass, breathing wrath and rhetoric, pointing decisive fingers into the evening air. Basil was a member of the Gold Standard Defence Association. Humphry supported the Bimetallic League.
>
> That summer of 1895 was the height of the Kaffir Circus boom. Shares in real and fictive seams of gold were feverishly traded. Basil dines with the Randlords and had made a fortune, in gold and in paper. Humphry publicly used the jibe that a mine was a hole in the ground owned by a liar. He also said in public that the financial press took underhand *douceurs* to promote and condemn prospectuses. Basil suspected Humphry of being responsible for pseudonymous articles in satirical journals, mocking Croesus, Midas and the Golden Calf.
>
> He also suspected him of confidential knowledge from his employment in the Bank of England to attack that institution. In 1893 it was rumoured that the Chief Cashier, Frank May, had made huge unauthorized advances to his son, a speculative broker. Worse, he had made advances to himself.

ACTIVITY 5

Reading

Barber, C. (1997) *Early Modern English*, 2nd edn, London: André Deutsch.

Cameron, D. (1992) *Feminism and Linguistic Theory*, 2nd edn, London: Macmillan, pp. 79–90.

Crystal, D. (2006b) *Language and the Internet*, 2nd edn, Cambridge: Cambridge University Press.

Fairclough, N. (1992) *Discourse and Social Change*, London: Polity Press.

Leith, D. (1997) *A Social History of English*, 2nd edn, London: Routledge & Kegan Paul, pp. 32–57.

Pauwels, A. (1998) *Women Changing Language*, London: Longman.

UNIT 6

Language and place

This unit:

- describes how various features of language are used in representing place in literary texts, drawing attention to different points of view such descriptions can create;

- introduces place-related speaker variation, including regional accent and dialect, and shows how such features of language use can combine in the repertoire of an individual speaker;

- assesses the importance of styles of speaking presented as the voice of a fictional narrator in a literary work;

- explores how linguistic construction of different voices in literary texts affects the depiction of social attitudes, especially in modernism and in post-colonial writing in English.

UNIT 6

Texts can create a sense of place in two main ways. First, they can describe places, incorporating many different sorts of detail. Where this occurs in fiction, the effect is what we think of as 'setting'. Second, place can be represented in how characters (or a narrator or poetic persona) are made to speak. This second way of representing place relies on connections we typically make between the distinctive properties of voices and the places with which they are conventionally associated. These two means of representing place work together, and can express complex beliefs, desires and fears about how human life fits into the natural and social environment (see Williams, 1985). There are also whole literary genres, such as the pastoral (Gifford, 1999), which use established but changing conventions to comment in this way (see **Unit 4, Recognizing genre**).

6.1   Describing places

Consider description (or 'setting') first. In Thomas Hardy's novels, the author precisely describes aspects of 'Wessex', Hardy's fictional name for the Southwest of England. In *The Mayor of Casterbridge* (1886), for example, the arrival in Casterbridge in Chapter 4 of Henchard's wife Susan, while searching for Henchard, offers an early opportunity for description of the town. Casterbridge, Hardy writes, is a place 'at that time, recent as it was, untouched by the faintest sprinkle of modernism'; and he continues:

> It was compact as a box of dominoes. It had no suburbs – in the ordinary sense. Country and town met at a mathematical line.
>
> To birds of the more soaring kind Casterbridge must have appeared on this fine evening as a mosaic-work of subdued reds, browns, greys, and crystals, held together by a rectangular frame of deep green. To the level eye of humanity it stood as an indistinct mass behind a dense stockade of limes and chestnuts, set in the midst of miles of rotund down and concave field. The mass became gradually dissected by the vision into towers, gables, chimneys, and casements, the highest glazings shining bleared and bloodshot with the coppery fire they caught from the belt of sunlit cloud in the west.
>
> From the centre of each side of this tree-bound square ran avenues east, west, and south into the wide expanse of corn-land and coomb to the distance of a mile or so. It was by one of these avenues that the pedestrians were about to enter.

Note in this passage the different kinds of detail that build Hardy's description: presentation of two viewpoints (eye-level and bird's-eye view); mapping of directions and layout ('east, west, and south'); the topography of the land ('rotund down and concave field'); and references to specific plants ('limes and chestnuts') as well as to colours ('reds, browns, greys, and crystals'). There is also close attention to architectural detail ('towers, gables, chimneys, and casements'), reflecting

Hardy's earlier chosen profession. Note also, however, a further dimension of the fictional sense of place: contrasts and boundaries that contribute to the novel's moral and political themes. A boundary is marked here, for example, between country and city (the two meet in Casterbridge 'at a mathematical line'); and reference is made to social changes that affect places over time (Casterbridge even at that recent time was, 'untouched by the faintest sprinkle of modernism'). As in much fictional writing, Hardy's description of Casterbridge here provides the novel not only with a specific geographical background or setting but also with important thematic or symbolic under-pinning that guide our search for meaning and significance in the narrative.

6.2   Point of view in describing place

One aspect of descriptions of place that is often overlooked is where the place in question is looked at *from*. To adopt the vocabulary of film or television, we might call this the 'camera-angle' for the descriptive 'shot'. In the passage above, two points of view are referred to: bird's-eye view ('to birds') and street-level view (the 'level eye of humanity'). By being compared with each other, these two viewpoints are suggested to be camera angles of a composite, 360 degree vision. Such an omniscient overview is commonly adopted in fictional descriptions of place, but may be subtly shifted in order to move a narrator's view closer to or further away from particular characters and events.

Indication of where the narrator is looking from comes partly from 'deictics' (or words whose meaning can only be interpreted by reference to the location of the speaker – the word **deixis** means pointing). As regards place, deictic words typically involve oppositions between relative closeness to, or distance from, the speaker: 'near'/'far'; 'here'/'there'; 'this'/'that', etc. (As regards time, time relative to the moment of speaking is contained in the meaning of words such as 'now', 'yesterday', 'soon', and phrases such as 'a week ago'.)

In fiction (as in film and television), places are not consistently described from the same point of view, even within one text. Nor are they always described straightforwardly from the viewpoint of the narrator. As an alternative to looking on, from a detached 'overview' position, the narrator can empathize with, or project himself or herself into, a point of view more closely aligned with one of the characters, and so begin to interpret events as if from a position within the world of the story (the 'text world'), rather than from outside it (for discussion of **deictic shift**, see Jeffries and McIntyre, 2010).

Consider by way of example two fairly typical brief passages slightly later in *The Mayor of Casterbridge*. The first is the opening sentence of Chapter 6, in which Susan Henchard and Elizabeth-Jane have their first encounter, in the King's Arms Hotel (and after a long absence), with the recently elevated Michael Henchard, Mayor of Casterbridge.

> Now the group outside the window had within the last few minutes been reinforced by new arrivals, some of them respectable shopkeepers and their assistants, who had come out for a whiff of air after putting up the shutters for the night . . .

The phrase 'outside the window' in this sentence locates the narrator's point of view *inside* the hotel. The 'new arrivals in the crowd', by contrast, have 'come out for a whiff of air' (note: not 'gone out' for a whiff of air) from shops located implicitly further away from the hotel, beyond the place they 'arrive' at, immediately 'outside'. Such details of description not only establish a point of view from which place and events will be observed, but also activate a process of mapping an imagined scene or landscape which the reader constructs as the world of the text. Interestingly in this excerpt, too, the phrase 'within the last few minutes' (in contrast with, for example, 'the previous few minutes') zooms the narrator's viewpoint towards Elizabeth-Jane's and her mother's time perspective, reinforcing a sense of involvement with the viewpoint of these two characters in time as well as space.

Similar use of deixis draws the reader into Elizabeth-Jane's hotel room to create a point-of-view that is significant in narrative terms in the first sentence of Chapter 9:

> When Elizabeth Jane opened the hinged casement next morning the mellow air brought in the field of imminent autumn almost as distinctly as if she had been in the remotest hamlet.

'Brought in' here indicates movement *towards* the deictic centre. Aligned in this way with Elizabth-Jane's room-centred view, we learn that she hears Henchard walking past and moves away from the window, preferring to look on from behind the window-curtains:

> Henchard, it appeared, had gone a little way past the inn before he had noticed his acquaintance of the previous evening. He came back a few steps . . .

Although Henchard has 'gone' a little way 'past' the inn (movement away), he then 'came back' (movement back towards the observation point, inside Elizabeth-Jane's hotel room) before entering into conversation with his 'acquaintance of the previous evening', a character called Donald Farfrae who has opened the window of the hotel room next to Elizabeth-Jane's own. That conversation, we now understand, is overheard.

6.3   How characters (and the narrator) talk

In tandem with descriptions of place of this kind, a further sense of place can be conveyed by how characters (and the narrator, where there is one) are made to speak. Such representation in a written text calls on an association we make between recognizable differences in grammar, vocabulary and pronunciation and how we suppose people speak in different places.

Creating a sense of place by incorporating regional speech mannerisms can be more problematic than description of place, however. Written representations of dialect or **accent** draw on, and sometimes exaggerate, conventional – sometimes stereotypical – images and connotations for varieties of language. While such images permit vivid and instant associations of voice with place, in doing so they trade on received ideas and contrasts, for instance the notion that some regional voices are more naive, stranger, rougher, more erotic or more authoritative than others.

6.4   Language variation

To investigate how we read such conventional 'imagery' of different textual voices, we must first consider how variation in language correlates with place. We can then explore more precisely how such variation is manipulated in literary works (as well as in non-literary and media texts) as a significant resource.

6.4.1   Variation within as well as between languages

The many languages of the world are related to each other in families (Indo-European, Dravidian, etc.). This family structure of languages involves overlapping and historically connected varieties, which in many cases have loaned each other words, sounds and structures. Even within what is called a single language, however, there is typically variation from region to region, as well as between classes, ethnic groups and genders (for a historical account of such development and interaction in relation to English, see Crystal, 2006a).

6.4.2   Dialect and accent

Variation within a given language can involve differences in the sound system, when speakers from a particular region (or social group) consistently pronounce words in different ways from other groups. Examples of this type of variation are the words 'rather' and 'farmer', which are pronounced differently in different parts of Britain. 'Tomato' and 'dynasty' differ between British and American English; and 'nothing' and 'hotel' differ between British English and Indian English.

Alongside differences in pronunciation, there can also be consistent differences in other aspects of the language. Different words are used in different places to refer to equivalent things or ideas. The word 'throat', for example, varies with 'gullet', 'thropple' and 'quilter' in different parts of Britain. A 'faucet' is what American English speakers call a 'tap'; 'pants' are 'trousers'; and 'suspenders' are equivalent to 'braces'. A 'cot' in India is an adult 'bed', not, as in British English, a child's bed. In South Africa, a 'robot' is a traffic light as well as an automaton. 'Outwith' in Scotland means the same as 'outside' or 'beyond' in England. **Dialect maps** of such variation can be drawn to show the traditional geographical distribution of different words representing the same (or closely similar) meanings.

Differences also occur in grammar. Scottish English, 'the potatoes need peeled', matches Southern English English 'the potatoes need to be peeled'. Yorkshire 'thou knowest' parallels Southern English English 'you know'. American English 'they did it Monday' parallels British English 'they did it on Monday'. British English 'I didn't like it either' matches Indian English 'I didn't like it also'.

When variations according to place are found exclusively in pronunciation, we speak of different accents; when variation according to region occurs simultaneously at the level of sound, vocabulary and grammar, we speak of different dialects. It is possible, therefore, to speak of a Yorkshire accent if we are referring only to pronunciation or of a Yorkshire dialect if we are referring to all the ways language in Yorkshire varies in relation to other regions. Similarly, we can speak of a 'West of Scotland' accent or dialect, and of a 'South East of England' accent or dialect.

The issue is complicated, however, by the fact that language also varies according to class (and, to a lesser degree, according to age, subculture and profession). Because these variations affect vocabulary and grammar as well as pronunciation, it is also possible to speak of class dialects and social dialects, as well as accents (see **Unit 9, Language and society**). The relation between regional dialects and social dialects is variable. Sometimes they reinforce one another; sometimes one will override the other. For example, the language of the upper classes in Scotland is likely to have more in common with that of the equivalent social group in England than with that of working-class speakers in Scotland.

6.4.3 Attitudes towards variation

What makes accent and dialect important – both in social interaction and in ways of reading – is that people feel very strongly, and also quite differently, about different varieties. Attitudes are often based on stereotypical contrasts between localities, for instance the contrast between rural and industrial. Such attitudes also rely on our ability to 'place' a language variety. When this is not possible, and judgement is made simply on the basis of the sound itself rather than on the basis of associated social knowledge, stereotypical views tend to evaporate. Conventional attitudes towards different language varieties also rely on an assumed fixed point of 'standard' pronunciation or grammar. The 'standard' variety is the one that is given most prestige. Pronunciation or grammar that is thought to stray from it is implicitly compared with it, and as a result perceived as 'non-standard'.

6.4.4   The repertoire of varieties available to individual speakers

The fact that language varies according to the regional and social identity of the user does not, however, result in each speaker being consistent in how he or she speaks or writes. In different situations, or when communicating about different topics, a speaker will automatically modify his or her language. Speakers shift – in response to subtle changes in situation and relationship – between different parts of the linguistic **repertoire** available to them. Variations that arise according to situation of use, rather than according to the identity of the user, are known as registers (see **Unit 7: Language and context: register**). Speakers who are able to use more than one dialect can manipulate those dialects as if they were registers, changing between them to achieve specific effects in any given situation (e.g. of appropriacy or marked inappropriacy). This type of shifting is especially common between a regional and a 'standard' variety. (For a literary example of this, see the discussion of *Lady Chatterley's Lover* in **Unit 9, Language and society**.)

6.5   Language variety in literary texts

Historically, the language in which literary texts might be written in Britain has been a troubled question. Quite apart from the issue of minority languages such as Welsh and Gaelic, it is worth noting that, before the sixteenth century, Latin and French were serious competitors to English. In the sixteenth century itself, English was not always thought good enough for literary work (though writing in it did take place).

During the period of the late Elizabethans and early Jacobeans (end of sixteenth and early seventeenth century), the attitude that English might not be good enough for literary work gradually changed, affected partly by celebration of existing writing in English (e.g. Shakespeare) and partly by changing attitudes towards Latin during the Reformation (the Protestant churches rejected the religious use by Roman Catholics of Latin). Little more than a century later, English was widely believed to have produced an especially eminent literature. Many of the arguments about which language to write in, in many parts of the world today, have in this way (despite their otherwise major differences) an analogue in the circumstances of English in Britain during the later medieval and early Renaissance period.

6.5.1   Dialect representation

In the history of literary writing in English, there have been clear but shifting constraints on which variety or varieties might be used and how. A criterion of

decorum was often invoked as a standard of appropriate style within a given genre, and this excluded a wide range of voices from serious literary writing. Dialect speakers were represented in many works merely as comic characters, with frequent jokes (including many specifically about dialect) made at their expense.

In tracing this history, it is important, however, to remember that accent is completely, and dialect largely, associated with speech rather than with writing. Representation of speech in writing cannot reproduce how people actually speak. Rather, it draws on conventions (such as modified spellings) that produce an illusion of speech (see **Unit 25, Performance and the page**), in order to signal that a character's speech is different from that of other characters in the text.

Dialect representation is more than a matter of how particular sounds should be represented, nevertheless. Differences between 'standard' and 'non-standard' voices set up a **hierarchy of voices** within a literary work. In nineteenth-century novels, for instance, the narrator and central characters tend to use Standard English, while regional or working-class characters – often minor characters in narrative and thematic terms – may speak with an accent or in a dialect. This raises the question of how far non-standard speech is used to reproduce the way people actually spoke in the place where the novel is set, and how far such use aims to accentuate contrasts of class or moral authority (in the way that other details, such as clothing and aspects of behaviour, also do).

Consider *The Mayor of Casterbridge* again. Hardy's Wessex novels are peopled with minor rural characters who speak in West Country dialect. Within this setting, however, Hardy typically explores the fate and fortune of middle-class characters, whose speech is more standard than that of the rural characters around them. In the following scene (from Chapter 15), Michael Henchard's changing speech style echoes his rise and fall from destitute rural worker to mayor of Casterbridge, then back to destitution, as Henchard chastises one of the workers on his farm for being late in the mornings:

> Then Henchard . . . declared with an oath that this was the last time; that if he were behind once more, by God, he would come and drag him out o' bed.
>
> 'There is sommit wrong in my make, your worshipful!' said Abel, '. . . I never enjoy my bed at all, for no sooner do I lie down than I be asleep, and afore I be awake I be up. I've fretted my gizzard green about it, maister, but what can I do? . . .'
>
> 'I don't want to hear it!' roared Henchard. 'To-morrow the waggons must start at four, and if you're not here, stand clear. I'll mortify thy flesh for thee!'

The worker's dialect is rendered here through non-standard spelling ('maister'), non-standard grammar ('no sooner do I lie down than I be asleep') and dialect phrases ('I've fretted my gizzard'). Interestingly, though, in his anger Henchard 'lapses' into dialect (and/or biblical language) in a way that reminds us of his origins ('thee' and 'thy' remain in use in dialects long after their disappearance from

Standard English). The narrative voice reinforces this shift. Henchard's comments begin in Standard English, using **indirect speech** ('Henchard declared with an oath that this was the last time'); then they switch into **free indirect speech**, in order to let Henchard's own, non-standard speech come through: 'by God, he would come and drag him out o' bed'. (For discussion of 'indirect' and 'free indirect speech' see **Unit 22, Speech and narration**.)

6.5.2   Modernist polyphony

One distinctive feature of twentieth-century modernist writing is that a wider range of voices is sometimes presented than was usual (or even possible) in earlier literary works in English. In many cases, the introduction of a wider range of voices takes the form of variety switching (as in James Joyce's *Ulysses* (1922)), or juxtaposition (as in T.S. Eliot's *The Waste Land* (1922)).

But a fundamental question about dialect representation then arises: Do such texts introduce their representation (or mimicry) of regional and class voices as a fundamentally new kind of polyphony, in which all those voices have become equal? Or is there still a hierarchy of voices in terms of relative seriousness and authority, with these extra voices included merely so that they can be finally subordinated to, or refined into, a reaffirmed, authoritative standard voice of the literary narrator or poetic persona? (The second of these alternatives is directly arguable in relation to T.S. Eliot's *The Waste Land*; for a discussion of this issue in *Ulysses*, see **Unit 7, Language and context: register** and **Unit 12, Juxtaposition**.) In such experimental writing, it is significant that regional varieties are used to create a schematic contrast between Standard and non-Standard English. Arguably it is only in forms of dialect writing linked to an expressed sense of place and regional identity (as in much Scottish writing since the early twentieth century) that dialect functions less to contrast with an established standard than to affirm a distinct regional idiom.

How dialect will be used in literary works in future is far from certain. In contemporary Britain, people have many quite different experiences of place from one another, partly because of the regional, class and ethnic diversity of the population. This seems likely to give rise to continuing experimentation with juxtaposition and mixing of language varieties. Also, people move from place to place and take their dialect with them. So interaction between the regional and social dimensions of dialect seems likely to result in changing and unpredictable connections between voice, region and sense of identity.

6.6   Post-colonial writing in English

In many **anglophone** post-colonial societies (such as India, Pakistan, anglophone Africa, the Philippines, Malaysia, the Caribbean and many other places), the idea of using English at all in creative writing has been contentious. Some influential writers (such as the Kenyan novelist and dramatist Ngugi wa Thiong'o (b. 1938), now resident in California) have argued that using a former colonial language merely reinforces the power of emerging neocolonial elites at the expense of developing a self-confident and emancipated local or national literature. Other writers have argued that the linking, 'transnational' function of a language such as English enables different communities (including different African communities) to become more aware of each other. In this second view, using English in literary and other contexts may open up new possibilities for redefining relations between communities in a way that would be impossible if they remained separated by walls of linguistic difference.

In some post-colonial writing in English, dialect is viewed in an almost opposite way. It serves as a kind of **anti-language**, or mode of expression deliberately adopted to mark it off from dominant traditions of writing that are being rejected. And in other kinds of writing again, an argument for using dialect is made in terms of authenticity, and an aspiration to give a true representation of the writer's identity (see **Unit 14, Authorship and intention**). Yet such a fixed conjunction of identity, dialect and place is difficult: dialect contrasts – as well as individual varieties – themselves vary as they travel from place to place. Forms of dialect spelling and **code-switching** to be found in such writing are likely to be read differently as they circulate beyond the region or country in which the variety being represented is actually used.

ACTIVITY 6

Like the passages from Hardy earlier in this unit, the passage below (from near the beginning of a novel) describes a specific place, the narrator's claimed birthplace: 'a small undistinguished seaside town' called Bacong, on the island of Negros Oriental, Southern Philippines. The passage is also narrated, we are told, at a specific time: in 'the late 1800s'. This activity explores techniques in the passage that contribute to, but at the same time complicate, the description of the island and the narrator's place in that description.

The outline of Negros Island much resembled an inverted silhouette of a lady with a powerful neck and a high bun on her head. Where the lady's eye would be, the taller peak of Cuernos de Negros rose to a craggy cloud-capped height.

When Pedro Saavedra, Spanish surveyor and heir to a brewery fortune in Galicia, stood on this peak in 1765 and thus came to the crowning culmination of seven months of geodetic cum geologic work on the island, he took one long sweeping look at the curving coastline to the south, where the island's head widened to the sea's hairdressing hands, and breathed deeply the way Galicians of high birth do before their first swig of malt at sundown.

'Ah, yesss . . .' Pedro Saavedra hissed softly, drawing in the lowlying clouds to view the neighboring islands of Siquijor and Cebu across the

continued

strait, and directly south the big one, Mindanao of the large promise despite the betelnutchewing, bloodred-spitting Muslims.

6,967 feet, inscribed Pedro Saavedra on his ledger. He turned about again to sweep the panorama of the island's southern end. Down from the peak the jungly growths began less than fifty feet away. Undulations of dark dipterocarp green descended gradually to a vast plain where a carpet of coconut palms stretched out towards the sea. A pair of eagles swooped in ritual romance down the slope and when they lofted farther along towards the faint steeple of Valencia, the town by the foothills, a roost of blackbirds darted quickly through their familiar course of dead trees. Wisps of smoke rose from the towns below: Zamboanguita, Siaton, Dauin, Bacong, and the large capital of Dumaguete. Thinner curls of rising noonday smoke could be seen across the foothills where bands of slash-and-burn farmers tended their season's patches of tubers and legumes.

Pedro Saavedra breathed deeply before scanning over the rest of the pages in his work ledger. Latitude 8°, longitude 123°, 28,432 feet at the island's widest, 131,848 feet at its longest, chromatic basalt studded by sulphur vents all along the serpentine vein of prehistoric crater activity . . . There, right about there, he squinted towards 8 degrees north-north-east, that crystal speck some three thousand feet away is the volcanic lake the natives called Balinsasayao for its dancing swallows, where black swans were also said to have once glided along the dark serene surface.

There is too much dark beneath this country's serene surface, Pedro thought to himself.

(from *Great Philippine Jungle Energy Café*, a novel by
Alfred A. Yuson (Adriana Printing Co, 1988))

---

1   Make a list of expressions in the passage that suggest an attempt to describe place as 'objectively' or precisely as possible. Examples might include specific place names; technical terms for describing layout, direction or orientation; scientific names for plants or animals; dates, numbers and measurements of distance, height, etc.

2   Make a list of expressions that suggest a less directly descriptive, more imaginative or poetic approach to creating a sense of place. Examples might include cultural analogies; informal or colloquial terms used to name places, plants, buildings or animals; poetic imagery and personification, etc.

3   Do these two forms of expression remain separate in the passage, or are they interwoven?

continued

4   The narrator, we know, is an inhabitant of the island, located in time in 'the late 1800s'. But the description in the passage is mainly presented through the attributed perceptions and actions of an earlier Spanish colonial occupier of the island: a character (Pedro Saavedra) who is simultaneously a surveyor and an heir to a brewery back in Galicia, a region of Spain. A third perspective is also alluded to, by characterization of one thing (a 'volcanic lake') as something that 'the natives called' something else: 'Balinsasayao', with an accompanying description. Are these different perspectives kept separate, or do they interact?

5   The passage ends with a switch of topic: from a description of swans gliding on a 'dark serene' lake surface to the suggestion by the colonial surveyor that there is 'too much dark beneath this country's serene surface'. What does this modulation from description into more speculative comment suggest about the possible direction or concerns of the novel?

Reading

Crystal, D. (2006a) *The Stories of English*, Harmondsworth: Penguin.

Gifford, T. (1999) *The Pastoral*, New Critical Idiom Series, London: Routledge.

Jeffries, L. and McIntyre, D. (2010) *Stylistics*, Cambridge: Cambridge University Press, Chapter 6.

Lodge, D. (1994) *The Art of Fiction*, Harmondsworth: Penguin.

Williams, R. (1985) *The Country and the City*, London: The Hogarth Press.

Language and context: register

This unit:

- introduces the concept of 'register', showing how to analyse and explain the significance of: linguistic medium, social relationship between participants, and the field or topic being talked about;

- examines the relationship between register and discourses associated with social class, as well as the potential created by register for switching within an individual speaker's repertoire;

- shows how different registers have been used in different periods of literary writing sometimes to create a particular kind of literary voice and sometimes to disrupt or undermine the creation of any such singular voice.

UNIT 7

The term 'register' is used to describe the fact that the kinds of language we use are affected by the context in which we use them. This takes place to such an extent that certain kinds of language use become conventionally associated with particular situations, and our tacit knowledge of these conventions of use allows us to judge whether what someone says or writes is 'appropriate' in a given context (Biber and Conrad, 2009). Our ability to judge spontaneously whether language choices match a given situation can be highlighted by the odd effect created when a text deviates from what seems an appropriate register, as happens towards the end of the following official passenger information announcement on a train:

> May I have your attention please, ladies and gentlemen. The train is now approaching Lancaster. Passengers for the Liverpool boat train should alight here and cross to platform one. Delays are being experienced on this train and passengers intending to use this service should consult the notice board on platform one to find out what the score is.

The slightly comic effect of the end of this passage is created by a sudden (presumably unintentional) switch of register in the last phrase. For the most part, the announcement keeps to typical language choices that British travellers associate with train announcements, though we may feel that the style is too elevated or 'high-flown' for what is only information about trains and platforms. Unintended humour creeps in when the announcer juxtaposes the formal opening of the announcement with its much less formal conclusion ('to find out what the score is'), thereby comically undercutting what has gone before. (See **Unit 12, Juxtaposition**.)

The most obvious way in which a text 'registers' its context is in selection of vocabulary. Our experience of language in context allows us to recognize that vocabulary items such as 'alight' and 'consult' are characteristic of a professional idiom that the railway company uses for communicating to the public, and we are equally sensitive to the fact that 'to find out what the score is' does not belong to that idiom. But differences in register involve differences in grammar as well. In the phrase 'Delays are being experienced', the use of an impersonal passive construction contributes as much as the vocabulary to the formality of the announcement's register.

Each of us experiences a variety of language situations every day, and from moment to moment: talking on the phone about financial matters, chatting to friends, speaking in a tutorial, writing an essay or email, or communicating with friends on Facebook. In each of these contexts, we adopt the appropriate register without effort, and are able to recognize when others do the same. By the same token, we are all sensitive to deviation in register.

7.1 Contexts that affect register

7.1.1 Medium

The medium of a text is the substance from which the text is made, or through which it is transmitted, or in which it is stored (the text may be spoken or written, live or recorded, on paper or in a digital format). For register, the most prominent difference in medium is between speech and writing (see **Unit 22, Speech and narration**). Speech is usually made up on the spot and interpreted as it is heard. Writing, on the other hand, may involve long periods of composition and revision and the resulting text may be read (and possibly re-read) in circumstances quite remote in time and place from the circumstances in which it was written. Written texts, therefore, tend to be more formal than spoken texts, which tend to be more provisional in their structure and to feel less formal. Speech and writing may also be shaped according to whether they pass through other media: a telephone conversation is not the same as a face-to-face chat; texts and blogs have recognizably different register features from letters or newspapers. In public settings, spoken texts may be carefully prepared in advance and may take on the formal characteristics of the written mode. The rail announcement above begins in this fashion, before slipping into something closer to everyday speech.

7.1.2 Tone (or tenor)

A second aspect of the context that affects register is that of the social roles prescribed for, or adopted by, participants in the communication situation. Differences in register result from whether the relationships between participants are informal or formal, familiar or polite, personal or impersonal. The tone of the text can also indicate the attitude or position adopted by the writer or speaker in relation to the reader or listener. In the train announcement, use of phrases such as 'ladies and gentlemen' (signalling politeness), the intricate syntax (which, together with words such as 'attention', 'approaching' and 'alight', signals formality) and the passive voice (which avoids reference to human agency – as in 'Delays are being experienced') are all features of an impersonal register. The suggestion that passengers should 'find out what the score is', by contrast, assumes a more informal and familiar relationship between speaker and addressee: one that seems to clash with the context previously established.

7.1.3 Field and role

A third aspect of context that affects register is the topic and role of the communication. Language can be used for a variety of purposes (to convey information, to express feelings, to cajole, to seduce, to pray, to produce **aesthetic** effects, etc.). Each of these purposes leaves its mark on what is said and how what is said is said. In addition, most human activities – law, science, religion, academic work, sport, and so on, as well as people involved in each of those fields – have their own characteristic registers, because they employ 'field-specific' vocabularies (or vocabulary specific to a distinct **semantic field**). In Britain, for example, train companies no longer address passengers as 'passengers' but as 'customers'. This involves a switch in field (and hence of register) from the notion of a public service, transport, to the field of shopping – subtly changing the assumed relationship between the rail company and the people who travel on its trains.

7.2 The social distribution of registers

Each of us is able to adopt the appropriate register for a wide variety of contexts: we have a repertoire of different registers at our command. We also have a passive familiarity with a larger range of other registers (those we recognize but do not normally perform, associated with legal documents, religious rituals, scientific discourse, etc.). The range of registers we feel comfortable with (in an active or passive capacity) may be affected by many factors, including our age, social background, education, gender, race and work status. Register has the effect of positioning, or can be used to position, participants in a dialogue differently according to who those participants are. At this point, any simple contrast between register and dialect as a contrast between *language according to use* and *language according to user* (see **Unit 6, Language and place**) begins to break down. The registers we become familiar with and learn how to manipulate in higher education, for example, might well be alienating to people who have not had access to those registers (and one of the purposes of higher education is to familiarize students with the specialized register of the discipline being studied.)

7.3 Conservative and liberal registers

Although linguistic usage changes with time, some historical periods, societies or professions try to preserve a 'purity' of particular registers, by maintaining rigorous hierarchical distinctions between them. Institutions such as the Church and the law have been relatively successful in maintaining their field-specific registers with relatively little alteration over the centuries, perhaps to maintain distinctions between initiates and non-initiates. Institutions that seek to preserve their particular registers and isolate them from linguistic changes taking place in the society around them may be said to act 'conservatively' in relation to register. Compared with such register behaviour, areas such as youth culture and literature adopt more 'open' or 'liberal' registers that change frequently, invent new words and phrases more often, and borrow from each other as well as from the 'conservative' registers around them.

7.4 Literature and register

Register impacts on literature in two main ways. First, the fact that literary works typically attempt to represent recognizable social worlds in convincing ways means that literary texts may draw on, or quote from, any of the non-literary registers that exist in the social world at the time of writing or in the period in which the text is set. Second, literature has its own, specialized register conventions that have been built up historically. Consequently, the reader of any literary text needs to be alert to the non-literary registers that it is 'voicing', and to the way that the text is engaging with literary registers (and so expectations of linguistic suitability) established in the history of literature.

7.4.1 The novel and non-literary registers

In his essay 'Discourse in the Novel' (first published in Russia in 1973), Mikhail Bakhtin argues that the novel as a genre is characterized by what he calls **dialogism.** Any novel, on this view, typically includes a multiplicity of different, and potentially conflicting, voices. Most obviously, novels include the voices of narrators and characters, and these voices will necessarily be marked by register. Who or what or where is the narrator supposed to be? Is he or she supposed to be speaking or writing? Is his or her narration 'literary' or not? What is the social identity of any given character? What **speech situations** are they placed within? Do they write letters, and if so to whom? Less obviously, though, Bakhtin also suggests that the palette of the novelist is precisely the whole range of possible registers. Bakhtin's list of the kinds of 'voices' that may be woven into a novel is, viewed in this light, effectively a list of registers:

(1)   direct authorial literary-artistic narration (in all its diverse variants);
(2)   stylization of the various forms of oral everyday narration (*skaz*);
(3)   stylization of the various forms of semi-literary (written) everyday narration (the letter, the diary, etc.);
(4)   various forms of literary but extra-artistic authorial speech (moral, philosophical or scientific statements, oratory, ethnographic descriptions, memoranda and so forth);
(5)   the stylistically individualized speech of characters.

(adapted from Leitch, 2001, p. 1192)

Bakhtin argues that the discursive material available to the novel is an almost inexhaustible range of registers:

> The internal stratification of any single national language into social dialects, characteristic group behavior, professional jargons, generic languages, languages of generations and age groups, tendentious languages, languages of the authorities, of various circles and of passing fashions, languages that

serve the specific sociopolitical purposes of the day, even of the hour . . . this internal stratification present in every language at any given moment of its historical existence is the indispensable prerequisite for the novel as a genre.

(Leitch, 2010, p. 1192)

7.4.2 The registers of *Robinson Crusoe*

To illustrate Bakhtin's argument, we might look at Daniel Defoe's *Robinson Crusoe* (1719), which is often regarded as one of the first novels in English. Although the novel is a first-person narrative, and although for a great deal of the novel the narrator is alone on a deserted island, *Robinson Crusoe* is a good example of the dialogic nature of the genre. This is because the narrator's mono-logue consists of a polyphony of various 'voices' or registers that were in circulation in early eighteenth-century Britain. Crusoe's narration contains, for example, features of Puritan spiritual autobiography of the period, along with features of another related contemporary genre – the private journal. Other contemporary registers in Crusoe's narration include that of seafaring and navigation – a promi-nent discourse at a historical moment when Britain's empire was being expanded by means of sea voyaging – as well as the registers of building, agriculture and husbandry as Crusoe exploits the natural resources of his island. Crusoe's response to his situation wavers between a register of Protestant self-examination, with its notions of sin, providence, divine retribution and salvation, and the twin registers of early capitalism (business and trade, profit and loss) and economic individualism (an emphasis on individual effort, rational calculation, trial and error, cause and effect). Crusoe's monologue is therefore riven by two of the dominant registers in English culture of the period. The two registers nevertheless converge when Crusoe writes up a balance sheet of his condition on the island:

> I now began to consider seriously my Condition, and the Circumstance I was reduc'd to, and I drew up the State of my Affairs in Writing, . . . and as my Reason began now to master my Despondency, . . . I stated . . . very impar-tially, like Debtor and Creditor, the Comforts I enjoy'd, against the Miseries I suffer'd, Thus:

Evil	Good
I am cast upon a horrible desolate Island, void of all hope of Recovery.	*But I am alive, and not drown'd as all my Ship's Company was.*
I am singl'd out and separated, as it were, from all the World to be miserable.	*But I am singl'd out too from all the Ship's Crew to be spar'd from Death; and He that miraculously saved me from Death, can deliver me from this Condition.*

In this passage, the register is partly that of Protestant faith ('he that miraculously sav'd me from Death, can deliver me from this Condition'), but its form – the balance sheet of 'Debtor and Creditor' – reflects the register of economic individualism. While these two registers and impulses sometimes went hand in hand in early eighteenth-century Britain (and sometimes do in *Robinson Crusoe*), Defoe's weaving of the two registers into Crusoe's narration sometimes suggests an incongruity between them as views of the world.

7.4.3   Register in Modernism

The registers that resonate in Crusoe's narration are 'motivated': in other words, there tend to be reasons for their use. For example, Crusoe uses the registers associated with seafaring and navigation when he is describing experiences at sea. Even the mixing of religious and rational/economic registers discussed above is motivated, in that these are the voices of Crusoe's inner conflict, and they also reflect the historical moment at which Defoe was writing. Use of motivated registers in this way is characteristic of realist novels. The experimentation that differentiates some Modernist literature of the early twentieth century from this type of realist register use, however, involves register mixing that largely abandons such motivation.

There is a connection, even so, between how a clash between registers expresses Robinson Crusoe's inner thoughts and turmoil and the more fundamental experimentation with register that takes place in Modernist fiction and poetry. Modernist writing was characterized by major uncertainty regarding the voice in which a literary speaker (whether fictional narrator or poetic persona) could credibly address readers, as if the accepted registers adopted in established literary genres, and the modes of thought and perception with which they were associated, were worn out.

The uncertainty of literary voice of the period was reflected in poetry by Modernist writers such as T.S. Eliot and Ezra Pound experimenting in ways that almost resemble an apprenticeship, with mimicking or imitating various, contrasting varieties of language out of which they might construct new, composite poetic voices (Pound even called his first collection of poems *Personae*). In a number of poetic works of the period, including T.S. Eliot's *The Waste Land* (1922), Ezra Pound's *Cantos* (begun in 1917 and left unfinished at the poet's death in 1972) and William Carlos Williams's long poem *Paterson* (published between 1946 and 1958), different registers collide with one another, ranging across the archaic, technical, political, conversational, conventionally poetic, and religious. Fragments of already existing discourse are also brought into these poems, as a kind of verbal collage consisting of translated excerpts, quotation from literary works of earlier periods (as well as, in Pound, from political, economic and philosophical discourse), and (in William Carlos Williams) scraps from local newspapers, letters received by the writer, public signs and notices.

The impact of such experimentation with different registers is a fundamental disruption of the impression that register helps to achieve in most discourse of a unified consciousness engaged in writing in a given situation and typically for a recognizable purpose. Instead, the characteristics of a text's language are fore-grounded: its deviant, exaggerated and fragmented forms clash with one another and result in multiple, broken-up voices and a kind of polyphony, rather than any more consistent, singular voice that could be suggestive of an expressive identity behind the writing.

Consider, for example, the following brief extract from Pound's 'Canto 50' (roughly halfway through his series of *Cantos*):

'Pardon our brief digression' saith Zobi:
America is our daughter and VashiNNtonn had civic virtues.
and Leopoldo meant to cut off two thirds of state debt,
to abolish it
              and then they sent him off to be Emperor
in hell's bog, in the slough of Vienna, in
the midden of Europe in the black hole of all
mental vileness, in the privvy that stank Franz Josef,
in Metternich's merdery in the absolute rottenness,
among embasterdized cross-breeds,

(Canto 50: 247)

In this short extract (apparently of historical exposition), we have polite register ('pardon our brief digression') presented in inverted commas as direct speech and followed by a reporting verb that is archaic ('saith'); we have fragments of polit-ical discourse ('America is our daughter' and 'cut off two thirds of state debt'); and we have abusive near-synonyms (from different registers) used to describe Imperial Vienna: 'hell's bog', the 'slough' of Vienna, the 'midden' of Europe, the 'black hole', the 'privvy' and 'merdery'. Although there is an explicit indication of a speaker for the first line (Zobi), and representation of a manner of speaking in the spelling of Washington as 'VashiNNtonn', no overall impression is created of a consistent **poetic speaker**: the various words and phrases that make up the passage seem unlikely to co-occur in any naturally occurring register, and create instead a fragmented voice that is only unified by the idea of poetic register as an absorption of many different voices.

The literary purposes served by such experimentation appear to have varied between different writers. One way of understanding register counterpoint, for example, is to imagine a process of sifting, or selection and synthesis, through which one register emerges as a standard against which others are judged. This is one way of looking at the polyphony of T.S. Eliot's poem *The Waste Land*, though the idea of synthesizing the literary past and showing its superiority to contemporary culture is tested almost to destruction by persistent imagery of personal breakdown (see also **Unit 12, Juxtaposition**). The register counterpoint of William Carlos

Williams's poem *Paterson* might be thought a means of bringing together various discourses circulating in a town, Paterson (where the poet worked as a doctor); so there may be a suggestion of social observation in its polyphony of different voices. Ezra Pound's *Cantos* appear labyrinthine in their range of different voices and languages; but the poet stressed, sometimes aggressively, that a clear line of meaning and precise definition should be evident throughout. The register fragments in James Joyce's *Ulysses* (1922) resemble a ragbag of odds and ends taken from a huge variety of often incongruous registers; and although our sensitivity to register incongruity is often triggered in the novel for comic effect (e.g. to deflate high or grand styles with sudden shifts to low, informal ones), Joyce's experimentation has a more far-reaching implication: that of making it uncertain what the relationship between registers is. Indeterminacy of register in the novel presents the narrator less as someone who has or is finding a voice in which to say something than as a position through which the various different voices of a society speak. As regards the significance of such experimentation, one consequence in relation to *Ulysses* is that the novel's register experimentation allows this work to be viewed either as an attempt to rejuvenate, and so continue, the novel genre or alternatively as a challenge to the genre's claims to be a singular or elevated discourse, so undermining it.

7.4.4 'Literary' register

Modernist fragmentation of register of the kind illustrated above reignited a wider, continuing debate in literary criticism about whether or not literature has its own, specialized register or registers (such that we should be able to identify one or more 'literary' registers, in the way we recognize technical register, medical register or religious register).

For long periods in the history of thinking about literature, the answer to this question would have been that literature does have its own distinctive registers. That idea was based on a notion of 'decorum': the belief that there is an appropriate language for each kind of subject matter and genre. Just as we expect a funeral sermon to be conducted in a particular kind of language, so literary critics from classical Greece through to the eighteenth century also felt that the subject matter of a literary text ought to dictate its register. The choice to be made was partly a matter of genre: each genre – epic, tragedy, comedy, pastoral, and so on – was linked to a particular register. The notion of appropriateness was also shaped by social, political and cultural factors. In the eighteenth century – a literary age characterized by reason, politeness and social distinctions – literature was governed for the most part by notions of decorum: the language of literature is typically educated, polite, upper middle class; and the period's assumptions about literary appropriateness were summed up by the poet Alexander Pope in 1711: 'Expression is the dress of thought, and still / Appears more decent, as more suitable' (*An Essay on Criticism*, II, 318–19).

By the end of the eighteenth century, however, when ideas of democracy and revolution had begun to challenge the stabilities of this earlier neoclassical period, a parallel revolution had begun as regards the register considered appropriate to literature. In the 'Preface' to *Lyrical Ballads* (1800 [1798]), Wordsworth explains that *Lyrical Ballads* 'was published as an experiment . . . to ascertain, how far . . . a selection of the real language of men in a state of vivid sensation' might be a suitable language for poetry; the language 'of low and rustic life' – suitably adopted and 'purified' – was chosen because 'such men . . . convey their feelings and notions in simple and unelaborated expressions'. In this way Wordsworth attempted to change the register of poetry and challenged the assumption that poetry should be the preserve of an elite readership.

In some of Wordsworth's other poems, however, such as 'Tintern Abbey' (1798) and *The Prelude* (1805), the poet developed his own, recognizably 'Wordsworthian' register that is now part of a larger 'Romantic' register that characterizes poetry from the late eighteenth to the early twentieth century and that is still *the* register of poetry for many readers. When Keats's poetic speaker addresses a Grecian urn (or a figure on its design) as 'Thou still unravished bride of quietness', we know we are in the presence of poetry – or at least of 'Romantic' poetry. However, just as modernist writers experimented with the registers of the novel, so modernist poets experimented with this poetic register, challenging the underlying notion that there is a special register for poetry. The opening lines of T.S. Eliot's 'The Love Song of J. Alfred Prufrock' (1915) created an early shock that is largely produced by the way the third line jars with our preconceptions about poetic register:

> Let us go then, you and I,
> When the evening is spread out against the sky
> Like a patient etherised upon a table.

While the first two lines are in a recognizably poetic register that seems appropriate to a love song, the third line provides a simile for the evening sky that comes from a wholly different and incongruous register: that of surgical operations.

'The history of modern poetry – and poetic theory – may be seen, linguistically, as a series of attempts to escape from the dominant (Romantic) poetic register. Yet, as St John Butler (1999) has argued, if a text (any text) is set out on the page as poetry that in itself serves as a signal of poetic register, regardless of what the words themselves are. When we see this typographic generic signal (poetic layout), we tend to read what we are presented with as poetry; and, if the content (the subject matter and the vocabulary) seems obviously non-poetic, this produces a clash between form and content. Rather than abandoning poetic register, such poems presuppose our knowledge of it in order to achieve their challenging effect.

We should be wary, nevertheless, of assuming that register mixing and clashing is somehow unique to modernist poetry and the more recent poetry that followed it. It could be argued that the practice of recycling and mixing registers is central to the literary process more generally. Pope, who was cited above as arguing that poetic language should be 'suitable', also exploits possibilities created by that very notion in order to produce comic irony. In *The Rape of the Lock* (1712/1714), the humorous effect created depends precisely on a reader's familiarity with the register used in epic poetry and ability to recognize the mismatch between Pope's use of this 'high' register and the 'low' subject matter of the poem. In a similar way, novels such as *Ulysses* or poems such as 'The Love Song of J. Alfred Prufrock' depend on the notion of appropriateness built into the concept of register to achieve their effects, which may serve to challenge established ideas about literature, or to make a joke, or both.

ACTIVITY 7

This activity focuses on Edmund Blunden's 'Vlamertinghe: Passing the Chateau, July 1917' (1928). Vlamertinghe is a village in Belgium, near Passchendaele, where some of the heaviest fighting of the First World War took place in 1917.

'And all her silken flanks with garlands drest' –
But we are coming to the sacrifice.
Must those have flowers who are not yet gone West?
May those have flowers who live with death and lice?
This must be the floweriest place
That earth allows; the queenly face
Of the proud mansion borrows grace for grace
Spite of those brute guns lowing at the skies.

Bold great daisies, golden lights,
Bubbling roses' pinks and whites –
Such a gay carpet! poppies by the million;
Such damask! such vermilion!
But if you ask me, mate, the choice of colour
Is scarcely right; this red should have been much duller.

---

1   Read the poem carefully, then identify the poem's register or registers by marking where you feel the register changes. To do this, you might want to ask the following questions of each phrase or line of the poem: does this sound like: (a) poetry or some non-poetic use of language? (b) written or spoken language? (c) the language of 1917, or language from an earlier period? (d) the kind of thing a soldier might say to another soldier in the First World War? or (e) something else (if so, what is that something else?).

continued

2   What features of the language influence your answers to question (1)? Are the distinctions you are making a matter of vocabulary and/or of syntax?

3   Try to add a 'register label' alongside relevant words, phrases, lines or sections of the poem. For example, if you think that parts of the poem, or even the whole poem, are in 'poetic' register, then write that label alongside the relevant phrase or lines.

4   Register variation is one of the best ways of spotting poetic allusion (see **Unit 13, Allusion and intertextuality**). Are there any lines or phrases in this poem that you think might be an allusion to another poem? Try out your hunches by doing an internet search on those phrases.

5   By tackling the previous tasks, you should have discovered that Blunden's poem makes three allusions to one of the most famous poems in the English language. Do you think that the language of the rest of Blunden's poem is: (a) seeking to imitate the register of that poem, or (b) commenting on the register of that poem in some way, or (c) developing a different register?

6   Are there any other registers in the poem that come from the poem's context, rather than from the individual speaker? If so, identify the relevant words or phrases and try to decide what register they come from.

7   Which of the registers in the poem is most closely associated with the voice of the speaker? On the basis of your answer to this, how would you identify the poem's speaker in terms of class, education or rank in the army?

Reading

Bakhtin, M. (1981) 'Discourse in the Novel', trans. C. Emerson and M. Holquist, in V.B. Leitch (ed.) (2010) *The Norton Anthology of Theory and Criticism*, 2nd edn, London and New York: Norton, pp. 1190–1220.

Biber, D. and Conrad, S. (2009) *Register, Genre, and Style*, Cambridge: Cambridge University Press.

Furniss, T. and Bath, M. (2007) *Reading Poetry: An Introduction*, 2nd edn, London: Pearson Longman, pp. 3–24.

Halliday, M.A.K. (1978) *Language as Social Semiotic: The Social Interpretation of Language and Meaning*, London: Arnold.

Leech, G. (1969) *A Linguistic Guide to English Poetry*, London: Longman, pp. 9–12, 49–51.

Simpson, P. (1997) *Language through Literature: An Introduction*, London: Routledge.

St John Butler, L. (1999) *Registering the Difference: Reading Literature through Register*, Manchester: Manchester University Press; New York: St Martin's Press.

UNIT 8

Language and gender

This unit:

- explores how language encodes gender roles, embedding particular stances towards women which literary texts may either reflect or challenge;

- describes how language typically presents the male as a norm, including through generic forms that are used to denote both men and women, and how such terms downgrade or derogate women;

- examines how far women's writing may be said to be different from men's writing, including how far it has developed new ways of using language: 'a woman's sentence'.

U N I T   8

Language plays a crucial role in signalling how we think about others and in displaying to others how we think about ourselves. Our relationships with others are largely managed through language; so in our choice of language items and styles of language we signify to others how we see ourselves as gendered, classed and raced individuals.

Since the 1970s, language has been of interest to feminist linguists because the use of certain types of language signifies particular attitudes towards women and men. Language seems systematically to encode a view of women as aberrant from a male norm. More recently, however, feminist linguists have stressed how, despite the embeddedness of certain stances towards women within language, words do not 'contain' meaning in any simple way. Instead, meanings are worked out contextually and can be contested. So while it is clear that sexist attitudes are still expressed, they no longer have such a normative feel to them; they must take their meanings in a context of contesting discourses, such as feminism, which have suggested alternative forms of expression. Those who wish to express sexist attitudes may also be driven to be more indirect, to use irony or presuppositions rather than being direct.

8.1   Male as norm

First, let us consider how language encodes women as a marked case and males as the norm. In many languages, reference to human beings is commonly made as if all humans were male (Pauwels, 1998). This happens partly through the operation of the noun 'man', when used generically to stand for the species, but also through use of 'he' as a **generic pronoun** (generic means general rather than specific – the generic 'he' is therefore supposed to include females as well as males). However, as Rosalind Coward and Maria Black (1990) have pointed out, if generic 'man' is genuinely inclusive then both of the following (numbered) example sentences should sound equally odd:

(1)   Man's vital interests are food, shelter, and access to females.

(2)   Man, unlike other mammals, has difficulties in giving birth.

In practice, however, sentences like (1) are more likely to be produced and accepted unreflectingly than sentences like (2). Even when operating generically, therefore, words such as 'he' and 'man' carry masculine connotations with them. This tendency also operates in more restricted kinds of reference, when generic 'he' is not intended to refer to the human species as a whole but to some non-gender specific group within it, as in the following examples:

(3)   When the police officer has completed his investigation, he files a report.

(4)   The modern reader may at first feel baffled by the over-punctuation, as it will feel to him that there are too many commas.

The conventions of usage of the generic pronoun say that we should understand the use of 'he' and 'his' in (3) as referring to all police officers (that is, including female officers). Similarly, in (4) the conventions of usage suggest that both male and female readers are being included in the reference. However, readers of sentences containing generic pronouns often do not read them as having general reference, but in fact read them as referring strictly to males. Kidd (1971), for instance, demonstrated that, when students are asked to visualize the referent of a generic pronoun, they almost invariably draw a male referent, even when the intended referent seems at first sight to be general.

A similar process may be seen at work in the following caption from an advertisement for Lufthansa airlines: 'What does today's business traveller expect of his airline?' Most people would read 'his' as having generic reference here, since it follows a **generic noun** 'business traveller'. But the picture that accompanies the advertisement makes it clear that the reference is only to males, since it shows a plane full of male business travellers relaxing on board an aeroplane; the only female on board is the steward who is serving them drinks. Thus, so-called generic nouns and pronouns are quite commonly not truly generic in practice. Apparently non-gender specific, they often turn out to be referring actually to males. This process makes women less visible in social and cultural activity; use, for instance, of the generic 'he' in example (3), or in the advertisement, serves to erase the fact that there are women who work as police officers, or who travel on business.

In some ways generic nouns (such as 'business travellers') that masquerade as non-gender specific terms are more insidious than the generic pronoun, 'he'. This is partly because there are so many of them; it is partly also because – unlike 'he' – they do not give any explicit signal that they might be excluding women. Because of this, such expressions become powerful ways of carving up social reality in implicitly masculine ways, without announcing that they are doing so. Cameron (1992), for instance, shows that even expressions such as 'astronaut', 'firefighter', 'lecturer', 'shop assistant', 'scientist', and so on, disguise a tendency to refer only to men – despite their apparently neutral generic potential. Cameron cites two newspaper reports:

(5)   The lack of vitality is aggravated by the fact that there are so few able-bodied young adults about. They have all gone off to work or look for work, leaving behind the old, the disabled, the women and the children. (*The Sunday Times*)

(6)   A coloured South African who was subjected to racial abuse by his neighbours went berserk with a machete and killed his next-door neighbour's wife, Birmingham Crown Court heard yesterday. (*The Guardian*)

In example (5), the generic expression is 'able-bodied young adults'. Yet it is clear from the rest of the sentence that what is really meant is 'able-bodied young men', since women and children are subsequently excluded from its reference. In the second example (6), the generic expression is 'next-door neighbour', since this word ostensibly means both male and female neighbours. Yet it is clear that, when used to refer to women, the expression needs to be modified to 'neighbour's wife'. So neighbour, rather than being a generic in this context, is in fact only referring to male neighbours.

Further evidence that generic nouns often refer solely to men comes from the way that, for example, women doing a job that is conventionally viewed as male are sometimes described as 'lady doctor', 'female engineer', 'woman pilot', etc. As more and more women take up jobs that have been conventionally seen as male, however, the most salient feature of their work will not continue to be their gender, and true generics such as 'firefighter' will be used to refer to both females and males.

Apart from this discrimination entailed in generic nouns and pronouns, expressions can also be ambiguous in their reference, as in the following sentence:

(7)   The more education an individual attains the better his occupation is likely to be.

It is unclear here whether the 'individual' is supposed to be a man or whether this is indeed a generic use (this is not resolved by 'his' – which may also be generic). Because the reference of generic nouns and pronouns is ambiguous, and because they make women seem invisible, feminists such as Dale Spender (1998), Casey Miller and Kate Swift (1979) have objected to their use. As Pauwels (1998) has noted, feminists have been active in campaigning against their use in official documents, so that, in the public sphere, at least, their use is much less common; and feminists have also developed alternative terms that are more acceptable to women. For example, many people now avoid the use of the generic 'he' pronoun and instead use 's/he'. Because this can be rather cumbersome over a lengthy text, more people are using the pronoun 'they' as if it were a singular pronoun, as in, 'Each police officer is equipped with a baton which they only use *in extremis*'.

Feminists have suggested a number of ways round the problem of the generic pronoun and generic reference. Some writers, for instance, have begun to avoid using generic 'he' entirely, by using the passivized form, as in the following example:

(8)   When a police officer has finished an investigation, a report should be filed.

Or the 'he' can be avoided by using plural 'they':

(9)   When police officers have finished their investigation, they should file a report.

In these sentences, it is clear that the reference is truly generic. But it is also possible to signal more positively that there may be female as well as male police officers:

(10) When the police officer has finished the investigation, he or she should file a report.

Some writers even use 'she' throughout their work to draw attention to the problems with generic 'he' usage. These forms are often contested, particularly the use exemplified in (10), and even though usage has changed greatly recently – since nearly all publishers, educational institutions and organizations have issued their staff with guidelines on language use to cover reference to gender and race – the topic of use of generics is still contested and debated.

8.2   Female as downgraded or derogated

There is a range of words that are used solely for males or females, and which are therefore **gender specific**. Many of these words have a slightly archaic feel to them now; this is an indicator of how language has been changing rapidly in this area in recent years (see **Unit 5, Language and time**). So, for example, the word 'poetess' is only used for women, and the word 'courtier' is usually only used for men. Many female actors, particularly those who are at the top of the profession, do not use the word 'actress' to describe themselves. They prefer to use the generic 'actor', which indicates the extent to which 'actress' is seen to be a demeaning word that describes someone who is not serious about her profession.

There are significant patterns in the use of gender-specific language, as can be shown in the way that pairs of gender-specific nouns are not always symmetrical. Instead, such pairs tend to downgrade (or derogate) women by treating them as if they were only sexual objects rather than full human beings; this can be seen in the following pairs:

  master/mistress
  courtier/courtesan
  host/hostess.

Terms on the male side have positive or neutral connotations, and seem to refer solely to an occupation. The female equivalents, by contrast, often have negative sexual connotations. There is a further asymmetry in the way that women are often referred to as 'girls'. In the following advertisement, from the English newspaper *The Guardian*, 'girl' is used as if it were the female equivalent of 'man' (whereas 'girl' generally refers to female children rather than adults):

EFL TEACHERS: required first week in February. Girl with driving licence for Italy; man with experience and girl with degree in German for Germany.

This form of description (not from a recent copy of the newspaper, and sounding slightly dated) remains common in sports commentaries, where adult women athletes are regularly described as 'girls' (or as 'ladies'). It should be remembered, however, that 'girl' is not intrinsically sexist, since it may be used playfully by women to refer to themselves; context will determine whether the terms are used to express sexism.

Women and men are also named in different ways. Women's marital status is signalled by the use of the terms Mrs and Miss, for which there are no current male equivalents (Mr does not indicate whether a man is married or single). To challenge this, feminists introduced the term Ms in the 1980s, so that women would be able to have an equivalent title to males. Use of Ms has become much more general in recent years, despite a great deal of opposition. Some women still feel wary about using it, because it is associated with feminism or is assumed to refer to women who are divorced or separated. Nevertheless, a large number of companies and institutions now offer Ms as an option for women to refer to themselves on forms and documents; and perhaps 'Miss' is now the term that is chosen less. However, this initiative to invent a new term to refer to women has resulted in there now being three terms rather than two, all of them posing problems for women when they are asked for their name.

There is also a covert asymmetry in the way that women are referred to in tabloid newspapers, where they are frequently identified by their marital or family status (wife, mother, grandmother) rather than by their profession. This is clear in a headline from another English newspaper, the *Daily Star*: 'MAD GUNMAN HUNT AS WIFE IS SHOT'. It is also quite common in British tabloid newspapers for women to be described in terms of their physical appearance (hair colour, body shape, and so on), whereas men are usually described by reference to their job and age.

Stereotypes about males and females inform the type of language that is used about them. Such stereotypes of masculinity and femininity can even influence the way that scientific reports are written, for example in assertions made about the activity of eggs and sperm (Martin, 1997) or when describing animals in nature programmes (Crowther and Leith, 1995). Martin describes how scientific reports tend to draw on stereotypical notions of male and female activity and passivity when analysing sperm and eggs. She claims that:

The egg is seen as large and passive. It does not move or journey, but passively 'is transported', 'is swept' or even 'drifts' along the fallopian tube. In utter contrast, sperm are small, 'streamlined' and invariably active. They 'deliver' their genes to the egg, 'activate the developmental program of the egg' and have a velocity which is often remarked upon. Their tails are strong and efficiently powered.

(Martin, 1997, p. 87)

Despite the fact that both egg and sperm play an active role in conception, and that both move, scientists still tend to represent conception in terms that accord with the notion of the female element being passive. In a similar way, Crowther and Leith have found that, in nature programmes on television, in descriptions of the way that lions organize themselves in social groups, terms such as 'harems' have been used to describe a situation where the female lions in a pride allow one male lion to mate with them, excluding all others. In this way, the stereotype of female passivity associated with the term harem is carried over into how lion communities are described.

8.3 Potential for reform

Some feminists, such as Dale Spender (1998), see such asymmetries in language as demeaning to women and have urged that language should be reformed accordingly. For many feminists it is important to suggest alternative terms to use: 'chairperson', for example, should be used instead of 'chairman'; and 'manager' should be used for both males and females. Others, such as Deborah Cameron (1992), have suggested that sexism cannot be eradicated simply by changing language items, since this only changes the surface manifestation of beliefs about women. (See also **Unit 5, Language and time**.)

8.4 Sexism

Until fairly recently, sexist statements were often treated as if they were rather trivial. If someone made a remark about a woman's driving abilities and asserted that women were necessarily worse drivers than men, this was often treated as if it were simply common sense. However, feminists have drawn attention to the systematic nature of this type of discrimination (Mills, 2008). Although sexism is now highly contested (who after all decides whether something is sexist or not?), in recent years it has become far more common for sexism in the public sphere to be taken more seriously. For example, a British sports commentator, Andy Gray, who worked for the broadcaster Sky Television, lost his job in 2011 because he made a disparaging and sexist comment about a female football referee, suggesting that she did not understand the game's offside rule. This action by Sky, as well as the public response to Gray's comments, suggests that the public considers sexism against women to be anachronistic.

8.5 The female sentence: a woman's writing?

Many writers and theorists claim that women's writing is qualitatively different from men's writing. For example, Virginia Woolf proposed that Dorothy

Richardson's writing had developed a new way of using language, which Woolf termed 'a woman's sentence'. Woolf did not describe in detail what this 'psychological sentence of the feminine gender' consisted of. But if we compare the following two extracts by Anita Brookner and Malcolm Lowry, it seems easy to argue that Brookner is using a 'feminine' style, while Lowry is using a 'masculine' style:

From the window all that could be seen was a receding area of grey. It was to be supposed that beyond the grey garden, which seemed to sprout nothing but the stiffish leaves of some unfamiliar plant, lay the vast grey lake, spreading like an anaesthetic towards the invisible further shore, and beyond that, in imagination only, yet verified by the brochure, the peak of the Dent d'Oche, on which snow might already be slightly and silently falling.

(Anita Brookner, *Hôtel du Lac*, 1984)

Two mountain chains traverse the republic roughly from north to south, forming between them a number of valleys and plateaux. Overlooking one of these valleys, which is dominated by two volcanoes, lies, six thousand feet above sea-level, the town of Quauhnahuac. It is situated well south of the Tropic of Cancer, to be exact on the nineteenth parallel, in about the same latitude as the Revillagigedo Islands to the west in the Pacific, or very much farther west, the southernmost tip of Hawaii.

(Malcolm Lowry, *Under the Volcano*, 1967)

The Brookner passage describes the landscape from a particular point of view: that is, as seen from a character's perspective rather than from an omniscient narrator's standpoint. This personalized account consists of descriptions of colours, and the effect that these colours have on the character. There also seems to be a certain vagueness about the description. Instead of facts, the account is concerned with what 'was supposed to be', what 'seemed' and what 'might be' happening. This modification or tentativeness is conventionally said to characterize a feminine style. In contrast, the Lowry passage seems far more distanced: the narrator dispenses facts, using a scientific objective passive voice ('it is situated . . .' and 'the town . . . is dominated'). The information emanates not from an identifiable character but from a seemingly objective, omniscient narrator. In fact, the style used is reminiscent of the **register** (see **Unit 7, Language and context: register**) of guidebooks or of geographical descriptions.

For many readers, the two passages may seem to characterize a feminine and masculine style respectively: one a personalized style, describing in detail relationships and the actions of characters; the other more concerned with factual descriptions of the world. Such a contrast accords with assertions made by Deborah Tannen that women tend to adopt certain strategies in speech that she calls rapport talk (talk that is concerned with maintaining relationships), while men adopt strategies that she terms report talk (talk concerned with giving information and establishing hierarchies) (Tannen, 1991). However, it is clear that these distinctions, although fairly easy to make, are based on stereotypical notions of gender difference (e.g. that women are supposed to be vague and concerned with relationships, whereas men are supposed to be precise and interested in facts). Not all male writers write like Lowry; and not all women writers write as Brookner does here. Iris Murdoch, for example, often writes in a manner more akin to Lowry's writing, and frequently uses a male narrator. Also, it should be noted that much of the imprecision of the Brookner passage arises from the fact that she is focusing on the impressions of a character who is unfamiliar with the landscape.

The idea that there is a masculine style and a feminine style, accordingly, appears to be based more on stereotypical notions of sexual difference than on any inevitable textual difference in the way men and women write. Although the way a person uses language (in writing as in speech) will be influenced by conventional stereotypes about gender, and although readers often apply these same stereotypes when reading literature, the stereotypes are neither natural nor inevitable. If women do sometimes use language differently, this is related to the way that women are derogated in language and the way that social pressures may encourage them to adopt certain speech styles. It may also be the case that women may choose to adopt feminine styles because those styles may be strategically more effective in a particular context. At the same time, women writers (like their male counterparts) may adopt different linguistic styles for particular artistic and political ends. Feminist critics and writers often employ language in ways that challenge the gender biases embedded in language and resist the derogation and disempowering of women. On the other hand, early twentieth-century writers such as Woolf, Richardson and Rosamond Lehmann can be seen as adopting a 'feminine' style precisely in order to subvert or question assumptions of 'masculine' objectivity. It is important, therefore, to be able to recognize masculine and feminine elements within language but to be aware that these may serve different objectives and call for different interpretations depending on the context.

1   Analyse the following passage from a novel and assess whether you think that the text is written by a male or female writer. Consider which elements led you to your decision, for example the sex of the narrator, the style, the representation of thought, the subject matter, genre, sentence length, and so on. Then consider how much your assessment has relied on stereotypical views of masculinity and femininity.

    A hand came from behind and went over his mouth. He wasn't afraid, he knew who it was. Gupta said:
        'Are you crazy?'
        'I'm not well.'

ACTIVITY 8

continued

Even in the dark he could see Gupta's bloody teeth when he spoke. They looked as if he'd been chomping on raw steak but in fact it was betel he chewed. All the money Hob had was exchanged for what Gupta produced, a zip lock bag holding a small block of something like a white pebble but rough and irregular, not smoothed by the sea. Automatically he thought of his strength and Gupta's fragility and of the other white stones in the yoghurt carton, enough to keep him well; for a long time. But it was no use. Retribution would be swift. He'd carried out some of it for them so he knew. They'd start by breaking his legs.

2   The extract is from Ruth Rendell's *The Keys to the Street* (1997), p. 5. If you felt that the above extract is particularly masculine in style and tone, do you think that there are particular genres in which women writers are likely to use this 'hard-nosed' style?

Reading

Bergvall, V., Bing, J. and Freed, A. (eds) (1996) *Rethinking Language and Gender Research: Theory and Practice*, London: Longman.

Cameron, D. (1992) *Feminism and Linguistic Theory*, 2nd edn, London: Macmillan.

Cameron, D. (ed.) (1998) *The Feminist Critique of Language: a Reader*, 2nd edn, London: Routledge.

Coward, R. and Black, M. (1990) 'Linguistic, Social and Sexual Relations: A Review of Dale Spender's *Man Made Language*,' reprinted in D. Cameron (ed.) *The Feminist Critique of Language*, London, Routledge, pp. 111–33.

Crowther, B. and Leith, D. (1995) 'Feminism, Language and the Rhetoric of Television Wildlife Programmes', in S. Mills (ed.) *Language and Gender: Interdisciplinary Perspectives*, London: Longman, pp. 207–26.

Holmes, J. and Meyerhoff, M. (eds) (2005) *Handbook of Language and Gender*, Oxford: Blackwell.

Kidd, V. (1971) 'A study of the images produced through the use of the male pronoun as generic' in *Moments in Contemporary Rhetoric and Communication 1: 25–30*.

Martin, E. (1997) 'The Egg and the Sperm: How Science has Constructed a Romance Based on Stereotypical Male–Female Roles', in L. Lamphere, H. Ragone and P. Zavella (eds) *Situated Lives: Gender and Culture in Everyday Life*, London: Routledge, pp. 85–99.

Miller, C. and Swift, K. (1979) *Words and Women*, Harmondsworth, Penguin.

Mills, S. (1996) *Feminist Stylistics*, London: Routledge.

Mills, S. (2008) *Language and Sexism*, Cambridge: Cambridge University Press.

Pauwels, A. (1998) *Women Changing Language*, London: Longman.

Spender, D. (1998) *Man Made Language*, 4th edn, London, Routledge and Kegan Paul.

Tannen D. (1991) *You Just Don't Understand: Women and Men in Conversation*, London: Virago.

Language and society

This unit:

- considers how language reflects and represents social structure, including class relations;
- draws attention to how particular linguistic patterns (especially those that convey 'transitivity') signal agency in events and actions, and in doing so assign power, passivity and responsibility to different social groups;
- explores how social structure (including class relations) is conveyed by a combination of details of language use in works of fiction.

UNIT 9

A language such as 'English' can be thought of as a group of closely related dialects. Those dialects have many elements in common, but differ to some extent in vocabulary and grammar. Dialects usually also differ from each other in a language by being associated with different accents: that is, different ways of pronouncing words. Which dialects and accents a person is able to use fluently, and when they use those dialects and accents, relates both to geography and to social class. As we see in this unit, where linguistic alternatives are possible the choice of one alternative over another has social implications, often relating to ideology, power and social status. The alternatives involved are not just dialect and accent, but also choice of interactional style.

9.1 Vocabulary in social history

Our experience of the world is shaped for us by our language. This is partly a matter of vocabulary. The emergence of particular vocabulary items in a language helps to bring aspects of reality into focus for speakers of that language, and alternative vocabulary items may reflect, or lead to a redefinition of, that reality. The history of a society, and the struggles within that society, are manifested in the vocabulary used by that society. Raymond Williams showed this in *Keywords* (1983), his vocabulary of culture and society that traces the history of certain words and shows how the histories of these words are also social histories (see also **Unit 5, Language and time**).

The word 'family', for example, has repeatedly been at the centre of political debates. While the word is often used as if it is unproblematic, this is not reflected in its complex history. 'Family' first entered English from Latin in the late fourteenth century, and at that time referred to a household (incorporating not only blood-relations but also servants, where applicable, all living together under one roof). The word was then extended in meaning to signify a house formed by descent from a common ancestor. This specialization of the term to refer to a small kin-group living in a single house is a fairly late development in the history of the word in English (between the seventeenth and nineteenth centuries), and reflects social changes, including the growing importance of the family as an economic unit in developing capitalism.

One of the reasons why words change their meanings through history is that they reflect transformations of social structure. Another reason is that society is never a single entity, but is always differentiated along lines of class, race and gender. Use of the term 'the family' in recent political debate tends to emphasize the heterosexual, parenting couple as a self-contained economic unit living in its own home independent of state and social support (the 'nuclear family'), a sense that excludes single parents, unmarried parents and homosexual couples. The fact that this narrower definition does not accord with how many people live in English-speaking societies in the twenty-first century goes some way to showing the kind of ideological work that language performs in attempts made to promote or legitimate particular versions of reality. Viewed in this way, language cannot escape being the site of social and political contestation. It gives us categories for organizing experience and for understanding the world that may seem neutral and unbiased, while being inevitably partial and particular.

9.2 Language and social relations

At the same time as language constructs a social reality for us, it also constructs and shapes our social relationships. When we speak or write, we speak or write *about something*; but we also speak or write *to someone*. Consequently, every time we speak or write we articulate our social identity in relation to the social identity of the hearer or reader. As Valentin N. Voloshinov (1973) pointed out, each utterance we make is a bridge between self and other. That bridge is constructed partly by means of our choice of address terms, and more generally by the way that the utterance we produce also codifies the position of its addressee (see **Unit 15, Mode of address: positioning the reader**). The incumbent of the White House is not addressed in press conferences as 'Barack', but as 'Mr President', or 'Sir', or even 'Mr President, Sir'. Similarly, exchanges in the Westminster Houses of Parliament follow elaborate codes of address in which speakers in the lower house refer to each other as 'the Right Honourable Lady' or 'my Right Honourable Friend', and refer to members of the upper house as 'my noble Lords'. Such formulations, involving titles and honorifics, encode social distance, formality and status in graduated ways. Title (Mr President) is more formal than Title + Last Name (President Obama), and this in turn is more formal than First Name (Barack). Collectively, the rules underpinning such formulations constitute a system of modes of address. Selecting from within that system is a way of defining (and redefining) the nature of the relationship between speaker and hearer, addressor and addressee. In addition to direct address, of course, the audience is also addressed by implication. In effect, texts project or invoke 'a position' – a framework of beliefs and common understanding – from which the text makes sense.

The two types of address – direct and indirect – work hand in hand. Consider, for instance, the following extract from Henry Fielding's novel, *Tom Jones* (1749), which uses direct address to define and redefine the relationship of the narrator to the reader:

> We are now, reader, arrived at the last stage of our long journey. As we have therefore travelled together through so many pages, let us behave to one another like fellow-travellers in a stage coach, who have passed several days in the company of each other; and who . . . mount, for the last time, into their vehicle with chearfulness and good-humour . . .
>
> And now, my friend, I take this opportunity (as I shall have no other) of heartily wishing thee well. If I have been an entertaining companion to thee, I promise thee it is what I have desired.
>
> (Fielding, 1749, Book XVIII, Chapter 1)

Notice that 'the reader' is not only addressed as such, but is also constituted, both directly and indirectly, in quite specific terms as singular ('thee'), as equivalent to a companion or friend, as capable of being 'chearful' and 'good-humoured', and so on. Indeed, the positive traits of sociability, benign good-humour, tolerance and conviviality that are so much espoused in the narrative world of the novel are also projected outwards onto its implied addressee.

This mode of address adopted in the *Tom Jones* extract is worlds apart from the less formal, offhand, and strictly impersonal opening of Forster's *Howards End* (1910):

> One may as well begin with Helen's letters to her sister.

Every text, spoken or written, organizes social relationships through its modes of address. That organization is achieved partly through address terms (gentle reader, Mr President, etc.); but it is also achieved by means of the capacity of language to perform actions through words in relation to the addressee. Words allow a speaker to question, command, state, challenge, promise, insult, offer, invite, request, and so on. Many of our most important institutions depend on using words to perform quite specific actions, whether those actions form part of a marriage ceremony, a Parliamentary debate, a job interview, legal proceedings or union negotiations.

9.3   Transitivity and notions of overt and covert agency

Speakers can align themselves with a social position not only by their choice of individual words, but also by how they combine those words into sentences. A sentence represents what is called an 'eventuality'. An 'eventuality' is a cover term used to describe an event, or an action, or a state of affairs; all sentences represent one or other of these three types of occurrence or situation. An event is something that happens. An action is something that is caused to happen: it involves an **agent**, a sentient individual, usually a person, who makes that something happen. A state of affairs just *is*; it has no agent. The important point for our purposes is that an eventuality that is being reported can be reshaped in the process of the reporting, such that, for example, an action can be made to seem more like an event.

Consider, for example, in Table 9.1, a two-page spread of headlines from a politically right-of-centre British newspaper. Each of these headlines is a sentence that represents an eventuality. All six eventualities are actions (as is clear when the articles are read: they all involve events initiated by agents). The headlines nevertheless present these actions *as* actions to different degrees: some are presented more clearly as actions than others. The clearest examples of actions are (c) and (e), where there are explicit agents. It may be significant that these are also the two eventualities where the editorial stance of the newspaper is most

TABLE 9.1 **Eventualities as depicted in headlines**

	The headline	The eventuality (extracted from news story)
(a)	Five held in hunt for animal rights desecrated grave	Police have arrested . . .
(b)	Greek and Latin become easier to pass	An exam board is to reduce vocabulary requirements . . .
(c)	Liberals delay appointing new bishops	Liberal bishops decided not to appoint . . .
(d)	*Who* guitarist's lover found dead from 'overdose'	She was found by a family member . . .
(e)	Parents of sick children dupe nurseries	Working parents are leaving sick children with nurseries . . .
(f)	Health warning over long working hours	The chief executive of a charity has said that . . .

disapproving; perhaps agency is emphasized when the action is considered unfavourably. In contrast, the police disappear as agents from action (a), which might as a result even be read as a representation of a state of affairs; and the warner (the agent of warning) disappears from (f).

The distinction between eventualities represented as actions and eventualities represented as events or states of affairs is, as expressed here, a rather crude one. A more multidimensional differentiation uses the notion of **transitivity** (see Jeffries, 2009). The core notion involved in transitivity is that of an action where an agent does something to someone or something else (called the 'patient' of the action). In traditional grammar, a transitive sentence is a sentence with both a subject and an object, such as 'Mary ate the cheese'; in this sentence, 'Mary' is the subject of the sentence and also the agent of the action, and 'the cheese' is both the object of the sentence and also the patient of the action. Core transitive sentences of this kind can be thought of as 'high in transitivity', and transitivity viewed as a gradient characteristic of a sentence (it can be greater or lesser). Some of the elements of a sentence that make it highly transitive are the following:

(1) The subject of the sentence (the phrase before the verb) expresses the agent of the action, and there is an object of the sentence (the phrase after the verb), which expresses the patient of the action. Passive sentences such as headline (d) above get a low transitivity score on this criterion, because they do not have objects (the patient of the action is expressed as the subject of the sentence).

(2) The action takes place at a moment in time; it is not currently ongoing, but has finished. On this criterion headline (e) is low in transitivity, though it is high in transitivity on criterion (1).

(3) The action is done on purpose. Purposiveness is an important component of being an agent; and the more clear it is that the action is purposeful, the higher its transitivity. Headline (b) scores low for transitivity in this regard, though it can be argued that the transitivity of the actual eventuality that it reports has been reduced in reporting it.

(4) The patient is an individuated entity that is totally affected by the action. For example, headline (a) scores high on transitivity in that five distinct people are individuated and affected by the action; in contrast, headline (c) scores low on this aspect of transitivity because no specific person is affected by the action.

These criteria allow us to assess the level of transitivity on various different dimensions. We can then interpret the results. For example, the fact that headline (a), about the arrests, is low by transitivity criterion (1) but high by criteria (2), (3) and (4) makes even more salient the fact that the agency of the police has been concealed. It is as though the police do not act as individual agents, but perhaps as collective representatives of the social order. In contrast, headline (c), about the delay in appointing gay bishops, is high by criterion (1) but low by criteria (2), (3) and (4). Here, despite the generally low transitivity of the eventuality (the action of delaying an action), the salience of the actors stands in interesting contrast to the absence of the police from the other headline. Here, perhaps, the salience of the bishops as actors suggests that they do not represent a collective social order (in the way that the police were collective representatives of social order), or at least that they do not represent a collective order to which readers of the paper may see themselves as belonging.

The extent to which it is possible to make political sense of how eventualities are portrayed is explored in the theoretical approach of 'Critical Discourse Analysis' (or CDA), particularly in relation to media texts. Such an analysis could, for example, be undertaken for the reporting of oil spills in the Gulf of Mexico by BP in 2010. The following advertisement appeared on the back of the *New Scientist* magazine in 2011, below a full colour (and oil-free) picture of oil rigs in the Gulf:

One year later. Our commitment continues

A year has passed since the Deepwater Horizon accident in the Gulf of Mexico. From the beginning, BP has taken responsibility for the clean-up. Much progress has been made and our commitment to the Gulf remains unchanged.

Reducing the impact of the spill

No oil has flowed into the Gulf since July 15th. As our efforts continue, all beaches and 98% of waters are open. Gulf seafood has been subjected to more rigorous safety testing, by independent experts, than any other seafood in the world. To date, BP has spent more than $13 billion on the clean up.

Restoring the environment

We helped organize over 48,000 people, 6000 vessels and 120 aircraft to clean up the water and coastline.

Learning and sharing the lessons

This was a tragedy that should not have happened. Our responsibility is to learn from it and share with competitors, partners, governments and regulators to help ensure that it never happens again.

In this text from the overall advertisement, BP stresses the scale of the work they are undertaking to clean up after the oil spill. The company uses verb forms such as 'has taken responsibility', 'progress has been made', 'our efforts continue', 'BP has spent $13 billion', and 'we helped organize people', which all represent BP as active. However, they represent the devastating oil spill in a way that diminishes their responsibility: they represent it as an 'accident' and as a 'tragedy'. The company states that they have 'taken responsibility for the clean-up', but they do not accept responsibility for the 'accident'. In the final paragraph, they state that 'this was a tragedy which should not have happened', using impersonal forms of the verb that diminish their responsibility for the spill. They also state that their responsibility is to 'learn from it' and ensure that 'it never happens again'. Twice in the text 'responsibility' is emphasized, but in both cases it is responsibility for the clean-up and responsibility to learn, rather than responsibility for the disaster.

9.4   Language and social structure in the novel

Among literary genres, the novel is more overtly 'social' than poetry (or drama). This is partly a matter of form, because novels present a range of different voices rather than the single consciousness typically expressed in poetry. The social emphasis of the novel is also a matter of the themes it tended to treat in the nineteenth century: typically the tensions that existed between different classes. Earlier in its history, too, the English novel served as a means of representing the rise of the middle classes during the eighteenth century.

The nineteenth-century 'realist' novel in Britain frequently dramatizes the (usually fraught) relations between three classes: the upper class, the middle class and the working class. The distinctions and struggles between these classes are typically registered in language as well as in themes, characters and plots. Charles Dickens's *Great Expectations* (1860–1), for example, explores class issues by having one character (the narrator Pip) cross the boundaries of social class. Pip is brought up in a working-class household by his sister and her husband Joe Gargery, a blacksmith with whom he develops strong ties in the first third of the novel. With the support of a mysterious benefactor, however, Pip becomes a 'gentleman', takes rooms in London, and begins to regard his humble past as an embarrassment.

When he receives word that Joe intends to visit him in London, for example, Pip anticipates meeting his old friend 'with considerable disturbance, some mortification, and a keen sense of incongruity':

> As the time approached I should have liked to run away, but . . . presently I heard Joe on the staircase. I knew it was Joe, by his clumsy manner of coming up-stairs – his state boots being always too big for him – and by the time it took him to read the names on the other floors in the course of his ascent. When at last he stopped outside our door, I could hear his finger tracing over the painted letters of my name . . . Finally he gave a faint single rap, and Pepper . . . announced 'Mr Gargery!' I thought he never would have done wiping his feet . . . but at last he came in.
> 'Joe, how are you, Joe?'
> 'Pip, how AIR you, Pip?'
> . . .
> 'I am glad to see you, Joe. Give me your hat.'
> But Joe . . . wouldn't hear of parting with that piece of property, and persisted in standing talking over it in a most uncomfortable way.
> 'Which you have that growed,' said Joe, 'and that swelled, and that gentle-folked'; Joe considered a little before he discovered this word; 'as to be sure you are a honour to your king and country.'
> 'And you, Joe, look wonderfully well.'
>
> (Charles Dickens, *Great Expectations*,
> Chapter 27)

Dickens uses a number of devices here to indicate the social distance that has come between the two characters. He registers Joe's uneasiness by highlighting the way Joe wipes his feet and holds his hat, and registers Pip's equally revealing attention to these details. But the social difference between Pip and Joe is also conveyed by their language: not only their different kinds of language but also their different relations to language. Joe's difficulty with the written language is foregrounded through Pip's acute consciousness of his ponderous attempts to read the names on the doors. Still more significant is the way Joe speaks. While Pip conceals his unease behind a register of polite affability (see **Unit 7, Language and context: register**), Joe reveals his sense of awkwardness in echoing Pip. In attempting to imitate his young friend's speech, Joe hypercorrects his own accent by revealingly overdoing the 'proper' pronunciation of 'are' (as 'AIR'). However, Joe then quickly 'forgets himself' and lapses into his usual accent in what we may take as a flood of genuine feeling and admiration. Pip, by contrast, continues in a polite register, which suggests an inability to respond with any intimacy to his old friend. Pip maintains the social stratification through language that this passage dramatizes alongside the other details of social class it picks out.

In the twentieth-century novel, such sociolinguistic stratification has often been challenged and undermined. D.H. Lawrence's fiction typically attempts to reverse the kind of hierarchy set up in the Dickens passage above, as can be seen in several places in *Lady Chatterley's Lover* (1928). Consider the following exchange between Lady Chatterley and her lover (who is a gamekeeper on her estate):

> 'Tha mun come one naight ter th'cottage, afore tha goos; sholl ter?' he asked, lifting his eyebrows as he looked at her, his hands dangling between his knees.
>> 'Sholl ter?' she echoed, teasing.
>> He smiled.
>> 'Ay, sholl ter?' he repeated.
>> 'Ay!' she said, imitating the dialect sound . . . .
>> 'Appen Sunday,' she said.
>> 'Appen a' Sunday! Ay!'
>> He laughed at her quickly.
>> 'Nay, tha canna,' he protested.
>> 'Why canna I?' she said
>> He laughed. Her attempts at the dialect were so ludicrous, somehow.
>> (D.H. Lawrence, *Lady Chatterley's Lover*, Chapter 12)

On one level, this exchange between the two characters presents a tender scene between two lovers in which the social difference in their ways of speaking becomes material for a lovers' game. At the same time, however, the social significance of the difference cannot be overlooked. At other points in the novel Mellors, the gamekeeper, uses the fact that he can move at will between the two ways of speaking as a weapon in a class war against the upper-class family that employs him. Lady Chatterley's attempt to imitate the dialect of a 'lower' social class (which reverses the situation in *Great Expectations* discussed above) can be read, by contrast, as a bid to escape from the restrictions of her own class. This interpretation gains some support from the fact that the gamekeeper's dialect is treated throughout the novel as if it were the authentic expression of desire, in contrast to the coldly mental, sexless language of the upper classes. In this respect, Lady Chatterley's imitation of her gamekeeper's dialect – an amusing failure in Mellors's eyes – is symptomatic of a wider failure, in the novel's terms, to achieve an authentic modality for the enactment of desire across the divide of social class (accent and dialect are also discussed in **Unit 6, Language and place**).

ACTIVITY 9

Read the following passage from Elizabeth Gaskell's *North and South* (1854–5). The central character of the novel, Margaret Hale, has recently moved from the south of England to Manchester (one of the main centres of industrial development in the nineteenth century); she is discussing an imminent strike at a local mill with a poverty-stricken leader of the union, Nicholas Higgins ('to clem' is a dialect term for 'to starve'):

'Why do you strike?' asked Margaret. 'Striking is leaving off work till you get your own rate of wages, is it not? You must not wonder at my ignorance; where I come from I never heard of a strike.'

. . .

'Why yo' see, there's five or six masters who have set themselves again paying the wages they've been paying these two years past, and flourishing upon, and getting richer upon. And now they come to us, and say we're to take less. And we won't. We'll just clem to death first; and see who'll work for 'em then.'

. . .

'And so you plan dying, in order to be revenged upon them!'

'No,' said he, 'I dunnot. I just look forward to the chance of dying at my post sooner than yield. That's what folk call fine and honourable in a soldier, and why not in a poor weaver-chap?'

'But,' said Margaret, 'a soldier dies in the cause of the Nation – in the cause of others.'

'. . . Dun yo' think it's for mysel' I'm striking work at this time? It's just as much in the cause of others as yon soldier . . . I take up John Boucher's cause, as lives next door but one, wi' a sickly wife, and eight childer, . . . I take up th' cause o' justice. . . .'

. . .

'But,' said Margaret, . . . 'the state of trade may be such as not to enable them to give you the same remuneration.'

'State o' trade! That's just a piece o' masters' humbug. It's rate o' wages I was talking of. Th' masters keep th' state o' trade in their own hands; and just walk it forward like a black bug-a-boo, to frighten naughty children with into being good.'

(from Chapter 17, 'What is a Strike?')

---

1   Make a list of words and phrases that Higgins uses to describe: (a) the mill owners; (b) the workers; (c) himself; (d) the mill owners' actions; (e) the workers' actions; and (f) his own actions. Using this evidence, describe Higgins's view of the strike (for example, by considering who does what to whom).

continued

2   Make a list of words and phrases that Margaret uses to describe: (a) the mill owners' possible actions; (b) Higgins's description of his own role; and (c) the actions of workers in a strike. Using this evidence, describe Margaret's view of the strike.

3   What is the difference between Margaret's suggestion that 'the state of trade' might not allow the owners to give the workers the same 'remuneration', and Higgins's response that he is not talking about the state of trade but 'rate o' wages'? How, in Higgins's view, do the owners use the term 'state of trade'?

4   What effect is created by Higgins speaking in a working-class northern dialect, while Margaret speaks in Standard English? Does this make Higgins's view of the strike more credible? Less credible? More authentic? Less authoritative?

Reading

Burton, D. (1988) 'Through Glass Darkly: Through Dark Glasses', in R. Carter (ed.) *Language and Literature: An Introductory Reader in Stylistics*, London: George Allen & Unwin, pp. 195–214.

Fabb, N. (1997) *Linguistics and Literature: Language in the Verbal Arts of the World*, Oxford: Blackwell, pp. 173–92.

Fairclough, N. (1992) *Discourse and Social Change*, London: Polity Press.

Montgomery, M. (2008) *An Introduction to Language and Society*, 3rd edn, London: Routledge.

Simpson, P. (1993) *Language, Ideology and Point of View*, London: Routledge.

Williams, R. (1983) *Keywords: A Vocabulary of Culture and Society*, 2nd edn, London: Fontana.

Attributing meaning

UNIT 10

Metaphor and figurative language

This unit:

- introduces the concept of figurative language;
- describes and illustrates metaphor, simile, metonymy, synecdoche, allegory and apostrophe;
- offers practical guidance on how to analyse the main kinds of metaphor, in order to bring out their implied meanings;
- discusses the pervasiveness, function and significance of metaphor in literature.

UNIT 10

Recognizing, and then analysing, figurative language (including local figures of speech) depends on a general distinction between literal and figurative uses of language. The notion of literal meaning does not imply that each word has only one meaning. In fact, the word 'literal' itself has several meanings. The *Shorter Oxford English Dictionary* indicates that one of the word's primary meanings is 'Of or pertaining to letters of the alphabet' or 'expressed by letters'. In this sense, all writing is literal. A related meaning is the theological notion of interpreting the Christian scriptures according to the letter: that is, 'taking the words in their natural and customary meaning'. In this sense, literal is distinguished from mystical or allegorical interpretation of scripture. This meaning, and the distinction it relies on, is related to how the term is used in this unit: literal is 'applied to taking words in their etymological or primary sense, or in the sense expressed by the actual wording of a passage, without recourse to any metaphorical or suggested meaning'. We are not concerned with the recent tendency to use the term 'literally' as an intensifier, or emphatic strengthening of what is being said (as in 'the house was literally five minutes away'). If treated as meaningful rather than emphatic, that use can result in absurdity (as in 'the news was literally an eye-opener'). This emphatic use needs to be avoided in literary criticism.

Literal tends to be defined in opposition to 'metaphorical' or 'figurative'. The term 'figurative' also has several meanings. One is related to the representation of figures in visual art: 'Pertaining to, or of the nature of, pictorial or plastic representation'. Another meaning relates to language use: 'Of speech: based on figures or metaphors; metaphorical, not literal'. In literary criticism, figurative language is a general term for a variety of non-literal uses of language. Although 'metaphorical' is also used in this way, 'metaphor' is a particular type of figurative language (as we will see below). So in a literary context it is better to use 'figurative' as the umbrella term, and to restrict 'metaphorical' to its specific meaning. (The use of 'umbrella' in the previous sentence indicates that figurative language occurs in all language uses, including student textbooks, and is not confined to literary works.) Typically, figurative language involves the use of words or phrases whose literal meaning (1) does not make sense, or (2) cannot be true, or (3) should not be taken as true, but implies a non-literal meaning that does make sense or could be true. So for example, it is not literally true to say that 'figurative language is an umbrella term', since a piece of language cannot be an umbrella; but the phrase nevertheless makes sense for reasons that it is possible to analyse and clarify.

10.1 Types of figurative language: metaphor, simile, metonymy, synecdoche, allegory, apostrophe

Discussion of figurative language has a long history, at least as far back as the study of **rhetoric** in classical Greece and Rome. Classical rhetoric was largely concerned with the art of persuasion, and as part of that study various kinds of figurative language were identified, and each given its own name. In literary studies today, focus is usually kept on a handful of specific figurative devices: metaphor, simile, metonymy, synecdoche, irony, allegory, apostrophe and a few others. (In linguistics and psychology, by contrast, the focus of investigation has shifted towards general cognitive mechanisms underlying figurative language, in ways that apply to all the various devices, see Croft and Cruse, 2004.) Irony is the topic of the following unit. In the present unit, we concentrate on the figurative devices named in the list above.

10.1.1   Metaphor

The word **metaphor** comes from a Greek word *metaphora*, 'to transfer' or 'carry over'. Metaphor occurs when a word or phrase in one semantic field is transferred into another semantic field, in order to talk about one thing as if it were a quite different thing and so blend two different ways of understanding something. For example, in a phrase such as 'to live a quiet life was the summit of his ambition', the term 'summit' has been transferred from the semantic field to do with mountains into a sentence concerned with a person's life aspirations. The highest point of the man's ambition is presented as if it were the top of a mountain. Metaphors work on the basis that there is some similarity between the two ideas that have been brought together; this can be seen in the similarity between 'highest point' and 'summit'. To interpret the metaphor, we identify the element of similarity between the non-literal word or phrase ('summit') and the implied idea (highest point), and transfer that element of similarity into the new context. At the same time, we still register implications of the dissimilarity between the two ideas: in the metaphor we are looking at, there may be ironic criticism in the perceived disparity between the ambition involved in climbing a mountain and the implied lack of ambition in the desire to lead a quiet life.

All metaphors work like this, and can be analysed in the way described. In the statement 'by the year 2020 manufacturing will be dominated by industries now at an embryonic stage', the word 'embryonic' seems initially not to fit in a discussion of industry and manufacturing (since it is a term for the offspring of an animal before birth or emergence from an egg). To make sense of 'embryonic' in this unusual context, we select those parts of its meaning that allow us to interpret the word in a discussion about industry. 'At an embryonic stage' becomes a metaphorical way of saying that the industries of the future are at an early, or rudimentary stage of their development. The idea of natural gestation is also transferred into the new context; so we are also invited to see the development of industry as in some way a natural process (and this perhaps offers a reassuring sense that the new industries are to be welcomed). In this way, metaphor can significantly affect how we perceive and respond to what is being described.

10.1.2   Simile

Simile is related to metaphor in that, as its name suggests, it draws attention to a similarity between two terms through words. What makes simile different from metaphor is that it does so explicitly, by means of words such as 'like' and 'as'. Simile does not always entail figurative language, in that both terms of a simile may be understood literally. The simile 'the sky is like a polished mirror', for example, invites the listener or reader to imagine how the sky might resemble a polished mirror. The difference between a simile and a metaphor in this respect can be demonstrated by turning a simile into a metaphor. If we say 'the sky is a polished mirror', this formulation can no longer be understood literally: we know that the sky is not really a polished mirror, though it might look like one; therefore, 'polished mirror' has to be read metaphorically. But simile is included in figurative language because there are many similes that cannot be taken literally. In 'To a Skylark' (1820), for example, Shelley describes the skylark through an extraordinary catalogue of similes, including the claim that the bird is 'Like a cloud of fire' (8) – a simile that cannot be understood literally, because 'cloud of fire' is itself a figurative rather than literal expression.

10.1.3 Metonymy

Metonymy (Greek for 'change of name') is distinguished from metaphor in that, while metaphor works through similarity, metonymy works through other kinds of association (e.g. cause–effect; attribute; containment, etc.). The sentence 'Moscow made a short statement' makes sense only if we understand it figuratively, taking 'Moscow' to stand for the Russian government. This figure is possible not because of any similarity between government and city, but because they are associated with each other (the government is based in the city). Metonymies can be formed through many different kinds of associative link. Typical dress, for example, can be used metonymically to stand for those who wear it: if someone says that 'a lot of big wigs came to the party', we understand 'big wigs' to refer to 'important people' (a metonymy that derives from the fashion among the upper classes in earlier centuries in Europe of wearing elaborate wigs in public).

10.1.4 Synecdoche

Synecdoche (Greek for 'taking together') is a sub-type of metonymy. It occurs when the association between figurative and literal senses is that of a part of the whole to which it belongs. 'Farm hands' is a common synecdoche for workers on a farm; 'a new motor' comes to mean 'a new car' by using one part of the car, its engine, to stand for the whole. (Note that 'big wig', above, is not a part of the person to which it belongs, and so would not be called synecdoche.)

10.1.5 Allegory

The term **allegory** comes from the Greek for 'speaking otherwise'. An allegory is

> a narrative fiction in which the agents and actions, and sometimes the setting
> as well, are contrived to make coherent sense on the 'literal', or primary, level

of signification, and at the same time to signify a second, correlated order of agents, concepts, and events.

(Abrams, 2011)

Allegory differs from the other kinds of figurative language we are looking at because an allegorical story makes sense at the literal level as well as indicating that it needs to be understood at a second allegorical level.

10.1.6 Apostrophe

An **apostrophe** is a variant on the general poetic speech situation in which a speaker or notional speaker addresses a reader. With apostrophe, the speaker is addressing either someone who is not there, or even dead, or something normally thought of as unable to understand language or to reply (e.g. an animal or an object). In 'To a Skylark', Shelley apostrophizes the skylark: 'Hail to thee, blithe spirit'. In 'Ode on a Grecian Urn' (1820), Keats apostrophizes a Greek urn and the figures in its design. One of the consequences of apostrophe is that it personifies the thing addressed, and is therefore similar to personifying metaphor (see below). Apostrophe also tends to involve the use of an archaic second-person pronoun and its associated verb form (as for instance in Shelley's 'Ode to a Skylark', 'Hail to *thee*, blithe spirit! / Bird *thou* never *wert*. . .' One of the effects of such archaism is to elevate the thing being apostrophized, partly because of the association of this pronoun and verb form with the Bible and with the mode of addressing God in Christian prayer: 'Our Father which *art* in Heaven, Hallowed be *thy* name' (see **Unit 5, Language and time**).

10.2 Analysing metaphors

Metaphor is the most important and interesting of the various kinds of figurative language to students of literature, and a great deal of scholarly and theoretical analysis has been devoted to the topic. The rest of this unit accordingly examines aspects of metaphor and various ways of reading metaphors in texts.

10.2.1 Metaphor and inferencing

One account of the way we understand figurative language is that we use the same kind of **inferencing** process we employ when trying to identify authorial intention (see **Unit 14, Authorship and intention**). Inferencing is a process of assigning meaning by making informed guesses based on evidence from the text and other sources. Deciphering figurative language in this way involves 'reading between the lines' to discover what the author is 'really' saying.

Most users of English are able to make sense of the statement that figurative language is an 'umbrella term'. Most of the time, we make sense of such metaphors without paying attention to how we do so. Often we are able to do this because we have heard or read, and made sense of, the figurative usage before. But we are also able, for the most part, to understand new metaphors without conscious effort. When we try to analyse how we do this, however, the process can suddenly seem strange and difficult to reconstruct.

In the case of 'figurative language is an umbrella term', we can break down the process of understanding into several stages. First, we notice that the literal meaning cannot be true. Second, we assume that the phrase, to be relevant in the communication, must have a potentially true meaning and that we should therefore invent or infer a non-literal meaning that is plausible. Third, we set about trying to infer that plausible, non-literal meaning. (Plausibility depends on a number of factors: the meaning must be capable of being true and it must fit in with the rest of the text.) In the 'umbrella' example, we ask what features or uses of an umbrella might be relevant in the phrase we are trying to understand. Keeping out the rain does not seem relevant. What is possibly relevant, in relation to 'figurative language', is the idea that an umbrella is designed to cover one person or more. The notion of something covering more than one other thing appears to fit, especially since we had already said, before using this expression, that figurative language is 'a general term for a range of different non-literal uses of language'.

10.2.2 Metaphors as different parts of speech

The process of inferencing can be guided by a recognition that metaphors may be formed with different parts of speech but that the inferred meaning of a metaphor needs to be formulated as the same part(s) of speech as the metaphorical expression itself. This requirement follows from the fact that metaphor works through a process of substitution, or comparison, of like with like. In 'figurative language is an umbrella term', 'umbrella' could be said to be substituting for other possible words that would make literal sense: 'general', 'all-encompassing', and so on. The substitutive relation is emphasized by the fact that 'umbrella', 'general' and 'all-encompassing' would all function in the sentence as adjectives (that is, they modify the noun 'term'). Yet 'umbrella', of course, is usually a noun, as in the following (also figurative) sentence: 'We need to develop a nuclear *umbrella* to defend the world against asteroid collision.' In this example, the metaphorical noun 'umbrella' could be substituted by another noun phrase, such as 'defensive system'.

10.2.3 Tenor, vehicle, ground

Recognizing that explicating a metaphor involves substituting a meaning-indicating expression that is also an equivalent part of speech is an important analytic step. As well as helping to explain the inferencing process described above as a kind of substitution, it also helps us to understand an influential procedure for analysing metaphors developed by the literary critic I.A. Richards (1893–1979). Richards's analysis involved identifying the different components of metaphor, which he called tenor, vehicle and ground. (Sharp readers, to use a metaphor, will notice that both 'vehicle' and 'ground' are themselves metaphors.) The word or phrase in a sentence that cannot be taken literally in the context is the 'vehicle'. The meaning that is implied, or referred to, by the vehicle is the 'tenor'. To work out the 'ground' of the metaphor (that is, the basis for the substitution) we need to identify what vehicle and tenor have in common: their 'common ground'. We can then filter out aspects of the vehicle that do not relate to the tenor. Re-describing our example 'Figurative language is an umbrella term' in these terms, the ground that links the vehicle (i.e. 'umbrella') and the tenor (i.e. 'general') is that both cover more than one thing.

10.2.4 Explicit and implicit metaphors

Another useful distinction in understanding metaphor is that between explicit and implicit metaphors. In an explicit metaphor (often involving the verb 'to be'), both the vehicle and the tenor are present in the text. In 'The M1 motorway is the artery of England', for example, the tenor is 'M1 motorway', the vehicle is 'artery', and the ground is the similarity between a motorway as a main channel of traffic flow and an artery as a main channel of blood flow. In an implicit metaphor, by contrast, while the vehicle is present in the text, the tenor has to be inferred: in 'figurative language is an umbrella term', the vehicle is 'umbrella' while the tenor (general, all-encompassing) has to be inferred.

10.2.5 Classifying metaphors: concretive, animistic, humanizing

Another important strategy in analysing a metaphor is to compare vehicle and tenor in order to describe what sort of transference of meaning, including connotations, goes on between them (see Leech, 1969). A 'concretive' metaphor uses a concrete term to talk about an abstract thing. Common examples include 'the burden of responsibility' and 'every cloud has a silver lining'. Religious discourse often uses concretive metaphors to make abstract ideas more vivid; heaven, for example, is often referred to as if it were a place or a building, as in, 'In my Father's house are many mansions' (John 14.2). An animistic metaphor uses a term usually associated with living creatures to talk about an inanimate thing. Common examples include 'the heart of the matter' and 'the screech of brakes'. A humanizing or anthropomorphic metaphor (sometimes called **personification**) uses a term usually associated with human beings to talk about a non-human thing. Common examples include the 'hands' of a clock and 'the dawn chorus'. As regards how metaphor gives expression to particular ways in which objects and processes are perceived and understood, humanizing metaphor is connected with the **pathetic fallacy** (the idea that the world reflects or participates in a person's emotions): 'the promise of spring' is a human projection onto the season (which cannot literally make a promise).

These are not the only kinds of transfer that can provide a basis for metaphor. Consider the phrase 'the nightclubs are full of sharks'. Given that it is unlikely that this will be true, we infer that the statement means that the men (and/or women) in the nightclubs behave in predatory ways, like sharks. In other words, human beings are metaphorically described as a kind of animal (rather than, as in **personification**, the reverse). In the statement 'the dog flew at the intruder's throat', the dog's action is described as if it were the action of a bird (hence, animal-to-animal transference). In general, though (and across languages), metaphors tend to represent abstract things – ideas, emotions, thoughts, feelings – as physical objects or processes, and to represent physical things or events in ways that reveal how we think or feel about them. Such metaphors make thoughts and feelings more vivid or tangible: they give a 'figure' to thoughts and feelings, and allow us to see them in new ways. This is why metaphors can be found in abundance in poetry and other forms of literature (as well as in jokes, advertising slogans, conversation and many other forms of discourse).

10.2.6 Extended metaphor

When a piece of language uses several vehicles from the same area of thought (or semantic field), this is called an extended metaphor. In the last two stanzas of the poem 'The Unequal Fetters' (1713), Anne Finch develops an extended metaphor to suggest that marriage ('Hymen') is a set of 'unequal fetters' (chains or bonds) for men and women and that, as a consequence, she intends to avoid it. The language of the stanzas creates a description of marriage through a series of metaphorical expressions which blend the conceptual field of marriage with the conceptual field of servitude:

> Free as Nature's first intention
> Was to make us, I'll be found
> Nor by subtle Man's invention
> Yield to be in fetters bound
> By one that walks a freer round.
>
> Marriage does but slightly tie men
> Whilst close prisoners we remain
> They the larger slaves of Hymen
> Still are begging love again
> At the full length of all their chain.

10.2.7 Mixed metaphor

Books on 'good style' often condemn mixed metaphor (i.e. the combination of two or more metaphors whose vehicles come from incongruous semantic fields) because they can have unintentionally ludicrous effects. Corny jokes often exploit mixed metaphor for precisely this reason. M.H. Abrams (1993), however, claims that mixed metaphor can have interesting effects in literature, as can be illustrated by the opening lines of the following sonnet, 'To the Pupils of the Hindu College', by Henry L. Derozio (1809–31):

> Expanding like the petals of young flowers
> I watch the gentle opening of your minds,
> And the sweet loosening of the spell that binds
> Your intellectual energies and powers
> That stretch (like young birds in soft summer hours)
> Their wings to try their strength.

In these lines, the effect of education on the pupils' minds is figured as the opening of flower petals (a dead metaphor), as release from a spell, and as the stretching of fledglings' wings in order to get ready for first flight. Yet this is not an especially incongruent mixing of metaphors, in that all the metaphors have a 'common ground' that could be labelled as growth, release, flight or escape, each used to signify an effort to find a suitable conceptualization that can give expression to the process being described.

10.2.8 Vital metaphors and dead metaphors

New metaphors are constantly being developed, whenever a new area of experience or thought needs new descriptive terms. Gradually, however, metaphors become familiar and can cease to be recognized as metaphors at all. When this happens, they lose their power as metaphors. Everyday language is full of such terms. A speaker of English would not normally be conscious of using two (very different) metaphors in claiming that 'things are looking up for the team since the landslide victory last week'. Yet both 'things are looking up' and 'landslide' have to be understood as metaphors, since they cannot be taken literally in the context. Words and phrases that are metaphorical, but cease to be regarded as metaphors, are called dead metaphors (the term 'dead metaphor' is itself a dead metaphor).

Dead metaphors tend to reproduce commonplace thoughts and do not require much imagination to be understood. By contrast, vitally new metaphors force us out of established ways of thinking. As Wallace Stevens suggests in a notebook, 'Reality is a cliché / From which we escape by metaphor'. An original metaphor that draws attention to itself can make demands on our powers of creative interpretation. Each time such challenging metaphors are produced, the way that language maps the world is altered. Domains that are usually kept separate, at least in language, are momentarily blended or fused, and new meanings brought into existence.

10.3 Reading metaphor in literature

It is sometimes suggested that literature uses language metaphorically while non-literary discourse uses language literally. This is clearly not the case. All kinds of non-literary discourses use figurative language. A more useful metaphor for thinking about how metaphor features in different kinds of language use is to imagine a spectrum of language types, ranging from discourses that consist mostly of literal usages and dead metaphors through to discourses that are highly conscious and innovative in their use of metaphor. Literature is generally at the highly conscious and innovative end of this spectrum; but we should be wary of thinking that only the vivid and strikingly new metaphors count. Not all literary texts are trying to break new ground in their use of figurative language. Sometimes, indeed, it is the quieter, almost imperceptible metaphors – those we might easily fail to notice – that do a lot of important work in a literary text by showing how – 'in what terms' – the topic is being perceived.

One consequence of becoming alert to metaphor is that we start to see metaphors everywhere, especially when looking closely at a literary passage. It is true that metaphor is everywhere, and that even the basic fabric of language is metaphorical (Lakoff and Johnson, 2003). But there can still be a danger that inexperienced readers of literary works begin to see significant metaphors where there are none. To avoid this, a good rule of thumb (to use a metaphor) is to say 'if an expression can be read literally, then treat it as literal, at least initially – only read something as a metaphor if it can't be taken literally'. But while this is a good general rule, it is not failsafe. Sometimes a text may make use of the ambiguity that can arise when something can equally be taken as literal or as metaphorical. This is very common in song lyrics, for example, where the capability of phrases to carry multiple meanings, especially when sung with pauses as part of a musical composition, creates much of their power. And sometimes, although it *is* possible to read an expression literally, there are hints in the text that it should be read metaphorically instead. In other words, reading for metaphor sometimes has to take the whole text – or certainly the immediately surrounding text and context – into consideration.

ACTIVITY 10

This activity looks at Toru Dutt's poem 'Our Casuarina Tree' (first published in India, in 1878).

> Like a huge Python, winding round and round
> The rugged trunk, indented deep with scars
> Up to its very summit near the stars,
> A creeper climbs, in whose embraces bound
> No other tree could live. But gallantly   5
> The giant wears the scarf, and flowers are hung

In crimson clusters all the boughs among,
Whereon all day are gathered bird and bee;
And oft at nights the garden overflows
With one sweet song that seems to have no close,   10
Sung darkling from our tree, while men repose.

When first my casement is wide open thrown
At dawn, my eyes delighted on it rest;
Sometimes, and most in winter, – on its crest
A gray baboon sits statue-like alone   15
Watching the sunrise; while on lower boughs
His puny offspring leap about and play;
And far and near kokilas hail the day;
And to their pastures wend our sleepy cows;
And in the shadow, on the broad tank cast   20
By that hoar tree, so beautiful and vast,
The water-lilies spring, like snow enmassed.

But not because of its magnificence
Dear is the Casuarina to my soul:
Beneath it we have played; though years may roll,   25
O sweet companions, loved with love intense,
For your sakes shall the tree be ever dear!
Blent with your images, it shall arise
In memory, till the hot tears blind mine eyes!
What is that dirge-like murmur that I hear   30
Like the sea breaking on a shingle-beach?
It is the tree's lament, an eerie speech,
That haply to the unknown land may reach.

Unknown, yet well-known to the eye of faith!
Ah, I have heard that wail far, far away   35
In distant lands, by many a sheltered bay,
When slumbered in his cave the water-wraith
And the waves gently kissed the classic shore
Of France or Italy, beneath the moon
When earth lay tranced in a dreamless swoon: 40
And every time the music rose, – before
Mine inner vision rose a form sublime,
Thy form, O Tree, as in my happy prime
I saw thee, in my own loved native clime.

Therefore I fain would consecrate a lay   45
Unto thy honour, Tree, beloved of those
Who now in blessed sleep for aye repose,
Dearer than life to me, alas! were they!

continued

continued

Mayst thou be numbered when my days are done
With deathless trees – like those in Borrowdale,   50
Under whose awful branches lingered pale
'Fear, trembling Hope, and Death, the skeleton,
And Time the shadow' and though weak the verse
That would thy beauty fain, oh fain rehearse,
May Love defend thee from Oblivion's curse.   55

(Note: in the last stanza, Dutt alludes to and quotes from Wordsworth's poem 'Yew Trees' (1815).)

---

1 Highlight or underline all the uses of figurative language that you can find in this poem; give each usage its appropriate label (simile, personification, etc.).

   1.1 Choose one of the metaphors you have identified and analyse it using the methods described above: (a) identify vehicle, tenor and ground; (b) is it implicit or explicit? (c) is it concretive, animistic or humanizing? (d) is it extended – i.e. are there other vehicles or non-literal terms in the poem that come from the same semantic field?

2 Rewrite the first stanza in order to eliminate all similes and metaphors. What is the difference between your stanza and Dutt's?

   2.1 How would you describe the image of the tree that Dutt's similes and metaphors create in this stanza?

3 Use the metaphors and similes of the third stanza as a way to identify why the tree is dear to the speaker. (You could also look at the first four lines of the final stanza.)

   3.1 Do the vehicles of the important similes and metaphors in the third stanza come from (a) the same semantic field, (b) related semantic fields or (c) different semantic fields?

   3.2 Where would you locate these metaphors on a scale ranging from vitally new metaphors, at one end, through to dead metaphors, at the other? What does your categorization suggest?

4 How does the use of apostrophe in stanzas three, four and five confirm or challenge your interpretation of the poem?

5 Is 'deathless' (line 50) metaphorical or literal? How will the tree become deathless? How does the wish that the tree should become 'deathless' relate to the overall meaning of the poem?

6 In the course of answering these questions have you: (a) discovered more metaphors and similes than you did when you answered question (1)? or (b) realized that some of the metaphors and similes you identified in answering question (1) are not actually metaphors or similes? What do you learn from this?

Reading

Abrams, M.H. (2011) *A Glossary of Literary Terms*, 10th edn, New York and London: Harcourt Brace Jovanovich.

Croft, W. and Cruse, D. (2004) *Cognitive Linguistics*, Cambridge: Cambridge University Press.

Fauconnier, G. and Turner, M. (2003) *The Way We Think: Conceptual Blending and the Mind's Hidden Complexities*, New York: Basic Books.

Furniss, T. and Bath, M. (2007) *Reading Poetry: An Introduction*, 2nd edn, London: Longman, Chapters 5–6.

Glucksberg, S. (with M. McGlone) (2001) *Understanding Figurative Language: From Metaphors to Idioms*, Oxford: Oxford University Press.

Kövecses, Z. (2010) *Metaphor: A Practical Introduction*, 2nd edn, Oxford: Oxford University Press.

Lakoff, G. and Johnson, M. (2003) *Metaphors We Live By*, 2nd edn, Chicago: University of Chicago Press, especially pp. 3–40.

Leech, G. (1969) *A Linguistic Guide to English Poetry*, London: Longman, pp. 147–65.

Lodge, D. (1989) *The Modes of Modern Writing*, London: Edward Arnold.

Richards, I.A. (1965) *Philosophy of Rhetoric*, Oxford: Oxford University Press, especially Chapters 5–6.

Semino, E. (2008) *Metaphor in Discourse*, Cambridge: Cambridge University Press.

Irony

This unit:

- introduces the concept of verbal irony, as a use of language in which we do not literally mean what we say;

- distinguishes the main kinds of irony, including situational irony and dramatic irony;

- explores modern uses of irony in which no underlying or intended meaning is expressed unambiguously, showing how such uses have a destabilizing effect on any particular point or world view that the text might otherwise appear to be communicating.

Irony involves the figurative, or indirect, interpretation of an utterance, text, situation or event because of something the interpreter already knows (or has been led to believe) which encourages them not to treat what they are interpreting at face value. Irony takes many forms, of which the clearest in texts is called verbal irony: that is, irony associated specifically with verbal communication.

11.1 Verbal irony

Verbal irony is a use of language in which we do not intend what we say or write to be taken seriously or as sincere. To understand how verbal irony works we need to consider first the various kinds of meaning that we communicate when we speak or write.

A communicated meaning can be analysed into two component parts: (1) a proposition, and (2) an attitude towards that proposition. A proposition is a sentence that makes a statement about the real world or about some fictional world. The most common attitude we have towards such a proposition (our **propositional attitude**) is that of belief: we tend to believe what we say (and in many cases say what we believe). But we can also express propositions that we don't believe. In this case, if we conceal our propositional attitude (now one of disbelief), then we are lying. If, on the other hand, we signal in some way that we ourselves do not believe what we are saying, then we are being ironic. In verbal irony, the speaker communicates a proposition and at the same time signals that he/she does not believe it to be true (often implying the reverse of what is actually said). There is no difference in the proposition itself: the difference is in the attitude that is communicated along with it.

Verbal irony is successful when the writer or speaker provides sufficient evidence to indicate that his or her attitude is one of disbelief, rather than the expected attitude of belief. Since disbelief towards what you are saying is not the normal state of affairs, there must be something unusual about the text to signal that the speaker disbelieves what he or she is saying. One of the available signals of verbal irony is obvious exaggeration of the proposition in question. In the first sentence of Jane Austen's *Pride and Prejudice* (1813), for example, irony is signalled by an exaggerated assertion of the truth of a proposition that is far from being clearly true:

> It is a truth universally acknowledged, that a single man in possession of a good fortune, must be in want of a wife.

The narrator here actually presents two propositions, and makes it clear that she believes neither of them. The core proposition is 'a single man in possession of a good fortune, must be in want of a wife'; this proposition is prefaced by another proposition: 'It is a truth universally acknowledged [that a single man in possession of a good fortune, must be in want of a wife].' The initial, prefatory proposition, by asserting so emphatically the truth of the second proposition, signals the narrator's disagreement with both.

In principle, any kind of signal might be used to indicate that a speaker, character or narrator has an attitude of disbelief towards a proposition. One signal of irony is where the register of a text or passage is clearly incompatible with the situation, subject matter or assumed speaker (see **Unit 7, Language and context: register**). In *The Rape of the Lock* (1714), for example, Alexander Pope treats a trivial incident in high society by using the elevated register and conventions associated with epic poetry. By doing so, he creates a 'mock epic' poem that ironically criticizes the frivolity of his age. Another possible signal of irony can be a clear contradiction between what is said and our **background knowledge**: that is, with what we already know (as, for example, in the opening sentence of *Pride and Prejudice*). Unless there is good reason to abandon our previous beliefs, we instead adopt an attitude of disbelief towards what is said. But this is still not enough on its own to give rise to irony. We might, for example, decide that the author has made a mistake. We must be convinced that the author *intends* us to see that the character or narrator does not believe what is said. This may be achieved, as we have begun to see, through exaggeration and overemphasis, including by means of hyperbole, extensive use of superlatives, and emphatic (insincere) statements of belief.

In verbal irony, the speaker/writer often implies not only that he or she does not believe the proposition but that someone else *does* believe it. The ironist simultaneously communicates his or her own attitude of disbelief and also suggests that someone else has a different attitude (of belief), irrespective of whether that someone else is identifiable or not. Irony often also involves an implication that the speaker or writer shares with us an amused attitude towards those misguided people and characters who believe the proposition in question. The opening sentence of *Pride and Prejudice* implies that some misguided people do believe that a single man in possession of a good fortune must be in want of a wife. Further reading of the novel reveals that quite a lot of the characters in it believe exactly this. But it is precisely these characters who are criticized and made fun of in the novel. In this way, verbal irony can be used as a tool of social criticism that is more subtle and powerful than straightforward condemnation, which is one of the reasons why it is often used in novels, plays and poems. By contrast, the two heroines (especially Elizabeth Bennett) resist the general presumption in the neighbourhood that marriage should be treated as a social arrangement based on money and social standing. Yet although the opening sentence of *Pride and Prejudice* is a clear example of verbal irony, one of the more subtle ironies of the novel is that Elizabeth does end up marrying the rich hero (Mr Darcy) when he finally realizes that he is indeed in want of a wife.

All varieties of verbal irony work in basically the same way: they signal that the overt statement is not believed by the speaker or writer and not to be believed by the listener or reader. In sarcasm, which is often called the lowest form of verbal irony, an exaggerated tone of voice communicates the attitude of disbelief. But the disbelief nevertheless remains implicit: the speaker does not actually *say* that they do not believe what they are saying. In irony the attitude of disbelief is always implicitly rather than explicitly communicated. The first sentence of *Pride and Prejudice* would not be ironic if it announced that 'Some of the characters in this book incorrectly believe that it is a truth universally acknowledged, that a single man in possession of a good fortune, must be in want of a wife.' Irony involves some tension between what is said and what is meant, and opens up a subtle game that authors and readers can play together.

11.2　Situational irony

Situational irony involves a mismatch between what two different people (or two groups of people) know. The participant in an event understands that event in a way that is not correct, while the viewer, audience or reader understands the event differently, and correctly. Viewers or readers are able to do this because they have an advantage over the participant, by virtue of being outside the situation of the participant and by having access to knowledge that the participant does not have.

One way of being outside the situation of a participant is to be historically later than the participant. Historical irony arises, accordingly, when a participant may have convictions about how events will play out in the future, but from our later perspective we know that they will turn out very differently. This kind of situational irony also occurs when we read a text whose **dénouement** we already know (either through having read it before or because it is well known). When we read characters' eager or anxious anticipations of a future we know will not happen, we see them as subject to situational irony. The participant is 'subject to situational irony' in that the reader or viewer sees the incongruity between what the participant says or does and their true situation. In verbal irony, the speaker means us to see the disparity between what is said and what is believed; in situational irony, the speaker's words and actions are based on sincere belief and it is we, as interpreters of what they say or do, who see that the belief is false or inappropriate.

Dramatic irony is a kind of situational irony that is typically generated in theatre (as well as in film and TV drama, see **Unit 24 Ways of reading drama**). A character on stage, who is involved in a dramatic action, has a specific belief about his or her situation that the audience knows to be false. Typically, that incorrect belief will be about some crucial component of the plot and will lead to comic or tragic irony.

Situational ironies of this kind, which are sometimes referred to more generally as **structural irony**, occur in everyday life as well as in literary texts, films, TV drama, and so on. They occur whenever we see that someone acts or speaks based on limited or false beliefs that are inappropriate to the situation. The participant can be a child or some other individual who is unable fully to understand their situation, while the onlookers or audience are developmentally more advanced than the participant – an older child or an adult, for example. In Henry James's *What Maisie Knew* (1897), the child Maisie responds to and thinks about the behaviour of the adults in her world without fully understanding their sexual implications; but adult readers can reinterpret her interpretations in the light of their more experienced understanding. Maisie is therefore subject to situational irony. Another kind of 'limited' participant might be someone with a cognitive impairment that prevents them fully understanding their situation, such as the autistic narrator of Mark Haddon's *The Curious Incident of the Dog in the Night-time* (2003), or the cognitively impaired narrator of Book 1 of William Faulkner's *The Sound and the Fury* (1929). Finally, the participant might be an animal or alien (e.g. a Martian visiting Earth, as used in jokes), unable fully to understand their situation, especially if that situation requires an attempt to understand the human world.

These ways of separating the reader from the participant can have the effect of 'othering' the participant: that is, defining the participant not just as different but also as somehow less than us. Or these 'othered' participants can encourage us to read the situational ironies in reverse, so that we identify with the character as having a special kind of knowledge that we lack. In such circumstances, it is as though we are temporarily allowed to look at ourselves through the eyes of others, thereby subjecting ourselves to a kind of situational irony. A child or animal character or narrator may be able to understand our adult human situation in ways that **defamiliarize** aspects of our world that we have not noticed or properly thought about. In Tolstoy's short story 'Strider' (1886), a horse narrator relates his life story to some other horses and in doing so defamiliarizes human customs – such as the ownership of horses – that puzzle and horrify him. In some novels, a foreigner describes our society in ways that show that we do not fully understand our situation, in this way subjecting us to situational irony. An example of this would be George Mikes's *How To Be an Alien* (1947), an 'othering' description of British society of the period written for a British audience from the perspective of a Hungarian immigrant. Use of such characters and narrators switches the situational irony onto the anticipated reader, and undermines that reader's assumed superiority.

11.3 Radical irony

As an illustration of some of the more complex possibilities of irony, consider Shelley's sonnet 'Ozymandias' (1819). This poem prompts a number of interpretive problems, among which is the identification and attribution of an irony associated with the inscription cited in lines 10–11:

> I met a traveler from an antique land
> Who said: Two vast and trunkless legs of stone

Stand in the desert . . . Near them, on the sand,
Half sunk, a shattered visage lies, whose frown,
And wrinkled lip, and sneer of cold command,   5
Tell that its sculptor well those passions read
Which yet survive, stamped on these lifeless things,
The hand that mocked them, and the heart that fed:
And on the pedestal these words appear:
'My name is Ozymandias, king of kings: 10
Look on my works, ye Mighty, and despair!'
Nothing beside remains. Round the decay
Of that colossal wreck, boundless and bare
The lone and level sands stretch far away.

If the inscription in lines 10–11 is interpreted as telling the mighty (kings, politicians, etc.) to despair 'because even my great works will come to nothing', then it is not ironic at all: rather, it is correctly believed by all parties concerned. But alternatively, if that same inscription is interpreted as telling the mighty to despair 'because my works are so great', then the proposition is falsely believed by Ozymandias but correctly disbelieved by us (because the works have vanished over the course of time, resulting in a historical irony). However, even if we identify the text as, in this way, ironically mocking the overweening arrogance of this 'king of kings', there is still a problem: who we attribute the ironic intention to (and so, who the ironist is). If Ozymandias, in adding these words to the pedestal, intended to boast of his superiority over all other kings, then the wasting powers of time have made his words ironic. But what was the attitude of the sculptor who 'mocked' Ozymandias? 'Mocked' here means 'portrayed in stone' (by producing a 'mock' or simulating image). But it can also mean 'made a mockery of'. If we assume that it was the sculptor who added the inscription, then was this action on the orders of Ozymandias, or the sculptor's own decision (and, if the latter, was the attitude of the sculptor reverential or ironic in performing this action)? It is also conceivable that the words were added by a later hand, at a point when the erosive powers of time had already made a mockery of Ozymandias' statue, in this way allowing a straightforward irony. The poem does not answer these questions. Rather, it leaves them hanging – and besides, it is not clear that they could be answered. What we can be sure of is that Shelley's poem exploits the ironic disparity between what the words say and what the ruined statue 'says'. Further contextual knowledge – of Shelley's radical politics, of the political anger of his other poems of the period and of his response to the recent 'Peterloo Massacre' (in which troops had charged on a political demonstration in Manchester in 1819) – seems to invite us to read the poem as offering an ironic message to Britain's oppressive government of the period.

11.4 Romantic irony

Irony contrasts with sincerity: it creates an appearance of sincerity while signalling that an utterance or action is not meant to be taken sincerely, and is often used to puncture the sincerity of others. Given that sincerity is one of the characteristic stances of Romanticism, then, the notion of '**Romantic irony**' might appear to be a contradiction in terms. Yet there is a strand of writing in European Romanticism that simultaneously presents itself as sincere and yet undercuts its own sincerity by foregrounding the fact that literature is not the product of a spontaneous overflow of powerful feelings but is 'made up' by the author–narrator, who appears in the text and engages in some kind of play with the reader.

The term 'Romantic irony' was introduced by the German critic Friedrich Schlegel. One of the clearest examples of sustained Romantic irony, however, is Byron's long poem, *Don Juan* (1819–24). The story of this mock-epic poem involves an ironic version of the Don Juan myth (which can be explored, as a myth, by following suggestions made in **Unit 2, Using information sources**). Byron's poem nevertheless prevents us from taking the story seriously by deploying a host of ironic techniques, including a creator–narrator who pretends to discuss the poem and his poetic technique with the reader as he goes along. Stanzas VI–VII of Canto I exemplify how the narrator foregrounds and plays with the epic conventions that he uses and abuses:

> Most epic poets plunge in 'medias res,'
>   (Horace makes this the heroic turnpike road)
> And then your hero tells, whene'er you please,
>   What went before – by way of episode,
> While seated after dinner at his ease,   (5)
>   Beside his mistress in some soft abode,
> Palace, or garden, paradise, or cavern,
> Which serves the happy couple for a tavern.
>
> That is the usual method, but not mine –
>   My way is to begin with the beginning;   (10)
> The regularity of my design
>   Forbids all wandering as the worst of sinning,
> And therefore I shall open with a line
>   (Although it cost me half an hour in spinning)
> Narrating somewhat of Don Juan's father,   (15)
> And also of his mother, if you'd rather.

(41–56)

Here, the ironic Byronic narrator uses verbal irony to undercut the seriousness of epic conventions. The final rhyme of each stanza, for example, deflates what the rest of the stanza sets up. The suggestion that epic heroes typically tell their back story while relaxing after dinner with their mistress, in the equivalent of a 'tavern', produces an incongruity that serves to mock the epic genre's high seriousness. But this internal irony is supplemented by a Romantic irony that both celebrates the narrator's creative liberty and subjects the creator–narrator, the poem itself and the reading process to destabilizing ironies.

The second stanza foregrounds the fact that the poem is a work of art, rather than 'real life'. It presents a self-conscious narrator who engages in a pretend dialogue with his reader, discussing his creative 'method' and suggesting that the poem's composition is an arbitrary, ongoing process that the reader might influence – especially when he tells us that he will 'open with a line' that cost him 'half an hour in spinning'. The narrator is also self-ironic, as in the pompous assertion that the regularity of his design 'Forbids all wandering as the worst of sinning'. Irony is signalled here partly by the exaggeration, but more importantly by the fact that *Don Juan* contains numerous examples of the narrator's penchant for arbitrary digressions that are often more interesting than the central narrative – a feature that undercuts the fictional illusion of the core story. Romantic irony in this way fits our general definition of irony: the creator–narrator both half-pretends that this is a serious poem and that he is sincerely concerned for the fate of his hero and, at the same time, offers a variety of signals that tell us not to take any of this seriously. *Don Juan*'s irony is radically destabilizing, in that it is directed not only against the moral and political hypocrisy that Byron saw in early nineteenth-century Europe, but also against the illusions of literature and the illusion that life itself makes sense. In Canto VII, the creator–narrator hopes 'it is no crime / To laugh at *all* things – for I wish to know / *What*, after *all*, are *all* things – but a show?' (stanza 2). Yet this philosophical irony is itself subject to irony, for instance when the narrator announces, 'There's no such thing as certainty, that's plain' (Canto IX, stanza 17) – a line that announces the certainty of radical uncertainty! Similarly, there is a delicious irony in the fact that *Don Juan* is a poem that undermines the seriousness of literature in seventeen long cantos of virtuosic poetry.

Romantic irony is not confined to the Romantic period or to poetry. Often-cited examples include Laurence Sterne's pioneering **metafictional** novel *Tristram Shandy* (1760–67), which narrates a story yet constantly disrupts and reflects on it, and Denis Diderot's *Jacques the Fatalist* (1771–78). Metafictional novels of the twentieth century, such as John Fowles's *The French Lieutenant's Woman* (1969) or Alastair Gray's *Lanark* (1981), break with nineteenth-century realist conventions by in many respects returning to the strategies of eighteenth- and early nineteenth-century Romantic irony.

11.5 Why use irony?

Verbal irony makes it possible for us to say something that we do not believe to be true, and by doing so to communicate a range of meanings that we *do* believe to be true. Irony is a more effective technique of social and political criticism than telling it straight – as the examples we have looked at show. Situational and dramatic irony can also function to express social and cultural critique, as in the uses of naïve but defamiliarizing narrators examined earlier.

These effects of irony can be seen, for example, in George Orwell's *Animal Farm* (1945). The narrator in *Animal Farm* apparently shares the naïve, optimistic viewpoint of the exploited worker-animals on the socialist farm, making the novel's criticism of Stalinist Russia all the more powerful. Situational and dramatic irony are also powerful techniques for producing tragedy and comedy. Depending on the situation depicted in a text, when we witness a character on stage or read about a character in a novel who speaks and behaves in ways that are incongruous in that situation we feel either pity or an impulse to laugh. Shakespeare's comedies frequently create comic situational irony, when we witness the ridiculous and inappropriate vanity of overweening fools (such as Malvolio in *Twelfth Night*). In Shakespeare's tragedies, by contrast, we read or watch with horror and pity as sympathetic characters behave in ways that are wholly inappropriate because those ways of behaving are based on fundamentally mistaken views of their situation – something we see when the hero of *Othello* murders his wife in the mistaken belief that she has been unfaithful to him (see **Unit 24, Ways of reading drama**).

ACTIVITY 11

This activity is based on Chapter II of Book I of Henry Fielding's *Tom Jones* (1749).

CHAPTER II

A short description of Squire Allworthy, and a fuller account of Miss Bridget Allworthy, his sister.

In that part of the western division of this kingdom which is commonly called Somersetshire, there lately lived (and perhaps lives still) a gentleman whose name was Allworthy, and who might well be called the favourite of both Nature and Fortune; for both of these seem to have contended which should bless and enrich him most. In this contention, Nature may seem to some to have come off victorious, as she bestowed on him many gifts, while Fortune had only one gift in her power; but in pouring forth this, she was so very profuse, that others perhaps may think this single endowment to have been more than equivalent to all the various blessings which he enjoyed from Nature. From the former of these, he derived an agreeable person, a sound constitution, a solid understanding, and a benevolent heart; by the latter, he was decreed to the inheritance of one of the largest estates in the county.

This gentleman had in his youth married a very worthy and beautiful woman, of whom he had been extremely fond; by her he had three children, all of whom died in their infancy. He had likewise had the misfortune of burying this beloved wife herself, about five years before

continued

the time in which this history chooses to set out. This loss, however great, he bore like a man of sense and constancy, though it must be confessed he would often talk a little whimsically on this head; for he sometimes said he looked on himself as still married, and considered his wife as only gone a little before him, a journey which he should most certainly, sooner or later, take after her; and that he had not the least doubt of meeting her again in a place where he should never part with her more. Sentiments for which his sense was arraigned by one part of his neighbours, his religion by a second, and his sincerity by a third.

He now lived, for the most part, retired in the country, with one sister, for whom he had a very tender affection. This lady was now some-what past the age of thirty, an era at which, in the opinion of the malicious, the title of Old Maid may, with no impropriety, be assumed. She was of that species of women whom you commend rather for good qualities than beauty, and who are generally called by their own sex, very good sort of women – as good a sort of woman, madam, as you would wish to know. Indeed, she was so far from regretting want of beauty that she never mentioned that perfection (if it can be called one) without contempt; and would often thank God she was not as handsome as Miss such-a-one, whom perhaps beauty had led into errors which she might have otherwise avoided. Miss Bridget Allworthy (for that was the name of this lady) very rightly conceived the charms of person in a woman to be no better than snares for herself, as well as for others; and yet so discreet was she in her conduct, that her prudence was as much on the guard as if she had all the snares to apprehend which were ever laid for her whole sex. Indeed, I have observed (though it may seem unaccountable to the reader) that this guard of prudence, like the trained bands, is always readiest to go on duty where there is the least danger. It often basely and cowardly deserts those paragons for whom the men are all wishing, sighing, dying, and spreading every net in their power; and constantly attends the heels of that higher order of women for whom the other sex have a more distant and awful respect, and whom (from despair, I suppose, of success) they never venture to attack.

Reader, I think proper, before we proceed any farther together, to acquaint thee that I intend to digress, through this whole history, as often as I see occasion; of which I am myself a better judge than any pitiful critic whatever; and here I must desire all those critics to mind their own business, and not to intermeddle with affairs, or works, which no ways concern them; for till they produce the authority by which they are constituted judges, I shall proceed to their jurisdiction.

---

continued

1   Describe the author–narrator's attitude towards Squire Allworthy in the first two paragraphs of chapter II. Is that attitude sympathetic or ironic?

2   In the light of your answer to question (1), what do you think the author–narrator's implied attitude is towards the comments made by Mr Allworthy's neighbours in the final sentence of the second paragraph? (The voices of the neighbourhood work as a kind of chorus, voicing general opinion throughout the novel.)

3   Describe the author–narrator's attitude towards Miss Bridget Allworthy, as suggested in the first half of the third paragraph.

4   What is the author–narrator's tone in the last two sentences of the third paragraph (beginning 'Indeed, I have observed . . .')?

5   Does the final paragraph of Chapter II (the direct address to the reader) employ or create any of the kinds of irony discussed in this chapter? Does this paragraph constrain our response to the many digressions contained in the novel?

Reading

Booth, W. (1975) *A Rhetoric of Irony*, Chicago: University of Chicago Press.

Colebrook, C. (2003) *Irony: The New Critical Idiom*, London: Routledge.

Fabb, N. (1997) *Linguistics and Literature: Language in the Verbal Arts of the World*, Oxford: Blackwell, Chapter 10.

Furniss, T. and Bath, M. (2007) *Reading Poetry: An Introduction*, 2nd edn, London: Pearson Longman, Chapter 8.

Furst, L. (1984) *Fictions of Romantic Irony in European Narrative, 1760–1857*, London: Macmillan.

Leech, G. and Short, M. (2007) *Style in Fiction: A Linguistic Introduction to English Fictional Prose*, 2nd edn, London: Longman, pp. 277–80.

Muecke, D. (1983) *Irony and the Ironic*, London: Methuen.

Juxtaposition

This unit:

- introduces the concept of juxtaposition, showing how strategic placing of linguistic elements side-by-side, or immediately one after another, can give rise to inferences that create specific meanings;
- illustrates meaning-creating juxtaposition in poetry and painting, as well as use of the technique of 'montage' in film;
- assesses the contribution made by different kinds of juxtaposition to unsettling meanings apparently conveyed by other features of a literary text.

Juxtaposition can be defined simply as the placing of elements side by side. In communication, juxtaposition of meaningful elements is both a routine and essential practice in the composition of messages, whether those messages are literary, non-literary verbal discourse, static images, video, or multimedia. At the same time, juxtaposition is also a major resource for the communication of indirect messages and implications.

12.1 Verbal (and poetic) juxtaposition

Consider verbal juxtaposition first. Sentence construction relies on observing close constraints in how words are put together; within such constraints, significant alterations in meaning can result from simple changes in the ordering or the placing of items in a sentence (for example, by pairing items, putting items into a list or locating items at opposite ends of the sentence). Similar effects can be achieved by rhetorical techniques that go beyond the simple placement of communicative elements side by side in sentences. In this more specialized sense, juxtaposition might be defined more precisely as:

> combining together two or more communicative elements in ways that emphasize the discontinuities or differences between them, thereby provoking some surprise or puzzlement at their close placement.

Some of the underlying principles at work in juxtaposition can be illustrated in the following translations of seventeenth- and eighteenth-century Japanese **haiku**:

Haiku 1

Harvest moon:
On the bamboo mat
Pine tree shadows.

Haiku 2

Wooden gate,
Lock firmly bolted:
Winter moon.

Each of these poems consists of three short lines; and in both cases the sense of the poem seems to rest on three separate elements: 'moon', 'mat' and 'shadows' in one; 'gate', 'lock' and 'moon' in the other. These elements are juxtaposed in such a way that the links between them are not especially obvious. Neither of the poems, for instance, consists of fully formed sentences; so the reader is required to make an interpretive effort to fill in the gaps and spell out connections between the main elements. The need for such effort is accentuated by the division of each poem into two sections around a major punctuation mark, a colon. In each case, as a result, there is only an implicit connection between elements on either side of the colon. Although it is possible to see a causal relation between a harvest moon and pine tree shadows, lack of an expressed connection forces the reader to make an inferential leap. Finding a connection between a locked wooden gate and a winter moon requires greater interpretive effort. But in each poem an element from nature has been juxtaposed with an element from culture: the moon with a bamboo mat; the moon with a bolted gate. The juxtaposition creates a tension in each poem between the first and the second part. Haiku poems typically revolve around a tension or puzzle produced by juxtaposing (without further explanation) a natural phenomenon with an event or object more closely related to the human world.

The poems above are translations from Japanese texts of the seventeenth and eighteenth centuries. But similar techniques can be identified in more recent, Western poetry. The following poem by Ezra Pound can be seen as influenced by the haiku form:

L'art, 1910

Green arsenic smeared on an egg-white cloth,
Crushed strawberries! Come let us feast our eyes.

Here we find a startling juxtaposition of something toxic (arsenic) with something delectable (strawberries), and between something green and something red. Simultaneously, things more normally defined by taste and toxicity are transformed into a publicly visual experience ('Come let us feast our eyes'), though choice of the word 'feast' also involves a play between seeing and eating. Note, of course, that the title makes these juxtaposed elements emblematic of a historically defined moment in art. At the core of the poem, as a result, is a pattern of juxtaposition not dissimilar to that involved in haiku. Indeed, the association is deliberate: 'L'art, 1910' was written when Pound was a leading figure of the 'Imagist' movement (roughly 1910–20): a group of writers in Britain and the United States who attempted to develop a new form of poetry strongly influenced by haiku (especially by its use of stark, unexplained juxtapositions). The new form of poetry that resulted was an early example of modernism, a period (1910–40) of experimentation across all the arts in which juxtaposition of startlingly different elements was a characteristic technique. Much of T.S. Eliot's poetry (such as *The Waste Land*, 1922) juxtaposes a wide range of different kinds of linguistic material (quotations from Wagner's operas, biblical language, diaries, language heard in a public house, etc.).

Although juxtaposition was particularly common in the verbal and visual arts of the first half of the twentieth century, it is not confined to that period. Juxtaposition is also found in texts, both literary and non-literary, from many periods and cultures. Techniques of juxtaposition may be seen to underpin the following example, also influenced by haiku, from the contemporary Scottish poet, Alan Spence:

> mouse tracks
> across the frozen lard
> in the frying pan
> remembering
> my father's death –
> cold november rain
>
> (from *Five Haiku*, 1986)

Juxtaposition is also used, to startling effect, in the following poem by Margaret Atwood (1971):

> You fit into Me
> you fit into me
> like a hook into an eye
> a fish hook
> an open eye

12.2 Visual juxtaposition: film

Use of juxtaposition based on tension between communicative elements is not limited to verbal texts. Indeed, one early theoretician of film, the Soviet director Sergei Eisenstein (1898–1948), made discontinuity between successive shots central to his account of how film should work. He described such juxtaposition as **montage** (that is, as the selection, cutting and piecing together of filmic material as a consecutive sequence). In contrast to the dominant strand of cinematic development of the time, associated with commercial cinema and Hollywood (in which editing aspires to continuity and smoothness of transition between shots), early Soviet cinema, and particularly that of Eisenstein, attempted to produce collisions rather than continuity between shots, precisely in order to create startling juxtapositions. Eisenstein argued that, by introducing a gap or tension between successive images, it was possible to generate meaning beyond those meanings contained in the successive shots themselves.

We can illustrate this filmic use of juxtaposition, as montage, by reference to two famous images in consecutive shots in Eisenstein's film *Battleship Potemkin* (1925). The first image shows a medium close-up of a woman's face, wearing pince-nez or glasses; the second image presents the same woman, but now with her eye bleeding and the pince-nez shattered. The overall effect is that of a shot hitting the eye, even though neither the act of shooting, nor the experience of being shot, is visibly represented. The two images form part of a longer episode, commonly referred to as the 'Odessa Steps sequence', in which soldiers brutally attempt to put down a popular uprising. Images of boots marching down steps, and of rifle volleys, are intercut with images of a child's pram rolling unattended down the steps, and of a small boy being trampled underfoot. (See Figure 12.1. Parts of this

FIGURE 12.1 Series of images from the Odessa Steps sequence, *Battleship Potemkin*
        (Sergei Eisenstein, 1925).

sequence may be viewed at the following internet address: www.carleton.edu/
curricular/MEDA/classes/media110/Severson/potemkin.htm.)

The stark juxtapositions created in this sequence create a powerful sense of
movement and confusion. But what is more important for Eisenstein is how they
force the viewer to make a connection between the soldiers' actions and the
suffering of defenceless people. In this way, montage in this sequence replicates,
in its collision between images, other, larger contradictions between contending
social forces related to the film's overall subject matter. Juxtaposition was in this
way for Eisenstein part of a self-consciously Marxist, dialectical approach to film-
making, which not only emphasized discontinuity between images but (as Bertolt
Brecht did in theatre, using equivalent devices) demanded active interpretive
engagement by an audience.

12.3 Sequential versus simultaneous juxtaposition

Visual juxtaposition in film, video and TV mostly works by exploiting a sense of
surprise or shock made possible by the juxtaposition of successive images. Where
media depend upon items occurring in this way in series, they may be said to rely
on temporal or sequential juxtaposition. The images from Eisenstein's film are

good examples of sequential juxtaposition, in that their meaning depends on the order in which the elements are presented. Any change in that order either changes the meaning, or results in nonsense (imagine the effect of reversing the sequence of the two images discussed above from *Battleship Potemkin*).

Juxtaposition is also used in other media; however, in ways that do not unfold as a sequence through time. Rather, juxtaposition is spatial (e.g. in photographs, paintings and cartoons). A precise analogue to Eliot's technique of literary **brico-lage** in *The Waste Land*, discussed above, may be found in the twentieth-century use of collage in pictorial art. Collage is an abstract form of art in which photographs, pieces of paper, string, etc. are placed in juxtaposition and glued to a pictorial surface. Works of **surrealism**, as exemplified in the work of Salvador Dali (1904–89) or René Magritte (1898–1967), often depict quite unrelated items in the same pictorial space, creating an atmosphere of dream or fantasy. Here, for instance, is how Magritte described his famous painting, *Time Transfixed* (1938) (see Figure 12.2), in which a steam locomotive emerges from an empty fireplace, on the mantelpiece of which rests a clock with its hands at 12.43:

> I thought about painting a picture of a locomotive. Given that possibility, the problem was this: how to paint the picture in such a way that it evoked mystery . . . the mystery that has no meaning . . . The image of the locomotive is immediately familiar, so its mystery passes unnoticed. To bring out its mystery another immediately familiar and hence unmysterious image – that of the dining room fireplace – was combined with the image of the locomotive . . . suggesting the mystery of beings that normally strike us (by mistake, through habit) as familiar . . .

The juxtaposed elements in this kind of art practice are simultaneously present for interpretation. We take them in at a glance, and, while there must always be an order of apprehension of elements within an overall image, the order in which they are read seems not to affect the image's overall meaning. So we can say that such media create their effect by means of simultaneous juxtaposition. As with verbal composition, such techniques – though prevalent – are not restricted to the modernist phase of the twentieth century. Paintings by the Flemish painter Hieronymous Bosch (*c.* 1450–1516), for example, which depict the delights of heaven and the horrors of hell, are full of startling, sometimes grotesque and fantastic, juxtapositions.

Any visual composition, of course, is bound to include elements placed side by side. In this sense whatever is found within the same visual frame has been 'juxtaposed', if only in a rather weak sense of the term. As pointed out above, however, the notion of juxtaposition is best reserved for cases where the relation between elements goes beyond the obvious and is active in creating a meaningful effect, especially where the placing of elements next to one another defies easy explanation and where the reader or viewer is called on to supply an inferential connection.

FIGURE 12.2 René Magritte's *Time Transfixed* (*La durée poignardée*) 1938 – Oil on canvas, 147 × 98.7 cm, Art Institute, Chicago (Joseph Winterbottom Collection).

Magazine advertising frequently uses juxtaposition in the sense we are describing here. In looking at a magazine advert, we see two or more entities depicted in an image, but at first sight there may be no obvious reason why such objects should be put together. The absence of an obvious connection presents a puzzle: an **enigma** that requires some interpretive effort to resolve. Juxtaposition of the objects within the same visual field somehow implies a correspondence between the objects that the interpreter needs to discover or construct. In inviting the reader to compare juxtaposed items in this way, visual juxtaposition appears to work in a similar way to metaphor (See **Unit 10, Metaphor and figurative language**). A visual or verbal link invites us to transfer selected attributes of one juxtaposed object onto the other object to which it is juxtaposed, just as a metaphor demands that we transfer selected attributes from vehicle to tenor. But in literary and artistic works that involve juxtaposition, what is involved is less a transfer from one element to the other than a kind of surprising conceptual blending: new effects of meaning are created that are somehow 'beyond' or 'between' the elements juxtaposed (in the haiku and imagist poems, for instance, the lack of a definite connection between images seems to open them up to a multiplicity of interpretations). With most adverts, by contrast, the transfer of attributes often takes place less between elements within the image than from the image onto the commodity or brand being advertised – a process of fixing a preferred reading of the image in which the accompanying text often plays an important role. Use of captions and straplines to anchor a particular meaning within a range of possibilities opened up by juxtaposed elements suggests that juxtaposition is both a powerful and an unpredictable device, since advertisers often find it necessary to control possibly divergent interpretations that might be created.

12.4 Effects of juxtaposition

It is not possible to predict a single effect for all cases of juxtaposition. But we can point to a range of characteristic, sometimes overlapping, effects. We have already seen that juxtaposition tends to open up a plurality of possible, meaningful connections between juxtaposed elements, precisely because simple or straightforward connections are omitted. Juxtaposition can also produce a characteristic sense of tension (as in Pound's imagist poem 'L'art, 1910' discussed above).

Because of its power to communicate strong and varied effects, juxtaposition can be thought of as a rhetorical strategy, in some instances similar to that of metaphor. The similarity between juxtaposition and kinds of metaphor (especially those kinds of metaphor that take the form A is B) is reflected in the humorous use of serial juxtaposition in films: a first image shows two people beginning to make love but the following image cuts to, say, volcanoes erupting or fireworks exploding. Juxtaposition of the second image with the first invites us to imagine that there is a metaphorical relation between the couple's love-making and the volcano erupting or the fireworks going off (i.e. the second image becomes a metaphor for the first). As this conventional example suggests, such metaphorical relations can range from the inventive or poetic, through to the trite and stereotypical. Other effects of juxtaposition can be characterized along the lines used to describe kinds of irony (see **Unit 11, Irony**), reinforcing a more general idea that juxtaposition may be used to encourage oblique, inferential interpretations.

12.4.1 Juxtaposition and tragic irony

An example of juxtaposition working to create tragic irony may be found at the end of Shakespeare's *King Lear* (1606). Edmund's dying attempt to revoke his command that Cordelia be murdered, and Albany's supplication 'The gods defend her!', are immediately juxtaposed with Lear's arrival carrying Cordelia, already dead, in his arms:

EDMUND:	He hath commission from thy wife and me
	To hang Cordelia in the prison, and
	To lay the blame upon her own despair,
	That she fordid herself.
ALBANY:	The gods defend her! Bear him hence awhile.

Edmund is borne off
Enter Lear with Cordelia dead in his arms; Edgar, Captain and others
following

| LEAR: | Howl, howl, howl. . . . |

(V, iii, 251–6)

The juxtaposition of on-stage evidence of Cordelia's death (and Lear's reaction to it) with Albany's immediately preceding prayer ('The gods defend her!') reinforces the tragic effect of this scene, and ironically casts doubt on the efficacy of prayer. Juxtaposition in this context undermines, or calls into question, one element through its immediate proximity with another.

12.4.2 Juxtaposition and comic irony

Sometimes the incongruity of a juxtaposition leads not to a tragic but to a humorous effect. In radio broadcasting, mixing between alternative sources (e.g. live studio talk and pre-recorded announcements or commercials) can lead to laughably unintended juxtapositions, as in the following examples:

'It's time now, ladies and gentlemen, for our featured guest, the prominent lecturer and social leader, Mrs Elma Dodge . . .' (*accidental cut to Superman*) . . . 'who is able to leap tall buildings in a single bound.'

'So remember, use Pepsodent toothpaste, and brush your teeth . . .' (*cut in to cleansing product commercial*) . . . 'right down the drain!'

In these examples, the comic effect requires that the cut-in text provides a grammatically well-formed completion of a sentence begun in the initial text, even though the topic of the cut-in text is discordantly at odds with that of the initial text. Humorous juxtaposition is often deliberately employed as a textual strategy in comic texts which shift from one register, usually a high register, to a low register that has the effect of undercutting a seriousness previously aimed at (see **Unit 7, Language and context: register**).

12.4.3 Juxtaposition and destabilizing irony

A different, less controlled kind of irony is sometimes created when elements from recognizably different discourse styles or texts are juxtaposed with one another. Where juxtaposed elements are presented as part of a complex pattern of parallelisms (e.g. as described above in relation to imagist poetry, surrealist painting, and T.S. Eliot's influential Modernist poem, *The Waste Land*), the reader's task of inferring relations between juxtaposed elements becomes especially challenging. Juxtaposed images, quotations and styles encourage perceptions that overrun a single meaning for the text, possibly to such an extent that there no longer appears to be a single, authoritative voice or consciousness directing how one element or fragment stands in relation to others.

Such a destabilizing effect has already been intimated above in relation to the bricolage presented in Eliot's *The Waste Land*. In the course of the poem's approximately 430 lines, elements are juxtaposed at many different levels: different registers (literary quotation from earlier periods, a more contemporary lyrical style, interludes of conversational speech); different periods (often in apparent contrast between a high literary past and a damaged present, or 'waste land'); different social classes (figures in an Elizabethan Royal barge on the River Thames, someone remonstrating with someone else in a pub about her need for dentures in order to have a happy married life); and different degrees of cultural status (Classical and seventeenth-century verse, excerpts from contemporary popular songs). The counterpoint created between such elements develops over the course of the poem; and one possible way of interpreting this (outlined in **Unit 7, Language and context: register**) is that the poem holds its various ironies in place. Some of the juxtaposed elements are called into question in order to affirm others; and the poem closes with a religious incantation ('shantih') in which all contradiction is finally resolved.

It is not clear, however, whether irony created by juxtaposed elements can be contained in this way. Consider, for example, an apparently minor textual feature of *The Waste Land*: the footnotes Eliot provides for his own poem. From one perspective, such notes are a framing device. They provide authoritative commentary on the poem's meanings and significance, and direct the play of possible meanings that is otherwise invited by the juxtaposed material. A 'footnote' discourse appears well suited to this function, in being not just generically informative but in this case highly learned: quotations are presented from different languages; page references are given to scholarly works; and a central role for the classical figure Tiresias in the text is asserted. At the same time, in a poem consisting of many juxtaposed registers with no obviously mediating poetic voice, the notes must also be acknowledged as a further, juxtaposed style: *part of* the field of ironic interaction between all the various discourses of which the poem consists.

The juxtaposition of several footnotes with the lines to which they relate seems to lend support to a view that the notes are another, ironized voice in this way, rather than a framing voice that carries the poem's 'truth'. The note for line 46, for example (a line that introduces a character called Madame Sosostris, a 'famous clairvoyante' who uses a 'wicked pack of cards' in making her predictions), tells us that the poet does not know the details of the Tarot card pack, 'from which I have obviously departed to suit my own convenience' and that a particular card

'I associate, quite arbitrarily, with the Fisher King himself' (a central symbolic figure in an anthropological study by Jessie Weston to which Eliot refers at the beginning of the notes).

Acknowledging arbitrariness and lack of information in a note that is to locate the meaning of a passage in the poem is unusual. But this could be explained in other ways than as destabilizing irony. This seems less the case, however, with the note to line 68 (a line that tells how the bell of the London church Saint Mary Woolnoth chimes the hours 'With a dead sound on the final stroke of nine'). The complete note informs us only that this is, 'A phenomenon which I have often noticed'. The redundancy of this observation – especially juxtaposed with a passage in the poem that shifts without comment in a few lines between the living dead of an 'unreal city', detailed directions in London, and the classical naval battle of Mylae between Rome and Carthage – suggests slightly more strongly that the footnotes may be functioning as one more ironized discourse (exaggerated for effect) among various other kinds of discourse that make up the poem's polyphony of voices and points of view.

A similar effect is created by the note associated with line 199. This line presents a snippet from a song about a Mrs Porter and her daughter, who 'wash their feet in soda water'. The note adds only that the poet does not know the origin of this ballad, along with the presumably intentionally unhelpful detail that, 'it was reported to me from Sydney, Australia'. And similarly again with line 309, a quotation from St Augustine. The note supplies a reference to St Augustine's *Confessions*, then adds – in a manner as likely to unsettle as to reassure a reader committed to making sense of the poem – that bringing together ascetic religious figures from east and west at this stage of the poem 'is not an accident'.

Are small details of this kind sufficient to suggest that the resulting irony is destabilizing? For a poet to add his or her own footnotes to a poem at the time of publication is certainly unusual, and therefore distinctive. The poem itself is also unusual – and was especially distinctive in 1922 – in consisting largely of juxtaposed materials without an obvious narrative or lyrical voice (partly the result of editorial cuts that had been made by Eliot's friend Ezra Pound). The redundancy of information provided in some of the footnotes – especially in contrast with the obvious interpretive challenge presented by the poem with which they are juxtaposed – implies less an information-bearing function than possible inclusion of the notes as an additional kind of discourse that makes claims on cultural authority and value alongside others also presented in the poem. We may choose to view such notes as anchoring the poem's polyphony; in such an interpretation, the irony created between juxtaposed note and the lines of the poem to which it relates is closed – the note supplies information and frames poetic meaning. Alternatively, we may see the notes as extending the ironic interaction that takes place between all the other discourses in the poem. Whether such ironic play is destabilizing would then depend on how far we infer a presiding poetic voice or point of view that can offer a focus for meaning and a limit on ironic effect.

ACTIVITY 12

Cut-up poems are created by juxtaposing elements drawn from two or more pre-existing texts, in order to create effects of tension or incongruity. Below are two extracts from the beginning and end of Adrian Henri's 'On the Late Late Massachers Stillbirths and Deformed Children a Smoother Lovelier Skin Job'. This poem is presented as a 'Cut-up of John Milton Sonnet XVIII On the late Massacher in Piedmont/TV Times/CND leaflet' (*TV Times* is a UK television programme-listings magazine; and 'CND' stands for 'Campaign for Nuclear Disarmament').

> The seven-day beauty plan:
> Avenge O Lord thy slaughter'd saints, whose bones
> Will cause up to 1 million deaths from leukaemia
> Forget not, in thy book record their groans
> Now for the vitally important step. Cream your face and
>   neck a second time
> No American president world-famous for beauty
>   creams
> responsible for the freedom and safety of so many
>   young offenders
> TODAY'S MEN OF ACTION
> The Triple Tyrant Macmillan Kennedy Watkinson
> The West governments are satisfied as to the moral
>   necessity to resume
> Racing from Newmarket
> . . .
> This baby's eyes and nose had merged into
> one misshapen feature in the middle of its
> forehead, lost 6″ from Hips
> sufferers can now wear fashion stockings
> Early may fly the Babylonian woe
> followed by
> TOMORROW'S WEATHER
> The Epilogue
> close down.

1 By examining features of language and style, identify the source of each phrase or line (i.e. whether it is from Milton's sonnet, or from the *TV Times*, or from the CND leaflet).

2 Pick out three cases of significant juxtaposition and describe the effect that each creates.

continued

3   What is the overall effect created by the use of juxtaposition in this poem?

4   Now construct a cut-up poem of your own. Do this by (a) selecting two short texts (one of which should be a poem); (b) cutting the two texts up into fragments; and (c) weaving the fragments together in such a way that the juxtaposition of different material creates effects of irony, humour, surprise, or enigma, or other effects that you feel are similar to those created in the Henri poem. For the best results, do not use two texts of the same type (two poems, two adverts, etc.). The reason for requiring a poem as one of your source texts is that this will help you to establish a poetic form for your cut-up poem; the other text needs to be significantly different in order to create possible tension and incongruity. Use the same wording as the original texts. But you need not use the whole of each text or to follow the original order.

5   When you have finished your cut-up poem, consider the following questions:

   5.1   What guided your choice of the two texts?

   5.2   How did you decide where to divide your texts up into fragments?

   5.3   What principles guided your attempt to reconstitute them as a cut-up poem (e.g. Why did you use the particular sections you included? Why did you not use other parts? Why did you juxtapose the material in the way you did?).

   5.4   What kind of new, overall effect do you think has been created by the juxtaposition of your two texts?

Reading

Burgin, V. (1976) 'Art, Common Sense and Photography', in S. Hall and J. Evans (eds) (1999) *Visual Culture: The Reader*, London: Sage/Open University, pp. 41–50.

Eisenstein, S. (1979a) 'The Cinematographic Principle and the Ideogram', in G. Mast and Cohen, M. (eds) *Film Theory and Criticism*, Oxford: Oxford University Press, pp. 85–100.

Eisenstein, S. (1979b) 'A Dialectic Approach to Film Form', in G. Mast and M. Cohen (eds) *Film Theory and Criticism*, Oxford: Oxford University Press, pp. 101–22.

Shklovsky, V. (1917) 'Art as Technique', in D. Lodge (ed.) (1999) *Modern Criticism and Theory: A Reader*, 2nd edn, London: Longman, pp. 16–30.

Allusion and Intertextuality

UNIT 13

This unit:

- describes how an allusion can be made in one text either to a cultural referent or to another text, and offers practical guidance on how to discover and account for such references;

- introduces the concept of 'intertextuality', which denotes the many different ways that texts interact with other texts, showing them not to be isolated, autonomous objects but woven into a fabric of existing kinds of discourse, including literary discourse;

- shows how allusions and intertextuality create resonances that signal sometimes important relationships between a text and other works or more general literary or discourse styles;

- explores the relationship between intertextuality and ideas of originality, both on the part of an author creating a work and on the part of a reader interpreting one.

An 'allusion' occurs when one text makes an implicit or explicit reference to another text. In an explicit verbal **allusion**, an actual quotation is made and signalled with quotation marks. In an implicit verbal allusion, no signal is given and the original wording is sometimes changed to suit the new context.

13.1   Allusion, tradition and value

The opening of Wordsworth's *The Prelude* (1805) alludes to the end of Milton's *Paradise Lost* (1667), without actually quoting from it:

> The earth is all before me: with a heart
> Joyous, nor scared at its own liberty,
> I look about, and should the guide I choose
> Be nothing better than a wandering cloud,
> I cannot miss my way.
>
> (*The Prelude*, I, 15–19)

> The World was all before them, where to choose
> Their place of rest, and Providence their guide:
> They hand in hand with wand'ring steps and slow,
> Through Eden took their solitary way.
>
> (*Paradise Lost*, XII, 646–9)

An allusion of this kind serves as a means of establishing a relation to a cultural or literary tradition. The allusion places a text (in this Wordsworth's poem) within a textual network of other works that make up a cultural tradition. Because an allusion can have this effect, it can be used simply as a way of adding a kind of cultural value to a text.

13.1.1   Allusions in advertising

Use of allusions in this way is a common device in advertisements, not only in literary works. For example, a fairly representative single issue of the *Observer* magazine selected for analysis (8 May 1988) contained four advertisements that used allusions in their captions. The advertisements included one for a Renault car advertised with the caption 'A room of my own'; and a brand of chocolate (produced at that time by the company Cadbury in an area of Birmingham called Bournville) advertised with the caption 'If Chocolate be the food of Gods, Heaven must be in Birmingham'.

One of the reasons for making such allusions, whether in adverts or in literary works and other kinds of text, is that they can invoke cultural connotations associated with the source text. By a process of transference, the connotations are (as with **juxtaposition** and **metaphor**) transferred onto the product being promoted. In the Renault car advert referred to above, women are encouraged to buy a Renault car with the suggestion that it will grant them some of the independence that Virginia Woolf was seeking for women in her novel *A Room of One's Own* (1929). Such allusions can also flatter readers, by offering those who recognize the allusion a sense of being superior to those who do not. The Cadbury's chocolate advert seems to imply, at some level of seriousness, that it is only 'highly cultured' people – those with sufficient 'good taste' to recognize an allusion to Shakespeare (the first line of *Twelfth Night*) – who will fully appreciate Bournville chocolate.

Allusive techniques and their effects are very common. In fact, they have become so common that they can appear dated as a marketing style (note that the examples above were taken from a 1988 issue of a magazine). Advertisements sampled in the *Observer* magazine fifteen years after those examined above (on 20 February 2005) were contrastingly light on allusions. There was only one: 'South American *Odyssey*' (advertising a holiday in South America), and even in this example it was perhaps not necessary for readers to realize that 'Odyssey' is a reference to one of Homer's epics, since the word 'odyssey' has been absorbed into English as meaning a long, eventful journey (sixteen nights, in this case!). The downward trend in frequency of openly allusive Sunday broadsheet newspaper adverts of this kind appears to have continued. In an analysis of the 30 January 2011 edition of the *Observer* magazine, no advertisement at all made use of an overt literary allusion. What is nevertheless striking in that issue, however, is that the article *titles* include 'The Alchemist' (an article about Goldie, but alluding to Ben Jonson's play), and 'A Womb of my Own' (an article about home birth, but alluding to Virginia Woolf's novel, as above). Allusions in titles were also common to non-literary sources: 'It's not easy being green' (ecological advice, alluding to a TV series); 'New model army' (an article about the car industry, alluding to the name of the parliamentary army in the English Civil War); and 'Wild at heart' (an article about alternative Valentine breaks alluding to a TV series about a vet and his family who emigrate to South Africa).

13.1.2   Allusions in titles

Allusions are now also very common in the titles of newspaper and magazine articles. An issue of *New Scientist* magazine for 20 March 1999 includes the following titles: 'Forever Young' (an article about the youthfulness of *New Scientist* readers); 'The Long Goodbye' (an article about the extinction of the North Atlantic right whale); 'Something Rotten . . .' (an article about bluebottles); 'For Your Ears Only' (an article about radio); 'Trouble in Paradise' (an article about ecological degradation in Caribbean islands); and 'Where No Chip Has Gone Before' (an article about the company Motorola). Each of the allusions here, made in each case to a widely recognized cultural reference, is likely to be easy to track down by means of an internet search. Allusions made in titles are typically to pop songs, films and television (all reaching back to the 1970s or before, and so possibly based on the life experience of a given readership), as well as to currently well-known literary works.

We might alternatively understand the apparent consistency in the range of such allusions as a product of authorship, rather than readership, arising from the identity of the magazine's production staff (perhaps one person with a particular kind of cultural knowledge wrote the titles). Such consistency is not only a reflection of what particular groups of people know, however. It has an extra effect: allusions position the reader by telling a reader who recognizes the allusions that this magazine is for him or her – that is, it is aimed at or addressed to a person of a certain age, background or interests who possesses a certain range of cultural knowledge (see **Unit 4, Recognizing genre**).

13.2 Types of allusion

Texts may allude to other texts in a variety of ways. The following ways are the most common:

(1)   Through a verbal reference to another text (as in the way *The Prelude* refers to *Paradise Lost* through a similarity of phrasing).

(2)   Through **epigraphs** (an inscription at the beginning of the text). T.S Eliot's poem 'The Hollow Men' (1925) has an epigraph taken from Joseph Conrad's *Heart of Darkness* (1899/1902): 'Mistah Kurtz – he dead'. This invites the reader to look for a significant relationship between the poem and the novel (possibly that both texts suggest there is hollowness at the heart of European 'man' in the early twentieth century).

(3)   Through names of characters. The name Stephen Dedalus, the central character in James Joyce's *A Portrait of the Artist as a Young Man* (1914), refers to Daedalus, 'a character in Greek mythology who made wings with which he flew from Crete across the archipelago . . . his name is perpetuated in our daedal, skillful, fertile of invention' (*Brewer's Dictionary of Phrase and Fable*).

(4)   Through choice of titles. The title of William Faulkner's novel *The Sound and the Fury* (1929) is an explicit allusion to Macbeth's despairing claim that life is nothing but 'a tale / Told by an idiot, full of sound and fury, / Signifying nothing' (*Macbeth* (1606), V, v, 26–8).

13.2.1 Media allusions

The process involved in allusion is not confined to literature and advertisements. It can also be found in most other cultural and artistic forms. Music may allude to earlier music (e.g. Stravinsky's allusions to Bach, or The Beatles' allusions to the French national anthem and 'Greensleeves' in 'All You Need is Love'). Woody Allen's films have frequently made allusions to literature and other films: *Play It*

Again Sam (1972) makes a series of allusions to *Casablanca* (1942). Francis Ford Coppola's *Apocalypse Now* (1979) presents a complex network of allusions to Conrad and Eliot: it is overall a kind of rewriting of *Heart of Darkness*, but towards the end the Kurtz character (played by Marlon Brando) reads Eliot's poem 'The Hollow Men', reversing the relationship between *Heart of Darkness* and 'The Hollow Men' noted earlier.

13.2.2 Allusion and the relationship between texts

Reading a literary or other cultural text involves seeing possible significance in how it interacts with earlier texts. By choosing the title *The Sound and the Fury*, Faulkner seems to invite readers to compare the events and themes of his novel with Macbeth's nihilistic despair. In *A Portrait of the Artist*, the name Stephen Dedalus invites the reader to look out for parallels between the novel and the story of Daedalus. Is there some connection with the notion of flight? Or is the link to do with Stephen's aspiration to be an artist (skilful, fertile of invention), or to do with his failure (since Icarus, the son of Daedalus, dies when the wings his father made melt when he flies too near the sun), or alternatively to do with the father–son relationship (a death of the son because the father's ingenuity fails)? A reading that approaches the novel with this range of questions in mind is likely to find some relevance for each.

13.3 How to read allusions

Thomas Hardy's novels seem to some readers to be overloaded with allusions. But some of those allusions are charged with such significance that arguably an adequate reading cannot afford to pass them by.

In *Tess of the D'Urbervilles* (1891), for example, Alec d'Urberville, Tess's eventual seducer, makes an allusion that, if she had spotted it, might have allowed Tess to avoid her tragedy. Early on in the novel, Tess's impoverished parents send her to work for a rich family to whom they mistakenly think they are related. Tess's new employer, Mrs d'Urberville, who knows nothing of the supposed kinship, sets her to work looking after her poultry and bullfinches. One of the responsibilities involved in looking after the bullfinches is to whistle to them in order to 'teach 'em airs'. Alec, Tess's so-called cousin, spies her vainly attempting to practise whistling and takes this as an opportunity to flirt with her:

> 'Ah! I understand why you are trying – those bullies! My mother wants you to carry on their musical education. How selfish of her! As if attending to these curst cocks and hens were not enough work for any girl. I would flatly refuse if I were you.'
>
> 'But she wants me particularly to do it, and to be ready by tomorrow morning.'

'Does she? Well then – I'll give you a lesson or two.'

'Oh no, you won't!' said Tess, withdrawing towards the door.

'Nonsense; I don't want to touch you. See – I'll stand on this side of the wire-netting, and you can keep on the other; so you may feel quite safe. Now, look here; you screw up your lips too harshly. There 'tis – so.'

He suited the action to the word, and whistled a line of 'Take, O take those lips away'. But the allusion was lost upon Tess.

The editor of the Macmillan edition of Hardy's novel provides an endnote, explaining that Alec is alluding to the first line of the Page's song in Shakespeare's *Measure for Measure* (1604), Act IV, scene 1. This information in itself, however, is not enough to show the import of the allusion. Without an understanding of the significance of the song in *Measure for Measure*, the allusion remains lost – on the reader as well as on Tess. It is only if we compare the situation in the novel with the situation in the text being alluded to that the significance of the allusion becomes apparent. We might assume initially, for example, that the reference is primarily a way of contrasting Alec's worldliness with Tess's simplicity and 'uncultured' life. However, the fact that the narrator directly calls the whistling an 'allusion' may suggest that the song's meaning has a more direct bearing on the situation. Later in the novel (when Tess has been seduced by Alec and abandoned by Angel Clare), we may recognize that, in the song's original dramatic context, the Boy sings these lines to Mariana after she has become a seduced and abandoned victim. It might accordingly be argued that, in the fictional world Hardy has created, the fact that the allusion is lost upon Tess proves fatal for her. Fuller understanding of the allusion on the part of the reader, by contrast, adds to a sense of the text's tragic irony (once we know how the novel ends – see also **Unit 11, Irony**).

It is possible to identify at least three separate stages in analysing the allusion in *Tess of the D'Urbervilles*:

(1) The reader must recognize that an allusion has been made. In Hardy's novel, this is made easy because we are told that 'the allusion was lost upon Tess'. But not all allusions are so explicit. To some extent the ability to spot an implicit allusion depends on a reader having read the text being alluded to (the reader may have the feeling of having read something vaguely similar). However, spotting an allusion is not so dependent on the chance of having read and remembered something as this suggests. It is often possible to detect the presence of an allusion because it stands out in some way from the text that surrounds it – perhaps through some difference of style or register. Ernest Hemingway, for example, quotes the seventeenth-century poet John Donne in the title of his novel *For Whom the Bell Tolls* (1940). But we do not need to know this fact in order to recognize that the title uses a more archaic and 'literary' phrasing than Hemingway usually employs (see **Unit 7, Language and context: register**).

(2) The next task is to trace the allusion. In the example from *Tess of the D'Urbervilles* the editor does this for us. But in most cases we will have to do our own detective work. The most obvious way to trace the allusion is to use the internet. For example, a Google search on the words 'Take, O take those lips away' takes us almost instantly to many websites that quote the whole lyric and give the information needed. We can then follow up that information in a variety of sources (see **Unit 2, Using information sources**) as far as we find it relevant and helpful to do so. Before the internet, the process of hunting for an allusion was far more laborious, and involved trips to the reference section of a library to consult concordances or dictionaries of quotations in book form. If this failed, it was often a matter of educated guesswork (or, picking up the point made above about readers recognizing their own cultural background or even presumed superiority in an allusion, of having had a sufficiently literary education).

(3) The third step involves close reading of the section of the source text in which the word or phrase originally appears, together with some investigation of its significance for the text as a whole. At this stage, the challenge lies in working out similarities and differences between the source text and the text being read. Such similarities and contrasts (kinds of parallelism, see **Unit 18, Parallelism**) should help to establish why the allusion is being made and what kind of relation exists between the texts. Only by further consideration of the source text (as the example from *Tess of the D'Urbervilles* shows) can we be aware of the possible implications of an allusion.

13.4 Intertextuality

The term **intertextuality** describes how texts interact with other texts. In particular, it stresses the idea that texts are not unique, isolated objects but are made out of numerous other texts, some known to the new text producer and some not directly known. Allusion is a form of intertextuality that works mostly through verbal echoes between texts. However, texts may also interact with one another through other kinds of formal and thematic echo, as well as by recycling the voices and registers of other literary texts and the general culture in which they exist.

13.4.1 Intertextuality through genre

The very idea of genre – that texts can be divided into different groups according to shared characteristics – necessarily involves a degree of interconnection between texts (see **Unit 4, Recognizing genre**). No text is an island. Any poem, for example, will draw on certain poetic conventions that will distinguish it from prose (even if only to undercut or resist those conventions). Such 'family relationships' are even stronger in the various sub-genres, such as the sonnet.

The sonnet, as we saw in **Unit 4,** was developed in medieval Italy and introduced into English poetry in the sixteenth century. Its first practitioners in English generally followed the formal and thematic conventions established by Italian poets such as Dante (1265–1321) and Petrarch (1304–1374). Thus most sonnets have fourteen lines of **iambic pentameter** (close to Petrarch's *endecasillabo* metre), arranged into an elaborate rhyme scheme and – at least in the Renaissance period – tended to have a male speaker who talks about or addresses an unavailable woman to whom he professes eternal love. Following the example of Petrarch, English Renaissance poets such as Spenser, Sidney and Shakespeare tended to arrange their love sonnets into sequences that chart the changing fortunes and feelings of the male sonneteer in his quest for his beloved. Although the thematic range of the sonnet has been greatly extended since then, the form continues to be associated with the unrequited passion of a male speaker for an unavailable woman.

A number of women poets in the twentieth century, however, such as Edna St Vincent Millay, wrote sonnets and sonnet sequences that engage with, challenge and sometimes reverse the historical conventions associated with sonnets. A recent example of this practice of simultaneously drawing on and changing an earlier literary convention associated with a particular form is the sonnet sequence 'Fifty Sonnets', in Eleanor Brown's *Maiden Speech* (1996). This sonnet sequence charts the changing fortunes of the woman speaker's love for a man.

Sonnet III of Brown's sequence directly announces its intertextual relationship to Dante's sonnets:

> When Dante first saw Beatrice, she wore
> a red dress – probably not much like mine.
> Allowing, though, for accident (design,
> and taste, and length, and Lycra), what he saw
> was more or less what you saw on the night
> when I decided you were mine. My dress
> was red in its intent and – more or less –
> red in its consequence. And I was right
> to wear it, and play 'queen' with those poor boys
> who didn't know quite what was going on,
> and deferentially provided noise
> of admiration and desire. These gone,
> certain of these, and certain of your bed,
> we left; and the rest is taken as read.

The direct allusion to Dante highlights differences and well as similarities between Brown's sonnets and Dante's. In *Vita Nuova* (1292–94), an Italian book made up of twenty-six sonnets, six other poems and some prose commentary, Dante reveals his long devotion to Beatrice, who he first saw when they were both nine years old, who remains virtually unknown to him, and who he never has a relationship with. In section II, Dante recalls that when he first saw Beatrice she wore a decorous red dress considered suitable for her age. In section III he tells us that he next saw her nine years later, dressed in white; afterwards, however, he entered into a reverie in his room in which love appeared to him as a lordly man carrying Beatrice in his arms, naked except for a crimson cloth loosely wrapped around her. Despite this erotic vision, Dante increasingly sees Beatrice as a chaste saint in the text, especially after she dies. Indeed, it is precisely his lack of a relationship with her that stimulates Dante's poetry.

Brown's speaker, by contrast, is a woman who addresses the man she has succeeded in seducing and reveals her seduction strategy, including wearing a sexy red dress. The speech situation and sexual politics in Dante's sonnets are in this way radically transformed in Brown's (interestingly highlighting social differences between medieval Italy and late twentieth-century Britain). Part of the impact of Brown's sonnet arises from the fact that the woman speaker rejects the role conventionally ascribed to women in such situations. But the sonnet's full effect can only be registered by a reader who realizes that the poet uses the sonnet form in order to transgress thematic conventions historically associated with sonnets. Part of the poem's dynamic meaning therefore derives from the intertextual relationship it sets up between itself and the sonnet tradition.

13.4.2 Intertextuality through parody

Intertextuality can also result in other effects that rely on relations with other genres, including parody, satire and mock forms. For example, Alexander Pope's satirical poem *The Rape of the Lock* (1712/14) depends on the reader's familiarity with the conventions of the epic genre that it mocks. The poem opens:

> What dire offense from amorous causes springs,
> What mighty contests rise from trivial things,
> I sing – This verse to Caryll, Muse! is due.

These lines echo the ritualistic opening gesture of the epic mode, an example of which we saw in the opening lines of *Paradise Lost* (discussed from another perspective in **Unit 2, Using information sources**).

> Of man's first disobedience, and the fruit
> Of that forbidden tree, whose mortal taste
> Brought death into the world, and all our woe,
> With loss of Eden, till one greater man
> Restore us, and regain the blissful seat,
> Sing heavenly Muse . . .

Whereas *Paradise Lost* uses epic conventions to deal with a suitably epic theme, however (the expulsion of humankind from paradise that results from the battle between God and Satan), *The Rape of the Lock* uses epic conventions in order to treat a 'trivial' event in high society (a man snips a lock of hair from a woman's head) *as if* it were an epic matter.

In such examples, we see that part of the significance of a literary text is not inherent (lying within itself); there is also significance in how it relates to other texts. Examples of this kind also show that the intertextual dimensions of cultural texts achieve their effects and meaning only through the active knowledge that a reader brings to them. Pope's poem has a much-reduced impact on readers unfamiliar with the epic tradition it parodies, since the intertextual relation is largely or wholly lost.

13.4.3   The changing role of intertextuality

Between the Middle Ages and the end of the eighteenth century, education in Britain was limited to a privileged minority and was largely based on the study of the literature of ancient Greece and Rome (the 'classics'). Authors assumed that their readers would recognize allusions to the 'authorities' (the classics, Aristotle, the Bible), and tradition was valued at least as much as innovation. For example, in the 'neoclassical' period (roughly 1660–1785), authors showed their respect for classical writers by writing thematic and formal imitations of their works. Examples include Andrew Marvell's 'An Horatian Ode' (1681) and Alexander Pope's 'Imitations of Horace' (1733–9).

In the Romantic period, by contrast (roughly 1790–1830), with its emphasis on 'originality' at a time when literacy and education in the vernacular (i.e. English rather than the classical languages) was rapidly increasing, the importance of the 'classics' as authorities began to diminish. The relation of authors to past texts became less one of reverential imitation and more an attempt to break with the past. Wordsworth's allusions to *Paradise Lost*, for example, both acknowledge Milton's importance and register his attempt to go beyond him (remember, in the allusion discussed above, that Wordsworth's poem begins where Milton's poem ends).

13.4.4   Intertextuality and originality

Allusion and intertextuality raise a wider question about originality: how far do literary texts originate in an author's mind, and how far are they composed out of other literature? In modernist literature (roughly 1910–40), allusion became a major principle of composition. If T.S. Eliot's *The Waste Land* (1922) is read alongside the notes that Eliot himself added to the poem, we form an impression of the poem as a collage of quotations from and allusions to other texts (though see also **Unit 12, Juxtaposition**). In what is often called the postmodern period (roughly 1960 to the present), writers such as Angela Carter (e.g. *The Magic Toy Shop* (1967)) and Umberto Eco (e.g. *The Name of the Rose* (1980)) appear to have set aside attempts to be original in the narrow sense, in order to participate in an intertextual free-for-all in which allusiveness and/or intertextuality is celebrated for its own sake.

13.4.5 Post-structuralist accounts of intertextuality

Literary criticism is often concerned with the texts that influenced a particular writer, and influence is usually established by tracing allusions. If an editor spots an allusion, he or she will typically say something like 'Keats is thinking of Shakespeare's *Venus and Adonis* here'. But this assumption begs a number of questions: how do we know that? What if the allusion were unconscious? Or accidental? Or created by the editor's own associations? If texts inevitably interact, then reading, as well as writing, may be necessarily an intertextual process.

For post-structuralist literary theorists such as Julia Kristeva and Roland Barthes, all language use was considered to be inevitably intertextual, in at least two main senses. First, individuals do not originate or invent language: we are born into a language or languages that precede us. Second, without pre-existing forms, themes, conventions and codes there could be no such thing as literature. For Barthes (1968), accordingly, 'a text is . . . a multi-dimensional space in which a variety of writings, none of them original, blend and clash. The text is a tissue of quotations drawn from the innumerable centers of culture.' In making this claim, Barthes sought to transform the idea of literary or cultural tradition, from being a selected body of earlier work available as a stable resource behind the text into a potentially infinite network of links and echoes between texts of all kinds. Such a notion of intertextuality is massively expanded from earlier understandings of the function and significance of allusion.

13.4.6 Intertextuality in children's literature

Our initiation into intertextuality, if we continue Barthes's line of argument, begins when we first encounter stories as children. The formulaic opening 'Once upon a time' signals to the young reader or listener that this is the beginning of a story, in that he or she has encountered the same formula before (from another point of view, we might say that such a story opening is part of a genre, see **Unit 4, Recognizing genre**). The formulaic story opening signifies because it is intertextual. Many children's books are intertextual in this way: they draw on and revise kinds of plot, character and setting that children become familiar with by listening to and reading other texts. Such partial overlap or repetition need not inhibit perceived originality, and is pervasive in some of the most successful and innovative children's books. J.K. Rowling's *Harry Potter* series (1997–2007), for example, mixes conventions associated with two long-standing children's genres: fantasy (with wizards and witches, and so on) and boarding school stories (which go back to *Tom Brown's Schooldays* (1857) and include classic children's series such as Enid Blyton's *Malory Towers* (1946–51)). Children do not have to be conscious of the intertextual relations in order to appreciate and enjoy the *Harry Potter* series, though subliminal recognition of them may contribute to their pleasure.

A more complex example is Philip Pullman's *His Dark Materials* series (1995–2000). This series of novels draws on Blake's poetry in order to re-read and critique works including the Book of Genesis in the Bible, Milton's *Paradise Lost*, and C.S. Lewis's *The Chronicles of Narnia* (1950–6), as well as presentations of institutionalized Christianity in general. Many of Pullman's young readers will not have read *The Chronicles of Narnia*, of course; and perhaps most will not have read Genesis, Milton and Blake, or be aware of the theological issues with which *His Dark Materials* engages. Nonetheless, *His Dark Materials* has been hugely successful with young readers, partly because it can be understood and enjoyed at the level of character and plot alone. In this case, allusion and intertextual context seem to lead to two levels of reading, with adult or more widely read readers being able to respond to Pullman's trilogy in a different way from readers who do not realize the work's intertextual significance.

Here is a sonnet by Edna St Vincent Millay:

> We talk of taxes, and I call you friend;
> Well, such you are, – but well enough we know
> How thick about us root, how rankly grow
> Those subtle weeds no man has need to tend,
> That flourish through neglect, and soon must send
> Perfume too sweet upon us and over throw
> Our steady senses; how such matters go
> We are aware, and how such matters end.
> Yet shall be told no meagre passion here;
> With lovers such as we forevermore
> Isolde drinks the draught, and Guinevere
> Receives the Table's ruin through her door,
> Francesca, with the loud surf at her ear,
> Lets fall the colored book upon the floor.

As with many sonnets, this sonnet is divided into an octave (first eight lines) and a sestet (last six lines); the division or *volta* (turn) is marked by the rhyme scheme and by the word 'Yet' at the beginning of the ninth line.

ACTIVITY 13

continued

1 Read the first eight lines carefully and identify: (a) the speech situation (who is speaking to whom); (b) what the speaker is saying to the person spoken to (the addressee); and (c) how the use of metaphor indicates a particular attitude towards, or representation of, what the speaker is talking about.

2 Read the last six lines carefully and underline or highlight all potential allusions.

   2.1 Using the internet and/or appropriate reference books, search on the key words of each potential allusion in order to confirm whether or not it is an allusion.

   2.2 For each allusion you discover: (a) take notes about what the internet source or reference book says about the source of that allusion; (b) where possible, read the original text or texts Millay's poem is alluding to; and (c) identify relevant similarities between the source text and Millay's poem.

3. Now consider the overall function or effect of the allusions in the sestet of Millay's sonnet:

   3.1 How would you describe the relationship between the sestet and the octave in Millay's sonnet?

   3.2 How does Millay's sonnet relate to general conventions of the sonnet genre?

   3.3 How does Millay's sonnet relate to general conventions of love poetry?

Reading

Allen, G. (2011) *Intertextuality: The New Critical Idiom*, 2nd edn, London: Routledge.

Barthes, R. (1968) 'The Death of the Author' and (1971) 'From Work to Text', in V.B. Leitch (ed.) (2010) *The Norton Anthology of Theory and Criticism*, 2nd edn, New York and London: Norton.

Bate, J. (1999) *The Burden of the Past and the English Poet*, London: Chatto & Windus.

Bloom, H. (1997) *The Anxiety of Influence*, 2nd edn, Oxford: Oxford University Press.

Eliot, T.S. (1919) 'Tradition and the Individual Talent', in V.B. Leitch (ed.) (2010) *The Norton Anthology of Theory and Criticism*, 2nd edn, New York and London: Norton.

Furniss, T. and Bath, M. (2007) *Reading Poetry: An Introduction*, 2nd edn, London: Longman, Chapter 13.

Gilbert, S. and Gubar, S. (2000) *The Madwoman in the Attic*, 2nd edn, New Haven, CT: Yale University Press.

Hutchinson, P. (1983) *Games Authors Play*, London: Methuen.

Orr, M. (2003) *Intertextuality: Debates and Contexts*, Cambridge: Polity Press.

Renza, L. (1995) 'Influence', in F. Lentricchia and T. McLaughlin (eds) *Critical Terms for Literary Study*, Chicago: Chicago University Press, pp. 186–202.

UNIT 14

Authorship and intention

UNIT 14

This unit:

- provides a brief history of ideas about 'the author' in literature;

- discusses the role of authorial intention in interpretation, as well as the relation between intention and two other determinants of meaning: the forms or codes used in the text itself; and readers' attributions of meaning by means of inference;

- distinguishes several important functions often confused with the general role of an author: persona, narrator and implied author;

- shows how new kinds of meaning and significance are created by manipulation in some texts of differences and gaps between these various, apparently 'authorial' roles.

A text, it seems obvious to say, is created by an author (or by a group of authors). It also seems obvious to assume that an author (or group of authors) has a particular intention about what that text means, and how it should be interpreted. The concepts of author and intention appear indispensable notions in understanding origin and meaning for any given text. Indeed, it is our sense that a text (or art object) was designed by human agency that encourages us to believe that it will be worth spending time interpreting it. The goal of our interpretive efforts, we tend to assume, is to discover (or recover) the author's intention. Despite these common sense assumptions, however, the concepts of author and intention turn out to be less straightforward than they seem.

14.1 The author

Our assumptions about intention and authorship are shaped by views we hold about what an author does in creating a text. One view is that the author is a sort of skilful craft worker, who draws on and reworks the conventions of a cultural tradition but always remains less important than that tradition. This view is associated with literary practices and criticism in Europe broadly from the Middle Ages up to the eighteenth century. Eighteenth-century neoclassicism, for example, placed emphasis not so much on an author's originality as on how a text conforms to the conventions of the literature of classical Greece and Rome and how far it reiterated established assumptions. This outlook is summarized in Alexander Pope's definition of 'true wit' (good poetry) in 1711: 'True wit is Nature to advantage dress'd; / What oft was thought, but ne'er so well expressed' (*An Essay on Criticism*, II, 297–8).

Towards the end of the eighteenth century, however, the intellectual and artistic movement known as Romanticism developed a significantly different view of the author and of creativity, which placed particular emphasis on originality, individual imagination and inner feelings. The Romantics viewed an author as someone who discovers original material for creative expression somewhere inside himself or herself, rather than in the tradition. In 'Preface' to *Lyrical Ballads* (1800 [1798]), Wordsworth defined poetry as 'the spontaneous overflow of powerful feelings'. The author becomes, in such a framework, the source of what might be called the text's authenticity: what makes it original, sincere and natural. This Romantic view of the author became influential throughout nineteenth-century Europe and beyond. It survives today as a popular 'common sense' assumption about artistic creativity.

The modernist aesthetic theory of early twentieth-century Europe and the United States largely rejected this Romantic view of authorship, however. In his influential essay 'Tradition and the Individual Talent' (1919), T.S. Eliot effectively resurrected and modified pre-Romantic views of the author in order to attack the Romantic focus on individual creativity. Eliot argues that the individual poet's mind is, and should be, subservient to the literary tradition. For Eliot, popular interest in a poet's individuality and personal emotions is misguided; he proposes instead that readers should focus on what he calls 'significant emotion, emotion that has its life in the poem and not in the history of the poet'. In effect, Eliot is calling for a shift in attention away from poets towards poetry, and suggesting that a poem's originality is derived not from the poet's inner life but from the way it both fits into and modifies a literary tradition. Eliot's thinking significantly influenced a whole generation of writers and scholars, especially the New Critics, who taught in British and American universities from the 1940s onwards.

In the 1970s, a number of critical groups in Europe and the United States began to examine what might be called the 'politics of authorship'. Their attention turned to how marginalized groups, such as female, black, working-class or gay writers, had to struggle in order to represent marginalized social and personal experiences. An area in which such work has been particularly influential is feminist literary history, which has drawn attention to many neglected women writers from earlier periods.

From the late 1960s onwards, post-structuralist theory – especially in the writings of Michel Foucault, Jacques Derrida and Roland Barthes – attempted to problematize or 'deconstruct' the notion of the author and authorial intention. In an essay provocatively called 'The Death of the Author' (1968), Barthes makes the following suggestions:

(1) The author is, by definition, absent from writing (in contrast with speech, which generally implies the presence of a speaker).

(2) A text is not a unique artefact, emerging through a kind of immaculate conception from a writer's brain. Rather, the conventions and language that make up a text are available to the writer precisely because they have been used before (see **Unit 13, Allusion and Intertextuality**). A text is 'a tissue of quotations', 'a multi-dimensional space in which a variety of writings, none of them original, blend and clash'.

(3) Primary focus on writers is an imposition of institutional control that limits interpretation and marginalizes readers: 'Classic criticism has never paid any attention to the reader; for it, the writer is the only person in literature'; 'to give a text an Author . . . is to impose a limit on that text'.

(4) A text's meaning is generated in the creative, playful processes of reading, not of writing. Barthes therefore seeks to transform reading into a practice in which the reader is liberated from the process of discovering, or pretending to discover, what the author intended.

(5) Encapsulating these arguments, Barthes concludes that 'the birth of the reader must be at the cost of the death of the Author'.

The notion of the author's 'death' is not, of course, to be taken literally. By announcing the **death of the author** Barthes was attempting to kill off a tendency in literary criticism and educational institutions to use the notion of an author, and his or her supposed intentions, to limit interpretive possibilities in reading. Yet reports of the death of the author seem to have been exaggerated. Many literary critics, students and general readers seem unable or unwilling to accept that reading can proceed without considering authorial intention. In recent years, there have been at least two book-length announcements of the 'return' or 'resurrection' of the author (see Burke, 2008, 2010 and Irwin, 2002). Critical debate about authorship looks set to continue as long as the category of 'the author' remains viable.

14.2   Intention

The concept of the author is closely bound up with the notion of intention. Critical appeals to a compound of these two notions – to authorial intention – are often made in order to authenticate the critic's particular interpretation. Such appeals perhaps highlight an anxiety that, if there were no way of accessing authorial intention, then there would be no limit to the kinds of meanings that might be found in a text, and so no way of judging whether we are misreading or over-interpreting. But is such an anxiety well founded? And if not, what factors other than authorial intention serve to guide or limit interpretation?

The history of literary criticism has typically approached the issue of textual meaning by focusing on three different aspects of the reading situation: authorial intention; the language, forms and codes of the text itself; and the attribution of meaning by readers (or viewers). Different theories of interpretation typically differ in the amount of priority they accord to one or more of these three elements. A consideration of each of these three orientations can open up different perspectives on the role of intention in shaping the meanings of a text.

14.2.1   Authorial intention

The assumption that literary works are products of conscious intention entails a particular way of reading, as encapsulated in another of Pope's couplets, again from his *Essay on Criticism*:

> In every work regard the writer's end
> Since none can compass more than they intend
>
> (*Essay on Criticism*, II, 255–6)

An alternative view, associated with Romanticism, is that authors are not always fully conscious of the meaning or implications of their own literary works, because those works were produced in moments of inspiration. William Blake, for example, claims that although Milton announces at the beginning of *Paradise Lost* that he intended to 'justify the ways of God to men', the poem itself reveals that

Milton was 'of the Devil's party without knowing it'. This Romantic notion of non-conscious intention still allows interpretation to be anchored in authorial intention, so long as intention is taken to include unconscious elements such as the mysterious working of the poetic imagination that are not always available for conscious reflection even by the author him- or herself.

In the early twentieth century, the view that creation emerges out of unconscious impulses was given fresh impetus by psychoanalysis. Sigmund Freud, C.G. Jung and others suggested that people are never fully conscious of their intentions, because the unconscious mind can have an effect on what we say – and don't say – without our being aware of it. For Freud and Jung – though in different ways – the unconscious mind plays a major part in artistic creativity; and artistic creations can be used to investigate the unconscious minds of their creators.

Some schools of criticism and theories of interpretation continue to treat intention as playing an important role in conferring validity on textual interpretations. But although some critics, teachers and readers habitually refer to an author's intention, it is always worth querying how they know what that author intended. Even if an author from an earlier period left a record of his or her intentions, we would still need to consider whether such statements are reliable or not (some authors leave false trails). And even if authorial statements about intention are reliable, there seems no need to accept them if the text undermines the author's recorded intention (as *Paradise Lost* did for the Romantic poets).

14.2.2 The conventional forms and codes of the text itself

A common argument against the notion that the author's intention is the ultimate arbiter of a text's interpretation comes from the fact that the language, codes and conventions that texts use are social rather than individual. The words of a language exist, and have conventional meanings, before any particular speaker or writer uses them. As a consequence, meanings should be discoverable within texts themselves, from the language, rather than only in authorial statements of intention. An influential formulation of this view is the New Critical argument made in W.K. Wimsatt and M.C. Beardsley's essay 'The Intentional Fallacy' (1946). Concentrating on poetry (though their arguments can be applied to other kinds of text), Wimsatt and Beardsley set out the following reasons for not going outside the text in search of authorial intention:

(1) In most cases it is not possible to discover what the poet intended.
(2) We are primarily interested in how a poem works, not what was intended.
(3) A poem is a public rather than a private thing because it exists in language – which is by definition social rather than personal; the author does not own the text once it has been made public, and therefore does not have permanent authority over its meaning.

(4) A poem's meaning can only be discovered from its language, 'through our habitual knowledge of the language, through grammars, dictionaries, and all the literature which is the source of dictionaries, in general, through all that makes a language and culture'.

(5) If the poet succeeded in doing [what he/she intended], then the poem itself shows what he/she was trying to do.

The last of these points summarized from Wimsatt and Beardsley confirms that they were not rejecting the notion of authorial intention in itself, but criticizing the practice of looking for intention outside the text itself, in diaries, anecdotes, biographies, and so on. For Wimsatt and Beardsley, a successful poem embodies what its author intended. If we need to look beyond the text to discover the author's intention, then the poem is a failure and not worth bothering with.

A further development of this notion that meaning does not originate in the intentions of individual minds, but in the shared conventions of language and culture, can be found in the structuralist literary approach that emerged in France during the 1960s. Extending Ferdinand de Saussure's claim (made in the early twentieth century) that individual speech acts are made possible by a pre-existing language system that is shared by all users of the language, structuralism argued that individual literary texts are made possible and meaningful by a pre-existing literary system that is made up of conventional techniques and devices (such as the conventions of genre, and other symbolic codes of the culture). Structuralist literary theory minimized the role of the author and authorial intention in order to focus on how particular literary texts relate to and help us understand the pre-existing literary system (see Culler, 2002).

14.2.2 The literary competence of the reader

At the beginning of this unit, the point was made that it is our sense of a text (or art object) as something designed by human agency that encourages us to believe that it will be worth spending time interpreting it. This point seems to survive the various critiques of authorship and intention that we have examined. Even if the author's conscious mind is reduced to juggling the promptings of the unconscious mind, on the one hand, and mixing and reworking available codes and conventions, on the other, successful authors do this with great skill and with conscious intentions about the effects and meanings that are likely to result. Readers assume that creative texts are produced by authors with some degree of competence in manipulating the available codes of language and literary conventions. But in order to interpret such texts, readers seem to require an equivalent literary competence. It is this literary competence that generates, but also constrains, interpreted meanings regardless of authorial intention. In fact, *Ways of Reading*, the textbook you are reading, is designed precisely to help you develop such literary competence.

14.3 Ways of reading 'authorship'

Although readers remain interested in authors and in authorial intentions, it seems advisable to be cautious when interpreting any given text in claiming that we have uncovered what the author intended. Some of the more obvious pitfalls with such claims can be avoided by distinguishing carefully between authors, on the one hand, and narrators and characters, on the other. Contemporary novelists often receive letters from enthusiastic readers who confuse the characters and narrators of their books with the authors themselves. The following ways of reading can help readers to avoid such mistakes.

14.3.1 Narrator, implied author and poetic speaker

The author of a literary text is not the same as the imaginary person who is supposed to 'speak' it. In novels, we differentiate between the author and a first-person or third-person narrator: the fictional person who narrates the novel. This distinction is clear in the case of the main narrator of Gloria Naylor's *Bailey's Café* (1992):

> I can't say I've had much education. Book education. Even though high school back in the twenties was really school; not what these youngsters are getting away with now ... I went to kindergarten on the muddy streets in Brooklyn; finished up grade school when I married Nadine; took my first diploma from the Pacific; and this café, well now, this café is earning me a PhD. You might say I'm majoring in Life.

The narrator here differs from the author in several ways. First, the narrator is male (Naylor is female); second, the narrator went to school in the 1920s (Naylor was born in 1950); and third, the narrator has not had much book education (but by the time *Bailey's Café* was published, Naylor had a BA in English from Brooklyn College, an MA in Afro-American Studies from Yale, had taught in various universities and had published four highly regarded novels).

In reading poetry, we need to distinguish between a poem's author and its poetic speaker, narrator or persona. Whereas the poet is the creator of the poem, the speaker is part of that creation: one of the poem's devices or techniques. This distinction is important even in first-person Romantic poems, despite emphasis in Romanticism on individual authorial expression. In the first stanza of Wordsworth's 'Lucy Gray' (1800), a poem that recounts the story of a young girl who drowned in a canal in a snowstorm, it may seem natural to assume that the speaker is Wordsworth himself:

> Oft had I heard of Lucy Gray:
> And, when I crossed the wild,
> I chanced to see at break of day
> The solitary child.

Scholars have shown, however, that this poem is not based on Wordsworth's own experience, but rather on Wordsworth's sister Dorothy's recollections of an incident that occurred during her childhood, when she was living in a different part of England from her brother. In other words, Wordsworth could not have seen Lucy Gray in real life. Although the poem implies that the speaker encounters Lucy's ghost, which haunts the moors where she died, it seems clear that this is an imagined encounter. To draw attention to this is not to suggest that the poem is based on a lie, but to say that the poem recounts an imaginary incident and that we need to see the 'I' of the poem not as Wordsworth himself but as a kind of imaginary Wordsworth – a persona.

14.3.2   Authorial irony and the implied author

One reason for distinguishing between author and narrator is that some narrative texts may present us with a narrator who is subject to authorial irony, or **situational irony**, by being shown to be at some level unreliable – perhaps in terms of his or her ability to understand events or in terms of his or her moral position (see **Unit 11, Irony**).

Huck, the narrator of Mark Twain's novel *Huckleberry Finn* (1884), for example, is presented from the outset as being unable fully to understand his own situation, including the fact that he himself is a fictional character:

> You don't know about me, without you have read a book by the name of *The Adventures of Tom Sawyer*, but that ain't no matter. That book was made by Mr Mark Twain, and he told the truth, mainly. There was things which he stretched, but mainly he told the truth.

Huckleberry Finn was published in 1884, but the novel is set 'forty to fifty years previously': before the American Civil War led to the emancipation of American slaves. Huck is presented as sharing a conventional view that slavery is natural, even though it conflicts with his personal friendship for an escaped slave called Jim. As the narrator of the novel, Huck articulates the resulting moral confusion, worrying for example about Jim's plan to emancipate his children from slavery. Ironically, Huck is shocked by hearing Jim

> coming right out flat-footed and saying he would steal his children – children that belonged to a man I didn't even know; a man that hadn't ever done me no harm.

Huck later recognizes that he would feel just as bad if he betrayed Jim to the authorities; so he abandons his attempt to resolve what for him is a moral dilemma. To suggest, however, that Huck's predicament is a moral dilemma for the novel itself, or for its real author, would be a misreading. Huck's interior monologue is both comic and tragic in its limited viewpoint, and in its aping of the flawed logic and morality that helped to sustain slavery. Since Huck cannot see the irony of his own reasoning, there seems to be a higher-level viewpoint in the novel that is not available to Huck himself. We might describe that viewpoint as a post-Civil War perspective that exposes the ironic contradictions and limitations of a pre-Civil War narrator whose love for an individual slave does not allow him to see the problem with slavery in general.

In order to capture the sense that there is another point of view hidden behind or above Huck's, which allows us to glimpse a 'true' moral position that differs from Huck's ironized position, we need to employ a concept such as the **implied author**. The implied author needs to be distinguished from the real author because the implied author is not the original producer of the text but rather a creation or *effect* of the text: an impression that it produces. The implied author can only ever be a critical fiction: a rationalization of the impression we have in reading a novel that we are being confided in by some specific human consciousness.

The distinction between an implied author and real author is sometimes difficult to sustain in practice. In *Huckleberry Finn*, it seems almost inevitable to say that the post-Civil War consciousness that is exposing the ironic dilemmas of the narrating character is none other than Mark Twain himself. Nonetheless, it needs to be stressed that this is not a claim about authorial intention: a close reading of *Huckleberry Finn* suggests that the text itself is working to ironize Huck's dilemma, even though there are no voices in the book from which that irony appears to originate. It is possible to say that the text ironizes its own narrator, but in saying this it is not essential to claim that this was Twain's intention.

14.3.3 Ways of reading authorial games

Literary texts can be seen as elaborate games that authors and readers play together. Authors continually revive old games and make up new ones; and readers have to identify those games and learn how to play them. In Gothic novels that flourished in the second half of eighteenth-century Britain, for example, authors would often pretend that the novels they had written were ancient manuscripts that they had found and edited. Most readers quickly learned that this game, presented in prefaces supposedly written by an 'editor', was part of the fiction, one more convention of the genre. Twenty-first century novelists continue to play versions of this game, especially in historical fiction. Margaret Elphinstone's *Voyageurs* (2003), for example, begins with an 'Editor's Preface', mischievously written by 'MNE', which claims that the narrative that follows is a transcription of a found manuscript written by an eighteenth-century Quaker in which he describes his voyage to North America in search of his sister. Yet, despite the fact that *Voyageurs* is subtitled '*A Novel*', many readers have assumed that Elphinstone really did find such a manuscript. Like their eighteenth-century counterparts, modern readers have to learn that such 'editors', and the manuscripts they supposedly discover, are part of the fiction and not to be taken literally.

14.3.4   Does the identity of the author matter?

Knowing information about an author can hinder rather than aid interpretation. Once readers discover that the Romantic poet Samuel Taylor Coleridge was addicted to opium, they sometimes see nothing in his poems other than the effects of that addiction. In other cases, making discoveries about an author's identity can have positive effects. Realizing that the nineteenth-century novelist George Eliot was a woman – Mary Ann Evans (1819–80) – may enhance or subtly change responses to her novels' moral analysis of nineteenth-century England. But tracking down an author's identity is not always helpful, either. A great deal of ink has been wasted over the question of whether Shakespeare really wrote the plays and poetry attributed to him, or whether 'Shakespeare' was a pseudonym for another, more educated or higher-class person from the period. In this case, it does not seem to have harmed the works that we know little about Shakespeare the man: the texts themselves do the talking.

The name of the author is nevertheless frequently an important factor in the experience of reading. Knowing that we are reading a text by 'Shakespeare' has an impact, whether positive or negative, on responses to that text. This is likely to be the case with all 'great' or canonical writers. The name of the author on the cover or title page of a book is part of that book, and influences how it is read. Different names, indicating different statuses, have different effects: whether the author is famous or relatively unknown; whether a reader has read other books by the same author; whether the author is male or female, from the past or the present, and so on. The name of the author, together with further biographical information on the cover, can signal his or her geographical or ethnic origins, and this may also affect how the text is read. Given that the name of an author can carry such a range of influential connotations, we need to consider how different the experience of reading anonymous texts can be, or texts that have been worked on by more than one author. There are some cases where knowing the identity of an author concealed behind a nom-de-plume may have a significant impact on reading a text.

One stark example of this phenomenon arises with the erotic novel *Story of O* (1954), by 'Pauline Réage'. This novel follows the experiences of a woman who subjects herself to the sexual whims of her 'master', so it seems important to know whether the text was written by a man or a woman: whether, that is, the name 'Pauline Réage' was a pseudonym for a male writer. A website about the novel suggests that this question is urgent for many readers:

> The *Story of O* has surrounded itself with secrecy, mystery and conjecture for fifty years. When it was published in Paris in 1954 it provoked all sorts of scandal and for forty years the true identity of its author 'Pauline Reage' (actually Dominique Aury) was kept secret by a handful of friends close to the writer. Speculation concerning the author's identity produced many candidates, among them André Malraux, Henry de Montherlant, Andre Pieyre de Mandiargues, Raymond Queneau, and Jean Paulhan for whom, it

183

turns out, the book was actually written. The fact that it was written by a woman gives the novel, it has been said, a special 'diabolical' aura.

(www.storyofo.info/wasOtrue.html)

It is revealing that readers assumed that the real author of the novel must have been a man, and that the revelation that it was actually a woman made the story seem more 'diabolical'. That same revelation might have made the novel seem less 'diabolical', in allowing readers to view the book as a woman's exploration of aspects of female sexuality rather than a man's fantasy about exploitation of women.

ACTIVITY 14

The following song was written anonymously in France during the thirteenth century. It is a motet: a musical composition for two, three or four voices, with each voice singing different words. The text – whose author remains unknown – was translated from Old French by Carol Cosman.

> I am a young girl
> graceful and gay,
> not yet fifteen when
> my sweet breasts may
> begin to swell;
>
> Love should be my contemplation,
> I should learn its indication,
>
> But I am put in prison.
> God's curse be on my jailor!
>
> Evil, villainy and sin
> did he
> to give up a girl like me
> to a nunnery;
>
> A wicked deed, by my faith,
> the convent life will be my death
>   My God! for I am far too young.
>
> Beneath my sash I feel the sweet pain.
> God's curse on him who made me a nun.

The activity focuses on the question of who the 'author' of this text might have been. You may find evidence about the writer's possible identity in features of the text, in the description given at the beginning of the activity and/or in what you know or can guess about the historical circumstances of thirteenth-century France and about people of the time (and the sorts of opportunities open to them).

---

continued

1 Give any evidence you can find (or can construct for yourself) for thinking that the speaker of the text is also the author.

2 Give any evidence you can find (or can construct for yourself) for thinking that the speaker of the text is *not* the author.

3 Are there aspects of your response to the poem that are affected by the fact that it is (a) anonymous, (b) written for more than one voice, (c) written in the thirteenth century and (d) a translation by a named translator?

4 Now temporarily assume that the author is not the speaker. Present any evidence you can find (or construct) in support of the idea that the author was (a) a woman, or (b) a man.

5 Below are simplified descriptions of two hypothetical authors. For each, describe how believing that this was the identity of the author would change how you read the poem (and the effects the poem has on you):

(a) imagined author X = a 25-year-old male

(b) imagined author Y = a 15-year-old female

Try to distinguish between kinds of effect you think may have been intended or anticipated by the author of the text, and kinds of response you are making that could not have been anticipated by the text's author.

Reading

Burke, S. (ed.) (2008) *Authorship: From Plato to the Postmodern: A Reader*, Edinburgh: Edinburgh University Press.

Burke, S. (2010) *The Death and Return of the Author: Criticism and Subjectivity in Barthes, Foucault and Derrida*, 3rd edn, Edinburgh: Edinburgh University Press.

Caughie, J. (ed.) (1981) *Theories of Authorship: A Reader*, London: Routledge & Kegan Paul and the British Film Institute.

Culler, J. (2002) *Structuralist Poetics*, 2nd edn, London: Routledge.

Gibbs, R. (1999) *Intentions in the Experience of Meaning*, Cambridge: Cambridge University Press.

Irwin, W. (ed.) (2002) *The Death and Resurrection of the Author?*, Westwood, CT and London: Greenwood Press.

Leitch, V.B. (ed.) (2010) *The Norton Anthology of Theory and Criticism*, New York and London: Norton. (Contains a number of essays on authorship, including the essays by Barthes, Eliot, Foucault, and Wimsatt and Beardsley mentioned in this unit.)

Maynard, J. (2009) *Literary Intention, Literary Interpretation*, Peterborough, Ontario: Broadview.

Newton-de Molina, D. (ed.) (1976) *On Literary Intention*, Edinburgh: Edinburgh University Press.

Mode of address: positioning the reader

UNIT 15

This unit:

- shows how a text's meaning emerges from interaction between the reader and the text, rather than being fixed in the wording on the page;

- distinguishes between the actual reader of a text and characteristics attributed to an 'ideal' or 'intended' reader by features and techniques that collectively amount to the text addressing that 'ideal' or 'intended' reader;

- outlines the concepts of direct address and indirect address, and illustrates effects that follow from such modes of address, both in literary writing and in other kinds of discourse such as advertising;

- examines the significance of gender in how readers are positioned by texts, and explores how readers can contest the positioning they are assigned by texts and in doing so generate alternative readings as 'resisting readers'.

A text's meaning is produced in a complex negotiation between reader and text. It cannot be said that one contributes more than the other, and much recent theorizing about literature suggests a finely balanced negotiation between the two in terms of who or what determines the interpretation that the reader arrives at. It is clear that readers bring a great deal of background information to reading, which they use in constructing their 'reading' of a text. But the focus of this unit is on a distinctive contribution made to how the reader reads by the text itself: how it addresses or positions the reader. Texts address readers in a variety of ways, either by addressing them directly or alternatively by using a range of means of encouraging them indirectly to agree with certain statements.

15.1 The implied reader

It is important to distinguish between the actual reader of a text and its **implied reader**. The actual reader is any person who reads the text, whereas the implied reader is an ideal or optimum figure anticipated or constructed by the text. In this sense, the implied reader is rather like a role that the real reader is encouraged to adopt; that role provides a 'position' from which the real reader can interpret the text. For example, in the following extract from Joseph Conrad's *Heart of Darkness* (1902), the main narrator (Marlow) makes the following statement:

> It is queer how out of touch with truth women are. They live in a world of their own, and there has never been anything like it, and never can be. It is too beautiful altogether, and if they were to set it up it would go to pieces before the first sunset. Some confounded fact we men have been living contentedly with ever since the day of creation would start up and knock the whole thing over.

Marlow is the main protagonist and narrator of this novel, and in general his views are not overly challenged by other views. It seems as if he, as narrator and character, is given a position from which the 'truth' of the situation is given (Rimmon-Kenan, 2002; Toolan, 2001). The role that the reader is called upon to adopt here – as implied reader – is a masculine role. This is cued for the reader by the use of 'we men', a reference that includes Marlow and a group of men that comprises his audience on board a boat, together with an imagined audience for the novel of presumed male readers. It is also cued by the reference to 'women' as 'they'. Use of 'they' signals to the reader that the narrator is referring to a group to which 'we' do not belong.

The reader may also be drawn in this passage into agreeing with what is said about women, since the statements are not modified in any way by qualifying phrases such as 'I think' or 'Maybe', or by counter-statements from Marlow's listeners. The narrator's views about women come from a position in which it is 'common sense', a 'matter of fact', that 'women . . . are out of touch with truth', that 'they live in a world of their own', and so on. In this way, we can say that the (actual) reader of *Heart of Darkness* is drawn into a position (that of the implied reader) where the obviousness of these stereotypes about women may be taken for granted. This is not to say that we, as readers, have to agree with the views put forward; we may well distance ourselves as real readers while recognizing the position of the implied reader.

15.2 Direct address

Most texts present themselves as ignoring the presence of a reader. Yet some texts do address the reader in a direct manner, for example, by calling him or her 'dear reader' or 'you'. Advertisements in particular commonly address the reader in a direct manner, as the following caption (taken from an issue of *New!* magazine) illustrates:

> Copy these A-listers and get your hair to shine by nourishing it both inside and out.

This caption calls on the reader directly by first ordering her to 'copy' celebrities, addressing her as 'you', and referring to 'your hair'. The caption makes assumptions about the reader that she can be included in a group of people who are concerned about their hair shining; it also assumes that she would like to emulate famous celebrities who have shining hair.

Some texts address only a small proportion of their potential audience, or a section within that potential audience, as in the following advert (for a 'Chocolate Tasting Club'):

> ATTENTION ALL CHOCOLATE ENTHUSIASTS! WHY DO WE LOVE IT
> SO MUCH? YOUR CHOCOLATE BLISS POINT EXPLAINED. THE MOST
> DELICIOUS DRINKING CHOCOLATE YOU WILL EVER TASTE.

It might be assumed that this advert copy is addressing everyone who likes chocolate. But nearly all the images in the advertisement are of women eating chocolate. Furthermore, the likelihood that the advert is primarily addressed to women is reinforced by the language used being that of sexual seduction ('good chocolate seduces . . . flooding our senses with a deep pleasure'; 'voluptuous . . . lusciously wicked') and by a history of adverts that equate chocolate with sexual stimulation for women. So while the direct address involves 'we' and 'you', the implied reader is in fact restricted to women who like chocolate. The real reader and the implied reader may in this way not always match up. As will be argued in the next section, however, although the reader is placed in the position of an 'overhearer', this may still have an effect on him or her, by encouraging them to agree with particular statements or ideas.

Direct address is also found in novels. Mark Twain's *The Adventures of Huckleberry Finn* (1884), for example, begins with Huck as narrator introducing himself to the reader: 'You don't know about me, without you have read a book by the name of *The Adventures of Tom Sawyer*, but that ain't no matter.' The narrator of Herman Melville's *Moby Dick* (1851) begins by inviting the reader to 'Call me Ishmael', then takes the reader on an imaginary journey, asking the reader to look and to respond to rhetorical questions. Sometimes, novels address the reader as 'reader'. Perhaps the most famous example is the first sentence in the final chapter of Charlotte Brontë's *Jane Eyre* (1847): 'Reader, I married him.' Such strategies of direct address work to position the reader in relation to the text and to the narrator, although the precise implications of such positioning need to be worked out in each case.

Even plays, which for the most part present action and dialogue as if there were no audience or reader, sometimes include a character who directly addresses the reader/audience. Such a character, in some cases acting collectively in the form of a **chorus**, is often detached from the play's action and acts as a type of narrator. The chorus in Shakespeare's *Henry V*, for instance, asks members of the audience to use their imagination to help the players present large-scale historical actions on stage:

> . . . let us, ciphers to the great account,
> On your imaginary forces work.
> Suppose within the girdle of these walls
> Are now confined two mighty monarchies.

We need accordingly to be wary of assuming that all instances in which a text addresses someone in the second person ('you') are directly addressing the reader. In poetry, for example, instances of direct address are more likely to refer to someone specific who is the 'addressee', rather than to an actual reader, because many poems are addressed (as either an actual or simulated utterance) to someone other than the reader.

15.3 Indirect address

While some texts address their readers directly by the use of 'you', others engage the reader in more subtle ways, by means of **indirect address**. An important aspect of the use of indirect address is the appeal to background knowledge and assumptions. All texts, even the most simple and explicit, assume some degree of shared knowledge between the reader and the producer of the text. Sometimes, these elements of knowledge or ideas are presented as if the reader is bound to agree with them, or they may be based on implicit assumptions that are difficult to object to.

An advertisement for Lil-lets tampons, for example, is headlined 'Lil-lets: the art of self-protection'. The advert shows two women in the background engaged in martial arts, and assumes that the reader will bring to bear on the image quite particular background assumptions about menstruation. In the foreground, the advertisement shows a ball and chain, representing the women as being imprisoned by periods, together with the statement 'the small key to freedom'. It is assumed that the reader will agree with the implicit assertion that periods are imprisoning, that menstruation is something that women want to be 'discreet' about, and that Lil-lets offer a way out of this imprisonment (represented by Lil-lets as a key to the clasp on the chain). Even those women who do not in fact see their periods in such a negative way will, in order to make sense of the text, be led to draw on this shared knowledge about menstruation (see Laws, 1990, for further discussion).

15.4 Dominant readings

Some strands in investigating how texts are interpreted, particularly in cultural/media studies, have drawn on work by the cultural theorist Stuart Hall on encoding and decoding (Hall, 1980; Van Zoonan, 1994). Hall's work showed how a message encoded in a text by the author is not the same as the message decoded by the reader. Despite this potential for different meanings, it is nevertheless possible to argue that there are still clues to what will constitute a **dominant reading**: that is, the reading that seems to be self-evident. The dominant reading is the one ratified by common sense or by other, prevalent ideologies available in the society of the time. So rather than simply assuming that the reader will have certain areas of knowledge that can help make sense of the text, the dominant reading makes sense only by activating larger 'stories' circulating through society. As in the Lil-lets example above, many texts produce a dominant reading that accords with conventional notions of femininity.

Consider another advertisement, this time for Lancôme eye make-up. The dominant reading is effectively that women who want to look like the person depicted in the image should use Lancôme eye make-up. On the right of the advert image there is a representation of a beautiful woman, and to the left the words

L'origine. Pebble grey, moss green, cedar wood, senna brown. These are the subtle harmonies of original colour, colours drawn from Nature herself.

Below these words, in the image, there is a representation of the eye make-up, linked to the depiction of the woman by Lancôme's trademark rose motif. In order to make sense of this Lancôme advertisement, we have to decode a range of elements. The first is that the 'natural' is good. This is signalled by the inclusion of references to colours that are 'drawn from Nature herself' and named after natural substances (pebble grey, cedar wood). That 'natural' means good is also signalled by inclusion of the Lancôme trademark, which is a white stylized rose running horizontally across the image, linking the woman and the make-up. Juxtaposition of the woman, natural elements, the supposedly 'natural' make-up and the fact that nature is referred to as 'her' contributes to creating a dominant reading (see **Unit 12, Juxtaposition**), which puts forward the following kinds of connection between elements:

- the make-up is coloured in the same way as nature;
- natural ingredients are good;
- feminine women have a special relationship with nature;
- women who would like to be thought to be feminine will buy the make-up.

These are not statements that the text makes explicitly. In order to make coherent sense of this fragmented text, however, the reader has to draw on such larger discourses about femininity and its relation to the natural. In this way, ideological assumptions that circulate and constitute systems of shared knowledge ensure that a preferred sense for a particular text appears self-evident.

While a text will normally offer one particular preferred or dominant reading, there is always scope for other, contrary readings of the same text (as will be explored below). If the text is to function as a coherent whole, however, the dominant reading is the one that readers will recognize most easily and that they are therefore likely to choose, unless they have political or personal reasons for challenging that reading.

15.5 Gender and positioning

The space or position that a text offers a reader, from which it makes most sense, can be of various kinds. But one kind of position that has received particular critical attention relates to the reader's gender.

15.5.1 Positioning of the reader as male

When women read literature, feminist writers such as Judith Fetterley (1981) and Elaine Showalter (1982) have argued, they often read as men, precisely because literature often constructs the implied reader as male. Women readers often assent to background assumptions that are really the shared assumptions of males masquerading as a kind of general knowledge that 'we all know' to be true. So, for example, when women readers read the passage from Conrad cited at the beginning of this unit (p. 187), they may well read it without questioning the sexism it contains because that sexism accords with stereotypical background assumptions.

In the text below – an advertising flyer for Trippet's Nail and Tan – a number of assumptions about girls are also to be found that the reader is urged to agree with in order to make sense of the text:

> Lost for an idea for a children's party? Look no further. Trippet's nail and tan are now available for children's beauty parties. £12 per head (includes goody bag). Treatments available – mini manicure and polish, nail art, mini facial, make-up samplings, temporary body tattoos. Full makeover for party girl.

In interpreting this flyer, the reader has first to assume that children's parties can include such activities as body tattooing and that girls should be trained in this way to see that they need beauty treatments. This assumes that, in much the same way as boys are given parties involving swimming or ten pin bowling, girls' sense of enjoyment comes from concentrating on their appearance. This background knowledge is not made explicit. But the reader is forced to construct it and may feel some sense of disjuncture between their own sense of what is appropriate for children and the seemingly 'common sense' assumptions about girls articulated here.

Like the flyer for Trippet's Nail and Tan, several of the earlier examples in this unit have come from advertising. But analogous positioning of the reader (and of the spectator of audio-visual texts) also occurs in other forms and media. In film theory it has been argued, for example (see Mulvey, 1981), that women characters in many Hollywood films are posed as objects 'to-be-looked-at'. The camera focuses on women characters from the perspective of male characters, and it is often a highly sexualized vision of the women that is produced. This means that women spectators watching the same films have to watch them as if they were male voyeurs. This may be a pleasurable experience for women spectators; but it may also make the woman spectator complicit with assumptions about women that she may not ordinarily share (see Stacey, 1994).

15.6 The resisting reader

No account of the positioning of the reader would be complete without also considering how readers can generate alternative readings. One influential approach to alternative readings is that developed by Judith Fetterley (1981), building on the term the **resisting reader**: that is, a reader who does not accept the assumptions and kinds of knowledge that the text presents in the dominant reading, but instead resists them in order to construct an oppositional reading. Both male and female readers can read critically or oppositionally. But it is often more in a woman's interest to read in this way, because of the dominance of certain forms of address outlined above. With the Conrad text discussed earlier, for example (pp. 187–8), a resisting reader may focus on those assumptions that seem to make the text intelligible (for example, by focusing on the use and effects of 'they' and 'we').

Many songs exhibit similar characteristics to the *Heart of Darkness* passage as regards mode of address, and are similarly open to being read in different ways. In the following extract from a song by Neil Hannon (of the band The Divine Comedy, first released in 1997), we can trace two distinct readings: a dominant reading and a resisting reading.

> If . . .
> If you were the road I'd go all the way
> If you were the night I'd sleep in the day
> If you were the day I'd cry in the night
> 'Cause you are the way the truth and the light
> If you were a tree I could put my arms around you
> And you could not complain
> If you were a tree I could carve my name into your side
> And you would not cry, 'cause trees don't cry
> If you were a man I'd still love you
> If you were a drink I'd drink my fill of you
> If you were attacked I would kill for you
> If your name was Jack I'd change mine to Jill for you
> If you were a horse I'd clean the crap out of your stable
> And never once complain
> If you were a horse I could ride you through the fields at dawn
> Through the day until the day was gone
> I could sing about you in my songs
> As we rode away into the setting sun
> If you were my little girl I would find it hard to let you go
> If you were my sister I would find it doubly so
> If you were a dog I'd feed you scraps from off the table
> Though my wife complains
> If you were my dog I am sure you'd like it better
> Then you'd be my loyal four-legged friend
> You'd never have to think again
> And we could be together 'til the end.

The dominant reading of this song is guided by a series of conditional propositions that involve the reader and the narrator in mapping out a position in which the singer and the audience are assumed to share certain attitudes towards romance. The reader is directly addressed, so that he or she has to decide whether to take up the position of the 'I' or the 'you', the addresser or the addressee (see Durant and Lambrou, 2009, Unit C3). The content of the song is not simple, however: at one and the same time, the singer articulates an excessively romantic form of love, while also ironizing the grounds on which those romantic utterances are made. In some ways the singer, in postmodernist fashion, can be seen to be pushing the expression of romantic feeling beyond the realms of current discursive norms. Instead of comparing the person he loves to flowers and birds, he compares her to horses and dogs. These unusual comparisons create the song's humour, since the singer uses a kind of language not generally permissible within romantic songs (for example, 'crap'), and also makes statements such as 'If you were a man I'd still love you'. In such a reading of the song, the singer seems to be making excessive, humorous statements that the reader is expected to identify with as ironizing and funny.

The resisting reading of this song might take issue with this position of postmodernist ironizing. Its playful instability may seem to offer no basis from which to criticize the song. In this seemingly playful song, the woman is still objectified as in more openly sexist songs: she is represented as a loyal dog who is given scraps, a passive horse who is ridden, a tree on whom the singer carves his name, and a drink consumed by the singer (albeit in a slightly distanced, conditional form). Perhaps the oddest lines in the song are to be found in the final stanza: 'If you were a dog I'd feed you scraps from off the table / Though my wife complains'. If the loved one were a dog she would be loyal and would 'never have to think again'. Female agency is deleted in this song, even though on the surface it seems to be gesturing towards a more playful and anti-sexist interpretation.

Resisting readings can be produced for most texts, and may focus on the representation of a range of issues including depictions of race, class and sexual preference. For example, Cora Kaplan has questioned the way that white women have assumed that Alice Walker's *The Color Purple* refers to women in general, rather than to black women in particular. In doing so, Kaplan challenged the universalizing discussions that have taken place on the book, discussions that erase questions of race that the text raises (Kaplan, 1986). Lesbian readers might argue for a foregrounding of elements in the same text that focus on the female characters' love for one another (Hobby and White, 1991).

Some post-colonial literary theorists, working along similar lines, have re-read canonical literary texts in order to focus on elements they contain such as slavery and complicity in colonialism, which earlier readers of the same texts had overlooked or tried to ignore (Said, 2007). Other post-colonial critics have shown how Eurocentrism (that is, a form of thinking that presumes that countries are lacking if judged not in their own terms but against Western criteria such as industrial development and scientific achievement) pervades much of the representational practice of Western culture (Shohat and Stam, 1994). By adopting a critical approach to assumptions concealed in a text's mode of address, the reader can first trace and describe the dominant reading of the text, then refuse that position in order to focus on other elements that the text may also suggest, often in its margins. A reader who resists the text in this way assumes power and responsibility in relation to the determination of the text's meaning. In contrast with a traditional view of the reader as a passive recipient of information, in this view the reader is enabled to construct meaning for him- or herself.

The text below is a horoscope for Libra and Aquarius (taken from an issue of the *Observer* magazine, a weekly magazine given away with a national Sunday newspaper):

Libra: There's quite a change unfolding now, what with the professional pressure back on and some patient, tender handling of your personal life being called for. Take care with your words; this week they can carry extra clout and can hurt. The Libran Moon on Friday/Saturday brings emotional issues to a combustible climax; you might as well go for broke, in every respect except financially.

Aquarius: Work: even if you are not in education, a teaching role plays in your favour. You'll have to bi-locate like a Gemini in order to field imminent information overload. Good time to sign contracts, do deals. Home: about to become one heck of a sight busier. Romance, not tonight Josephine – but you can raise quite a rumpus come Friday and Saturday. Yes, you wild thing. Enjoy.

———————

1   Construct a number of different readers' lives with which these predictions could be made to fit (e.g. someone thinking of leaving a relationship; someone thinking of changing jobs). For example, consider the range of possible interpretations of, in the Aquarius section, 'a teaching role plays in your favour' or, in the Libra section, 'you might as well go for broke'.

2   Find evidence for characteristics that the readers of this horoscope are stated or implied to share (e.g. income, class, age, relationship).

A C T I V I T Y   1 5

Reading

Durant, A. and Lambrou, M. (2009) *Language and Media: A Resource Book for Students*, London: Routledge.

Fetterley, J. (1981) *The Resisting Reader: A Feminist Approach to American Fiction*, Bloomington, IN: Indiana University Press.

Hall, S. (1980) 'Encoding/Decoding', in S. Hall, D. Hobson, A. Lowe and P. Willis (eds) *Culture, Media, Language: Working Papers in Cultural Studies*, 1972–79, London: Hutchinson, pp. 128–39.

Kaplan, C. (1986) 'Keeping the Colour in *The Color Purple*' in C. Kaplan (ed.) *Sea Changes: Culture and Feminism*, London: Verso, pp. 176–87.

Laws, S. (1990) *Issues of Blood: The Politics of Menstruation*, Basingstoke: Macmillan.

Mills, S. (ed.) (1994) *Gendering the Reader*, Hemel Hempstead: Harvester Wheatsheaf.

Mills, S. (1996) *Feminist Stylistics*, London: Routledge.

Said, E. (2007) *Culture and Imperialism*, New York: Vintage.

Shohat, E. and Stam, R. (1994) *Unthinking Eurocentrism: Multiculturalism and the Media*, London: Routledge.

Showalter, E. (1982) *A Literature of Their Own: British Women Novelists from Bronte to Lessing*, revised edn, London: Virago Press.

Stacey, J. (1994) *Star Gazing: Hollywood Cinema and Female Spectatorship*, London: Routledge.

Toolan, M. (2001) *Narrative: A Critical Linguistic Introduction*, 2nd edn, London: Routledge.

Van Zoonan, L. (1994) *Feminist Media Studies*, London: Sage.

Poetic form

UNIT 16

Rhyme and sound patterning

This unit:

- explains how visual marks on the page (letters) are translated into mental representations of sounds;

- offers a description of the elements that make up a syllable – onset, nucleus and coda – and relates these elements to more familiar categories such as consonants and vowels;

- describes different sound patterns commonly found in poetry (as well as in proverbs, adverts, taglines and other forms of discourse), especially rhyme and alliteration;

- outlines the main views commonly taken of the significance of sound patterning, including arguments about the contribution made by sound symbolism to poetic effect;

- offers practical guidance on how to develop local interpretations based on sound symbolism, while urging caution in doing so.

U N I T 1 6

As we read words on a page, we translate visual marks (letters) into mental representations of sounds (phones, or phonemes). This is because English uses a 'phonetic-alphabetic script', in which letters stand for sounds: letters serve to represent particular patterns of sound. For example, the letter 'p' in 'pin' stands for a single sound (which we write phonetically as [p]); the two letters 'th' in 'thin' stand for a single sound (which we write phonetically as [θ]); the letter 'i' in 'time' stands for a combination of sounds called a diphthong (which we write phonetically as [a ɪ]). We can represent the way a word is made up of sounds using a phonetic script. It is then possible to compare the letter-spelling of a word with the phonetic structure of that word:

letter-spelling:	thing	queen	come
phonetic structure:	θ ɪ ŋ	k w i n	k ʌ m

In this unit we are interested in the phonetic structure of words rather than their spelling. Because of the relatively small number of distinct sounds used in a language, the sounds of a text inevitably occur and recur as we read. Such repetitions make up a sort of kaleidoscope of recurrence and permutations. In casual conversation and in most kinds of written texts, this repetition of sounds occurs for the most part apparently randomly, ordered only by the historical accidents governing which sounds make up which words. But it is possible for speakers and writers to organize the sounds of utterances in more systematic ways, ranging from motivated but irregular instances through to fully predictable patterns, in order to achieve certain effects. Many different types of discourse employ such sound patterning: poetry, jokes, slogans, proverbs, advertising copy, sound-bites in political speeches and interviews, pop lyrics, rapping, etc.

16.1 Structure of the syllable

In **Unit 17, Verse, metre and rhythm**, we will see that the metrical form of a poem involves control over the syllables of the line, and that syllables are also relevant in the organization of sound patterning. **Rhyme** and **alliteration**, arguably the two basic kinds of sound patterning, involve different parts of the syllable. A syllable is divided into three parts (of which only the nucleus is essential): an onset, a nucleus and a coda. Table 16.1 illustrates this division of the syllable into three parts, using monosyllabic words.

Table 16.1 shows several things about syllables and sounds.

(1)   An onset can have any number from zero to three consonants, while a coda usually has between zero and two consonants. But there is always a nucleus.

(2)   The number of written letters before or after the nucleus is irrelevant; syllable structure is a matter of sound, not spelling, so both 'bite' and 'fight' have a one-consonant coda.

TABLE 16.1 **Three-part structure of the syllable**

Onset	Nucleus	Coda	[Word]
b	a ɪ	t	bite
f	a ɪ	t	fight
pl	a ɪ	t	plight
spl	æ	t	splat
p	e ɪ	st	paste
p	e ɪ		pay
	æ	t	at
	a ɪ		I

(3)   While the nucleus of a syllable is almost always a vowel, there are some written vowels that are not syllable nuclei, because they are not pronounced as vowels: 'paste' is a monosyllabic word based on the nucleus vowel [a], and the final written 'e' is irrelevant to its syllable structure.

The nucleus of the syllable is usually a vowel. Sometimes the nucleus of the syllable is a diphthong, which is two vowels pronounced together as in 'wheel', which is a single-syllable word with a two-vowel diphthong as its nucleus (in phonetic representation it is [i ə]). The nucleus can also be a highly 'sonorant' consonant. Sonorance is a vocal quality of vowels, but some consonants such as [r] and [l] and the nasal consonants [m] and [n] also have sonorance, so they can be syllable nuclei. For example, the word 'bottle' has two syllables, the second of which has [l] as its nucleus.

16.2   Types of sound pattern: rhyme and alliteration

We can group various kinds of sound patterning into larger groups. These larger groups we can call types of rhyme and types of alliteration. Types of rhyme involve the end of the syllable; types of alliteration involve the beginning of the syllable.

Strict rhyme involves the [nucleus+coda]. Thus 'bite', 'plight' and 'fight' (from Table 16.1) can all rhyme, because they have the same nucleus and coda. Where just the [nucleus] is repeated and the coda varies, this is called 'assonance'. While 'I' does not rhyme with 'bite', because the coda is different, the identity of the nucleus makes this an example of assonance. Where just the [coda] is repeated and the nucleus varies, this is called 'consonance'. Though 'at' does not rhyme with 'bite', because the nucleus is different, the similarity of coda makes this an example of 'consonance'. Various issues relating to rhyme can be examined by using the following stanzas from Shelley's, 'To a Skylark' (which has been discussed from other points of view in **Unit 2, Using information sources**, and **Unit 10, Metaphor and figurative language**).

> Hail to thee, blithe spirit!
> Bird thou never wert,
> That from heaven, or near it,
> Pourest thy full heart
> In profuse strains of unpremeditated art.
>
> Higher still and higher,
> From the earth thou springest
> Like a cloud of fire;
> the blue deep thou wingest,
> And singing still dost soar, and soaring ever singest.
>
> (Percy Bysshe Shelley, 'To a Skylark', 1820)

In the first stanza, we can see an exact repetition in 'heart' and 'art'. This is a rhyme (because nucleus+coda are the same in both words). But is 'wert' part of the same rhyme? One question we might ask is whether Shelley *pronounced* this word as he pronounced 'heart'. Vowels have changed in the course of the history of English, and a pair of words might once have rhymed even if they do not rhyme now. (However, in this case a check in *Walker's Pronouncing Dictionary* shows that 'wert' and 'heart' are listed at that time as having different pronunciations, at least in one standard accent of English.) If Shelley did not pronounce the two words alike, then we could describe the relation as an example of consonance between 'wert' and 'heart': consonance is the repetition of just [coda], here the final consonant [t] (or [rt] if the r is pronounced, as it is in some accents of English). It is often the case that in accounts of poetry a consonance is 'upgraded' to count as a rhyme, if there is supporting evidence. If we look at the rest of the poem – including the second stanza quoted here – we find that the second, fourth and fifth lines characteristically rhyme with each other; this gives us some reason to think of the 'wert'/'heart' match as a slightly defective rhyme, rather than as a true consonance. In this way we see that – as with metre – the abstract description of the form as 'rhyme' conceals some variation in actual pronunciation. We might similarly allow 'spirit' and 'near it' to count as rhyme, in that here we have a shared sequence of nucleus-onset-nucleus-coda, thus involving two syllables.

The kind of rhyme where two syllables are involved, and where the first syllable is stressed but the second is unstressed, is known as a **feminine rhyme**. Rhymes involving just a final stressed syllable are traditionally called masculine rhymes. Rhyme is often used systematically in English verse, and we then say that a poem has a 'rhyme scheme'. The rhyme scheme for this poem would be written down as ABABB for each stanza, a labelling that shows which lines rhyme in each five-line stanza. Some types of rhyme scheme have their own names: AABBCC patterns are called 'couplets'; and AAABBB, etc. patterns are known as 'triplets'.

Combinations of specific metres with specific rhymes also have specific names. The combination of iambic pentameter with (rhyme) couplets is called 'heroic verse', while the use of iambic pentameter *without* rhyme is called **blank verse**. Special types of stanza also have specific rhyme schemes, and some poetic genres, such as the sonnet, also have specific rhyme schemes. Finally, remember that it is the sounds (not the spellings) that produce rhyme. So 'cough' rhymes with 'off', not with 'plough'. Words like 'cough' and 'plough', whose spelling suggests that they ought to rhyme (even though they do not rhyme as pronounced), are called 'eye-rhymes'.

The second major class of sound patterning is **alliteration**. In its prototypical form, alliteration involves repetition of the onset, as in 'paste' and 'pay', or 'plaster' and 'plight'. For the most part in English, we can say that there is alliteration if just the first consonant in the onset is repeated. This is the kind of alliteration we see in Shelley's poem: 'pourest' and 'profuse' and 'blithe' and 'bird'. In a stricter variant, the whole onset must be repeated. In that stricter version of what constitutes alliteration, 'blithe' and 'bird' would not alliterate with each other, but 'blithe' and 'blood' would, or 'bide' and 'bird'. In a third variant, the onset must be in the first stressed syllable of the word. This concept of alliteration is seen in the notion of the 'three Rs': 'reading, writing and arithmetic'. Here the 'r' in each word is the complete onset of the first stressed syllable in that word (in 'arithmetic', this syllable is the second actual syllable in the word). A fourth variant of alliteration involves not only the onset but also the nucleus, as in 'cash' and 'carry'. Leech (1969) calls this variant 'reverse rhyme'. It is the standard type of alliteration (or reverse rhyme) in, for example, Finnish and Mongolian poetry, but is not common in English poetry. If we look at the alliteration in Shelley's poem we see that, although it is quite widespread, it is not systematic. We could not talk about an 'alliteration scheme', to parallel the rhyme scheme in the poem. In fact, English poetry has not had systematic alliteration since the medieval period (it is, however, the rule in Old English poetry, was revived in the Middle Ages, and is occasionally imitated in more recent poetry).

In analysing alliteration it is especially important to remember that you are analysing sounds, not letters. 'Seek' and 'shape' do not alliterate with each other because they begin with different sounds, even though their spelling makes them look similar. There is nevertheless a tradition of using line-initial (or stanza-initial) letters as an organizing device; while this is not a kind of alliteration (because it uses letters and not sounds), it is worth noting. The Latin poem *Altus Prosatur* (written on the Hebridean island of Iona during the sixth century) has each stanza beginning with a different letter of the alphabet, an effect that makes it what is called an 'abecedarian' poem.

We can broadly distinguish, then, between rhyme as the repetition of the end of the syllable (and usually the end of the word) and alliteration as repetition of the beginning of the syllable (and usually the beginning of the word). It is technically possible to have both the beginning and the end of the syllable repeated. This effect is called 'pararhyme' (and sometimes also called 'consonance'); it can be seen in 'send' and 'sound', and 'beat' and 'bite'.

16.3 The significance of sound patterns

So far, we have simply identified possible patterns and presented ways of describing them. In order to investigate how such patterns work as a stylistic resource, we need now to consider what kind of significance or function they might have. Five alternative possibilities are presented below. Each possibility should be considered for each case of sound patterning identified in a text:

(1) Patterning may serve no particular function. It may simply be the accidental result of random distribution of the small number of distinct sounds that make up the language. This is especially likely in spontaneous conversation. It is also likely where there is some distance in the text between instances of the sound taken to create the effect: functional sound patterning depends on proximity between the words involved, since readers (or listeners) are unlikely to recognize sounds repeated far apart. Moving to a more formal type of description (see Fabb, 1997), we can express this another way by saying that a closeness constraint seems to operate on some or all kinds of sound patterning, and that this closeness constraint is required in order to ensure that such patterning is noticeable, or perceptually 'salient'.

(2) Patterning may serve a 'cohesive' function. It can bond words together as formulaic, fixed phrases or units. This extra bonding at the level of sound can enhance the memorability of an utterance, as it does in riddles, catch phrases and proverbs ('action-packed'; 'a stitch in time saves nine'; 'be Indian, buy Indian', etc.).

(3) Patterning may have the effect of emphasizing or 'foregrounding' some aspect of the text. Patterning that involves repetition, for example, sometimes serves to make a passage seem as though it expresses great feeling, as is often the case in political rhetoric. Sometimes attention is drawn by means of the patterning to the physical existence of the utterance as a linguistic construct, as with tongue twisters such as the alliterative 'Peter Piper picked a peck of pickled peppercorns'. Notice incidentally that the alliteration here is set against a strange kind of counter-alliteration: the [p] sound and the [k] sound are made at opposite ends of the mouth, which is what creates the tongue twister.

(4) Patterning may have the effect of creating or reinforcing a parallelism. In this case, words that are linked together on the basis of shared sounds are also linked in terms of their meanings (they typically have similar or opposite meanings). This technique is common in jokes, advertising and some types of poetry (e.g. Augustan verse). Consider, from this point of view, such phrases as 'chalk and cheese' and 'cash and carry'. Or recall Blake's 'marks of weakness, marks of woe', an example of this effect in Romantic poetry (see **Unit 3, Analysing units of structure**).

(5) Patterning may contribute **sound symbolism**. Such effects are based on a belief that the sounds that make up words are not arbitrarily related to their

meaning, as most linguists think, but are motivated in some way by being loaded with resonance or with extra value that comes from connotations or associations.

A number of points are worth noting about the notion of sound symbolism:

(a)   The linguistic view that the sounds of language are arbitrary is supported by evidence such as the fact that the same meaning is expressed in different languages by words with very different sounds ('tree', 'arbre', 'Baum', etc.), and that the sounds of words change over time. Such evidence suggests that sounds are merely conventional aspects of the formal system of a language.

(b)   The view that sounds in language may have symbolic meanings or expressive effects, on the other hand, is based on a musical belief that sound itself carries meaning, as well as on the idea that individual sounds are felt differently because the way we make them with the voice differs for each sound. Consider three types of much-discussed evidence for this:

    (i)   Here are three imaginary but possible 'words': 'la', 'li' and 'lor'. If you had three tables of different sizes to label with these words, which would you call which? Research has shown that most people – across a wide range of different cultures – label the small table 'li', the middle-sized one 'la' and the largest 'lor'. This tendency probably reflects the fact that sounds are made differently in the mouth: 'lor' is a 'big' sound (mouth open, tongue back, large mouth cavity); 'li', by contrast, is a 'small' sound (mouth relatively closed, tongue up and forward, etc.).

    (ii)   Some clusters of words have both their sound and their general area of meaning in common (this effect is traditionally called 'onomatopoeia'). 'Clatter', 'clang' and 'clash' all suggest one thing striking against another; 'sneeze', 'snore', 'snooze' and 'sniffle' are all to do with breathing through the nose, and might be considered to sound like the actions they refer to (though consider 'snow' and 'snap' as counter-examples).

    (iii)   A hypothesis of gradience, or continuum, between linguistic sounds is sometimes made, from 'hard' through to 'soft'. The so-called hardest sounds include [p], [b], [t], [d], [k] and [g] (these are technically called stops or plosives, and all involve completely stopping breath coming out of the mouth, then releasing it suddenly). The so-called softest sounds are the vowels (these do not impede the air-flow out of the mouth at all, but simply reshape it), plus sounds such as those commonly produced from the letters 'w' and 'l'. The idea that words contain hard and soft sounds is sometimes then used as the basis for making links between sound and meaning.

(c)   Sound symbolism involves attributing conventional meanings or resonances to sound patterns. In Keats's famous line in 'To Autumn' (1820), 'Thou watchest the last oozings hours by hours', the repeated 's' and 'z' sounds are often taken to represent the oozing of cider being made in the press. In an equally well-known line from Tennyson, 'The murmuring of innumerable bees' (from 'The Princess' [1853]), the repeated 'm' sounds are taken to represent the sound of bees. But such associations of sound and meaning are not fixed: the sounds 's' and 'z' could equally be taken to stand for the buzzing of bees, if they were in a poem about bees. Meaning in this way contributes significantly to the apparent effect of sound symbolism in a poem.

16.4 Making interpretations on the basis of sound patterns

Having looked at how sound patterns may function, we need now to consider how the identification of sound patterning can be used in ways of reading, and to assess some of the possibilities and problems that may be involved in doing this.

Understanding the conventions underlying many idioms or genres requires that we recognize aspects of their use of sound patterning. Contemporary rapping involves rhyming as one of its main organizational principles, for instance. Headlines and advertising slogans also have characteristic ways of using sound patterns. Many texts written within established literary traditions draw on specialized conventions of sound patterning (and sometimes sound symbolism) as a conventional compositional resource. Traditions of interpreting these texts draw on the same network of conventions.

The conventional register of poetic language (see **Unit 7, Language and context: register**) has itself fluctuated throughout its history in the use made of sound patterning. Some periods and poets have preferred highly complex effects, for example. Such poets include Gerard Manley Hopkins, whose use of sound patterning is evident in the opening lines of 'The Windhover' (1877; published 1918):

> I caught this morning morning's minion, king-
> > dom of daylight's dauphin, dapple-dawn-drawn Falcon, in his riding
> > Of the rolling level underneath him steady air, and striding
> High there, how he rung upon the rein of a wimpling wing
> In his ecstasy!

The complexity of sound patterning in these lines contrasts strongly with, for instance, Wordsworth's aspiration for poetic language (or 'diction'): that it should approximate to the ordinary language of speech, a view famously presented in the 'Preface' to *Lyrical Ballads* (1802 [1798]), roughly half a century earlier than Hopkins. We should nevertheless be careful about generalizations as regards the contribution made by sound patterning to poetic styles. Caution is needed partly because sound patterning intersects in complex ways with rhythm and with other aspects of register. It is also partly because writers are not always consistent in their practice. Wordsworth's view of poetic language set out in *Lyrical Ballads*, for example, and his co-authorship of that volume with the poet Samuel Taylor Coleridge, did not stop Coleridge producing one of the most celebrated instances of intricate sound patterning in English verse around the same time: the first lines of 'Kubla Khan' (written 1797, published 1816):

> In Xanadu did Kubla Khan
> A stately pleasure-dome decree:
> Where Alph, the sacred river, ran
> Through caverns measureless to man
> Down to a sunless sea.

In attempting to interpret sound patterns, it is useful to distinguish between two different levels of effect: first, fairly systematic and predictable patterns that serve to define a form (such as rhyme schemes and local kinds of ornamentation); and second, patterns that have locally marked effects which seem to serve expressive or symbolic functions (such as extra memorability or special suggestiveness). One problem with trying to interpret the second kind of pattern is that the expressive or symbolic significance of sound effects cannot simply be read off from a text in a series of mechanical equations between sound and sense (as we saw with the examples from Keats and Tennyson above). A sequence of words beginning with the same sound may suggest one thing in one context but quite a different thing in another context. Priority in such circumstances should be given to the context and meaning of the words that appear to create the local, expressive effect. Only after considering meaning and context in this way is it safe to suggest how sound may support (or perhaps undercut) the sense.

More generally it is rarely, if ever, possible to *prove* an effect of sound patterning or sound symbolism. Caution is therefore needed in putting forward interpretive arguments based on the connotations or symbolic qualities of sounds. Arguments regarding the expressive or symbolic qualities of sound in a text become persuasive when they are based on some kind of mutual reinforcement that can be shown between properties of the text at different levels (between its sounds, grammatical structures, vocabulary, etc.). Arguments are generally less convincing when appeals are made either directly to fixed symbolic values attributed to sounds, or to a reader's personal sense of a sound's resonance.

Finally, when writing about a text there is little point in simply listing aspects of its sound patterning (e.g. its rhyme scheme, or the fact that two words alliterate). Comments along these lines are merely mechanical. Comment on sound effects only becomes interesting when it is linked to one of two kinds of argument: either an observation contributes to identifying a text's genre or form, where for some reason this is in question or worth establishing; or else the comment about sound effects supports a case for some local interpretation, in which the evocative effect of the sound connects with other indicators of what is meant.

To explore the practical challenge of identifying and commenting on sound patterns in a poem, look again at the first five lines of 'Kubla Khan', quoted above (now with slightly more space between them):

> In Xanadu did Kubla Khan
>
> A stately pleasure-dome decree:
>
> Where Alph, the sacred river, ran
>
> Through caverns measureless to man
>
> Down to a sunless sea.

_____

1   Label the rhyme scheme present in these lines (re-read section 16.2 above for help on how to label rhyming lines if you need to).

2   Find some examples of alliteration (check the core definition of alliteration outlined above in section 16.2, as well as different ways of viewing minor variations on that definition).

3   Now consider one sort of difficulty that can arise as a result of language variation and/or language change. Consider examples of assonance in the extract (and check the definition of assonance above, p. 201, if you are not sure exactly what assonance is). Which of the following vowels does the vowel in 'Khan', in the first line, assonate with?

    (a) the vowel in the second syllable of 'Kubla'?

    (b) the vowel in the second syllable of 'Xanadu'?

    (c) the vowel in the first syllable of 'Xanadu'?

    Using a suitable table of phonetic symbols (you can find one at the front of most dictionaries), represent what you think the sound in each of these cases is, using an appropriate symbol. Do you think that most other readers you know would be likely to share your intuitions regarding which is the best match? Explain your answer to this question as fully as you can.

4   Now draw up a list which shows as much local sound patterning in the five lines as you can see (or hear!). To do this, you will probably find it helpful to copy the extract and circle vowels, consonants and/or syllables that you believe will sound the same when uttered. Draw lines on your copy connecting repeated sounds; then compile your list, adding a classification of the resemblances you are noting.

continued

5   How many of the repetitions you have noticed occur between two or more stressed syllables? You may find it helpful here to distinguish stressed syllables from unstressed syllables using a highlighter pen (refer to **Unit 17, Verse, metre and rhythm** if you need clarification of verbal stress). How many of the repetitions you have noted occur between unstressed syllables? And how many occur between one or more stressed and one or more unstressed syllables? Does the relation between sound resemblance and verbal stress affect how prominent or salient the repetition of a sound is in any given case?

6   Does sound patterning need to occur between syllables that are fairly close together, if their relationship is to come to your notice (in section 16.2, we referred to the possibility of a 'closeness constraint' on the saliency of sound effects)? Or are echoes created in these lines between phrases some distance apart (e.g. in different lines)?

7   The poem 'Kubla Khan' was sub-titled 'A Vision in a Dream' when re-published in 1834 (as well as 'A Fragment' – a note added in 1816). In some respects, such framing allowed a lot of creative freedom as regards how the poem would develop (e.g. who or what might be introduced into it next), including in order to create felicitous sound effects. Coleridge also added a prefatory note to the poem for publication in 1816, describing how it had come to be written: he had fallen asleep and dreamt the poem; but while writing it down when he woke up, he was interrupted by 'a person on business from Porlock' (a nearby village) and subsequently forgot the rest of the dream – and so could not complete the poem. Consider this later prefatory note alongside the poem itself. Does the phrase 'person on business from Porlock' suggest anything about the relationship between the prefatory note and the poem itself, because of the sound patterning it contains? If it does, could we consider this an 'argument from sound patterning' along the lines discussed in this unit?

8   'Kubla Khan' is celebrated as an exceptional example of sound effects being created at different levels. But what about sound patterning in kinds of poetic discourse that may be more constrained than a 'A Vision in a Dream': for example, kinds of lyrical poem that develop a more obviously coherent rhetorical position, reflection on experience or argument? Consider the following poetic fragment, also written by Coleridge and also left unfinished (the fragment was never published in Coleridge's lifetime but was discovered in his Notebooks and was probably written a few years after 'Kubla Khan' [written 1797], in 1804–5):

> What never is, but only is to be
> This is not Life:–
> O hopeless Hope, and Death's Hypocrisy!
> And with perpetual promise breaks its promises.

continued

9 Carry out tasks 1–2 and 4–6 again, as now applied to these lines.

10 Consider in particular the following details of this poetic fragment:

(a) Does the second syllable of 'hopeless' assonate with 'Death' (and so also with the vowel in the first syllable of 'never'); or does it approximate to the vowel in the third syllable of 'Hypocrisy'? Or somehow *both*?

(b) What effect does sound repetition between 'promise' and 'promises' create, when linked to a contrast of meaning between these expressions: from abstract 'promise' to concrete and countable 'promises'?

(c) Does wording such as oxymoronic 'hopeless hope', or the twist of meaning conveyed by the move from 'is' to 'is to be' illustrate how sound effects may merge into the processes of thought that poetry is capable of expressing?

Reading

Fabb, N. (1997) *Linguistics and Literature: Language in the Verbal Arts of the World*, Oxford: Blackwell.

Furniss, T. and Bath, M. (2007) *Reading Poetry: An Introduction*, 2nd edn, London: Longman, Chapter 4.

Leech, G. (1969) *A Linguistic Guide to English Poetry*, London: Longman, Chapter 6.

Verse, metre and rhythm

This unit:

- reviews the concept of syllable and adds the idea of stress-creating beats that play a major role in poetry in English;
- explains how stress relates to syllable structure and to the creation of different sorts of poetic line;
- describes the main kinds of poetic foot involved in metre (iambic, trochaic, etc.), as well as the main kinds of line structure (as classified on the basis of the number of 'feet' that a line contains: tetrameter, pentameter, etc.);
- discusses different rhythmic effects created by variation from fixed metre, for example by 'foot substitution' or the addition or omission of syllables;
- concludes with discussion of what 'free verse' means, in relation to the concepts introduced in this unit, and gives advice on what to look for in analysing verse effects in poetry.

The following short poem, 'Rain' (1885) by Robert Louis Stevenson', is an example of metrical verse:

The rain is raining all around	(iambic tetrameter)
It falls on field and tree,	(iambic trimeter)
It rains on the umbrellas here,	(iambic tetrameter)
And on the ships at sea.	(iambic trimeter)

This is **verse** (rather than prose) because it is divided into lines. It is *metrical* verse because each line follows a metrical pattern (here iambic tetrameter or iambic trimeter); a metrical pattern partially controls how many syllables there are in each line, and what the rhythm of the line is. In order to understand English metre, it is necessary first to understand the two aspects of English words that are controlled by metre: syllables, and relative stress on syllables.

17.1 Syllables and stress

Syllables can be thought of as 'beats' in speech. A word with three syllables, such as 'umbrellas', consists of three beats. You will discover this if you tap as you say the word out: um-brel-las.

In English, the nucleus of a syllable usually consists of a vowel or diphthong (two vowels spoken together), or a triphthong (three vowels spoken together) (see **Unit 16, Rhyme and sound patterning**). The nuclei of the three syllables of 'umbrella' are 'u', 'e' and 'a'. However, a syllable can also be based on vowel-like consonants, such as 'l' or 'n' or 'r'; the second syllable of the two-syllable word 'bottle', for instance, has its second syllable based on 'l'.

Words may be monosyllabic or polysyllabic:

Monosyllables

1 syllable: in, up, man, heart, score, feet, smelt, death, wheat

Polysyllables

2 syllables: ready, pieces, upset, apple, monstrous, ending, fearsome
3 syllables: umbrellas, undertake, manicure, randomness, gentlemen
4 syllables: monstrosity, repulsiveness, menagerie, telescopic, dissertation
5 syllables: unreality, fortification, structuralism, nationality, philosophical
6 syllables: encyclopaedia, psychotherapeutic
7 syllables: environmentalism, autobiographical

Some words have a variable number of syllables, depending on pronunciation (e.g. 'literature' usually has three, but it can be pronounced with four; 'Wednesday' can be pronounced with two or with three). Such variation is one of the ways in which dialects can differ.

To test your understanding of syllable counting, try to identify how many syllables there are in each word in the Stevenson poem on p. 212; then add up the syllables in each line. You should find that there are 8+6+8+6.

One characteristic of being metrical (which means 'measured') is that the number of syllables in each line is controlled (though with some variation). An iambic tetrameter line will have eight syllables, and an iambic trimeter line normatively has (i.e. is required to have) six syllables, as in the poem quoted above. Adoption of a metrical pattern in this way places a constraint on composition: in the metrical pattern used in 'Rain', the one-syllable word 'field' could not be replaced by a two-syllable word such as 'garden' without creating tension between the line and the underlying metrical pattern.

To represent the organization of syllable patterns in poetic lines visually, we propose to write an 'x' (or asterisk) under each syllable in the line (if you do this on a computer, use an evenly-spaced font such as *Courier* to control vertical alignments; also avoid using the tab key):

```
The rain is raining all around
  x   x   x   x x   x    x x

It falls on field and tree,
x    x   x   x    x      x

It rains on the umbrellas here,
x    x    x     xx    x  x    x

And on the ships at sea.
x    x   x    x    x   x
```

The second aspect of metricality involves placement of stress. In any sequence of spoken syllables, some syllables are experienced as being more prominent than others: they may be slightly louder, have a higher pitch and/or be slightly longer than surrounding syllables. This is true of all the polysyllabic words in the above list. In each, it is possible to identify one syllable as more strongly stressed than the others. Dictionaries usually represent the pronunciation of polysyllabic words by putting an inverted comma before the syllable with the greatest stress relative to the other syllables. We can do the same for some of the words in the above list:

'ready, 'readiness, 'monstrous, mon'strosity, unre'ality, encyclo'paedia, environ'mentalism.

Try doing this for all the words in the list, then check in a dictionary if you are unsure.

When words are put together in a spoken sequence, the relative stress of syllables can also vary between words. In a sequence of monosyllables, for example, you will find that some monosyllables (e.g. the nouns) have more stress than others (e.g. articles such as 'the', or prepositions such as 'of', tend not to be stressed relative to surrounding words). When you tap out a word, you will find that you need to tap loudest on the syllable with greatest stress. Syllables with weak stress are often reduced in 'vowel quality': that is, they may be shortened or even no longer clearly distinguishable. How far this happens partly depends on dialect. Some kinds of Welsh and Scottish English have less reduction of unstressed vowels than some kinds of English English. In English English, the second syllable of 'Bournemouth' is reduced, while in Scottish English the same second syllable is given virtually the same stress as the first syllable.

We are now in a position to develop our metrical analysis of Stevenson's 'Rain'. We have indicated the stressed syllables in polysyllabic words with inverted commas (we have also underlined them). These syllables will automatically have stress in an oral performance of the poem. We have also underlined the mono-syllables that are likely to have stress in oral performance (try reading the poem aloud to check that this notation reflects how the lines would usually be spoken):

```
The rain is 'raining all a'round
  x   x   x    x   x   x   x  x

It falls on field and tree,
x  x    x  x      x      x

It rains on the um'brellas here,
x  x    x  x   x x    x    x   x

And on the ships at sea.
x   x   x   x    x   x
```

17.2 Iambic metre

What is striking about the stresses in 'Rain' is that they tend to be two syllables apart. Only the third line fails to show this pattern (and even there we could choose to stress 'the' and so make the rhythm fully regular). This degree of patterning suggests that, as far as the organization of stress is concerned, the syllables are grouped into pairs. It is also clearly the second (the rightmost or final) syllable of each pair that tends to have stress. In the most common method of metrical analysis, a pair of syllables like this is called an **iambic foot**, and this poem would be said to consist of 'iambic feet'. The poem's iambic feet are divided off in the diagram below by putting a closing bracket after every second cross (the crosses below the stressed syllables), so that the crosses are grouped into pairs. This notation produces what is called a 'scansion' of each line: a representation of its metrical structure:

> The <u>rain</u> is <u>rain</u>ing all <u>around</u>
>   x x) x   x) x x)   x x)   (four iambic feet)
>
> It <u>falls</u> on <u>field</u> and <u>tree</u>,
> x x) x x)   x   x)   (three iambic feet)
>
> It <u>rains</u> on the <u>um</u>brellas <u>here</u>,
> x x) x   x)x   x) x   x)   (four iambic feet)
>
> And on the <u>ships</u> at <u>sea</u>.
> x   x)   x   x) x   x)   (three iambic feet)

In this notation, the crosses and brackets mark out the poem's metre: that is, its underlying metrical pattern. The closing brackets divide the lines into iambic feet. But they also indicate that the beat falls on the second part of each foot.

17.3   Metre and rhythm

We can now point out the difference between metre and rhythm. The rhythm is what the lines sound like when read aloud (or heard in the head); the rhythm is indicated by underlining the syllables that would normally be stressed in an oral perform-ance. The metre of a poem is an abstract organization to which the rhythm approximates: the underlying metrical pattern as indicated by the pattern of crosses and brackets. The metre of each line is given a name (see below) that indicates:

(1)   the type of foot in the line;
(2)   how many feet there are in the line.

In Stevenson's poem, the metre alternates between iambic tetrameter (four iambic feet) and iambic trimeter (three iambic feet). This particular metrical pattern is sometimes called 'ballad metre', because it is often found in ballads. But the same metre can also be found in much 'art' poetry as well. Not all metrical poems vary their metre in this way; in most metrical poems, the metre is the same in every line.

The fact that the majority of the stressed syllables in 'Rain' coincide with beats in the underlying metrical pattern (the crosses marked by brackets) shows that the rhythms of this poem tend to fulfil the requirements of the metrical pattern. However, there are a few discrepancies, or tensions, between the poem's metre and its rhythm. Although the first and third lines are both in iambic tetrameter, they have slightly different rhythms. This can be seen by looking at the pattern of stressed and unstressed syllables. While the word 'the' in the third line coincides with the expected beat of the underlying metre, it is unlikely to be stressed in performance (though there is nothing to prevent a performer from stressing it). Also, although our scansion of the final line makes it a neat fit with the metre, it is possible to imagine two other fairly natural-sounding stress patterns in performance, either stressing 'and' instead of 'on' or stressing neither:

```
And  on  the  ships  at  sea
x    x)   x   x)    x   x)

And  on  the  ships  at  sea
x    x)   x   x)    x   x)
```

In this way, there is potential variation between the underlying (and unpronounced) pattern of the metre (its abstract structure) and the pronounced pattern of the rhythm (how it is realized in a given performance). When we read or listen to a metrical poem, we may attempt to match the abstract pattern (the metre) in our head against the actual pattern (the rhythm) that we are hearing or performing, so producing various kinds of local mismatch or 'metrical tension'. Metrical tensions ensure that the oral performance of poetry will not normally sound like a repetitive mechanical sound, or clockwork. Such tensions also have other effects: they can foreground complex relationships between sound and meaning; they can draw attention to key aspects of meaning and emphasis; and they can produce aesthetic, musical effects.

17.4 Possible metrical patterns and their names

We have seen that metrical patterns (metres) are conventionally named after the type of foot and the number of feet in a line. So far, we have looked at iambic trimeter and iambic tetrameter. But there are other possible line lengths:

dimeter	two feet
trimeter	three feet
tetrameter	four feet
pentameter	five feet
hexameter	six feet
heptameter	seven feet

There are also other possible kinds of foot in English: two binary (or duple) feet, and two ternary (or triple) feet:

iambic foot (iamb)	two beats, second is stressed (rising duple)
trochaic foot (trochee)	two beats, initial is stressed (falling duple)
anapaestic foot (anapaest)	three beats, third is stressed (rising triple)
dactylic foot (dactyl)	three beats, first is stressed (falling triple)

Consider the first verse of Christina Rossetti's 'In the Bleak Midwinter' (1872). This poem follows a trochaic metre, but has varying numbers of feet in each line:

> In the bleak mid-winter
> Frosty wind made moan,
> Earth stood hard as iron,
> Water like a stone;
> Snow had fallen, snow on snow,
> Snow on snow,
> In the bleak mid-winter
> Long ago.

Lines 5–7 can be scanned as follows (note that line 7 permits various other possible rhythms, some closer to the metre and some further from it). Because the initial beats of trochaic feet are stressed (rather than the second beats, as in an iambic metre), the bracket – now shown as an opening bracket – comes before the initial cross of each foot:

```
Snow had fallen, snow on snow,
 (x   x  (x  x    (x  x   (x     = trochaic tetrameter

Snow on snow,
 (x   x   (x                     = trochaic dimeter

In the bleak mid-winter
(x   x   (x    x  (x   x         = trochaic trimeter
```

In these lines we see another kind of variation. In two cases, a foot at the end of the line contains only one syllable when it might be expected to contain two. This shortening of a foot at the end of a line is called 'catalexis'; it is one of the conventional variations in English verse. In trochaic metres the short foot comes at the end of the line, whereas in iambic metres it comes at the beginning.

The metrical pattern of Lady Mary Wortley Montagu's 'The Lover: A Ballad' (1747) is anapaestic tetrameter (four-beat rising triple metre). This can be seen clearly in the second stanza:

```
But I hate to be cheated, and never will buy
 x  x  x)   x  x   x) x   x   x)x   x    x)

Long years of repentance for moments of joy.
 x     x)   x   x x) x    x    x)x    x    x)

Oh was there a man (but where shall I find
 x   x)    x   x  x)    x   x)    x   x  x)
```

```
Good sense and good nature so equally joined?)
 x    x)   x    x    x)x    x x)x   x   x)

Would value his pleasure, contribute to mine,
 x     x)x   x   x)  x    x   x)x   x   x)

Not meanly would boast, nor would lewdly design,
 x    x)  x   x    x)    x    x    x)   x  x  x)

Not over severe, yet not stupidly vain,
 x  x)x   x x)   x   x    x)x   x  x)

For I would have the power though not give the pain.
 x   x   x)   x     x  x)x    x    x)  x    x   x)
```

In these lines, the stressed syllables tend to be three syllables apart; so they form three-syllable feet, in which the final syllable tends to be stressed. Three-syllable feet with a final stress (rising triplets) are called anapaests (see above); so the underlying metrical pattern of these lines is anapaestic tetrameter (because there are four anapaestic feet in each line). Note that the initial foot in the lines sometimes consists of only two syllables (rather than three); this indicates catalexis, and hence variation between lines. Metres are rigid templates that nevertheless open up various opportunities or 'loopholes' for variation, in length or rhythm. Metre also makes possible, as we have seen, some interesting tensions between underlying pattern and oral performance.

While there is a general tendency in the lines quoted for the third syllable of the foot to be stressed, in conformity with the metrical pattern, other syllables might also be stressed as well. This appears to be the case in the final line, where a stress on 'I' rather than 'would' would subtly change the meaning and sets up a tension between rhythm and metre. The possible stressing of 'I' in oral performance (or in how the line is heard in the head when reading silently) would largely depend on the performer's sense of where the emphasis (of rhythm and meaning) should lie. Note also how the third foot of the third line breaks with the metrical pattern, by consisting of only two syllables ('but where'); this variation perhaps enhances the speaker's sense of urgency or despair at finding a man of good sense and good nature.

The fourth kind of foot, dactyls (or falling triplets), is quite rare in English. The poet Samuel Taylor Coleridge devised a way of remembering their metrical pattern, and the typical effect or association they create: 'Dactyls are stately and classical'. Thomas Hood's 'The Bridge of Sighs' (1844) is written using dactylic dimeter:

```
Look at her garments
(x    x   x  (x   x

Clinging like cerements;
 (x   x    x    (x x  x
```

```
Whilst the wave constantly
 (x     x  x  (x   x   x

Drips from her clothing;
 (x     x  x  (x  x

Take her up instantly,
(x    x  x (x   x   x

Loving, not loathing.
(x x     x  (x   x
```

The feet are dactyls because the stressed syllables tend to fall three syllables apart and the stressed syllable comes first. The lines are in dactylic dimeter because there are two dactylic feet per line. Yet the metre allows for considerable metrical and rhythmic variation. The final feet in the first, fourth and sixth lines fall short; and in a performance we might want to stress 'wave' in the third line, even though it does not coincide with a stressed beat in the metrical pattern. Lines that are in the same metre can nevertheless vary both in length and in rhythm.

17.5 'Foot substitution'

The most common method of metrical analysis, which we are modifying a little here, includes a notion of 'foot substitution'. We explain below why we do not adopt this aspect of metrical analysis here, but first we should explain how the notion of 'foot substitution' is supposed to work. The following lines come from 'Epistle I' of Alexander Pope's *An Essay on Man* (1733–34), a long poem in iambic pentameter:

```
And catch the manners living as they rise
x    x)    x  x) x   x)x   x)   x   x)

Eye Nature's walks, shoot folly as it flies,
x   x)x      x)     x    x) x x) x    x)
```

Establish metre first: Pope's poem is in iambic pentameter because the vast majority of its lines have five iambic feet: five beat rising duple metre. When we read a poem that keeps to a regular metre, we internalize that pattern and notice when a line deviates from it. Once the pattern is established, mismatches between the regular metrical pattern and the more flexible rhythm are recognized as rhythmic variations. In the first of these lines, a mismatch of this kind is created by the word 'as', which would not normally be stressed but which coincides with the stressed beat of the underlying metre. In the second line quoted, there are then more drastic mismatches between rhythm and metre, involving the first and fifth syllables: both carry stress but are in positions in the metre that do not require stress. There is also a mismatch in the eighth syllable, which does not carry stress but is in a position where the metre requires stress.

To account for the way in which the rhythm in the second of these lines gets so out of step with the metre, a traditional method of metrical analysis would typically claim that the metrical form had changed to match the rhythm, by replacing the expected iambic feet with other types of foot:

```
Eye Na   ture's walks,  shoot fol ly as    it flies,
x    x) x      x)       x   x)  x x)   x    x)
spondee iamb             spondee  pyrrhic iamb [substitutes]
```

In the notation here, the likely rhythm in performance has been indicated by underlining the syllables that would be stressed; the expected iambic pattern is shown by the crosses and brackets. Underneath, we have indicated the names of the feet that traditional analysis would claim have replaced the iambs.

Traditional analysis would suggest that two of the iambic feet have been replaced with 'spondees' (feet with two successive stressed beats) and that another iambic foot has been replaced with a 'pyrrhic' foot (a foot with no stressed beats). These two 'mutant' feet (spondee and pyrrhic) are found in English verse only as substitutions; that is why we did not mention them in 17.4 above. There is a problem with this approach to metrical analysis, however. It is based on an assumption that feet are a component of the *rhythm* of the line. We have suggested that this is not the case. Feet are a component of *metre*. Rhythm – the actual performance of the line – does not consist of feet, but should be thought of as an oral or imagined performance that may conform to or deviate from the underlying metrical pattern.

The only occasions when the notion of 'foot substitution' remains useful occur when the notion is used to describe particularly common rhythmic variations that benefit from being given a name; the most common of these is when an iambic line begins with a 'stressed–unstressed' sequence, as in the following lines from Aemilia Lanyer's 'The Description of Cooke-ham' (1611). The lines are addressed to Margaret Clifford, Countess of Cumberland, who lived in the house being described in the poem:

> The trees with leaves, with fruits, with flowers clad,
> Embraced each other, seeming to be glad,
> Turning themselves to beauteous Canopies,
> To shade the bright sun from your brighter eyes

The poem as a whole is in iambic pentameter. But *rhythmically* the third of these lines begins with a stressed–unstressed sequence that is in counterpoint to the iambic pattern. If this sequence were to be continued through the whole line, then we might describe the line as a trochaic pentameter line that stands out from the dominant iambic pentameter pattern. However, the deviation only occurs in the first two syllables. A conventional analysis would call this effect 'trochaic substitution' or 'trochaic inversion'. To this extent, the term remains perhaps a useful shorthand, or indicator of a common variation in iambic pentameter.

17.6 Extra (and missing) syllables in a line

We have seen how metrical verse allows for catalexis, when one or two syllables go missing at the beginning or end of a line and a metrical foot falls short as a result. We now look at two ways in which metrical lines can vary by including additional, so-called 'extrametrical' syllables. Both of these ways of having 'extra' syllables are fairly common in English verse, particularly in iambic verse.

In iambic verse, an extra syllable can optionally appear at the end of the line:

> With fingers light the lingering breezes quiver
> Over the glowing of the still, deep river,
> Whose water sings among the reeds, and smiles
> 'Mid glittering forests and luxuriant isles.
>
> (John Ruskin, untitled, 1836)

The first two lines of this extract can each be divided into five iambic feet plus an extrametrical syllable at the end. The extrametricality of the final syllable is cued by the fact that it forms part of a so-called 'feminine rhyme' (a multisyllabic rhyme word in which the final syllable is unstressed, see **Unit 16, Rhyme and sound patterning**):

```
With fingers light the lingering breezes quiver
 x    x) x   x)     x  x)   x      x) x   x) x
```

This line also illustrates a further respect in which a syllable can be 'extra'. The word 'lingering' normally has three syllables; but here it counts as two. This suggests that one syllable is ignored when the syllables are grouped into metrical feet. It is possible to mark out the 'ignored' syllables (while remembering that they do not affect the actual foot size), by writing a different kind of symbol beneath them (here we use a delta, a little triangle, to mark the uncounted syllable):

```
With fingers light the lingering breezes quiver
 x    x) x   x)     x  x) Δ x      x) x   x) x
```

The seventeenth-century poet John Donne made extensive use of uncounted syllables, particularly vowels before vowels. His use is so extensive, in fact, that many readers have found it difficult to work out the relation between the performed rhythm of some of his poems and their underlying metre.

17.7 Strong-stress or accentual metre

This unit began with a clear claim: that metrical verse controls both the number of syllables and the number of stresses per line. For this reason, such metre is described as accentual-syllabic (where 'accent' is another word for 'stress'). We have also seen, however, that accentual-syllabic metre does allow limited metrical and rhythmical variation, including both the losing and gaining of syllables. There is also another way of having 'extra' syllables that constitutes an entirely new metre: one we have not looked at so far. The resulting metre has been given many names: 'Christabel metre', 'dol'nik' or 'iambic-anapaestic metre'. We will call it 'strong-stress' or 'accentual' metre, because its dominant feature is that, while it controls the number of stresses in lines (usually four), it can vary considerably in the number of syllables that appear in lines.

Variation in the number of syllables between stresses in 'strong-stress' or 'accentual' metre is made possible by the fact that the four-beat pattern is so insistent. The pattern is very familiar, because it is found in virtually all popular (i.e. non-classical) song forms: nursery rhymes, folk songs, ballads, hymns, blues, pop songs, rock songs, and so on. Four-beat strong-stress metre is also found in poetry that derives from songs or imitates song forms. It features, too, in much folk poetry, particularly ballads and nursery rhymes, as well as in art poetry that imitates folk poetry such as William Blake's *Songs of Innocence and of Experience* (1794), and in much twentieth-century metrical verse.

Consider the beginning of a nursery rhyme, 'The love-sick frog' (recorded since 1809), which is discussed from another point of view in **Unit 2, Using information sources.** The extract illustrates the metre, but also shows up shortcomings in the descriptive terminology used above:

A frog he would a-wooing go,	[loose iambic tetrameter]
Heigh ho! says Rowley,	[loose iambic trimeter]
A frog he would a-wooing go,	[loose iambic tetrameter]
Whether his mother would let him or no.	[loose iambic tetrameter]
With a rowley, powley, gammon and spinach,	[loose iambic tetrameter]
Heigh ho! says Anthony Rowley.	[loose iambic trimeter (?)]

The line 'With a rowley, powley, gammon and spinach' shows why the metre is sometimes called 'iambic-anapaestic': there seems to be a mixture of iambic and anapaestic feet in it:

```
With a rowley, powley, gammon and spinach
 x   x  x) x    x) x    x) x  x    x)x
```

Like most of the other lines, this line cannot be fitted into any one of the metrical templates we have looked at so far. The only pattern that does remain constant in strong-stress verse is the organization of the number of stresses in each line. In this nursery rhyme, stresses vary irregularly between three and four (whereas, in a ballad stanza as we have seen, the stress pattern regularly alternates between three and four stresses). In strong-stress verse, we might say, rhythm and metre are much more closely related to one another than in the metres we have looked at above. The 'counterpointing' of a varying rhythm against a strict metre seems not to be what is happening. Instead, the rhythm largely determines where the metrical beats fall. As a general principle, wherever there is a strongly stressed syllable in the line this is treated as the realization of a stressed beat. The number of unstressed syllables between the strongly stressed syllables can vary from none to three. So it is possible for two strongly stressed syllables to be immediately next to each other:

```
Heigh ho! says Rowley,
 x)    x)   x    x) x
```

(Note here the extrametrical syllable at the end of the line.) Because rhythm significantly determines metre here, different performances will give the line different metrical forms; here are two alternatives for the last line:

```
Heigh ho! says Anthony Rowley.
 x      x)  x   x)   x x  x) x

Heigh ho! says Anthony Rowley.
 x)     x)  x   x)   x x  x) x
```

Variability in the number of syllables in strong-stress verse is highlighted in a more obviously literary context in the first stanza of Blake's 'Nurse's Song', from *Songs of Innocence* (1789), in the form of a **ballad stanza**:

> When the voices of children are heard on the green
> And laughing is heard on the hill,
> My heart is at rest within my breast
> And everything else is still.

While the first line has twelve syllables (and four stresses), the third line has only nine syllables (and four stresses). A still more striking version of strong-stress metre was developed by the poet Gerard Manley Hopkins, which he called 'sprung rhythm'. In Hopkins's poetry, even longer stretches (of three or more syllables) are permitted between beats.

17.8 Free verse

In metrical verse, the length of a line is measured according to a predetermined pattern of syllables and stresses (or of stresses only, in strong-stress verse). Verse whose lines are not measured in this way is non-metrical verse, or **free verse**.

In free verse, there is no predetermined pattern to control how the text is divided into lines. Consider, for example, the following lines from William Blake's 'Vala, or the Four Zoas' (1797–1807):

> They sing unceasing to the notes of my immortal hand.
> The solemn, silent moon
> Reverberates the living harmony upon my limbs,
> The birds & beasts rejoice & play,
> And every one seeks for his mate to prove his inmost joy.

A count of the syllables and stresses in these lines shows that there is no underlying metrical pattern. We might therefore ask what the principle of line division is. Lineation (or division into lines) does not coincide with units of syntax, for instance, as some lines are sentences but others are not. Some lines end on pauses, while others do not. Nor is there any rhyme, or sound patterning, or parallelism to organize the lines, in the way that a metrical pattern would do. Such lack of a consistent pattern in how a text (that is in some way still poetry) is divided into lines results in it being thought of as 'free verse'. The King James Bible arguably consists of verse of this kind, and is a known influence on Blake. Since the early twentieth century, free verse has become a common type of verse.

17.9 The significance of metre

When reading verse texts, one question worth asking is whether different kinds of structure in it match up, or whether they involve some kind of mismatch. What kind of relationship, we might ask, is there between division into metrical lines and division on the basis of syntax (i.e. into sentences, clauses, phrases)? Matches or mismatches between line division and syntax may give rise to aesthetic effects created by **coherence** or tension; and the overall tendency in a text towards or away from such tension might reflect aesthetic attitudes characteristic of the time of writing.

One kind of mismatch, where the grammar of a sentence continues across a line ending, is called 'enjambment'. This effect can be found throughout Wordsworth's *The Prelude* (1805), as in the following lines:

> And there, with fingers interwoven, both hands
> Press'd closely, palm to palm, and to his mouth
> Uplifted, . . .

(V, 395–7)

Each line ends with a noun; but the syntax leads us to expect that a verb or modifying phrase will follow those nouns, and this expectation leads us to read on across the line ending, rather than seeing the line ending as fully an ending. Such mismatches between syntactic structure and line structure are common in this poem; and they give the impression that verse and thought are unconstrained by formal conventions – an effect that fits with the Romantic poets' emphasis on what Wordsworth called 'the spontaneous overflow of powerful feelings' and what Shelley called 'unpremeditated art'. For much of the eighteenth century, by contrast, especially in work influenced by neoclassical values, priority in poetry and in other arts was accorded to values such as rational control, balance and predetermined artistic rules. The opening lines of Oliver Goldsmith's 'The Deserted Village' (1770) were published in a period when the assumptions of neoclassicism were in decline; but they reveal a very different metrical aesthetic from that of *The Prelude*, despite the fact that both poems are in iambic pentameter:

> Sweet Auburn! loveliest village of the plain,
> Where health and plenty cheered the labouring swain,
> Where smiling spring its earliest visit paid,
> And parting summer's lingering blooms delayed.

Each of the first two lines of this opening passage of the poem ends with a noun, as in the extract from *The Prelude*. But those nouns complete the syntax of the line of which they are the final word. The first line could easily be re-punctuated as a sentence in its own right. Alternatively, the first two lines together could be punctuated as a complete sentence. There is no enjambment and no sense that thought and feeling are overflowing, or are in tension with, the confines of line structure. A sense of stability within the constraints of the metre is reinforced by use of rhyming couplets, and the overall effect created is of a very different kind of aesthetic ideology from that of the Romantic poets.

For each text below, identify the metre by:

1 counting the number of syllables per line;

2 counting the number of stresses per line;

3 identifying the type of foot, and the number of feet per line;

4 selecting an appropriate label for the metre using the terminology presented in 17.4 above.

ACTIVITY 17

continued

Text A

Come, and mark within what bush
Builds the blackbird or the thrush;
Great his joy who first espies
Greater his who spares the prize.

(from Hannah More, 'Inscription in a Beautiful
Retreat Called Fairy Bower', 1774)

Text B

The boy stood on the burning deck
Whence all but he had fled;
The flame that lit the battle's wreck
Shone round him o'er the dead.

(from Felicia Dorothea Hemans,
'Casabianca', 1826)

Text C

Sweet are the blossoms the summer adorning
Shed in profusion o'er meadow and lea,
Decked with the charms of the dew-sprinkled morning
Ere the sun's spangles dry blossom and tree.

(from John Clare, 'Ballad', 1835)

Text D

The critics say that epics have died out
With Agamemnon and the goat-nursed gods;
I'll not believe it. I could never deem,
As Payne Knight did (the mythic mountaineer
Who travelled higher than he was born to live,
And showed sometimes the goitre in his throat
Discoursing of an image seen through fog),
That Homer's heroes measured twelve feet high.

(from Elizabeth Barrett Browning,
Aurora Leigh, Book 5, 1857)

Text E
Sing on there in the swamp,
O singer bashful and tender, I hear your notes, I hear
   your call,
I hear, I come presently, I understand you,
But a moment I linger, for the lustrous star has detain'd me,
The star my departing comrade holds and detains me.

(from Walt Whitman, 'When Lilacs Last in
the Dooryard Bloom'd', 1881)

Reading

Attridge, D. (1996) *Poetic Rhythm: An Introduction*, Cambridge: Cambridge University Press.

Attridge, D. (2004) *The Rhythms of English Poetry*, London: Longman.

Carper, T. and Attridge, D. (2003) *Meter and Meaning: An Introduction to Rhythm in Poetry*, London: Routledge.

Fabb, N. (2002) *Language and Literary Structure*, Cambridge: Cambridge University Press, Chapters 1, 2 and 4.

Fabb, N. and Halle, M. (2008) *The Meter of a Poem: A New Theory*, Cambridge: Cambridge University Press.

Furniss, T. and Bath, M.(2007) *Reading Poetry: An Introduction*, 2nd edn, London: Pearson Longman, Chapters 2 and 3.

Fussell, P. (1979) *Poetic Meter and Poetic Form*, New York: McGraw-Hill.

UNIT 18

Parallelism

UNIT 18

This unit:

- introduces the concept of 'parallelism', as a contrived combination of similarity and contrast between elements in a text that serves to create additional meanings and effects;

- shows how to analyse parallelism through a worked example;

- describes and assesses the main functions of parallelism, as well as the different kinds of texts (both literary and non-literary) in which it commonly occurs.

Parallelism occurs where two close or adjacent sections of a text are presented as being similar or contrasting in some respect that is relevant to their interpretation. The fact that the elements in question are arranged close to one another gives parallelism a resemblance to the wider phenomenon of juxtaposition (see **Unit 12, Juxtaposition**). But with parallelism the closeness of elements concerns more than adjacency: it also involves structural similarity.

18.1   Kinds of parallelism

Sometimes the relation between the parallel elements in a text is one of lexical similarity: the arranged words are similar (or opposite) in meaning. Sometimes the similarity is formal (e.g. likeness in terms of rhyme, alliteration or metre). The limit case of similarity is exact repetition; but most cases of parallelism involve partial similarity: a combination of similarity and difference.

A combination of similarity and difference can be seen in the following example from John Donne's 'Sermon at St Paul's', 1625:

> so in the agonies of Death, in the anguish of that dissolution, in the sorrows of that valediction, in the irreversableness of that transmigration, I shall have a joy which shall no more evaporate than my soul shall evaporate, a joy that shall passe up and put on a more glorious garment above, and be joy superinvested in glory.

In this passage there are several parallelisms. The first – between 'in the agonies of Death' and 'in the anguish of that dissolution' – involves all three kinds of parallelism mentioned above. The syntactic structure is virtually the same (in the X of Y); the words are similar in meaning ('agonies'/'anguish'; 'Death'/'dissolution'); and there is the formal parallelism of the alliteration. (There are further parallelisms in the passage, too, which you may find it instructive to look for.)

Parallelisms can be distinguished according to different levels of textual material or structure they involve. At the level of narrative structure, we can talk about parallelism between plots, or parallelism between characters. A narrative has component parts, such as distinct sub-plots, episodes, characters and objects, and any or all of these components can be involved in parallelism. It is not uncommon, for example, for a sub-plot to parallel a main plot (as happens in Shakespeare's *A Midsummer Night's Dream* (1596)). A narrative might be arranged in parallel episodes, possibly organized according to some numerical principle such as 'in pairs' or 'in triplets' (e.g. two incidents of one kind, followed by two incidents of another, or alternatively three of each). It is also common to have characters in a narrative who are similar at some level of abstract description, while being opposites on the surface: there may for example be a parallelism between the hero and the villain (e.g. in the *Harry Potter* series there are a number of parallelisms between Harry Potter and Voldemort).

At different levels of language we can also distinguish kinds of parallelism. 'Lexical parallelism' involves parallelism of meaning between words (hence 'lexical'); 'syntactic parallelism' (parallelism of sentence structure) is parallelism between two sections of text that have similar syntactic form; and 'phonological parallelism' is parallelism involving sounds. Within phonological parallelism there are then several kinds; and of these some are also found in prose, not only in poetry (as we have seen in the extract from Donne's sermon). The most common type of phonological parallelism in English literature consists of the repetition of units of sound at the end or beginning of nearby syllables, as in rhyme and alliteration (see **Unit 16: Rhyme and sound patterning**). Another type, which is developed systematically in some literary traditions, is parallelism between two longer sequences of sounds; this is a sort of 'parallelism between parallelisms', and could be called sound-pattern parallelism. Examples are found in the technique of *cynghanedd* ('harmony') in Welsh poetry, where a sequence of consonants in the first half of a poetic line is repeated in the second half of the line. The Welsh-born poet Gerard Manley Hopkins adapted this technique in some of his English-language poems. Another type of phonological parallelism is metre. As we saw in **Unit 17, Verse, rhythm and metre**, although the lines of a metrical poem will differ in their meanings, syntax and sounds, they will nevertheless be rhythmically similar to one another to the extent that they conform to an underlying metrical pattern.

Most parallelisms have two members, and so are called 'binary parallelisms'. Others have three parts ('ternary parallelisms'), and some more than this. The following passage from Longfellow's *The Song of Hiawatha* (1855) is characteristic of the text as a whole in employing extended parallelism. Note how lines 2 and 3 form a binary parallelism; how line 4 contains a binary parallelism; and how lines 4–8 make up a four-part parallelism:

> Should you ask where Nawadaha
> Found these songs so wild and wayward,
> Found these legends and traditions,
> I should answer, I should tell you,
> 'In the bird's-nests of the forest,   (5)
> In the lodges of the beaver,
> In the hoofprint of the bison,
> In the eyry of the eagle!'
>
> (Henry Wadsworth Longfellow, *The Song of Hiawatha*, 1855)

The lines quoted here also contain alliterative parallelism: 'wild and wayward', 'beaver' and 'bison', and 'eyry' and 'eagle'. They also contain metrical parallelism, in that all the lines are in trochaic tetrameter (four-beat falling duple metre).

When words are brought together by parallelism, the words in question are typically similar in some respect but different in another respect. One level of similarity or difference between them that is of particular interest is the level of meaning. A pair or larger set of words belonging to the same 'area' of meaning are said to form part of a 'semantic field': a set of words with various kinds of relation to one another, including likeness or even interchangeability of meaning (synonymy), instances of a more general type (a hyponym is a particular case of a wider class), part of a whole (a meronym is a part or aspect of some larger whole) and opposition of meaning (antonymy). Where the two meanings are in opposition what is created is 'polar parallelism', because the words are at opposite poles as far as meaning is concerned. Such polar opposition contrasts with non-polar parallelism, of a kind that can be seen in the opening lines of Wordsworth's 'Tintern Abbey' (1798):

> Five years have past; five summers, with the length
> Of five long winters!

We can illustrate the parallelism in these lines by means of the following layout:

	Five	years	have past;
	five	summers,	with the length /
Of	five	long	winters!

In this example, there is a triple parallelism. The first two members ('years' and 'summers') are in a whole-to-part relation (because a year contains a summer); the second and third members ('summers' and 'winters') are in polar opposition (because summer is the opposite of winter). Polar parallelisms often draw on pre-existing cultural oppositions, such as culture versus nature, or masculine versus feminine, and allow thoughts, beliefs and attitudes to be conveyed without being directly stated.

In structural parallelism (that is, parallelism in the structural arrangement of elements in a sentence, or grammar), the parallel elements need not be structured identically. One member of the parallelism can omit a word or phrase (in an 'ellipsis') which is supplied from the context. Consider this proverb:

> Excellent speech becometh not a fool;
> Much less do lying lips a prince.

(Proverbs, 17, 7)

The parallelism can be shown as follows:

	Excellent speech becometh not	a fool;
Much less do lying	lips	a prince.

The second member of the parallelism has no verb; but it is easy to supply that verb ('becometh') from the previous line ('becometh' here means 'suit' or 'fit').

As a result, the second member can be read as 'much less do lying lips *becometh a prince*'. (Ellipsis can also occur in the first member of a parallelism, where the missing word or phrase has to be inferred from the second member.)

A **chiasmus** (or chiasm) is a syntactic parallelism in which the order of elements out of which the parallelism is created is reversed. ('Chiasmus' comes from the Greek 'chi', the name for the Greek letter χ, which in this context emblematically represents the crossing over of the parts.) Chiasmus occurs in the proverb quoted above, in that the syntactic sequence of the first line (which places the negating word 'not' after the noun and verb) is partially reversed in the second line (where the negating phrase 'much less' comes before the noun). Or consider the following example:

> Oft did the harvest to their sickle yield,
> Their furrow oft the stubborn glebe has broke;
> > (Thomas Gray, 'Elegy Written in a Country Churchyard', 1751)

To draw attention to the parallelism, we can set out these lines as follows:

> Oft did the harvest to their sickle yield,
>   A   B   C   D
>
> Their furrow oft the stubborn glebe has broke;
>   C   A   B   D

Here, 'the harvest' and 'the stubborn glebe' (an area of farm land) are lexically parallel: one is the product of the soil, the other is the soil itself. 'Their sickle' and 'their furrow' are also lexically parallel: they both relate to farming activities. But the two parallel pairs are reversed in the two lines, and so create an instance of chiasmus. Note too that a further parallelism occurs between 'did ... yield' and 'has broke', in which the former member ('did ... yield') is split in the line, with other words in between.

18.2 Analysing parallelism

Parallelisms typically work together, sometimes in highly complex ways. As a sustained example, consider the beginning of Pope's *An Essay on Man* (1733):

> Awake, my St. John! leave all meaner things
> To low ambition, and the pride of kings.
> Let us (since life can little more supply
> Than just to look about us and to die)
> Expatiate free o'er all this scene of man;   5
> A mighty maze! but not without a plan;

A wild, where weeds and flow'rs promiscuous shoot;
Or garden, tempting with forbidden fruit.
Together let us beat this ample field,
Try what the open, what the covert yield;   10
The latent tracts, the giddy heights explore
Of all who blindly creep, or sightless soar;
Eye Nature's walks, shoot folly as it flies,
And catch the manners living as they rise;
Laugh where we must, be candid where we can;   15
But vindicate the ways of God to man.

This is a highly-parallelistic poem on a phonological level: it takes the form of rhyming couplets in iambic pentameter. In addition, the poem makes intensive use of syntactic parallelism, as can be seen by rearranging parallel segments on the page, one above the other wherever possible. In cases where there are parallelisms between parts of text at some distance from one another, parallelism can still be reflected in layout, but is more difficult to see (e.g. between 'leave all meaner things' (in line 1) and 'expatiate free o'er all this scene of man' (in line 5)). Further, the text appears to be divided into four sections, each of which is internally consistent as regards meaning (see **Unit 3, Analysing units of structure**). In the notation below, we use forward slashes to indicate line boundaries. It is possible to analyse any parallelistic text in this way: you do not need any special knowledge (e.g. of grammar), and can carry out an analysis by looking at meanings alone. (If you try to set out parallelisms using a computer, use an evenly-spaced font such as Courier to control vertical alignments, and avoid using the tab key.)

A (lines 1–2):

```
Awake, my St. John!
leave                   all meaner things /

To     low   ambition,
and          the pride of kings. /
```

B (lines 3–8):

```
Let us ...
Expatiate free o'er  all this scene of man; /

A mighty maze!  but not without a plan; /
A         wild,  where weeds
                    and flow'rs promiscuous shoot; /
Or        garden, tempting with forbidden fruit. /
```

C (lines 9–14):

```
Together
        let us beat                                    this ample field, /
                Try what the open,
                    what the covert yield; /

        The    latent    tracts,
        the    giddy     heights   explore /
Of all who blindly    creep, or
                sightless   soar; /

        Eye    Nature's walks,
        shoot folly                       as it flies, /
And    catch the manners      living as they rise; /
```

D (lines 15–16):

```
        Laugh                          where we must,
        be candid                      where we can; /
But vindicate the ways of God
                                to man. /
```

(Note: 'expatiate' (5) means both to wander freely and also to write about at length; and 'wild' (6) is used here as a noun. Section C employs an extended metaphor from hunting: beating the field with sticks to drive the animals being hunted into view.)

By laying out a poem in this way, we can see clearly some of the ways in which parallelism works in this text:

(1) Note the placement of line endings: often a member ends at the end of a line; alternatively, two members are sometimes found in the same line. In this way parallelism (in this poem and in many others) varies in how it operates relative to line boundaries, but generally respects or is sensitive to line boundaries.

(2) The parallelisms are generally binary (two members); but ternary parallelisms (i.e. ones involving three members) appear at the end of the sections we have looked at (sections B, C and D). These sections were distinguished on the basis that they have a unified meaning; but we can see that use of ternary rather than binary parallelism can function as a formal cue to the end of a section.

(3) There are some chiasms (though not many). Most prominently, 'low ambition' forms one with 'the pride of kings', where we have an AB:BA pattern, if we interpret 'low' to mean 'associated with people of low social rank', and therefore to contrast with 'kings'.

(4) Parallelism is sometimes obvious, but sometimes much less obvious. In this extract, the whole passage employs a parallelism involving members that are exhortations or commands. 'Leave all meaner things' has a parallel in section B, '(let us) expatiate free o'er all this scene of man', as well as in section C, 'let us beat this ample field', and in section D, 'laugh ... be candid ... vindicate the ways of God to man'.

(5) Parallelism does not necessarily respect syntactic (grammatical) structure. For instance, the adjective 'low' functions as an opposite to the noun 'kings', so different word classes can be involved. Also, members of a parallelism are not always coherent syntactic units, as in 'Try [what the open :: what the covert] yield'. These units would only be coherent syntactically if they were structured as 'Try [what the open yields :: what the covert yields]'. In this way parallelism largely respects syntactic structure, but can sometimes violate it.

(6) The passage draws extensively on the semantic field of 'looking' (e.g. 'look about us', 'blindly', 'sightless' and 'eye'). This semantic field overarches the other parallelisms, as a kind of extended parallelism of its own.

(7) There are some highly conventional parallelisms. Here most clearly there is the parallelism between 'God' and 'man', which is very common in English poetry. Implicitly there is also a culture–nature parallelism (also very common elsewhere) in, for example, the opposition between the 'wild' and the 'garden'.

(8) Underlying and shaping all these parallelisms is a highly parallelistic use of closed couplets and iambic pentameter.

Summing up such an analysis, we might say that parallelism is an organizational principle that matches, to some extent, other organizational principles in the passage, such as its lineation and syntactic structure, but which is also in a kind of 'counterpoint' with them. (We introduced the notion of such matching and counterpointing effects in **Unit 17, Verse, rhythm and metre**, when discussing the tension that can be created between rhythm and metre in poetry.) Formal complexity can itself be part of the goal of a poem, functioning as a display of compositional skill and giving pleasure. But the passage quoted here also has an argumentative purpose: it is an 'essay on man'. Its foregrounding, by means of parallelism, of similarities and differences between man and animals, between God and man, and between culture and nature is a technique through which form and content are interrelated.

18.3 Functions of parallelism

Parallelism is a formal practice, or technique. This means that it is a way of organizing the material from which a text is made: both the forms of the language (the words and sentence structures) and the text's meanings. As a formal practice, parallelism is widespread in most kinds of English literary discourse, as well as in the literature of other languages. In the verse traditions of some languages, semantic and syntactic parallelism play an organizational role equivalent to (and often instead of) parallelism of metrical form (for detailed discussion see Fabb, 1997). Parallelism is also found in different genres. In English it can be found not only in poetry, but also in religious texts (such as the 'Authorized' translation of the Bible of 1611), in advertising, in political speeches, in spoken anecdotes and jokes, and so on. Martin Luther King's 'I have a dream' speech at the Lincoln Memorial, Washington DC (28 August 1963), is also known for making striking use of parallelism in calling for full civil rights for black people in the United States. Aspects of parallelism worth noting include its amount of repetition, and the fact that its four-unit structure concludes with a unit that, unlike the others, does not participate fully in the parallelism previously established: 'I have a dream today!' In this closing variation, we see use of formal difference to mark the end of a section (in the extract from Pope's poem quoted above, the formal difference that achieves this involved not less but more parallelism).

In the nineteenth century, Gerard Manley Hopkins suggested that parallelism accounted for virtually all aspects of verbal art in poetry:

> The artificial part of poetry . . . reduces itself to the principle of parallelism. . . . But parallelism is of two kinds necessarily . . . the first kind . . . is concerned with the structure of verse – in rhythm, the recurrence of a certain sequence of syllables, in metre, the recurrence of a certain sequence of rhythm, in alliteration, in assonance and in rhyme. Now the force of this recurrence is to beget a recurrence or parallelism answering to it in the words or thought and, speaking roughly, . . . the more marked parallelism in structure . . . begets more marked parallelism in the words and sense. . . . To the [other] kind of parallelism belong metaphor, simile, parable, and so on, where the effect is sought in likeness of things, and antithesis, contrast, and so on, where it is sought in unlikeness.
>
> (quoted in Jakobson, 1990, pp. 82–3)

Interestingly, Hopkins points out that figurative language (metaphor, simile and parable) constitutes a kind of parallelism. He also suggests that formal parallelism 'begets' (causes or creates) parallelism in words or thought. As we have seen, syntactic or phonological parallelism invites the reader actively to look for similarity or difference in meaning between the two or more segments of text that the parallelism brings together for consideration.

The influential linguist and literary commentator Roman Jakobson (in whose work the Hopkins passage above is quoted and who was influenced by Hopkins) suggested that parallelism functions to draw attention to the form of verbal art in its own right, not only as a neutral 'vehicle' for conveying meaning. In normal language use, we select words and phrases and combine them in a syntactic sequence. When selecting a word such as 'normal' in the previous sentence, we also reject a number of other equivalent words that could have served the same function: e.g., 'everyday', 'conventional', 'regular', 'non-poetic', and so on. But in poetry, and other forms of verbal art, we can combine together two or more items that might normally function as alternatives and put them one after another. This practice is reflected in Jakobson's suggestion that 'The poetic function projects the principle of equivalence from the axis of selection into the axis of combination' (1990, p. 71). In the Pope passage above, 'blindly creep' and 'sightless soar' combine ways of describing a living thing's blind movement; instead of stating one or the other, Pope states both in sequence. Jakobson suggests that this technique foregrounds a formal characteristic of language: a characteristic which makes possible what he called the 'poetic function'. That 'poetic' function is dominant in poetry, but is also a characteristic of texts that can be found extensively in non-literary texts as well.

Parallelisms in a text often reflect conventional cultural parallelisms, especially polar parallelisms (oppositions). In doing so, they can reinforce the culturally influential oppositions that such parallelisms communicate. Or alternatively, they can create new contrasts. As we have seen, for example, Pope's *An Essay on Man* explores conventional oppositions between human and animal, culture and nature, and human and God. Whether or not he reinforces such oppositions, or undermines or renegotiates them, is a matter that can only be established by reading and interpreting the whole poem. Either way, the poet's exploration of such culturally central oppositions contributed to prevailing understandings of concepts and the relationships between them circulating in the society of the time. The anthropologist Claude Lévi-Strauss argued that parallelistic structures (especially oppositions) may be fundamental to the way that cultures think, and, because of how they think, how they are organized. Arguments put forward by Lévi-Strauss about the implications of oppositions suggest that parallelistic texts may act out general ways of thinking about the world, rather than only commenting on the particular topics (such as culture and nature) they seem to be exploring.

In general, we tend to assume that a text must hold together as a whole: that it must be 'coherent'. Coherence is partly a matter of interpretation; and readers or listeners can try to impose coherence on a text that may not appear to be coherent. But coherence can also be created by 'cohesive devices' within the text itself (see Halliday and Hasan, 1976); and parallelism can also function in this way. Consider, for example, the use of parallel plots (e.g. main and sub-plot) in narrative texts (in novels, plays, films or TV drama): similarities between such plots create a sense of internal coherence for the text as a whole.

Parallelism, especially metre and rhyme, may also function as a way of making a text easier to remember. This may be one reason why poetry employs parallelism (especially in oral cultures) and why religious texts adopt highly parallel structures. It may also be one of the reasons why proverbs (such as the one quoted earlier), and other kinds of 'wisdom literature' from different cultures, commonly deploy parallelistic structures. Repetition of similar but different phrases can also have persuasive effects, as in sermons (such as Donne's) and political speeches (as in King's). Political speeches in Shakespeare's plays often make memorable use of parallelism, as in Mark Antony's speech in *Julius Caesar* (Act III, scene 2) beginning 'Friends, Romans, countrymen, lend me your ears'; and a famous, more recent example is Winston Churchill's speech to the House of Commons during the Second World War:

> We shall go on to the end. We shall fight in France, we shall fight on the seas and oceans, we shall fight with growing confidence and growing strength in the air, we shall defend our island, whatever the cost may be. We shall fight on the beaches, we shall fight on the landing grounds, we shall fight in the fields and in the streets, we shall fight in the hills; we shall never surrender . . .

Finally, parallelism has an implied relationship to intertextuality or allusion (see **Unit 13, Allusion and intertextuality**). The formal practice of parallelism may be employed simply because it has been used before in powerful or prestigious texts. The Bible has been especially influential on English literature in this respect, especially the 'Authorized Version' of 1611. In the eighteenth century the first theorist of parallelism, Robert Lowth, described how the original Hebrew texts (those that were translated into English as the 'Old Testament') were governed by parallelism (a characteristic of many other texts of the ancient Near East, including Egyptian texts). The English translation known as the Authorized Version preserves that principle of parallelism to such an extent that it is possible to open the Old Testament at any page and find instances of parallelism. Here is a typical example:

> Every valley shall be exalted, and every mountain and hill shall be made low: and the crooked shall be made straight, and the rough places plain:
> And the glory of the Lord shall be revealed, and all flesh shall see it together: for the mouth of the Lord hath spoken it.
>
> (Isaiah 40, 4–5)

Because the Bible employs parallelism in such powerful ways, the technique has carried a highly distinctive cultural value in literary writing in English, such that a text can acquire an additional kind of cultural value simply by echoing this aspect of its style.

This activity uses a poem by Emily Dickinson, written about 1863:

> Because I could not stop for Death –
> He kindly stopped for me –
> The Carriage held but just Ourselves –
> And Immortality.
>
> We slowly drove – He knew no haste
> And I had put away
> My labor and my leisure too,
> For His Civility –
>
> We passed the School, where Children strove
> At Recess – in the Ring –
> We passed the Fields of Gazing Grain –
> We passed the Setting Sun –
>
> Or rather – He passed Us –
> The Dews drew quivering and chill –
> For only Gossamer, my Gown –
> My Tippet – only Tulle –
>
> We paused before a House that seemed
> A Swelling of the Ground –
> The Roof was scarcely visible –
> The Cornice – in the Ground –
>
> Since then – 'tis Centuries – and yet
> Feels shorter than the Day
> I first surmised the Horses' Heads
> Were toward Eternity –

(Note: a 'tippet' is a garment (for the shoulders), and 'tulle' and 'gossamer' are lightweight materials; a 'cornice' is a decorative structure on the ceiling of a room.)

––––––––––

1   Lay out this poem in a way that highlights its parallelisms (e.g. by using the method illustrated above for *An Essay on Man*).

2   For lexical parallelisms that you identify, distinguish polar parallelisms (opposites) from non-polar parallelisms. How do the lexical parallelisms, both polar and non-polar, help to develop and clarify the meaning of the poem? Do the polar and non-polar parallelisms seem to achieve the same effect or different effects?

continued

3 Identify any examples of chiasmus. How do such chiasms help to structure the poem and develop its meaning?

4 Now look more generally at the phenomenon of parallelism in the poem. How do the parallelisms you have identified relate to other structural aspects of the text: e.g. its division into stanzas, and its division into lines?

5 Describe as clearly as you can how the sound parallelisms in particular (e.g. rhyme, alliteration, metre, etc.) relate to the other kinds of parallelism.

Reading

Aitchison, J. (2007) *The Word Weavers: Newshounds and Wordsmiths*, Cambridge: Cambridge University Press.

Berlin, A. (2008) *Dynamics of Biblical Parallelism*, Grand Rapids, MI: Eerdmans Publishing.

Fabb, N. (1997) *Linguistics and Literature: Language in the Verbal Arts of the World*, Oxford: Blackwell, Chapter 6.

Fox, J. (ed.) (1988) *To Speak in Pairs: Essays on the Ritual Languages of Eastern Indonesia*, Cambridge: Cambridge University Press.

Furniss, T. and Bath, M. (2007) *Reading Poetry*, 2nd edn, London, Longman, pp. 122–42.

Halliday, M.A.K. and Hasan, R. (1976) *Cohesion in English*, London: Longman.

Jakobson, R. (1990) 'Linguistics and Poetics', in K. Pomorska and S. Rudy (eds) *Language in Literature*, Cambridge, MA: Harvard University Press.

Leech, G. (1973) *A Linguistic Guide to English Poetry*, London: Longman, Chapter 5.

Deviation

This unit:

- reviews the notion of 'convention' in literary texts, showing how conventions exist at different linguistic levels: letters and sounds; words and the combination of words into sentences; meanings;

- shows how some literary works 'deviate' from such conventions, by breaking rules at a given linguistic level, in order to disrupt readers' expectations and create new possible meanings or effects;

- assesses whether there is a general significance in literary deviation, for example an effect of 'defamiliarization', or tendency to draw attention to how language conveys meanings in ways that are otherwise taken for granted.

Literary language, especially poetry, frequently differs from everyday language because of its manipulation and exploitation of linguistic norms or rules. In this unit we consider the types of linguistic rule that underpin ordinary communication and explore how such rules are manipulated and exploited. We also consider why writers choose to manipulate communicative norms in the ways they do.

19.1 Convention and deviation in everyday language

Everyday verbal communication depends on following underlying rules. Those rules form the grammar of the language being used to communicate (**see Unit 3, Analysing units of structure**.) When linguists study a language, they aim to describe these rules or norms, and in this way help to account for our capacity to achieve mutual intelligibility when we communicate with others using a common language. Linguists emphasize that the rules they describe 'constitute' the language, in the way that the rules of football or chess constitute those games. Such constitutive rules need to be distinguished from prescriptive rules, or rules you are required to follow, such as 'don't split your infinitives', 'don't drop your aitches' or 'say "it is I" rather than "it is me"'. The prescriptive rules formulated about a language often bear little relation to the underlying grammar of the language that makes communication possible.

19.1.1 Components of grammar and types of linguistic rule

Three levels at which a language is organized are often distinguished: the levels of substance, form and meaning. *Substance* refers to the physical medium in which expression takes place: articulated sounds in speech, or marks on paper in writing. *Form* refers to how those sounds become organized into words, and words into phrases and sentences. *Meaning* refers to the propositions that are encoded in form and substance. In linguistic analysis, each level has a different subsection of the grammar associated with it.

The subsections of the grammar consist of different kinds of rules. The level of substance (sounds or letters) is analysed in terms of phonological and graphological rules: i.e. rules dealing with pronunciation and spelling. Form (the patterning of words into phrases and sentences) is analysed in terms of syntactic rules. Meaning is studied through semantic rules. The overall picture is as set out in the diagram on the facing page.

Formulating the grammar of a language consists of stating what rules govern its operation at each of these three main levels. There will be phonological and graphological rules that state permissible patterns at the level of substance (i.e. patterns that are possible within the language, and recognized as parts of it): in English, for instance, we do not find the sound /n/ followed immediately by /g/ at the beginning of a word. There are rules of syntax, which govern how words combine into sentences: in English, for instance, definite articles (i.e. 'the') come

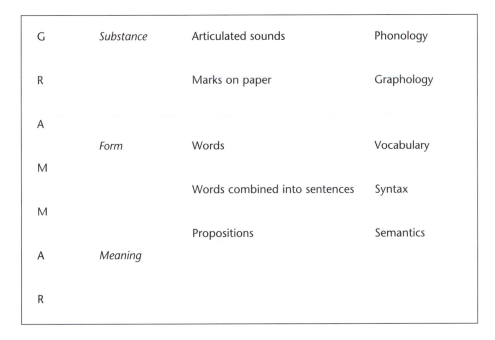

G	*Substance*	Articulated sounds	Phonology
R		Marks on paper	Graphology
A			
	Form	Words	Vocabulary
M			
		Words combined into sentences	Syntax
M			
		Propositions	Semantics
A	*Meaning*		
R			

before the noun, not after ('the car', not 'car the'). And there are semantic rules governing the properties of propositions: e.g. a speaker cannot promise or predict things that have already happened.

In practice the grammar, or rule system, is not always rigidly observed. In rapid speech, for instance, we constantly make mistakes: slips of the tongue, false starts, unfinished sentences and other kinds of production error. But our background awareness of the rule system helps us to decipher or edit out mistakes, with the result that in practice we are hardly even aware of them. Children learning their first language also – unsurprisingly – make mistakes. They build up the adult grammar or rule system over a period of time, using interesting approximations to it on the way. Such mistakes (e.g. 'me go home') are not merely random errors. Children make similar kinds of approximation, in the same developmental order, as they build up their adult rule system. Finally, in addition to performance errors and developmental errors, other kinds of mistake may be traced to particular kinds of impairment (such as aphasia or dyslexia), which disrupt specific aspects of the rule system. In all cases, however, the resulting linguistic errors or deviations are unintended; and speakers in general attempt to avoid them.

These various kinds of deviation all differ from another kind: that of intended, playful departures from the rule system. An everyday example of manipulating an aspect of the rule system – in this case that of spelling – can be found in text-messaging: 'be' may be written as 'b', 'you' becomes 'u', 'great' becomes 'gr8', and 'bcnu' means 'be seeing you'. At one level these departures from normal spelling are measures adopted for speed and to save money. But there is also a measure of inventiveness, innovation and play involved, as in 'F2F' ('face to face') or 'H2CUS' ('hope to see you soon'). Such deliberate, rule-breaking playfulness occurs in many everyday contexts of communication. But it is particularly common in literature. Indeed, the language of literature is influenced by two general principles: that of rule-making, on the one hand, and a principle of rule-*breaking*, on the other. In **Units 16–18** (**Rhyme and sound patterning**, **Verse, metre and rhythm** and **Parallelism**), we have looked at aspects of rule-making, or the superimposition of *extra* patterning in literary language on the sorts of structure that govern everyday discourse. In the rest of this unit we focus on the opposite tendency: rule-breaking, or deviation.

19.2 Convention and deviation in literature

To a greater or lesser extent, literary discourse distinguishes itself from other uses of language by bending the rules of everyday communication. Indeed, literature might be seen as operating within a spectrum of degrees of linguistic deviation. Some authors, and some periods and genres, tend to be more deviant than others. The literature of the first half of the twentieth century, for instance, involved more conscious linguistic experimentation, and hence deviation, than that of the first half of the eighteenth century.

Whatever pleasure we derive from linguistic deviation in everyday language depends on our knowledge of norms or conventions of ordinary usage. Linguistic deviation is only enjoyable and interesting, as a practice, if we know what is being deviated *from*. The same is true of deviation in literature. In this case, however, there is a complicating factor. In literature, deviation operates against a background of two different sets of norms: the conventions or norms of ordinary usage; and the conventions or norms of literary usage. What at first appears deviant and 'original' in literature can quickly become conventional. Writers continually invent new kinds of deviations in an attempt, as Ezra Pound put it, to 'make it new'.

We now examine some common types of linguistic deviation in literature, considering instances of deviation under the categories introduced above of substance, form and meaning.

19.2.1 Deviation in substance

In modern (as opposed to traditional, pre-literate) societies, literature in English exists primarily as a body of relatively fixed printed works, rather than as a varying series of oral performances. Since the principal mode of literary expression is now writing rather than speech, deviation at the level of substance is primarily a matter of typography, layout, punctuation and spelling.

Deviation in the substance of written language presupposes, of course, a norm against which such deviation, as a kind of breaking of convention, is to be judged. Poetry, for instance, routinely adopts its own distinctive layouts; these might themselves be considered deviations, in relation to the continuous flow of prose. But because many of those layouts have become conventionally established, and evidently follow rules of their own that are not unique to a single text, the layout of poetry (including features such as short lines indented on the page, and so on) has over time become conventional. As a result, this apparent deviation from a typical written discourse layout can function as a baseline against which further deviations may be measured.

Conventional use of spaces to indicate boundaries between words, for example, can be violated, as it is in Edwin Morgan's significantly titled poem 'Message Clear' (1967), by the insertion of spaces within words as well as between them. The result in Morgan's poem is that in each line of a poem 55 lines long spaces within words are made, of irregular length and randomly distributed, with no regard to conventional word-boundaries. Such deviation may initially seem trivial, or at least a purely visual effect. But by making the text resistant to being read, the deviation effect draws attention to levels of complexity in a poem being called 'Message Clear' when the reader has to work hard not only to see what message is being conveyed by the words and phrases but even to make sense of its substance as written language in the first place (because that substance as written language depends on conventions of typography, layout and punctuation).

With Morgan's 'Message Clear', it is only when, after 54 lines of irregularly placed fragments, the reader reaches the final line, 'i am the resurrection and the life' that a larger picture drops into place: that all the previous lines were variations on this last line. But the preceding lines look different because some of the letters that make up the final line have been left out, leaving blank spaces instead. The letters that remain appear to be randomly distributed, because they are still located in the same vertical position as they appear in the final line, rather than being closed-up together. If the irregular spacing of the letters in each line is looked at differently, however, words and phrases begin to appear, in ways that suggest many shorter utterances somehow 'contained in' what the last line says.

Some of the revealed expressions are illustrated in the following table of some selected lines:

Word position:	1	2	3	4	5	6	7
Line 1		am		i			
Line 26				o			life
Line 49	i			resurrect			
Line 51	i	am		in			life
Line 54	i	am					
Final line (= 55)	i	am	the	resurrection	and	the	life

Once these other words and phrases in the poem are revealed we see that each line anticipates the final line, not only by using letters from it selectively but by making an additional series of statements that, it turns out, can be interpreted as partial but compatible versions of the message expressed by the final line. The poem's title, accordingly, 'Message Clear', may seem initially an ironic comment on the reader's struggles. But if a different way of reading is adopted, then those deviations offer an additional kind of sense, such that the 'message' does finally begin to become 'clear'.

19.2.2 Deviation in vocabulary

Deviation in vocabulary occurs in literature when new words are created for particular effect. This can be done in various ways. The most straightforward strategy is simply to paste words or elements of words together, forming new combinations. Many words in English are formed in this way:

fortunate	=	fortune+ate
unfortunate	=	un+fortune+ate
unfortunately	=	un+fortune+ate+ly

We can see from these examples that even the small elements, or affixes (such as un-, -ate and -ly) have a fairly predictable meaning in the structure of a word. The affix un- usually means 'not'; -ate usually signals 'quality' or 'characteristic'; and -ly usually suggests 'manner'. These basic patterns of word construction and meaning allow us to make sense of words we have not encountered before. They also offer poets and others opportunities for verbal innovation.

When the Victorian religious poet and Jesuit priest, Gerard Manley Hopkins, refers in *The Wreck of the Deutschland* (1875) to the sea as 'widow-making, unchilding, unfathering deeps', he is exploiting the ordinary possibilities of affixation and compounding to form 'one-off' neologisms, or new words. These new words offer a resource for conveying, in a particularly compressed way, how the sea can take husbands from their wives, children from their parents, and fathers from their children. Similarly, when T.S. Eliot in *The Waste Land* (1922) puts a neologism into the mouth of the blind seer Tiresias, so that he says, 'And I Tiresias have foresuffered all', our knowledge of the conventional function of 'fore-' means that we are able to derive a meaning from the otherwise unfamiliar form 'foresuffer'. (Tiresias is claiming that his prophetic powers mean that he not only 'foresees' events, but that he has also suffered or endured them before they even happen.)

We make sense of neologisms in the same way that we make sense of other kinds of deviation: by using our implicit knowledge of underlying conventions of the language. This principle of estimating significance of a use of language from underlying conventions that have not been followed allows us to produce and understand puns in everyday life. It also extends as far as helping in our attempts to interpret the sustained deviations in word formation to be found throughout James Joyce's *Finnegans Wake* (1939), a novel in which the author uses what Lewis Carroll called 'portmanteau' words (so-called because they pack several meanings into one word, in the way that a portmanteau is filled up with different things). The word 'notwithstempting', to take simply one example from a continuous texture of such portmanteau words running over hundreds of pages, can be read as containing both the word 'notwithstanding' and the words 'not tempting'.

19.2.3   Deviation in syntax

Conveying meanings depends not only on the choice of one word rather than another, but also on how individual words are arranged into phrases and sentences. If a string of words is to make sense, strong constraints apply as regards how those words can be combined (see **Unit 3, Analysing units of structure**). These constraints make up the syntax of the language.

The importance of syntactic conventions in English can be illustrated by how even small changes of word order can significantly alter the meaning of sentences. In the following example, the change from a statement (saying something you claim to know) to a question (asking about something you don't know) is brought about by a change of order of the initial two items, subject and verb:

This is the ten o'clock news.

Is this the ten o'clock news?

Poets and experimental novelists, no less than other language users, must follow syntactic conventions if they are to be understood. Even when they deviate from syntactic conventions, they depend on our tacit knowledge of those conventions in order to achieve their effects. In poetry, however, inversions of normal word order are quite common, and may be motivated by considerations of rhyme and rhythm. Such inversions are accepted by readers of poetry, if they are not considered too awkward or intrusive. Consider the following lines:

Silent is the house: all are laid asleep:
One alone looks out o'er the snow-wreaths deep . . .
(Emily Brontë, 'The Visionary', 1846)

A more conventional order for the words that make up these lines would be:

The house is silent: all are laid asleep:
One alone looks out over the deep snow-wreaths . . .

This more conventional order, however, misses opportunities for patterning in rhyme and metre that are exploited by the poet.

An extended example of deviant word order can be found in the poem 'The Paschal Moon', by E.J. Scovell (1907–99):

> At four this April morning the Easter moon –
> Some days to full, awkwardly made, yet of brazen
> Beauty and power, near the north-west horizon
> Among our death-white street lamps going down –
> I wondered to see it from a lower storey   (5)
> Netted in airy twigs; and thought, a fire
> A mile off, or what or who? But going higher
> I freed it (to my eyes) into its full glory,
> Dominant, untouched by roofs, from this height seen
> Unmeshed from budding trees; not silver-white   (10)
> But brazed or golden. Our fluorescent light,
> That can change to snow a moment of the young green
> In the maple tree, showed ashen, null and dead
> Beside such strength, such presence as it had.

Formally, this poem conforms to most of the conventions of the sonnet genre. There are fourteen lines; and, despite some half rhymes ('moon'/'down'; 'dead'/'had') (see **Unit 16, Rhyme and sound patterning**), the rhyme scheme is that of an English sonnet, with three quatrains (abba, cddc, effe) and a concluding couplet. In order to meet these norms of the sonnet form, however, the poem deviates markedly from normal word order in English. When making statements, for instance, English clauses or sentences usually follow a pattern of subject followed by verb followed by object (as, for instance, in 'Usain Bolt [S] broke [V] the record [O]'); this is why English is described as an SVO language. The opening of the poem, however, deviates from this usual syntactic pattern. If we turn the opening into something closer to everyday English, it will read like this:

> I wondered to see the Easter moon at four this April morning from a lower storey, netted in airy twigs, going down among our death-white street lamps near the north-west horizon, awkwardly made, yet of brazen beauty and power, some days to full.

This revision restores a more normal order for the core constituents of an English clause or sentence: the subject comes first (in this case 'I'); the subject is followed by the verb (or verb phrase) ('wondered to see'); after the verb comes the object ('the Easter moon'). These elements are then followed by syntactically optional elements relating to time, place and circumstance of the action ('at four this April morning from a lower storey . . .', etc.). In the poem, however, the conventional order of the main elements is reversed: syntactically non-essential elements relating to circumstances are presented first. Indication of the object is delayed; and we do not come to the subject and main verb until line 5. Only then does the structure and sense of the poem's first sentence fall into place.

This kind syntactic 'suspense' is relatively unusual in everyday speech. It does occur in writing, under various circumstances, but is more characteristic of poetry, especially where the poet – as here – is working against, or within self-imposed limits of, a tight poetic form.

The **diction** (or choice of words) of 'The Paschal Moon' is also curious. There are, for example, turns of phrase that would be surprising in everyday prose. Again we can compare the opening of the poem with a revision into more everyday prose:

> I was surprised to see at four o'clock in the morning – around Easter time – the moon silhouetting the outline of a tree, descending among white street lamps near the north-west horizon. It was not yet a full moon, was awkwardly made, and was of brazen beauty and power.

Some of the phrasing of this more everyday prose version can be compared with the poem by setting changes out as in the columns below:

'I wondered to see'	'I was surprised to see';
'netted in airy twigs'	'silhouetting the outline of a tree'
'some days to full'	'not yet a full moon'

In each case the phrasing of the poem seems deviant by comparison with the more usual linguistic choice. For instance, words that more typically combine with *wondered* are:

wondered + if
wondered + what
wondered + why

Accordingly, the combination *wondered + to* (as in the poem) is likely to seem unusual. We can test our impression empirically by checking the frequency of occurrence of particular combinations in a large corpus of English text, such as the *Collins Online Birmingham University Corpus of English* (COBUILD). This corpus can be searched online for the likely occurrence of phrases (it consists of fifty-six million words of contemporary spoken and written text, including books, newspapers, magazines and transcribed speech from everyday conversation and radio; for further details, see www.collins.co.uk/Corpus/CorpusSearch.aspx). In the corpus, *surprised to see* (a combination in our prose version) occurs more than a hundred times; but *wondered to see* (as in the poem) does not occur even once. Although *wondered + to* does occur, it only occurs in combinations such as *I wondered to what extent* or *I wondered to what degree*.

Or consider 'netted in airy twigs'. This is a highly distinctive word combination in the poem. If we search COBUILD again, we find that 'netted' usually occurs either in angling contexts, or in relation to money, prizes and other financial gains, as in:

> netted the carp

> netted this eleven pounder

> having netted £66 million from the re-release

'Netted in', we learn, is extremely rare, and so likely to stand out as deviant in our impression of the poem.

Two further significant examples of deviation in Scovell's poem are the poem's title, 'Paschal Moon', and the reference to the moon's 'brazen beauty and power'. The word 'Paschal' relates to the Jewish festival of Passover and the related Christian festival of Easter. It typically combines (or collocates) in religious contexts with words such as 'joy', 'mystery' and 'optimism' – but not with 'moon'. 'Moon' commonly collocates with 'full', 'half' and 'blue'. The phrase, 'Paschal Moon', combining the notion of lunar cycle with a Judaeo-Christian religious festival is almost certainly unique to this poem.

'Brazen beauty' is a similarly distinctive phrase that is out of step with everyday usage. In COBUILD we find typical phrases such as:

> brazen cheek
> brazen deception
> brazen boasting
> brazen denial
> brazen crooks
> brazen con-man

A common association of 'brazen', accordingly, is with negative activities, including deception, boasting and criminality. In the poem, however, we find precisely the opposite kind of association, in an unusual combination with 'beauty' (our COBUILD search shows that the combination 'brazen beauty', while undoubtedly a grammatically possible combination, occurs only once within the corpus). The combination 'the brazen beauty and power' of the moon points to a paradox in the poem. The paschal moon is depicted as dominant: something of beauty and power, and glory and strength – in contrast with the ashen, fluorescent street lamp. Yet when we look at actions associated with her, she is on the receiving end of such actions: she is 'awkwardly made', 'netted in airy twigs', 'freed' and 'seen unmeshed'. The nearest thing to a positive action attributed to the moon occurs in the last few words of the poem: 'such presence as it had'. So the poem attributes to the moon contradictory characteristics, as something contemplated, experienced and acted upon by others, and as something of special power and beauty. This complex meaning is never directly asserted, but is a cumulative meaning that follows from a series of unusual linguistic choices which deviate from the patterning of everyday speech and writing.

19.2.4   Deviation in semantics

Each of the cases of literary deviation we have considered so far has *consequences* for meaning and interpretation. Breaking rules of punctuation, for instance, affects how we read and make sense of a text. But it is also possible to find cases of direct manipulation of conventional meanings. Joseph Heller's novel, *Catch 22* (1961), is particularly rich in this kind of deviation. Set during the Second World War, it derives its title from a paradox (Catch 22) used by the authorities depicted in the novel to keep American pilots flying an ever-increasing number of bombing missions. Although pilots can appeal to be grounded on grounds of insanity,

> [t]here was only one catch and that was Catch 22, which specified that a concern for one's own safety in the face of dangers that were real and immediate was the process of a rational mind. Orr was crazy and could be grounded. All he had to do was ask; and as soon as he did, he would no longer be crazy and would have to fly more missions. Orr would be crazy to fly more missions and sane if he didn't, but if he was sane he would have to fly them. If he flew them he was crazy and didn't have to; but if he didn't want to he was sane and had to.

Conventionally, the expressions 'sane' and 'crazy' are opposite in meaning. Part of the fascination (and the humour) of *Catch 22* is how the novel constructs conditions under which opposites can, under certain circumstances, both be true at the same time. Love and hate are conventionally opposite; yet the novel tells us that 'Dunbar loved shooting skeet because he hated every minute of it and the time passed so slowly.' Examples of such semantic deviation in the novel are frequently structured like jokes in two parts:

> Doc Daneeka was Yossarian's friend
> and would do just about nothing in his power to help him.

The profusion of semantic anomalies in the opening chapters of *Catch 22* creates an impression of a world in which war has undermined the rational basis of social and moral action.

Another way in which literature produces and exploits deviation in meaning is through its use of figurative language, since figures of speech may be thought of as deviations from literal meaning (see **Unit 10, Metaphor and figurative language** and **Unit 11, Irony**). Figures of speech play a large part in other kinds of discourse, but in the context of everyday language they tend to be treated as conventional, without any direct apprehension of their 'deviance'. In literature, on the other hand, figurative language tends to be more innovative and to draw attention to how it deviates from literal usage or conventional figures.

19.2.5 Literature as deviant discourse

Perhaps the most fundamental kind of deviation that characterizes literature is not so much its manipulation of linguistic rules as the peculiarity in how it can relate to experience and the world at large. Such peculiarity includes:

1   how literary texts construct imagined worlds;
2   how literary texts construct imagined speakers;
3   how literary texts address imagined addressees.

Most kinds of discourse – news, problem-pages, research reports, gossip, even advertising – operate under certain conditions of truth. We expect their assertions to be true, or at least to amount to a reasonable claim. Literature, on the other hand, is full of statements that look like assertions about the world but which contradict our everyday sense of what the world is like. Literary discourse is accordingly deviant in a sense not considered above: it is non-referential and, even when it claims to refer to things in the world, we are not (or at least not always, see **Unit 23, Narrative realism**) expected to take those claims seriously.

Consider, for instance, the opening sentence of George Orwell's novel, *Nineteen Eighty-Four* (1949):

It was a bright cold day in April and the clocks were striking thirteen.

To a British readership, the notion of there being a bright cold day in April may be completely unremarkable. But the fact that the same sentence tells us that 'the clocks were striking thirteen' places the events of the novel – and the world it creates – outside that readership's everyday world. Although for many years the title of the book (which was written in 1948, and published 1949) looked *forward* to a date in the future, the past **tense** of the first sentence refers backwards, as if to events that have already happened. Most readers will not interpret the first sentence as the beginning of a factual record of events that have really happened, but will realize that Orwell's point was that such events could conceivably come to pass, in a hypothetical future.

19.3 Effects of literary deviation: defamiliarization

We have seen how literature reworks conventions and codes of the language and is potentially deviant in a number of different respects. This need not mean, however, that literature can say nothing about the ordinary world. Use of deviation may allow us to see the world from unfamiliar and revealing angles. Russian Formalist critics called this effect **defamiliarization**; and in his *Tractatus Logico-Philosophicus*, 1922, the philosopher Ludwig Wittgenstein (1889–1951) wrote that 'the limits of my language mean the limits of my world'. In everyday communication we are usually content to leave the limits of language, and so the conventions of how we view the world, alone. Literature, by contrast, may extend the boundaries of the taken-for-granted world by deviating from habitual modes of expression. By subverting common sense links between utterances and their situations of use, deviant literary discourse invites exploration of kinds of identity, forms of relationship and ways of seeing the world.

ACTIVITY 19

Here is a poem by the American poet Emily Dickinson (1830–86) which describes a storm. The language of the poem deviates from everyday English in various respects.

> The Clouds their Backs together laid
> The North begun to push
> The Forests galloped till they fell
> The Lightning played like mice
> The Thunder crumbled like a stuff
> How good to be in Tombs
> Where Nature's Temper cannot reach
> Nor missile ever comes

———————

1   Underline instances of deviation in punctuation in the poem. How is the punctuation deviant and what effect or effects can be attributed to such deviation?

2   Identify an instance of unusual word order. Describe what motivates the deviation and what effect it creates.

3   The following are representative kinds of word combination, taken from the COBUILD corpus, involving the phrase 'to push':

   –   you don't even need a free hand to **push** the button to open the door

   –   Any attempt to **push** the boat upwind at more than 18 knots resulted

   –   have surrendered after a drive by the army to **push** them out of the eastern part of the country.

   –   She lay in bed, swallowing, trying to **push** back the acid bile that rose in her throat.

   –   From this position, try to **push** your hands further away from you and hold the

   –   Pressure is put on the upper arm to **push** it to the floor whilst the opposite hip is

continued

- that some boundaries exist. We continue to **push** boundaries in any new relationship throughout

- coming in with lots of money and trying to **push** people around.

- right at the end of the session to **push** Coulthard's team mate Damon Hill into third

- longer effective and couldn't bring myself to **push** the line. This commitment to a product line is

- and the spell was broken. They all began to **push** their chairs back and reach for plates

(COBUILD Corpus Concordance Sampler, www.collins.co.uk/Corpus/CorpusSearch.aspx)

3.1 What is unusual or distinctive in how the phrase 'to push' is used in the poem's second line?

3.2 Describe as precisely as you can what is unusual about the phrase 'the forests galloped'.

4 Now consider the extract below, which comes from the opening page of *The White Tiger*, by Aravind Adiga (2008). List the ways in which the writing is deviant (consider, for example, the addresses that are given, and how letters are usually represented in literature).

For the Desk of:
His Excellency Wen Jiabao,
The Premier's Office,
Beijing,
Capital of the Freedom Loving Nation of China

From the Desk of:
'The White Tiger'
A Thinking Man
And an entrepreneur
Living in the world's centre of technology and outsourcing
Electronics City Phase 1 (Just off Hosur Main Road)
Bangalore, India

Mr Premier,
Sir.
Neither you nor I can speak English, but there are some things that can be said only in English.

Reading

Erlich, V. (1981) *Russian Formalism: History – Doctrine*, 3rd edn, The Hague: Mouton.

Garvin, P. (ed. and trans.) (1964) *A Prague School Reader in Aesthetics, Literary Structure and Style*, Washington, DC: Georgetown University Press.

Leech, G. (1969) *A Linguistic Guide to English Poetry*, London: Longman, Chapters 2, 3.

Lemon, L. and Reis, M. (eds) (1965) *Russian Formalist Criticism: Four Essays*, Lincoln, NE: University of Nebraska Press, especially the Chapter by Shklovsky (1921), 'Sterne's *Tristram Shandy*: Stylistic Commentary', pp. 25–57.

Widdowson, H. (1992) *Practical Stylistics: An Approach to Poetry*, Oxford: Oxford University Press.

Narrative

SECTION 5

Narrative

This unit:

- introduces the idea of narrative as a sequence of related events, presented from a particular point of view and suggesting underlying patterns and causes that are stated or implied to be significant;

- offers guidance on how to distinguish the form of a narrative from its content, and illustrates the importance of distinguishing between these two aspects of storytelling;

- describes different roles in narratives played by characters, including conventional characters, as well as by typical events, or motifs, which recur in narratives that in other ways seem very different from one another;

- draws attention to the significance of how narratives begin and end, showing how close attention to these two key moments can help in interpreting the narrative as a whole.

UNIT 20

Narratives – which are not confined to storytelling in novels but also take many other forms – are stories involving a sequence of related events. There are various kinds of relationship between those events. The most obvious kind is where one event causes another. Such causal connection links one event with another and serves partly to give unity to the narrative, partly to allow the narrative to draw or imply moral conclusions about the consequences of actions it depicts.

The simplest narrative texts present a single series of events, with causal connections between them. More complex narrative texts may be compounded from two or more simple narratives narrated simultaneously (perhaps as plot and sub-plot); or they may present narratives in a sequence, only loosely connected (perhaps through sharing the same basic character, as in **picaresque** narratives).

20.1 Narrative form and narrative content

A lot of thinking about how narratives work distinguishes between two dimensions or layers of interest, which we might call 'narrative form' and 'narrative content'. The content of a narrative is its collection of represented events, along with the participants in those events and the circumstances of those events. The form of a narrative is how those events are represented through a particular narrative medium (usually spoken or written language, and/or images). Many narratives show a tension between content and form, as we will see in this unit.

The distinction between content and form is felt in different ways for different aspects of narrative. If we consider narrative events, we need for example to distinguish between the content order of events and the form order of events. The 'content order' is the chronological order of events (events in the sequence in which they supposedly 'really' occurred, as might be represented in a timeline). The 'form order' is the order in which the narrative presents these events to us. In the simplest narratives, the presentational or form order is the same as chronological or content order. If there is nothing to indicate otherwise, we assume that the orders are the same, and hence that, if we are told first one thing and then another, the first thing we heard about happened first and the second thing happened second. So if a narrative simply states,

The queen died. The king died.

then we typically assume that the queen died before the king, and that probably the latter's death was somehow a consequence of the former's death. However, it is also possible for narratives to present events out of chronological sequence. For instance,

The king died. Only a month earlier the queen had died in child birth.

This presentation of events (i.e. the order in which they are given in the narration) does not match their chronological occurrence. There is a mismatch between form order and content order, with content being presented in a new and different sequence. Complex narratives, such as we commonly find in films and novels, tend to manipulate their presentation of events. Detective fiction, for instance, may begin with a crime, then spend the rest of the narrative uncovering the chain of events leading to it. Flashbacks in film similarly manipulate form order and content order. A film – for example, the film *Sunset Boulevard* (1950) – may begin with a body floating in a pool, but then go on to show events that occurred earlier than this first image of the body in the pool.

Various terms are used to describe the distinction between form order and content order in a narrative. One terminological distinction that is widely used is between 'story' (= the content order of events, or order in which they supposedly happened) and 'discourse' (= the form order of events, or order in which they are presented in the narrative as it is told).

Creating a mismatch between content order and form order is an example of an 'aesthetic strategy': a strategy typically used in creating an aesthetic object such as a novel or film, and also employed in some oral narratives and anecdotes. It is rarely possible to pin down a single function for an aesthetic strategy. Instead, the strategy may serve any combination of a number of functions. The strategy of mismatching content order and form order, for example, may be used to create kinds of enigma (in that we are told consequences before we are told what brought them about); to create suspense (the order of events is interrupted by a flashback that leaves readers in a state of anticipation of what happens next); to help organize our understanding of the content (crucial background history is delayed until we need to know it), and so on. The Russian Formalists, a group of linguists concerned with how literature works and writing in the early twentieth century, focused their energy on trying to establish what makes a text 'literary'; one basic idea, for them, was that a text is literary to the extent that our attention is drawn to its aesthetic strategies. One very noticeable aesthetic strategy is the kind of mismatch described here between form order (which they termed *sjuzhet* – something like 'story' above) and content order (which they called *fabula,* something like 'discourse' above). In this way, such a mismatch serves a further purpose beyond those already described: it helps to define a text as literary.

The mismatch between form and content can have consequences for narrative pace or tempo. Minor events in the narrative may be dwelt on at length, and major events treated briefly or compressed. Spelling out minor events in detail can create an effect of dramatically slowing down the narrative. Conversely, condensed treatment of a crucial event seems to speed the narrative up.

George Orwell's account of an execution in Burma ('A Hanging', 1931) deals with events that last only a very short time. A prisoner is picked up at eight and is pronounced dead by eight minutes past eight. Orwell's account, however, dwells in detail on small events that retard the progress to the execution. A dog runs out to interrupt the procession; the prisoner steps aside to avoid a puddle; his final prayer seems to last forever.

Here is how Orwell dwells on one of these moments that slow down the narrative:

> And once, in spite of the men who gripped him by each shoulder, he stepped slightly aside to avoid a puddle on the path.
>
> It is curious, but till that moment I had never realized what it means to destroy a healthy, conscious man. When I saw the prisoner step aside to avoid the puddle, I saw the mystery, the unspeakable wrongness, of cutting a life short when it is in full tide. This man was not dying, he was alive just as we were alive. All the organs of his body were working – bowels digesting food, skin renewing itself, nails growing, tissues forming – all toiling away in solemn foolery. His nails would still be growing when he stood on the drop, when he was falling through the air with a tenth of a second to live. His eyes saw the yellow gravel and the grey walls, and his brain still remembered, foresaw, reasoned – reasoned even about puddles. He and we were a party of men walking together, seeing, hearing, feeling, understanding the same world; and in two minutes, with a sudden snap, one of us would be gone – one mind less, one world less.

But when the end finally comes, it comes swiftly:

> Suddenly the superintendent made up his mind. Throwing up his head he made a swift motion with his stick. 'Chalo!' he shouted almost fiercely.
>
> There was a clanking noise, and then dead silence. The prisoner had vanished, and the rope was twisting on itself.

So, just as dwelling on some events can slow a narrative down, compressing major events can create an impression of acceleration. The effect is created of the narrative decelerating when things are described very slowly and in detail (an effect seen also in slow motion sections of films), and accelerating or jumping when two events separated in the narrative content by major gaps in time are placed next to each other (a strategy used for example by Virginia Woolf in *To the Lighthouse* (1927)). Various functions may be ascribed to this aesthetic strategy, which again highlights and exploits the difference between narrative form and narrative content.

What we perceive as 'narrative coherence' involves recognition that we are being told one unified story: that we understand why we are told each event, that we understand how events fit together, and that we see how, if there are sub-stories inside the main story, these sub-stories make sense in terms of the overall story, perhaps by commenting on it (as is frequently the case with sub-plots in a Shakespeare play, or with a story that one character tells another during an ongoing narrative).

An interesting test of the coherence of a narrative is to try formulating the whole narrative as a single sentence, or even as a single word. This exercise brings out quite abstract, thematic kinds of coherence. The title of a narrative, where it has one, often carries out this function, either explicitly or by implication. Even the author of a narrative, however, may not find this sign-posting of coherence easy to achieve. F. Scott Fitzgerald worked through a series of titles for his most famous novel, including *Among the Ash-Heaps and Millionaires*, *Trimalchio in West Egg*, *Trimalchio* and *The Golden-Hatted Gatsby*, before finally settling on *The Great Gatsby* (1925). In retrospect, his final choice is considered by many to capture the novel's core meaning in ways eluded by those earlier attempts.

A further distinction we might draw between form and content in a narrative is that form is typically more coherent than content. If we take narrative content to correspond at some level to reality, then we must acknowledge its complexity, density and multiplicity; reality is something complex and messy rather than a singular and coherent thing. Narrative content takes on, and is likely to reflect to varying degrees, this inherent messiness. In contrast, the organization of such content by the selection and ordering of elements in a narrative involves an imposition of order: a fitting together or making sense of things, and in general a creation of coherence. The process is however not only one of selection and simplification; it also has a forward movement, or unfolding over the course of the narrative. Narratives tend to move from some kind of lack towards a resolution: from some particular kind of beginning towards a particular, selected end. But these characteristics are formal features designed to give a narrative its coherence. The implied reality represented by the narrative (its narrative content) inevitably lacks coherent movement from a particular kind of beginning to a particular kind of end, since the stream of lives and events continues beyond whatever narrative frame is imposed. The closure of a narrative is something imposed on it by the process of narration, commonly in order to fill a gap in understanding, or to offer some form of explanation of a particular aspect of life or events.

Another kind of mismatch between narrative form and narrative content is brought about by selection of 'narrative point of view' (see **Unit 21, Narrative point of view**). Events in narrative content occur, but they do not occur inherently from some particular vantage point for seeing them. In a particular narrative, by contrast, the selection of events (and so how they are described and interpreted) interacts with a choice made by the storyteller from whose perspective events will be described. In Henry James's ghost story, *The Turn of the Screw* (1898), crucial events are presented from the perspective of the governess. From her perspective, the children in her charge are in danger of demonic possession from ghostly apparitions. But readers may wonder if the apparitions are being claimed to exist in the world created by the narrative, or are presented as merely creations of the governess's particular view of events, in this case as figments of a neurotic imagination. Readers find it difficult to decide what happens in the narrative because of the dominant position given to the governess's point of view, which is the view of a character supposedly involved in whatever events are taking place (and hence a particular angle on them). In very many narratives, the narrator stands outside the events of the story, commenting rather than appearing to participate.

Use of a narrator is in this way an aesthetic strategy. Like all such strategies, choice of narrator can be used in various ways and for different purposes. Point of view may be switched in the course of the narrative, for instance. One consequence of this might be that we are made uncertain as to narrative content because what the content is alters, depending on which point of view is taken. Because narrators are fictional constructions, it is also possible to create narrators who are fantastic in various ways: the narrator may be an animal, or a dead person (the body in the pool in the film *Sunset Boulevard* referred to above is also the film's narrator).

Narrative form varies in how far it appears constrained by a need to stay close to narrative content. In some genres and periods, narrative form seems rigidly constrained in this way, with variation limited to flashbacks, while in other cases it appears to be the content that is constrained and the form that is unconstrained (e.g. where narrative pace is radically altered by acceleration and deceleration).

20.2 Typicality of characters and events

The 'raw material' of narrative, we might say, consists of events with their associated actors and circumstances. These elements comprise the basic content of a narrative, and are shaped into its narrative's form by the process of ordering and reordering of their sequence and by selection of a point of view from which actors, events and circumstances will be presented. Another characteristic of narrative, however, is that the events they contain are often typical or even stereotypical, with particular events and characters standing for more general kinds. To some extent the genre of a narrative requires certain kinds of typical event: a marriage, a murder, a chase, a disguise uncovered, a false accusation, and so on. Such typicality of the events represented (sometimes only in outline but sometimes in great detail) moves those events from the level of narrative content to the level of narrative form, in that they become components from which the narrative form is built. There is then a resulting conflict, as regards narrative events, between the demands of individuality, uniqueness and realism associated with narrative content (especially important historically, in the origin of the novel; see Watt, 2010) and the demands of typicality (a formal characteristic encouraging representativeness). A marriage in a narrative is (at least apparently) a specific marriage, which happens in all the complex and individual detail represented in the fictional world. At the same time, however, it is also a typical event, with all that individuality stripped off it in order to serve its purpose as a building block in the narrative (and frequently as one of the components that helps the narrative to end). Typical events in a narrative are called motifs; and folklorists catalogue such motifs in folktales (naming and numbering them, and tracing their occurrence across the social history of storytelling).

Just as events in a narrative are both individuated and yet typical, so are characters. On the one hand, characters are supposedly real people in the fictional world represented by the narrative. On the other hand, characters are parts of the mechanism that drives the narrative forwards, from beginning to end. In this second sense, they can be labelled according to their function in the narrative. This approach of treating characters as representatives of particular narrative tasks that they perform is associated especially with the work of Vladimir Propp, who suggested that typical characters in a corpus of Russian fairy tales he analysed perform typical functions. Propp identifies 'character function' on the basis of the character's involvement in specific types of event; for example, for Propp the 'hero' is a character function performed by a character who, in the fairy tales under discussion:

- is forbidden to do something;
- is sent off to resolve a lack;
- acquires a magical object;
- fights the villain;
- is marked (e.g. injured, or given something such as a ring);
- is pursued;
- arrives somewhere unrecognized;
- is married and ascends the throne.

Propp lists seven character functions, not all of which will be useful in narratives of different kinds. One in particular, however, 'the donor', does appear to be very frequently found. A specific character in the narrative is particularly important in enabling the narrative to move from lack to fulfilment. Donor (= giver) is the name given to this character, and typically the donor(-function) will give the hero (-function) some object (either real or intangible, such as information or inspiration) that allows the hero to conclude the narrative by restoring the lack. In Propp's fairy tales, the gift is often magical: a cloak of invisibility, or a special weapon. But if we move beyond fairy tales to more realistic narratives, we still find that there may be something magical about a gift that is not magical in an obvious sense: e.g. it may function unexpectedly, such as a Bible carried in a shirt pocket that deflects a bullet. A particularly common type of donor is an old person who gives the hero something in exchange for a favour. Sometimes the gift may be only a small piece of information (e.g. when a dying character in a thriller gasps out some crucial bit of information with his or her last breath).

If we try to trace Propp's character functions in more realistic texts than traditional folktales, we often need to adapt them, interpreting the name of the character function rather abstractly. The 'princess', for example, is a character who is searched for by the hero, possibly because that character has been snatched by a villain. 'Villain' also requires reinterpretation. The princess-character may for example have been kidnapped by their relationship with someone who takes on the 'villain' function. Some degree of gender transposition is also possible in assigning roles: the 'princess' function may be served by a young boy, for instance, and if the only family member otherwise involved is the boy's mother then she might be classified as 'the father of the princess'. This is the power of Propp's approach: it allows us to understand characters functionally, in terms of their role in the narrative, rather than only realistically in terms of their described, particular identity.

Narratives permeate culture as a way of making sense, packaging experience in particular ways for particular groups and audiences. A society's common narratives as a result provide collective focus for self-understanding, and are often laden with beliefs, attitudes and values. As part of such self-representation and imagining, an individual may be classified, for narrative purposes, on the basis of some characteristic: race, ethnic group, gender, age, sexuality, size, skin colour, etc. And the fit between character, characteristic and narrative function differs between genres and periods. In this respect, it is interesting to look at the relationship between the particular classificatory characteristics of a character and the function that the character plays in a given narrative. For example, in many contemporary American films an African-American character serves the function of donor. The donor typically has a minimal presence in the narrative (usually appearing briefly), but has a crucial role in allowing the narrative to develop and come to its conclusion. In any particular film, we might interpret the use of an African-American donor as making a historical claim: that African-Americans function as donor for the development of the 'narrative' of US society and the US economy. Or we could interpret this same narrative effect in terms of an apparently contradictory position taken by the film with regard to racism: the film seems to permit racial discrimination at the level of employment (the actor gets a small part), while carrying a positive message at the level of meaning (without the African-American character, the narrative could not be resolved).

20.3 The narrative arc: from lack to resolution

Narratives are typically about change. We can begin to think about change like this:

situation A   changes to   situation B

The changes in a narrative are typically (though not exclusively) brought about by human actions; and the notion that actions are causes that have effects is an important part of many narratives. Often in a narrative the changes that take place – particularly the important ones – need also to be understood in terms of the initial situation (situation A) being a lack or disruption, which is then restored or resolved by situation B. So we can think of many narratives as having arcs, or directions of development, like this:

situation A	changes to	situation B
lack	leads to	restoration

The lack may occur, for instance, when a family member leaves home. Such a lack is restored if the family is reunited at the end (this need not involve exactly the same people; the crucial point, for the narrative, is that a 'lacking' family is replaced by a 'restored' family). Or the lack may involve the loss or theft of an object, which is hunted and finally recovered. The lack may be a personal lack: the hero or heroine may begin in ignorance and end in wisdom, or begin in isolation and end in a relationship or community. There are many variations on the basic pattern of lack and restoration, but movement from one to the other is typically the driving force of a narrative.

With restoration comes the ending, or closure of the narrative, closely linked with the narrative's unity and coherence. Closure is a 'tying up' of the narrative, whereby loose ends are dealt with, problems solved and questions answered. Few narratives are completely without closure (and if they are, we tend to think of them as experimental or avant-garde). Nevertheless, because most narratives involve a number of lacks and possibly several levels or kinds of restoration, there is typically some lack of closure: a few issues (though not usually central ones) may remain unresolved. Occasionally the narrative ends with closure but at the very end of the text a new lack opens up; at the moment of its conclusion, the text opens up a new narrative (perhaps leading to a new text – a sequel – that will bring closure to that lack, which forms the beginning of the new narrative).

The existence or non-existence of closure in a text may be thought to suggest a moral or ideological position. For example, if a narrative can be closed by the major male and female characters getting married, then that narrative potentially conveys a message about the virtues of marriage. Or similarly, we might look at what constitutes or causes a 'lack' or disruption in the terms of a particular narrative in the first place. If the absence of a father at the beginning of a novel or film constitutes its initial lack, then the narrative may be read as a story advocating that nuclear families should stay together.

20.4   How narratives begin and end

So far, we have looked at how narrative form involves the management of whatever narrative content it represents. We now consider some of the ways in which narrative form is a response to the context in which the act of narration takes place, and in particular how narratives are started and how they finish. We can call the movement from lack to resolution described above the 'narrative proper'. The text of the narrative may, however, begin before its opening lack is revealed, and may end some time after that lack has been resolved. The extra material at each end serves to lead into and out of the narrative proper. The hearer or reader must 'enter' a narrative, and must then 'exit' from that narrative at the end; and there are characteristic strategies for achieving this entry and exit. We conclude this unit by considering first some 'entry strategies', then some 'exit strategies'.

Entry strategies include the title of the narrative itself, along with material quoted from elsewhere (an epigraph). Such 'text attached to the text', or **paratextual** material, may function to establish the leading idea of the narrative: the core notion that will provide its narrative coherence. There may occasionally be an initial 'abstract', or summary of what is to come. Very often, on the other hand, the text begins by setting the scene through a kind of illustration. This is called the 'orientation' of the narrative, and may include a representation of the place where the narrative is to take place and perhaps some initial details about the characters. Orientations can be stereotyped: fairy tales may begin with the stereotyped orientation, 'Once upon a time there was . . .'; and many films begin with a camera panning across a city towards a particular locality in which the action will be inferred to take place.

Exit strategies are ways of ending the text, once the lack has been restored. This material is generally called the 'coda', and can contain elements that mirror the 'abstract' (e.g. by offering a final summary) or the 'orientation' (e.g. by showing some kind of departure from the scene). The coda can also be stereotyped, as in the fairy-tale coda, 'And they all lived happily ever after . . .'. Sometimes codas fill a historical gap, between an explicitly historical narrative content and the time of narrating and reading/hearing. Commonly a film will end by telling us (typically by means of captions) what happened to various characters between the end of the narrative proper and now.

ACTIVITY 20

Consider the following extract from J.M. Coetzee's novel *Summertime*. Compare the techniques used in the passage with aspects of narrative technique outlined in the unit, and assess how the extract defeats your expectations of what a novel consists of. The character's name is J.M. Coetzee.

1 September 1972

The house that he shares with his father dates from the 1920s. The walls, built in part of baked brick but in the main of mud brick, are by now so rotten with damp creeping up from the earth that they have begun to crumble. To insulate them from the damp is an impossible task; the best that can be done is to lay an impermeable concrete apron around the periphery of the house and hope that slowly they will dry out.

From a home improvement guide he learns that for each metre of concrete he will require three bags of sand, five bags of stone, and ten bags of cement, which will entail six trips to the builders' yard, six full loads in a one ton truck. Halfway through the first day of work it dawns on him

continued

that he has made a mistake of a calamitous order. Either he misread the guide or in his calculations, he confused cubic metres with square metres. It is going to take many more than six trips. It is going to take many more than ten bags of cement plus sand and stone, to lay ninety six square metres of concrete; he is going to have to sacrifice more than just a few weekends of his life.

To be expanded on: his readiness to throw himself into half-baked projects: the alacrity with which he retreats from creative work into mindless industry.

Reading

Briggs, K. (1970) *A Dictionary of British Folk Tales in the English Language*, London: Routledge.

Fabb, N. (1997) *Linguistics and Literature: Language in the Verbal Arts of the World*, Oxford: Blackwell, Chapters 7–8.

Finnegan, R. (1992) *Oral Traditions and the Verbal Arts: A Guide to Research Practices*, London: Routledge.

Murray, J. (1998) *Hamlet on the Holodeck: The Future of Narrative in Cyberspace*, Cambridge, MA: MIT Press.

Onega, J. and Garcia Landa, J. (eds) (1996) *Narratology: An Introduction*, London: Longman.

Propp, V. (1968) *Morphology of the Folktale*, Austin, TX: University of Texas Press.

Toolan, M. (2001) *Narrative: A Critical Linguistic Introduction*, 2nd edn, London: Routledge.

Narrative point of view

This unit:

- reviews the distinction between the form and content of a narrative, showing the significance of 'narration' as the set of techniques adopted in telling a particular story in one way rather than another;

- examines the concept of 'point of view' in narration, illustrating the main differences between first-person narration and third-person narration;

- introduces more specialized techniques of 'focalization' used in literary narratives, showing how this concept can be used in developing a reading of a particular passage or work.

The term 'point of view' has been used in a variety of ways when applied to narrative prose fiction. It can be used literally to refer to visual perspective: the spatial position or angle of vision from which a scene is presented. It can also be used, metaphorically, to designate a text's ideological, philosophical or theological 'world view' (e.g. 'the point of view of an emergent bourgeoisie', or 'a Puritan perspective'). Finally, it can be used as a term for describing and analysing the narrative point of view from which a tale is told. The three uses overlap, but in this unit we concentrate on the third of these meanings, examining point of view as a 'mode of telling' before exploring that mode of telling as a way of seeing.

21.1 Point of view and narrative technique

A basic distinction in discussing narrative point of view is that between first-person 'I-narration' and third-person 'he-she-they-narration'. The latter is called 'third-person' because the narrator never refers to him- or herself using a first-person pronoun; instead, the narrator refers to all characters using third-person pronouns. The distinction can be illustrated simply. A narrative event such as 'the end of a relationship' could be presented in at least two ways:

Third-person: She texted him to say it was all over.

Or:

First-person: I texted him to say it was all over.

The terminology of 'first-person' and 'third-person' narration is based on the personal pronoun system in English, in which pronouns that refer to or include the speaker (I, we) are termed 'first person'; pronouns that refer to the addressee (you) are termed 'second person'; and pronouns that refer to anyone or anything other than the speaker and the addressee are termed 'third person' (he, she, it, they).

Given the options available in the pronoun system, we might wonder if second-person narration ever occurs. While it is extremely rare, some examples do exist. The best known, perhaps, is Italo Calvino's *If on a Winter's Night a Traveller* (1981). One reason that second-person narration is so rare relates to the difficulty of restricting the reference of second-person pronouns to characters in the narration, since such pronouns also seem to refer to the reader, outside the narration, as in the following example:

Second-person: You texted him to say it was all over.

This sounds more like a statement to a co-conversationalist (internal or external to the text), rather than description of a narrative event. Given the rarity of second-person narration, we deal below only with features of first- and third-person narration.

21.1.1 First-person narration

First-person narration is found in a wide range of novels that are are otherwise quite different in style and period. Such novels range from Daniel Defoe's *Robinson Crusoe* (1719) to Alice Walker's *The Color Purple* (1983). In most such novels, the I-narrator is also the main protagonist of the tale; so the person central to the action of the story is also telling it. For example, the core narrative of James Hogg's *The Private Memoirs and Confessions of a Justified Sinner* (1824), a document titled 'Private Memoirs and Confessions of a Sinner', is supposedly written by the 'sinner' himself. It begins,

> My life has been a life of trouble and turmoil; of change and vicissitude; of anger and exultation; of sorrow and of vengeance. My sorrows have all been for a slighted gospel, and my vengeance has been wreaked on its adversaries. Therefore in the might of heaven I will sit down and write . . . I was born an outcast in the world, in which I was destined to act so conspicuous a part.

In many first-person novels, it follows, the narrating character plays a 'conspicuous' part in the tale. But a first-person narrative can alternatively be told not by the central protagonist but by a subsidiary character. The 'Private Memoirs and Confessions of a Sinner' is itself framed by such a first-person 'Editor's Narrative', which was supposedly written by the editor and discoverer of the sinner's 'confessions' narrative.

F. Scott Fitzgerald's *The Great Gatsby* (1922) is a well-known case of a story told in first-person narration by a subsidiary character. Although Nick, the narrator, relates the story in the first person, he remains on the margins of the story's main events, which involve the central figure – Jay Gatsby – whose story is in this way narrated with some degree of narrative distance. Here, for instance, is Nick's final description of Gatsby and Daisy, whose reunion he has helped, almost unwittingly, to make possible:

> As I went over to say goodbye I saw that the expression of bewilderment had come back into Gatsby's face, as though a faint doubt had occurred to him as to the quality of his present happiness. Almost five years! There must have been moments even that afternoon when Daisy tumbled short of his dreams – not through her own fault, but because of the colossal vitality of his illusion. It had gone beyond her, beyond everything. He had thrown himself into it with a creative passion, adding to it all the time, decking it out with every bright feather that drifted his way. No amount of fire or freshness can challenge what a man can store up in his ghostly heart.
>
> . . .
>
> They had forgotten me, but Daisy glanced up and held out her hand; Gatsby didn't know me at all. I looked once more at them and they looked back at me, remotely, possessed by intense life. Then I went out of the room and down the marble steps into the rain, leaving them there together.

The narration here is full of circumspect observations, which foreground limitations of the narrator's knowledge: 'I saw that the expression of bewilderment had come back into Gatsby's face, *as though a faint doubt* had occurred to him'; or, 'There *must have been* moments'.

First-person narration, then, has in-built restrictions. These become especially evident when the narrative is related from the viewpoint of a minor character, although even a central narrating character may be presented as being ignorant about key events and may be compelled to appear to interpret the inner lives of other characters through their actions, words and gestures. These are not limitations to be regretted, since novelists exploit them to generate additional meanings and aesthetic effects of mystery, suspense, and so on. First-person narrators may also show a degree of unreliability or naivety, and so can be subject to situational irony (see **Unit 11, Irony**). On the other hand, first-person narration can also offer the reader a sense of having direct access to the inner consciousness of the narrating character, who reports events from a defined observer's position.

Another, less common version of first-person narration can be found in the epistolary novel, a genre in which the narrative is conveyed entirely in the form of letters supposedly written by the central character or characters. The techniques adopted in an epistolary novel create an impression that we are given privileged access to different characters' points of view, and can be used variously to produce a sense of intimacy or to foreground the limits of particular individuals' viewpoints. Mismatch between the various points of view presented in different letters contained in an epistolary novel can also be used to create comic or tragic effects, through situational irony (see **Unit 11, Irony**). Samuel Richardson's *Pamela; or, Virtue Rewarded* (1740) and *Clarissa* (1747–8) are the most well-known epistolary novels in English, along with Tobias Smollett's *The Expedition of Humphry Clinker* (1771). The form is not exclusively an eighteenth-century one, however. Malorie Blackman's *Noughts and Crosses* (2001), a novel for young adults that consists not of letters but of alternate diary entries by the two central characters, foregrounds tragic limitations of individual points of view in a racially divided society.

21.1.2 Third-person narration

Third-person narration, which is at least as common as first-person narration, is found in a wide range of novels, from Jane Austen's *Pride and Prejudice* (1813) or George Eliot's *Middlemarch* (1874) through to the *Harry Potter* series by J.K. Rowling (1997–2007). In contrast with first-person narration, third-person narration appears to offer a transparent window on events in a story. Because the role of a narrator is effaced, this mode of narration creates an impression of impersonal, but all-seeing, objectivity. The opening of William Golding's *Lord of the Flies* (1954), for example, gives this impression in the way it introduces an unnamed boy from the point of view of an outside, unnamed observer:

The boy with fair hair lowered himself down the last few feet of rock and began to pick his way towards the lagoon. Though he had taken off his school sweater and trailed it now from one hand, his grey shirt stuck to him and his hair was plastered to his forehead.

This kind of third-person narration offers a very different perspective on the boy and his actions from the one we would get if the novel were told by the boy himself, in first-person narration. A description such as 'The boy with fair hair' is clearly presented as if observed from without. It would be difficult to re-cast this passage in first-person form, as told from the boy's own perspective. A phrase such as 'my hair was plastered to my forehead' sounds odd precisely because the boy would simultaneously have to be the subjective agent of the narration and also an object under its scrutiny. He would, in effect, have to be talking about looking at himself from outside.

The opening passage of the novel continues in a similar vein:

All round him the long scar smashed into the jungle was a bath of heat. He was clambering heavily among the creepers and broken trunks when a bird, a vision of red and yellow, flashed upwards with a witch-like cry; and this cry was echoed by another.

Although the narration remains in third person, however, the sensations described here begin to appear to be those of the boy. It seems likely to be the boy who feels the long scar in the jungle as a bath of heat; who sees the red and yellow 'vision' of the bird; and who hears the bird's cry as 'witch-like'. If we transform these sentences into first-person, they do not sound at all odd: for instance, the sentence 'All round me the long scar smashed into the jungle was a bath of heat' reads quite plausibly.

In this respect, third-person narration enjoys a technical advantage over first-person narration. First-person narrators have to provide a warrant for knowing what they narrate; they cannot see into the minds of other characters, unless they are telepathic. By contrast, if the narrator is not defined as an individual 'I', and instead operates anonymously in third person, the narrative does not need to provide a warrant for presenting everything that is going on in the story, whether in the mind of a character or not. Part of the fiction of third-person narrative is in this way that it can appear omniscient: such narration can know everything that affects the story, and can have access to the inner experience and thoughts of one, more, or any of the characters.

Third-person narration in this way is capable of a variety of possibilities as regards point of view. We may sum these possibilities up in the following oppositions:

INTERNAL	versus	EXTERNAL
RESTRICTED	versus	UNRESTRICTED
KNOWLEDGE		KNOWLEDGE

Internal/External: The illustration of third-person narration taken from *Lord of the Flies* begins by observing the boy and his actions from outside (externally). It then shifts, to give us a sense of partial access to the boy's inner experience. Third-person narration by this means offers access to the consciousness of characters by revealing how they think and feel. This applies to, and can take on further properties or capabilities in, many novels.

Much of D.H. Lawrence's *Lady Chatterley's Lover* (1928), for example, despite its title, adopts Connie Chatterley's perspective rather than that of her lover, Mellors. The following passage is presented as being in this respect fairly representative of the novel as a whole:

> Now she came every day to the hens, they were the only things in the world that warmed her heart. Clifford's protestations made her go cold from head to foot. Mrs Bolton's voice made her go cold, and the sound of the business men who came. An occasional letter from Michaelis affected her with the same sense of chill. She felt she would surely die if it lasted much longer.
>
> Yet it was spring, and the bluebells were coming in the wood, and the leaf-buds on the hazels were opening like the spatter of green rain. How terrible it was that it should be spring, and everything cold-hearted, cold-hearted. Only the hens, fluffed so wonderfully on the eggs, were warm with their hot, brooding female bodies! Connie felt herself living on the brink of fainting all the time.

Although this passage is consistently in third person, it is nonetheless devoted primarily to the inner sensations and perceptions of the character being described. Much of the passage is told in a form of presentation called 'free indirect thought': a technique whose characteristic feature is that passages can be translated back out of such free, indirect representation into the direct thought of the character by changing third-person pronouns to first-person and changing past tense verbs into present tense (see **Unit 22, Speech and narration**). The final sentence of the first paragraph, 'translated' in this way, would read: 'I felt I would surely die if it lasted much longer'. Third-person narration, as a result, has the option of presenting internal or external points of view. It can even switch sometimes within the same text, and merge the voices of narrator and character.

Restricted/Unrestricted: A second distinction may be made within third-person narration between narration with no restriction on what is knowable (so-called 'omniscient narration'), and narration in which point of view is signalled as limited in some way. A narration may be told in third person, yet be wholly or partly limited to the experience, thoughts and feelings of a single character.

Consider for example the following passage from Henry James's *Daisy Miller* (1879). In this passage, the eponymous heroine (i.e. the heroine whose name is also the name of the novel) is observed by a subsidiary character, a young man named Winterbourne who is romantically attracted to her, while she is in conversation with an Italian companion ('her cavalier') named Giovanelli:

Winterbourne stood there; he had turned his eyes towards Daisy and her cavalier. They evidently saw no one; they were too deeply occupied with each other. When they reached the low garden wall, they stood a moment looking off at the great flat-topped pine-clusters of the Villa Borghese; then Giovanelli seated himself, familiarly, upon the broad ledge of the wall. The western sun in the opposite sky sent out a brilliant shaft through a couple of cloud bars, whereupon Daisy's companion took her parasol out of her hands and opened it. She came a little nearer, and he held the parasol over her; then, still holding it, he let it rest upon her shoulder, so that both of their heads were hidden from Winterbourne.

At some points, this passage can be read as neutral, unrestricted third-person narration. The following section taken in isolation, for example, shows no indication of expressing any one individual's perspective:

The western sun in the opposite sky sent out a brilliant shaft through a couple of cloud bars, whereupon Daisy's companion took her parasol out of her hands and opened it. She came a little nearer, and he held the parasol over her.

Yet the passage as a whole makes it clear that the actions of the characters are perceived from Winterbourne's point of view: 'he had *turned his eyes towards* Daisy and her cavalier. They *evidently* saw no-one.' The third-person narrative is in this way confined to what Winterbourne can see: after the opening of the parasol, for example, 'their heads were hidden from Winterbourne'. Restricting at crucial moments the description of a central action to what a subsidiary character can see is an important structural device in a novel. Like Winterbourne in this case, we are left at this point in the narrative in a state of uncertainty concerning the exact nature of Daisy's relationship (sexual or merely close?) with her 'cavalier' (courtly gentleman or lover?). Third-person narration need not always embody objectivity, therefore. Sometimes it can limit itself to internal, subjective and restricted positions, in order to create specific narrative or aesthetic effects. In his reflection on novelistic practice, *The Art of the Novel* (1934), Henry James described the perceiving character in his third-person narratives more generally as a 'focus' or 'centre of consciousness'. As we will see, James was in this regard anticipating an important development in modern theories of narrative.

21.2 Focalization

The distinction between first-person and third-person narration is not sufficient, in itself, to account for all the different types of point of view to be found in narrative prose fiction. Person-related terms indicate who *tells* the narrative, but narrative point of view is also a matter of who *sees* or experiences the narrated events.

Some accounts of narrative have for this reason refined their analysis of point of view by developing an additional concept: that of 'focalization'.

Focalization describes the way that a text represents the relationship between who 'experiences' and what is experienced. The character who experiences is called the **focalizer**, and what the focalizer experiences is called the 'focalized'. Focalization then falls into two main types: external focalization, in which an anonymous, unidentified voice situated outside the text functions as focalizer; and character focalization, where phenomena are presented as experienced by a character within the story.

The different possibilities for focalization in narrative prose fiction can be shown using the following notation:

F'r	=	Focalizer
E	=	External
C	=	Character
1	=	First-person
3	=	Third-person
F'd	=	Focalized phenomenon

The elements of this notation can be combined to show various kinds of narrative situation:

External focalizer	=	EF'r
Character focalizer (first-person)	=	CF'r1
Character focalizer (third-person)	=	CF'r3
Focalized phenomenon	=	F'd

The resulting classification can be illustrated by means of the following, invented examples:

(a) Despite closing the windows, I could hear noises from the beach all that sleepless night.
(b) Even with the windows closed, she could not shut out the noises from the beach.
(c) Even with the windows closed, the noises from the beach were audible all night.

In each of these example, 'noises from the beach' are the focalized phenomenon (or F'd). In (a), the first-person narrating character ('I') is the focalizer (or CF'r1). In (b), a third-person character ('she') is the focalizer (or CF'r3). In (c), no-one is identified as the focalizer, and the noises are reported by an unidentified narrator from a position seemingly somewhere outside the experience being reported (hence EF'r). The focalization structures of the three examples would be notated as follows:

(a)   CF'r1 ('I') → F'd ('noises from the beach')
(b)   CF'r3 ('she') → F'd ('the noises from the beach')
(c)   EF'r → F'd ('the noises from the beach')

As we saw in more general terms above, focalization in third-person narrative may shift from sentence to sentence, or even within the same sentence. The advantage of a notation of the kind presented here is that it can be used to highlight such shifts.

Crucial evidence for deciding who is focalizing comes from the presence or absence of verbs of experiencing, including 'look', 'see', 'touch', 'smell'. Consider the following example from Rosamund Lehmann's *The Weather in the Streets* (1936), in which the sentences have been numbered for ease of reference:

> (1) She [Olivia] ran down to the next floor, telephoned for a taxi, then opened the door of Etty's bedroom, adjoining the sitting room. (2) Silence and obscurity greeted her; and a smell compounded of powder, scent, toilet creams and chocolate truffles.

In the first of the two sentences that make up this passage, Olivia and her actions are focalized from without, by an unidentified focalizer. In the second sentence, however, the smell and silence are impressions that belong to Olivia, rather than to the external focalizer of the first sentence. The focalization has shifted, therefore, from external focalization (EF'r) to character focalization (CF'r). In the notation introduced above, the shift would be represented as follows:

> Sentence (1): EF'r (unspecified) → F'd (Olivia)
>
> Sentence (2): CF'r3 (Olivia/She) → F'd (silence, smell, etc.)

Similar shifts can be seen in the following passage from the same novel:

> (3) Between stages of dressing and washing she [Olivia] packed a hasty suitcase. (4) Pack the red dress, wear the dark brown tweed, Kate's cast off, well-cut, with my nice jumper, lime green, becoming, pack the other old brown jumper – That's about all.

Again, this extract begins as externally focalized. But in the second sentence there is a switch to Olivia's 'inner speech' or thoughts as she does her packing. Moving into the character's consciousness in this way entails a change of focalization, from external focalization to character focalization. In notation, we would say:

> Sentence 3: EF'r (unspecified) → F'd (Olivia packing)
>
> Sentence 4: CF'r1 (Olivia/my) → F'd (Olivia packing)

On this occasion, the notation highlights not just a shift in focalization, but also how Olivia comes in this passage to be the focalizer of her own actions. For a brief moment, she is the object of her own subjective consciousness, in a way that is simultaneously intimate and distanced. Examples such as this show how the concept of focalization can offer a powerful means of tracking shifts, developments and balances of point of view within a particular text. The novel *The Weather in the Streets* moves between external focalization and character focalization centred primarily on Olivia. As a result Olivia sometimes features as a third-person character, but sometimes as a first-person consciousness. The subtle and repeated variations of point of view adopted in this novel, as in narrative prose fiction more widely, can construct a character as either a subject or an object, or as simultaneously both a subject *and* an object of the narrative being related.

In this activity we explore narrative point of view in Daniel Defoe's *Robinson Crusoe* (1719). By changing referring expressions such as names and third-person pronouns ('he'/'him', etc.) into first-person pronouns ('I', 'me' and 'my') – and vice versa – we can rewrite selected passages in order to view events from one or other of the two main characters' perspectives, or alternatively from that of a 'detached' narrator.

The title page of Defoe's book, which is often considered an innovative early novel but also overlaps with the genres of travel journal and autobiography, reads as follows: 'The Life and Strange Surprising Adventures of Robinson Crusoe, of York. Mariner'. To this already long title Defoe adds a subtitle: 'who lived eight and twenty years, all alone in an uninhabited island on the coast of America, near the mouth of the great river of Oronoque'. And to this subtitle is added an explanation: 'having been cast on shore by ship-wreck, wherein all the men perished but himself', and a supplement: 'with an account of how he was at last as strangely delivered by pirates'. At the end of all this we are told that the book was 'written by himself'. *Robinson Crusoe*, then, is narrated in the first person, by Robinson Crusoe. In the passages below he is interacting with the only other inhabitant of the island, Friday, who he has rescued from cannibals.

1   In the following passage, change the first-person pronouns referring to Robinson to third-person pronouns (e.g. 'I' to 'he', 'me' to 'him', 'we' to 'they); and replace third-person pronouns referring to Friday with first-person pronouns. Switch the phrase 'Friday and I' to 'Robinson and I' at the beginning. The 'same narrative' is now presented through the mouthpiece of Friday rather than Robinson. (You may find it helpful to make a photocopy of the passage in order to make these changes.)

ACTIVITY 21

continued

After Friday and I became more intimately acquainted, and that he could understand almost all I said to him, and speak fluently, though in broken English, to me, I acquainted him with my own story, or at least so much of it as related to my coming into the place, how I had lived there, and how long. I let him into the mystery, for such it was to him, of gunpowder and bullet, and taught him how to shoot: I gave him a knife, which he was wonderfully delighted with, and I made him a belt, with a frog hanging to it, such as in England we wear hangers in; and in the frog, instead of a hanger, I gave him a hatchet, which was not only as good a weapon in some cases, but much more useful upon other occasions.

I described to him the country of Europe, and particularly England, which I came from: how we lived, how we worshipped God, how we behaved to one another; and how we traded in ships to all parts of the world. I gave him an account of the wreck which I had been on board of, and showed him as near as I could the place where she lay; but she was all beaten in pieces before, and gone.

I showed him the ruins of our boat, which we lost when we escaped, and which I could not stir with my whole strength then, but was now fallen almost to pieces. Upon seeing this boat, Friday stood musing a great while, and said nothing; I asked him what it was he studied upon; at last says he, 'Me see such boat like come to place at my nation.'

---

2   Write down any peculiar or incongruous sentences that result from this transposition of point of view and try to explain why they are peculiar. What overall effect is created by the changes you have made as regards the balance of interest shown in the thoughts and feelings of each of the two characters?

3   Now work through the original passage again. Replace first-person pronouns with the name Robinson (leaving some associated use of third-person pronouns for stylistic variation). Where third-person pronouns in the passage refer to Friday, replace them with the name Friday (again allowing for stylistic variation by leaving some associated use of third-person pronoun forms). The narrative should now appear to be told by a detached narrator, in a kind of external focalization.

4   Again, note any peculiarities or incongruities that result from this transposition into the viewpoint of a detached narrator.

5   Now repeat (1) (above) on a second passage, which occurs shortly after the one just looked at. In this passage, Robinson has walked with Friday

continued

up to the highest point on the island, from where they can see land on the horizon which Friday believes to be his own country. At this point, Robinson has taught Friday to be a Christian but now begins to wonder more about Friday's thoughts and values. (Note that in reversing point of view in this passage so that we hear the voice of Friday, you will need to change the second use of 'Friday' to 'I', but not the first use.)

> I observed an extraordinary sense of pleasure appeared in his face, and his eyes sparkled, and his countenance discovered a strange eagerness, as if he had a mind to be in his own country again; and this observation of mine put a great many thoughts into me, which made me at first not so easy about my new man Friday as I was before; and I made no doubt but that if Friday could get back to his own nation again, he would not only forget all his religion, but all his obligation to me; and would be forward enough to give his countrymen an account of me, and come back perhaps with a hundred or two of them, and make a feast upon me, at which he might be as merry as he used to be with those of his enemies, when they were taken in war.
>
> But I wronged the poor honest creature very much, for which I was very sorry afterwards. However, as my jealousy increased, and held me some weeks, I was a little more circumspect, and not so familiar and kind to him as before; in which I was certainly in the wrong too, the honest grateful creature having no thought about it, but what consisted with the best principles, both as a religious Christian, and as a grateful friend, as appeared afterwards to my full satisfaction.

5   In rewriting this second extract from Friday's point of view, you will have had to deal with two difficult expressions: 'poor honest creature' and 'honest grateful creature'. Both are ways of referring to Friday. Why do these expressions present a difficulty that does not arise with a pronoun like 'he' or 'him', or with a name like Friday?

6   Are the results of your re-writing different in relation to this second passage from when you made equivalent changes to the first passage, in (1) and (2) above? If so, how – and why?

7   Now compare the three different narrative points of view you have looked at during this activity: Crusoe's, Friday's, and a detached narrator's. Does each perspective involve an implicit bias? What have the rewriting exercises revealed about Crusoe's first-person narrative point of view? What significance, if any, should we attribute to an author's choice between alternative narrative points of view?

Reading

Bal, M. (2009) *Narratology: Introduction to the Theory of Narrative*, 3rd edn, Toronto: Toronto University Press, Chapter 2.8, pp. 145–65.

Branigan, E. (1985) *Point of View in the Cinema*, New York: Mouton.

Fowler, R. (1996) *Linguistic Criticism*, 2nd edn, Oxford: Oxford University Press, Chapter 9.

Furniss, T. and Bath, M. (2007) *Reading Poetry: An Introduction*, 2nd edn, London: Longman, Chapter 7.

Genette, G. (1980) *Narrative Discourse: An Essay in Method*, tr. J.E. Lewin, Ithaca, New York: Cornell University Press, Chapter 4.

James, H. (1934, 2011) *The Art of the Novel*, Chicago: University of Chicago Press.

Rimmon-Kenan, S. (2002) *Narrative Fiction: Contemporary Poetics*, 2nd edn, London: Methuen, Chapter 6.

Semino, E. (1999) *Language and World Creation in Poems and Other Texts*, London: Longman.

Simpson, P. (1993) *Language, Ideology and Point of View*, London: Routledge.

Speech and narration

This unit:

- examines the role of speech within a narrative, both by an imagined narrator and between characters in the story;

- contrasts direct speech, indirect speech and free indirect speech, offering practical guidance on how to analyse these different techniques in a given passage;

- explores the relationship between different ways of presenting speech in a narrative and different narrative genres, relating speech-presentation techniques to wider questions of how fiction presents thought, including as a kind of narrator's 'inner speech'.

Characters and events (as we saw in **Unit 20, Narrative**) are the building blocks of narratives. As in life, characters in narratives leave home, fall in love, sleep and wake up, live and die. But characters also speak. They argue, persuade, seduce, flatter and entertain each other; and storytelling – whether in the novel or in everyday anecdote – reflects this, by incorporating the expressive and dramatic potential of speech and quotation.

22.1 Spoken narrative

Spoken narrative in particular has specialized strategies for capturing characters' speech. The storyteller, for instance, can mimic tones of voice and pitch in order to convey emotion, and even to distinguish between one speaker and another.

Here, for instance, is a fragment of anecdote as told by a young casualty doctor:

> They come bustin' through the door – blood is everywhere
> on the walls
> on the floor
> everywhere
> [raised pitch]
> It's okay Billy it's okay we're gonna make it
> [normal voice]
> What's the hell wrong with you?
> We look at him. He's covered with blood y'know?
> All they had to do was take a wash cloth at home and go like this
> [pause for wiping action]
> and there'd be no blood . . .

The teller of the tale switches here between narration of action and the speech of protagonists. Indeed, in such spoken narratives pivotal moments in the action are often marked by this kind of embedding of enacted dialogue. The successful performance of the tale requires performance of the voices of those who inhabit it in order to bring the story fully alive for the audience.

In written narrative, of the kind we explore in this book, speech is no less important than in oral narrative. But writers have had to evolve specialized techniques to tackle the management and embedding of characters' voices and speech within the narrative as a whole.

22.2 Speech and writing

In presenting speech, writers have had to find ways of replacing the expressive possibilities of the voice with techniques for quotation, if such speech is to identify and individuate speakers. Techniques for achieving such effects developed slowly in the history of the novel, and are highly conventionalized: writers of narratives rarely attempt to render in detail actual, 'real-time', conversational speech, or **dialogue**. For one thing, conversation is full of false starts, repetitions, pauses, unfinished sentences and self-correction; so real-time speech looks messy if reproduced in more detail on the page. Here, for instance, is someone talking in ordinary conversation about arrangements for making telephone calls from a payphone:

> well you see (.) I'm sure it would have
> I'm sure it would have been possible
> if they had known anyone who was a post office engineer
> to install (.) a um er (.) rig
> so that the the the (.)
> where you can actually dial from the from the from that phone (.)
> er and if you (.) but that could be you know locked away
> and the er something like that (.)
> so that you could actually dial from that one
> by-pass the coin mechanism

A more 'written' version of this snatch of conversation – smoothing out its apparent disfluencies – might look like this:

> I am sure it would have been possible, if they had known anyone who was a post office engineer, to install the type of pay-phone where you can, if you wish, use a key to by-pass the coin mechanism and still dial out.

Such smoothing out of seemingly extraneous features of speech is generally what writers of narrative do. They conventionalize the raw immediacy of speech, even where (as we saw in **Unit 6, Language and place** and **Unit 9, Language and society**) a writer still accentuates differences between the narrative voice and the voice of a particular character, by attributing vernacular forms to characters and reserving standard dialect for the narration.

22.3   Speech presentation in prose fiction

In addition to techniques for smoothing out speech disfluency on the page, writers have evolved various ways of presenting the speech of characters. These methods vary considerably, from giving as much autonomy to the words attributed to a character as possible (rendering them, as it were, directly) through to filtering a character's speech through the report of the narrator – or another character – rendering the words indirectly.

22.3.1 Free direct speech

One influential technique in novels is that of free direct speech, in which there is hardly any evident intrusion or filtering by the narrator. With free direct speech, we nevertheless know that we have switched from the words of the narrator to words spoken by a character because of various clues, including indentation on the page and use of quotation marks. But there is little description of whose words the words in question are, or how they are spoken. The words seem to be allowed to speak for themselves. Consider this extract of free direct speech from Doris Lessing's *The Golden Notebook* (1962), and note the absence of any reporting clauses such as 'he said', 'she replied':

> They talked about his work. He specialised in leucotomies:
> 'Boy, I've cut literally hundreds of brains in half!'
> 'It doesn't bother you, what you're doing?'
> 'Why should it?'
> 'But you know when you've finished that operation, it's final, the people are never the same again?'
> 'But that's the idea, most of them don't want to be the same again.'

22.3.2 Direct speech

Direct speech (no longer 'free') is enclosed within quotation marks. In this respect, it resembles many examples of free direct speech. But direct speech is introduced by, or presented in the context of, a reporting clause (such as *she said/declared/commanded/asserted*, etc.):

> She said: 'Well there's nothing I can say to that, is there?'
> He leaned forward and said: 'I'm going to give you another chance, Anna.'
>
> (Doris Lessing, *The Golden Notebook*, 1962)

The strategy for representing speech adopted here makes a clear distinction between the words of the narrator ('He leaned forward and said') and words spoken by a character ('I'm going to give you another chance, Anna'). The technique also opens up possibilities for comment or evaluation on the character – implicitly or explicitly – by the narrator. In the exchange above, for example, the details of manner supplied by the narrator, as well as the words themselves, suggest a vaguely intimidating move in the dialogue. We have words spoken by the characters. But we also have, through the words of the reporting clause, the narrator's perspective.

22.3.3   Indirect speech

Indirect speech shifts perspective further away from the speaker towards the narrator. It differs from direct speech in a number of ways:

1   quotation marks are dropped;
2   some kind of subordinating **conjunction** such as *that* may be used;
3   there is a switch from first- and second-person pronouns (e.g. *I* or *you*) to third-person (*she, he, they*);
4   there is a shift in the tense of the verb, 'backwards' in time (e.g. from *is* to *was*);
5   temporal expressions also shift backwards in time (e.g. *now* becomes *then*);
6   **demonstratives** shift from close to distal (distant) ones (e.g. *here* becomes *there*).

Following the guidelines given here, the piece of dialogue in direct speech from *The Golden Notebook*, given above, can be converted into indirect speech fairly simply, as follows:

> She said that there was nothing she could say to that. He leaned forward and said that he was going to give her another chance.

Optionally, especially in a more informal style, the two uses of 'that' which introduce the reporting *that*-clauses could be omitted: 'she said there was. . .' and 'leaned forward and said he . . .'). Notice that the narrative voice is now more dominant than before, with consequent reduction, or attenuation, of the immediacy of the original dialogue.

22.3.4   Free indirect speech

Free indirect speech is a mixed form. It consists partly of direct speech and partly of indirect speech, in which – because of the omission of some of the distinguishing signals – it is difficult to separate the narrator's voice from the voice of the character.

In the following short extract from Chapter 16 of Dickens's novel, *Dombey and Son* (1846–8), we find features including 'backshifting' of tense ('the motion of the boat . . . *was* lulling him to rest') and some pronoun shift ('me' becomes 'him'); these features are characteristic of indirect speech, and emphasize the presence of a narrator who filters the speech of characters. At the same time, some sections of the passage sound close to the direct speech of a character (e.g. 'how bright the flowers growing on them, how tall the rushes!'):

> Presently he told her the motion of the boat upon the stream was lulling him to rest. How green the banks were now, how bright the flowers growing on them, and how tall the rushes! Now the boat was out at sea but gliding smoothly on. And now there was a shore before him. Who stood on the bank!

With a few changes, it is fairly straightforward to convert the free indirect speech of this passage into direct speech, moving the use of speech in the narrative closer to the perspective of the character:

> Presently he told her: 'The motion of the boat upon the stream is lulling me to rest. How green the banks are now, how bright the flowers growing on them, and how tall the rushes! Now the boat is out at sea but gliding smoothly on. And now there is a shore before me. Who stands on the bank!'

Free indirect speech is in this way an ambiguous mode, in that it blurs the distinction between a character's speech and the narrative voice. This ambiguity has made it attractive to many novelists, from Jane Austen onwards. Some writers – such as James Joyce in *Dubliners* (1914) or Jane Austen in *Emma* (1816) – are especially known as exponents of this technique of free indirect speech. As a technical device, it offers writers a way of presenting words that seem to come simultaneously both from inside and outside a character. Such words can be given the emotional weight of the character's perspective, while at the same time preserving a degree of narrative distance or ironic detachment from the character in question.

22.3.5 Speech and thought

Many of the distinctions in representing speech discussed above also apply to representation of characters' thoughts, to an extent that, in many respects, thought may be considered in narrative as a kind of 'inner speech'.

The different modes of presentation of speech and thought can accordingly be set out in a single table which shows how far a character's speech or thought is filtered through the narrator:

FREE DIRECT SPEECH/THOUGHT ('Come here tomorrow')	UNFILTERED BY NARRATOR
DIRECT SPEECH/THOUGHT (She said to him, 'Come here tomorrow.')	SOME FILTERING
FREE INDIRECT SPEECH/THOUGHT (She said to him to come tomorrow)	MORE FILTERING
INDIRECT SPEECH/THOUGHT (She said that he was to come there the next day)	MOST FILTERING

Because of the varying degree of connection between modes of presentation and relative closeness to or distance from the viewpoint of the character or narrator, ways of presenting speech in prose fiction are more than techniques that simply allow variety in the handling of characters' voices. Each different technique creates its own effect and seems to carry a different value, ranging from allowing the character to speak as if in his or her 'own words' to filtering those words through the narrator's overall perspective. While free indirect speech, for example, lends itself to ironic distance between the words of a character and those of the narrator, free indirect thought, on the other hand, can create a sense of empathy with the character. The different kinds of interplay between the narrator's voice and the speech of a character make techniques used in speech presentation important not only in themselves, but also for the way they connect with other topics in narrative such as fictional 'point of view' (see **Unit 21, Narrative point of view**).

22.3.6 Speech presentation and genre

Subtle differences in the presentation of speech can serve as indicators of different 'genres' of prose fiction (see **Unit 4, Recognizing genre**). Consider, for example, the following reporting clauses that frame direct speech (which are all drawn from within a few pages of each other in a single novel; the speech itself has been omitted):

> '. . . ,' she replied sharply.

> '. . . ,' she stuttered.

> '. . . ,' she wailed gaspingly.

> '. . . ,' he murmured huskily.

> '. . . ,' she asked as calmly as she could.

> '. . . ,' he said with chilly emphasis.

> '. . . ,' he countered silkily.

Readers familiar with the genre from which these reporting clauses are taken will instantly recognize them as commonly associated with popular romance (in fact, they are quoted from Susan Napier's *The Counterfeit Secretary: A Vivid Story of Passionate Attraction*, published by Mills and Boon (1986)). How the manner of speech has been foregrounded in the reported clauses listed, by means of adverbial phrases such as 'gaspingly', 'huskily', 'with chilly emphasis', and so on, is genre-specific to such popular romance. The stylistic distinctiveness can be seen by comparing the reporting clauses above with how speech is presented in the following short scene from Nancy Mitford's 'literary' novel *The Pursuit of Love* (1945):

> '*Allô – allô.*'
>> 'Hullo.'
>> 'Were you asleep?'
>> 'Yes, of course. What's the time?'

'About two. Shall I come round to see you?'

'Do you mean now?'

'Yes.'

'I must say it would be very nice, But the only thing is, what would the night porter think?'

'*Ma chère*, how English you are. *Eh bien, je vais vous le dire – il ne se fera aucune illusion.*'

'No, I suppose not.'

'But I don't imagine he's under any illusion as it is. After all, I come here for you three times every day – you've seen nobody else, and French people are quite quick at noticing these things, you know.'

'Yes – I see –'

'*Alors, c'est entendu – à tout à l'heure*'.

Both *The Counterfeit Secretary* and *The Pursuit of Love* are concerned with romantic relationships; and dialogue in each novel serves as an important vehicle for registering fluctuations in degree of emotional attachment. These similarities make the difference in how dialogue is handled all the more striking. *The Counterfeit Secretary* employs some free direct speech. But more of the dialogue consists of direct speech, in which information about the speaker's manner is foregrounded in explicit narrative comment. *The Pursuit of Love* makes more use of free direct speech, in which the characters' words have to achieve their own significance without being mediated by direct comment from the narrator.

Comparison between the two techniques suggests that, for popular romance, shifting grounds of emotional attachment may be carried in the *manner* of the speech, as much as by the speech itself – by what is said. For readers of *The Pursuit of Love*, on the other hand, the ebb and flow of emotional confrontation has to be deciphered in nuances of the wording of the dialogue. The contrast functions as a formal marker of generic distinctness; it may also signal a difference of attitudes towards language and meaning in the 'implied readerships' of the two works (see **Unit 15, Mode of address: positioning the reader**). The implied readership of *The Pursuit of Love* is, for instance, more class-based than that of *The Counterfeit Secretary*. The passage from the former presupposes not only some knowledge of French (very much a minority skill in Britain in 1945, restricted mostly to the middle and upper classes) but also – for its humour to be intelligible – some acquaintance with the distance between French and English sexual mores of the time. Free direct speech, furthermore, can be seen to make greater demands on the reader, since the significance of the dialogue has to be worked out from the wording of the speech itself, without interpretive guidance regarding tone and manner supplied by the narrator. In this way, differences in narrative presentation of speech in prose fiction may point to contrasts between popular and minority genres that are not confined to ways of telling the story but relate to how stories of particular kinds are interpreted.

'Thought' in fiction, this unit has suggested, may be considered a kind of 'inner speech', in that presentation of thought is accomplished by means of the same array of techniques that are used in presentation of speech. Direct speech, for example, is similar in its manner of presentation to direct thought, except that the reporting verbs will differ:

Direct speech:
She said, 'Well there's nothing I can say to that, is there?'

Direct thought:
She thought, 'Well there's nothing I can say to that, is there?'

In the following extract from Doris Lessing's *The Golden Notebook* (1962) two characters, Tommy and Anna, are having a confrontation. Tommy is the adult child of Anna's close friend; he is challenging Anna about her writing, and specifically about her way of organizing her work in four notebooks.

'Don't put me off, Anna. Are you afraid of being chaotic?'

Anna felt her stomach contract in a sort of fear, and said, after a pause: 'I suppose I must be.'

'Then it's dishonest. After all, you take your stand on something, don't you? Yes you do – you despise people like my father, who limit themselves. But you limit yourself too. For the same reason. You're afraid. You're being irresponsible.' He made this final judgement, the pouting, deliberate mouth smiling with satisfaction. Anna realised that this was what he had come to say. This was the point they had been working towards all evening. And he was going on, but in a flash of knowledge she said: 'I often leave my door open – have you been in here to read these notebooks?'

'Yes, I have. I was here yesterday, but I saw you coming up the street so I went out before you could see me. Well I've decided that you're dishonest, Anna. You are a happy person but . . .'

'I, happy?' said Anna, derisive.

———————

1 Identify the type of speech presentation used in the following excerpts from the passage:

(a) Anna . . . said, after a pause: 'I suppose I must be.'

(b) In a flash of knowledge she said: 'I often leave my door open – have you been in here to read these notebooks?'

Rewrite each as indirect speech. Make a note of the changes needed in order to do so. Now compare your rewritten version with the original.

continued

Is there any significant difference between them, in terms of meaning or effect? If so, make a note of what that difference is.

2   Identify the type of presentation of speech used in the following excerpt:

> 'Yes, I have. I was here yesterday, but I saw you coming up the street so I went out before you could see me. Well I've decided that you're dishonest, Anna. You are a happy person but . . .'

Rewrite this excerpt as free indirect speech. Make a note of the changes needed in order to do so. Now compare your rewritten version with the original. Is there any significant difference between them, in terms of meaning or effect? If so, make a note of what that difference is.

3   Identify how inner-speech/thought is represented in the following excerpt:

> Anna realised that this was what he had come to say. This was the point they had been working towards all evening. And he was going on . . .

Is there any uncertainty as to how much of this extract represents the character's thought, and how much is the narrator's report of events, or comment on them? If there is uncertainty, where does ambiguity as to whose voice is being presented begin? How could you resolve such ambiguity? Try to rewrite the passage as direct thought ('inner-speech'). Compare your rewritten version with the original. Do they differ in effect? If so, how?

4   Substitute your rewritten versions into the original, and read the whole (substantially rewritten) passage through. Does the passage work as well as the original? If it doesn't, why not? Being able to offer an answer to this question suggests that you have gone a long way towards under-standing why the author may have made those particular technical choices as regards speech presentation in the first place.

Reading

Fludernik, M. (1993) *The Fictions of Language and the Languages of Fiction: Linguistic Representation of Speech and Consciousness*, London: Routledge.

Leech, G. and Short, M. (2007) *Style in Fiction: A Linguistic Introduction to English Fictional Prose*, 2nd edn, London: Longman.

Semino, E. and Short, M. (2004) *Corpus Stylistics: Speech, Writing and Thought Presentation in a Corpus of English Writing*, London: Routledge.

Toolan, M. (2001) *Narrative: A Critical Linguistic Introduction*, 2nd edn, London: Routledge, pp. 90–145.

Narrative realism

This unit:

- reviews received senses of 'realism' as a measure of the fit between a text and the situations and events it depicts, and introduces a more specialized sense of narrative realism: as the set of techniques used in creating a reader's perception of what appears 'real';

- summarizes structuralist views of realist conventions as used in literary works;

- assesses the contribution made by influential Marxist traditions in analysing literary realism;

- examines non-realist contemporary writing, showing how such writing interacts with (and challenges) readers' expectations based on a tradition of classic realism.

When the term 'realism' is used to describe the effect of a text, or of a kind of text, it is often meant to convey a relationship between text and reality that is felt to be immediate, close and direct. Examples of realistic types of text are commonly genres such as 'the nineteenth-century novel', 'the Hollywood film', or 'popular fiction'. An alternative way of thinking about realism has developed in critical theory, however. In this view, realism means the adoption of a set of devices or techniques that *create* a sense of something being 'real'. Realism in this second meaning is a style of composition, which need not be considered to have any necessary reference to or connection with an external reality. The adjective 'realistic' points both ways: we need to distinguish between 'realistic', as commonly used to mean something such as 'close to how I see reality', or 'life-like'; and 'realist', in a more technical sense of conforming to conventions for presenting something in a narrative (in effect, passing it off) as real. Even future fantasy and science fiction draw on conventions of realism, stylistically or formally, and so can be 'realist'. 'Realistic' is a matter of evaluation of a narrative, while 'realist' is a description of its formal characteristics.

23.1 Traditional views of realism

'Realism' is the name of a literary movement, mainly involving novels, which flourished between about 1830 and 1890. That movement is usually considered to include the work of George Eliot, for example, as one of its major British exponents. 'Realism' is also the name of a wider 'genre' of writing (see **Unit 4, Recognizing genre**). In that genre, formal features associated with realist texts in the 'movement' sense of 'realism' are displayed in a given work. Until fairly recently, this was the view of realism held by most realist writers and critics. In this traditional view, it is possible to see realism in either of two ways: as direct imitation of the facts of reality; or as some special reconstruction of such facts of reality, a kind of reconstruction that Eric Auerbach (1953) called **mimesis**. If realism is direct imitation, then it can be seen as a style of writing that merely acts as a window onto the world, mirroring events almost as if writing is a matter of direct transcription of events in the real world. In the 'mimesis' view, on the other hand, while the reader recognizes a view of reality as being presented by the narrative (since the narrative includes elements from external reality with which he or she is familiar), what is presented is considered a more generalized or universalized version of the reality that the reader habitually experiences. It is this generalized, or universalized, version of reality that is taken to be of most value. Mimesis, in this sense, does not simply describe 'a' reality; it teaches or enlightens readers about 'reality' in general.

In **Unit 4, Recognizing genre**, we assessed the possibility of listing characteristics for particular genres. In the traditional view of realism outlined here, realism primarily consists of two elements: subject matter (what novels choose to depict); and message about that subject matter (typically thought of as a matter of moral intentions). The subject matter of realist novels is mostly concerned with what is considered, in the West, to be 'ordinary life': novels deal with the home, work, human relationships and stages of life. Most events described are not heroic deeds but seemingly ordinary events in the lives of ordinary people. One of realism's aims, accordingly – generalized from such typical topics and themes – is that of showing how ordinary people are complex and multifaceted, even when the events they are involved in are unexceptional or even mundane. Although realist texts are *about* individual characters and their lives, their message, which is often developed in terms of a secular, socially based morality, tends to be presented as containing a wider truth for all readers.

23.1.1   Language in reality and representation

In the approach to realism described so far, little attention needs to be given to the language of a text. In fact, such language may be thought of as **non-self-reflexive language**: that is, language that avoids drawing attention to itself *as* language. Instead, the language of the text is treated as merely a transparent medium, or conduit, for transmitting a message, as if language is capable of simply reflecting reality. The relation between texts, particularly literary texts, and reality is far more complex than mere reflection, however. As the stylisticians Leech and Short put it: 'The myth of absolute realism arises from a mistaken attempt to compare two incomparable things: language and extra-linguistic realities' (2007, p. 152). Realist texts are verbal constructs; but to appear reflective of reality their textual nature has to be ignored. Challenging such neglect of the role played by language in such texts, some critics have shifted the emphasis of their enquiry to realism: they examine not so much the relation between the words of the text and the material world outside that text, which it purports to show, as the relations between words within the text which make this impression possible.

23.1.2   How traditional realism shapes ways of reading

The view according to which realist texts describe the reality of a period or place is common in literary criticism and the teaching of texts. Readings developed along such lines can be insightful, but they run the risk of being limited by stereotypical views of the position of particular people within the reality being represented.

Realism, as described so far, has strong connections with stereotypical notions of authenticity, according to which certain experiences and individuals are held to be more 'real', or closer to 'life', than others. The so-called 'gritty' realism of a novel about working-class life in an inner city, for example, is often considered somehow more authentic than close examination of refined middle-class behavior in a leafy suburb.

Whole classes of texts are assumed to be more or less 'realist' for stereo-typical reasons. Novels written by women, for example, are often interpreted (including when they are included on university courses) as though they must be autobiographical, despite the reliance in such an assessment on the stereotypical notion that women are restricted to the private sphere and must be concerned with description of the personal, intimate intricacies of relationships. Novels by working-class writers are often read as documentary accounts (based on a stereo-type in which working-class people see everyday reality as it really is, but are unable to transcend the particularity of their viewpoint). And novels by black writers are often read as documenting inevitable personal struggles against oppression, even if those novels are concerned with more universal issues that concern both white and black people.

23.2 The structuralist view

The general view of realism outlined so far was described as 'traditional' because it has been challenged and to some extent displaced by other approaches. Structuralist critics such as Roland Barthes (1986) and David Lodge (1989), for example, redirected attention away from the relationship between text and reality towards 'textual' qualities of realism. They showed how literary convention is crucial in the composition and reading of realist novels. In this more recent view of realism, whether or not a text is 'realist' (i.e. whether it exhibits formal charac-teristics of realism) is not necessarily related to whether it is 'realistic' (i.e. whether it presents to the reader an approximation to some kind of recognized reality). Rather, a narrative is 'realist' if it uses conventional techniques to produce an appearance of being real: a **reality effect**.

23.2.1 Conventions

Literary texts are composed in large part by being assembled on the basis of a system of textual conventions or rules. Our notion of which genre a text belongs to, in turn, is founded on recognition of a particular set of conventions that the text draws on in its composition (see **Unit 4, Recognizing genre**). When a writer sets out to produce a realist narrative, there is already in place a set of conventions governing the main choices to be made. For example, the writer of a narrative will be constrained by the following broad narrative conventions (each of which invites examination in much greater detail):

(1) events in the text are arranged in roughly chronological order;
(2) there are complex, 'rounded' and developed characters, who develop throughout the narrative;
(3) there is generally a narrator who will adopt a consistent position within the text;
(4) there will be an ending that draws the various strands and sub-plots of the narrative together;
(5) events will be included on the basis of clear relevance to plot development.

Point (3) is particularly important (see **Unit 21, Narrative point of view**). The presence of a reliable or omniscient narrator serves the function of creating a hierarchy of different kinds of discourse in the narration, which in turn guarantees that at least one view of events narrated in the novel will be interpreted as offering the reader a view of 'the truth', or 'reality'. Although the conventions of realism can be experimented with, undermined, and altered – as they often are in novels – those conventions provide a basis for the construction of realist texts, and a baseline against which much fictional experimentation is interpreted.

23.2.2 Characteristics of realism

David Lodge (1989) suggests that realist texts achieve their 'reality effect' not so much because they are *like* reality, but because, in their conventions, they resemble texts that we classify as non-fictional. Lodge shows this by examining two different descriptions of capital punishment: one by George Orwell entitled 'A Hanging' (discussed in **Unit 20, Narrative**); and one which appeared as an article in *The Guardian*, a British newspaper. Lodge analyses similarities between the realist fiction text and the non-fictional report, and shows that:

(1) in neither case are features of language foregrounded in such a way that they become a focus of attention;

(2) the narrator does not draw attention to his or her role in interpreting events; rather, the events seem to speak themselves, or to present themselves to the reader without mediation;

(3) there is an emphasis on detailed description of the context of the event (the exact time, place and setting) and of the preparation for the execution.

It is almost impossible, Lodge concludes, to distinguish one text from the other, if attention is confined to the strategies they adopt in depicting the event. He suggests that realist texts draw on the same conventions used to construct non-fictional texts, in order precisely to convince the reader that they are describing reality: a strategy whose significance is that it lends authority to realist texts. Generalizing from his analysis, Lodge proposes a working definition of realism in literature as, 'the representation of experience in a manner which approximates closely to descriptions of similar experience in non-literary texts of the same culture' (1989: 25).

Specialized techniques at work in achieving realism also extend into other areas of narration. Dialogue is represented in literature, particularly in realist narrative, according to a specific set of conventions rather than by reference to how people actually speak in real life (a topic discussed in **Unit 22, Speech and narration**). Many elements of genuine speech are omitted (e.g. hesitation, interruption, repetition), while other elements are introduced, or even emphasized, in order to signal to a reader that they are reading 'real speech' (e.g. use of inverted commas, use of colloquialism).

Other conventions at work in realist narrative concern description. Roland Barthes noted, for example, how in most classic realist texts there is a profusion of descriptive detail. In most cases narratives tend to include a descriptive section that sets the scene in which the action takes place; this functions as a kind of necessary context. But Barthes points to the presence in realist narratives in of details that seem to be included for the sole purpose of signalling to the reader that what is being described is 'the real'; such details create a kind of 'verisimilitude' (or likeness to something being real).

In the following extract from *The Well of Loneliness*, by Radclyffe Hall (1928), for example, some details in the description serve the purpose of setting the principal character within a certain social class: the estate is 'well-timbered, well-cottaged'; there are two large lakes in the grounds; the house has 'dignity and pride'; and so on. But other elements of the description do not appear functional in this way, and seem to be included simply because of a more general convention of making the passage 'appear real':

> Not very far from Upton-on-Severn – between it, in fact, and the Malvern Hills – stands the country seat of the Gordons of Bramley; well-timbered, well-cottaged, well-fenced, and well-watered, having in this latter respect, a stream that forks in exactly the right position to feed two large lakes in the grounds. The house itself is of Georgian red brick, with charming circular windows near the roof. It has dignity and pride without ostentation, self-assurance without arrogance, repose without inertia; and a gentle aloofness that, to those who know its spirit, but adds to its value as a home.

The aside in the first sentence – 'between it, in fact, and the Malvern Hills' – serves no apparent informational purpose. Rather, it conveys a general sense of the real, reflected in observation and an attention to detail that is reflective rather than an act of creation. Similarly, description of the house as being built of Georgian red brick and as having circular windows seems far more than is needed by the narrative purpose of the passage. Such details may accordingly be seen as functioning as what Barthes calls 'realist operators': such operators, he suggests, serve to produce a 'reality effect': they convey to the reader that this is a realist text. These 'reality operators' also help to reinforce for the reader a sense that the text is anchored in some recognizable, pre-existent reality rather than the text being something merely made up.

Barthes sees a further significance in such 'reality operators'. He suggests that, in incorporating extra detail, realist texts implicitly draw on a **cultural code**, or set of statements whose meaning in the narrative is 'decoded' by the reader on the basis of conventions that the reader already knows (and is taken to share with the writer). The code allows a kind of translation of statements that appeal to assumed stereotypes, and background and 'common sense' knowledge. Statements of this kind either appear immediately self-evident, or else they function because the reader recognizes them as what *should be* shared knowledge and so assents to them, at least for the purpose of making sense of the passage in which they occur.

To see more clearly how such effects are achieved, consider how the passage quoted above from *The Well of Loneliness* continues:

> To Morton Hall came the Lady Anna Gordon as a bride of just over twenty. She was lovely as only an Irish woman can be, having that in her bearing that betokened quiet pride, having that in her eyes that betokened great longing, having that in her body that betokened happy promise – the archetype of the very perfect woman, whom creating God has found good.

The description of Anna here is presented as something the reader will instantly recognize as fitting a stereotype of the perfect woman. The reader is expected to draw on background assumptions about the loveliness of Irish women, and to recognize the details about Anna's eyes and body which the text presents as self-evidently constituting perfection in women (e.g. having quiet pride, embodying happy promise, and so on). This material is presented as information 'we all know'. To make sense of the passage in a coherent way, we are obliged to draw on such presumed background knowledge (even if we have to construct it, rather than in fact already 'knowing' it). In interpreting in this way, according to Barthes, we draw on a cultural code, or organized repository of common sense knowledge and stereotypes, in that the ideas we employ in making sense of the passage are not ideas we make up for ourselves but ideas we take to be already around us, in society generally. Through its operation in reading, the cultural code at work in realist texts confirms conventional views of reality, which may nevertheless have only slight correspondence with how things really are. Realist texts in this way create rather than reflect reality, and so one way of responding to them is to see them as shaping (rather than reflecting) our views of what is real or true.

The reality effect of narrative fiction is perhaps at its most powerful when a novel ends. At that point, a story typically faces a kind of 'closure', or ending by means of which the problems explored in the work are resolved (but in a way that is potentially unconvincing or unrealistic, see **Unit 20, Narrative**). In nineteenth-century realist novels, plots are frequently resolved by death or marriage; and sometimes coincidence is a further, strong motivating factor in how most, if not all, loose ends in a plot are knitted together so that the reader is left with few or no unresolved questions about the characters. In twentieth- and twenty-first-century realist texts, by contrast, closure is a convention that writers appear to feel they can experiment with or reject altogether. Narrative resolution tends to be less complete. Coincidence in particular is less commonly used as a device to bring narrative to a close, in this way exposing further divergence between realism as convention or technique and realism as perceived impression. For many readers, however, narrative closure is pleasurable, and they may feel unsatisfied or even cheated if a text leaves them with too many unresolved plot elements.

23.3 Questioning how things are: Marxism and realism

Over a fairly long historical period, Marxist criticism had a major impact on discussion of realism, especially regarding the potentially manipulative nature of claims expressed by realistic techniques as to how things are. Marxist literary criticism accordingly attaches a great deal of importance to questions of realism, and to the progressive or reactionary character of realism as a technique. (This issue has also been extensively debated in feminist circles; see, for example, Coward (1986) for an overview.)

For some critics, such as Georg Lukács (1962), realist novels can present readers with a vision of a greater harmony in the face of capitalist fragmentation. Novels that do so can spur people to action, since they point out problems in the present social system, and expose tensions between the individual and society in such a way as to foreground points of tension and ideological contradiction. Lukács went so far as to champion the cause of realism against the rival claims of modernism, rejecting the claims of the latter to be politically progressive because of its subjective, fragmentary and disconnected modes of representation, which he felt amounted to a retreat from society into pathological individualism. The dramatist Bertolt Brecht, by contrast, viewed realist novels as a form of anaesthesia (Brecht, 1977). Readers become hypnotized, he argued, by realist narrative and become uncritical of values expressed in the text that also exist in the wider social system. As an alternative, he proposed a new form of art: one that would deny the reader the comfort of realist narrative and encourage him or her instead to act on the contradictions in capitalism. Lukács is in this respect closer to a traditional view of realism, and Brecht closer to a structuralist view.

23.4 Non-realist texts

Many contemporary literary works play with conventions of realism. Such experimentation may serve to challenge traditional notions of realism (as in surreal works, or in science fiction or fantasy texts). Or alternatively it may challenge notions of what reality is, for example by representing the perspective of narrators or characters with different or altered states of consciousness. Many such **non-realist texts** force the reader to question both their sense of what counts as realism in a text *and* what is real.

In Mark Haddon's *The Curious Incident of the Dog in the Night-Time* (2003), for instance, the central character and narrator is not the conventional middle-class educated narrator of classic realist fiction, as is evident in this extract:

> Then the police arrived. I like the police. They have uniforms and numbers and you know what they are meant to be doing. There was a policewoman

and a policeman. The policewoman had a little hole in her tights on her left ankle and a red scratch in the middle of the hole. The policeman had a big orange leaf stuck to the bottom of his shoe which was poking out from one side. The policewoman put her arms round Mrs Shears and led her back towards the house. I lifted my head off the grass. The policeman squatted down beside me and said 'Would you like to tell me what's going on here, young man?' I sat up and said 'The dog is dead.' 'I'd got that far,' he said. I said 'I think someone killed the dog.' 'How old are you?' he asked. I replied, 'I am 15 years and 3 months and 2 days.' 'And what precisely were you doing in the garden?' he asked. 'I was holding the dog,' I replied. 'And why were you holding the dog?' he asked. This was a difficult question. It was something I wanted to do. I like dogs. It made me sad to see that the dog was dead. I like policemen too, and I wanted to answer the question properly, but the policeman did not give me enough time to work out the correct answer.

Evidently this passage is not an example of conventionally realist technique, although it does share certain features of realism. There is a certain amount of descriptive information given about the characters, for instance, yet this information seems not to be the type of relevant character-revealing information we typically find in realist texts. Instead, the reader is presented with information about the police officers that appears random: the policewoman has a hole in her tights and there is a scratch on her leg; the policeman has a leaf stuck to his shoe. This type of information seems to conform to Barthes's idea that a reality effect is created by 'reality operators', in that the detail gives excessive, non-necessary information; but in this passage any relevance of the information to plot development or character must be in question. In a similar way, we are not told that the character/narrator is lying on the ground; rather, we are forced to work this out when he says 'I lifted my head off the grass'. Realist narrators, we expect, spell out what is happening clearly to the reader. The fact that the protagonist gives the police officers either too much information (about his age) or too little (about his reasons for being in the garden) leads the reader to surmise that this is not the trustworthy narrator of **classic realism**. We are obliged to assume instead that the narrator's perspective is merely one of many different possible views of the events; in this way, the hierarchy of discourses essential to classic realism appears undermined. The narrator presents us with the 'truth' of the events; but his perspective has to be set alongside the perspective of the police officers. Contemporary texts that experiment in this way with realist conventions may be non-realist in the sense that they play with the conventions of classic realism; or they may be non-realist in the sense that they attempt to represent different 'realities', whose expression requires new and different forms of representation; or they may be both.

The aim of this activity is to analyse two pieces of narrative (which you choose for yourself) and to identify in them markers of realism and non-realism.

1   Choose two pieces of narrative: one that you would consider to be an example of realism, the other an example of what you would think of as non-realism. Don't worry if your impressions of the contrast are not precise; this is part of the point of the activity. Your two pieces should be from the same medium (i.e. both from novels, or both short stories, or both from television, film, videos, comic strips, photo-reportage, etc.). You will need to look closely and repeatedly at the two texts you choose; so if you choose a moving image you will need to have it in a video format that lends itself to repeat viewing.

Here is a reminder of some features that have been claimed to be characteristic of different sorts of realist text (for more detail see discussion in this unit, above):

- the subject matter is generally drawn from 'everyday', 'ordinary' life;
- the characters are ordinary people presented as complex individuals who are shown to be capable of change and development;
- there is a moral position from which the events depicted are viewed;
- there is a consistent point of view from which the events are evaluated (there may be more than one but each is consistent);
- the narrator presents a non-contradictory reality;
- the narrator does not draw attention to himself or herself;
- the language used in the narration does not draw attention to itself;
- events are arranged in roughly chronological order (there may be flashbacks, but the sequence of events is clear);
- the narrative reaches some kind of decisive resolution;
- detailed description is provided of material objects (clothes, faces, furniture, etc.);
- there are 'reality operators' (i.e. the inclusion of apparently arbitrary extra details);
- the narrative appeals to understanding based on a cultural code (views we are supposed to share or believe to be generally held).

2   Examine the 'realist' text first, and check which of these characteristics are present.

3   Add any other general characteristics of realism that occur to you as you examine your selected 'realist' text.

4 Now examine the 'non-realist' text. Check which of the characteristics are absent. Cross off the list any characteristics that your examination suggests may be features of all texts, not just realist ones.

5 For the two particular texts you have chosen, what reasons occur to you as regards why each text should draw on, or reject, conventions of realism (i.e. what specific effects it creates by being realist or non-realist)?

continued

Reading

Barthes, R. (1989) *The Rustle of Language*, Oxford: Blackwell, pp. 141–8.

Brecht, B. (1977) 'Against Georg Lukács', in T. Adorno, W. Benjamin, E. Bloch, B. Brecht and G. Lukács (eds) *Aesthetics and Politics*, London: Verso, pp. 68–85.

Coward, R. (1986) 'This Novel Changes Lives: Are Women's Novels Feminist Novels?' in M. Eagleton (ed.) *Feminist Literary Theory: A Reader*, Oxford, Blackwell pp. 155–60.

Emmott, C. (1999) *Narrative Comprehension: A Discourse Perspective*, Oxford: Oxford University Press.

Gavins, J. (2007) *Text World Theory: An Introduction*, Edinburgh: Edinburgh University Press.

Leech, G. and Short, M. (2007) *Style in Fiction: A Linguistic Introduction to English Fictional Prose*, 2nd edn, London: Longman.

Lodge, D. (1989) *The Modes of Modern Writing*, London: Arnold, Chapter 3, 'Realism'.

Lukács, G. (1962) *The Historical Novel*, London: Merlin.

Mills, S. and Pearce, L. (1996) *Feminist Readings/Feminists Reading*, 2nd edn, Hemel Hempstead: Harvester, especially chapter on 'Authentic Realism'.

Toolan, M. (2001) *Narrative: A Critical Linguistic Introduction*, 2nd edn, London: Routledge.

Drama and performance

Ways of reading drama

This unit:

- contrasts a perception of plays as relatively fixed literary works, like novels or poems, with an alternative view of plays as notation for a performance that must significantly supplement what is written with theatrical strategies and devices;

- draws attention to ways of reading dramatic techniques such as stage directions, dramatic irony and soliloquies, as well as incorporation into a play of a prologue and/or epilogue;

- discusses features of dramatic performance that potentially disrupt uncritical absorption in the theatrical spectacle, including cross-dressing and role-doubling, as well as a general strategy (associated with the work of Bertolt Brecht) of producing a so-called 'alienation effect'.

There are two basic ways of reading drama. Each is based on a specific conception of what a play is: a play can be considered either as a dramatic performance, or as a dramatic text (a piece of dramatic literature published in a book). For most actors, directors, theatre-goers, theatre critics, teachers and students of theatre studies, along with many teachers of literature, a play is something that takes place on a stage rather than on a page. Teachers of drama tend to see the printed text of a play as merely a preliminary script, or set of guidelines, that contributes just one element to the total live performance. Teachers of literature similarly assume that their students need at least to imagine how a dramatic text's meanings and effects might be realized on stage. From this point of view, reading the text of a play is different in important ways from reading a novel or a poem.

24.1 Stage or page?

The notion that we need to analyse a play on the stage rather than on the page is compatible with most of the ways of reading developed in the present book (partly because we have extended the notion of 'reading' to include investigation of speech, songs, advertisements, films and TV, and so on).

An extended notion of reading of this kind makes it perfectly possible to talk about 'reading' the products of performative arts such as stand-up comedy, dance or dramatic performance. Many of the effects achieved in such forms draw on devices including for instance metaphor, irony, sound patterning, and so on. In this unit, however, we concentrate on exploring ways of reading dramatic texts not as scripts for performance, or as a kind of discourse incorporating techniques we have looked at in other units, but as fully readable 'texts' in their own right. Most of the time, we suggest, reading dramatic texts involves employing general reading skills and strategies outlined in the present book for reading other kinds of literary and non-literary discourse but also adapting those skills and strategies to suit the specific needs and context of drama.

24.2 Reading dramatic texts

Reading dramatic texts involves attending only to those aspects of theatrical performance which are written into, or cued by, the dramatic text itself. In other words, where features of performance are not specified in the dramatic text (as is usually the case with details of costume, lighting, gesture and music) we consider that such elements are added to the dramatic text, theatrically, for the purpose of dramatic performance, and for this reason call for a separate extended, semiotic exploration of theatre rather than a reading of the drama.

In taking this position, we are echoing one of the earliest and most influential discussions of drama in the history of criticism: Aristotle's *On the Art of Poetry* (fourth century BC). Aristotle identifies six constituents in the tragic drama of classical Greece: plot, character, diction, thought, spectacle and song. After discussing the first four constituents, however, he more or less dismisses the last two as having more to do with theatrical production than with drama in itself:

> Of the remaining elements, the music is the most important of the pleasurable additions to the play. Spectacle, or stage-effect, is an attraction, of course, but it has the least to do with the playwright's craft or with the art of poetry. For the power of tragedy is independent both of performance and of actors, and besides, the production of spectacular effects is more the province of the property-man than of the playwright.

Following this general view, we suggest in this unit that the power of dramatic texts is, as Aristotle argued for tragedy, largely independent both of performance and of actors; most theatrical devices and techniques employed in a production of a play, we consider, are 'pleasurable additions' rather than intrinsic elements of the play itself.

This distinction can be made clearer by looking at a passage from Shakespeare's *Othello* (*c.* 1602). The play *Othello* is set in Venice and Cyprus, and concerns the tragic downfall of Othello, a Moor (a Muslim from North Africa) who has entered military service as a general with the Duke of Venice. For reasons that never become fully clear, Iago – Othello's 'Ancient' (his ensign or standard bearer) – hates Othello and tries to destroy him. Iago convinces Othello that he is a trustworthy ally and then induces him to believe that his wife Desdemona has been unfaithful. In Act IV, when Othello is finally led to believe that Desdemona has betrayed him by having an affair with Cassio (his honourable lieutenant), he accuses Desdemona of being a whore and then leaves the stage. Desdemona, who the reader/audience knows is innocent, is bewildered and thrown into despair by Othello's behaviour. At this point, Iago and his wife Emilia (Desdemona's faithful maid) enter the stage. The audience/reader knows that Iago is a villain and has duped Othello; but, while his wife is beginning to suspect him, Desdemona still thinks of Iago as Othello's loyal servant. Desdemona at this point turns to Iago for help:

> O God, Iago,
> What shall I do to win my lord again?
> Good friend, go to him, for, by this light of heaven,
> I know not how I lost him. Here I kneel:
> If e'er my will did trespass 'gainst his love,
> Either in discourse of thought or actual deed,
> . . .
> Comfort forswear me!
>
> (*Othello*, IV, ii, 150–61)

Consider in this passage the words 'Here I kneel'. In their introductory textbook, *Studying Plays*, Wallis and Shepherd point out (2010:10) that this expression serves as an implied stage direction: in other words, it guides the actor playing the part. Although Shakespeare's plays include a minimum of explicit stage directions (which might be considered notation for theatrical production), they do often embed implicit stage directions in characters' speeches. But such stage directions are as useful for readers as they are for actors and directors. 'Here I kneel' allows a reader to imagine Desdemona's posture and its implications in context. The phrase has a function on the page as well as on the stage. Although a reader may try to imagine how the scene might look and work on a stage, he or she can just as well imagine that the scene takes place in Cyprus, and so imagine Cyprus rather than the stage of a theatre. In other words, reading and interpreting the passage need not be essentially different from reading an equivalent passage in a novel, though some of the triggers to meaning and effect may be dramatically specific.

24.2.1 Dramatic or situational irony

Perhaps the most important dramatic technique or effect in the passage from *Othello* is that of 'dramatic irony' (see **Unit 11, Irony**). Dramatic irony has been defined as

> a plot device according to which (a) the spectators know more than the protagonist; (b) the character reacts in a way contrary to that which is appropriate or wise; (c) characters or situations are compared or contrasted for ironic effects, such as parody; or (d) there is a marked contrast between what the character understands about his acts and what the play demonstrates about them ... Tragedy is [especially] rich in all forms of dramatic [irony]. The necessity for a sudden reversal or catastrophe in the fortunes of the hero means that the fourth form of [irony] (form d) is almost inevitable.
> (Preminger and Brogan, 1993: 635)

Dramatic irony is produced, crucially, when an audience knows something important that one or more of the characters in a play do not know. If the character did have this piece of knowledge, it would change his or her behaviour and/or attitude towards other characters. In a comedy, this effect can lead to humour at the expense of the uninformed characters. In a tragedy, such as *Othello*, the effect usually leads to a tragic **dénouement**: the character or characters only discover what they need to know when it is too late. In *Othello*, dramatic irony results from the virtuous characters (Othello and Desdemona) being fooled by Iago into believing that he is also virtuous, and that he is doing his best to help them, when the audience knows that the opposite is the case. In the scene we are examining, for example, the audience knows that Iago is the cause of Desdemona's suffering and will therefore experience a sense of dramatic irony when she kneels and supplicates him to help her.

Dramatic irony, as outlined here, would seem to be an inherently theatrical effect, in that it is produced by a difference between what the characters know about their situation and what the audience knows. Yet it is perfectly possible for a reader not in the theatre to experience an equivalent ironic effect. An attentive reader of the passage above (provided that he or she has read the rest of the play up to this point) will recognize or experience the same sense of tragic irony that an audience at the theatre will. This is partly because written texts, including both novels and dramatic texts, commonly employ techniques of 'situational irony' whose conditions are virtually the same as those for dramatic irony (see **Unit 11, Irony**). While an audience will experience dramatic irony in witnessing Desdemona's speech and actions in this scene, we might say, a reader will experience a corresponding situational irony.

24.3   Formal analysis of drama

While we might say that the distinctive feature of a dramatic text is that it is a script for theatrical performance, it may therefore be more useful to define dramatic texts in purely *formal* terms, by highlighting their differences from narrative prose fiction and most kinds of poetry.

The three main genres of literature (see **Unit 4, Recognizing genre**) can be distinguished from one another by different ways in which they present themselves as speech, and how they present the speech of the characters they depict. Lyric poetry presents itself as the unmediated speech of a first-person speaker. Narrative prose fiction typically presents itself as the speech of a number of different characters, mediated through a narrator. Drama differs from lyric poetry and from narrative fiction by typically presenting itself as the direct speech or dialogue of a number of different characters, without a mediating narrator.

The difference between presentation with, and presentation without, a narrator can be seen by noting how the scene from *Othello* examined above continues. Iago responds to Desdemona's supplication like this:

IAGO	I pray you, be content, 'tis but his humour;
	The business of the state does him offence
	And he does chide with you.
DESDEMONA	If 'twere no other –
IAGO	'Tis but so, I warrant.

(*Othello*, IV, ii, 167–70)

In this exchange, there is no narrator to mediate the characters' speech or to guide the reader. So there are no reporting clauses ('she said, anxiously'), and no descriptions of the characters and their behaviour ('she knelt with her head in her hands'). Reading dramatic texts can in this way be more demanding than reading narrative prose fiction, in that the reader is required to picture what is happening and to gauge the characters' emotions and motives by picking up on clues embedded in the characters' speech (as in 'Here I kneel') and in other features of the dialogue between them. It is usually straightforward for a reader to do this, however, without needing to see or imagine the scene acted out theatrically.

24.4 Narrative in dramatic texts

It is helpful to characterize drama as dialogue unmediated by narration. But this general statement does need to be qualified. Dramatic texts also make use of a number of narrative devices or strategies that perform various functions: guiding actors, directors or set designers; guiding an audience; and guiding readers.

24.4.1 Narrative effect of implied and explicit stage directions

Implied stage directions in characters' speeches, of the kind outlined above, guide actors. But they also guide readers, by performing a narrative function. Explicit stage directions can also be read as both performance guidelines and as functioning like a narrative voice. In the scene from *Othello* discussed above, the text continues as follows:

> IAGO   'Tis but so, I warrant.
> > [*Trumpets.*]
> > Hark how these instruments summon to supper.
> >
> > > (*Othello*, IV, ii, 170–1)

In a novel, this passage might have been written to achieve a similar effect as follows:

> ''Tis but so, I warrant,' Iago replied. As he was speaking they heard the sound of trumpets calling them to supper.

In the naturalist and realist drama of nineteenth-century Europe (which typically presented crises in middle-class life as if through a transparent 'fourth wall' of a living room), stage directions became more extensive and began to resemble the narrative voice of realist novels of the period. One reason for this was that such plays were beginning to be published before they were performed. So they began to be written in anticipation of this form of circulation, as self-sufficient texts independent of dramatic performance.

Henrik Ibsen's *A Doll's House* (1879), for example, begins with two paragraphs of stage directions. The first paragraph describes in detail a middle-class, nineteenth-century European drawing room, in which all the on-stage action will take place. The second paragraph describes Nora Helmer arriving back from a Christmas shopping trip. Such detailed stage directions offer directors, set designers and actors explicit instructions as to the staging of the play. But they can also be read less as a description of a theatrical set than of an actual drawing room, with real people in it. For example, the first two sentences of the second paragraph are as follows (translated into English):

> The front door-bell rings in the hall; a moment later, there is the sound of the front door being opened. NORA comes into the room, happily humming to herself. She is dressed in her outdoor things, and is carrying lots of parcels which she then puts down on the table, right.

This passage is mostly indistinguishable from the kind of narrative **exposition** that features in the nineteenth-century realist novel, except that: (1) it is in present rather than past tense; (2) the narrative voice seems confined to, or located in, the room; and (3) the table is said to be 'right' – that is, stage right, as viewed from a position in front of the stage.

24.4.2 Narrative exposition in dialogue

Dramatic texts also use the characters they present as a means of offering the reader/audience elements of narrative exposition. Such exposition takes the form of the dialogue characters engage in with other characters.

When Iago says to Desdemona 'Hark how these instruments summon to supper', he says this as much for the benefit of the reader/audience as he does for Desdemona's benefit (after all, she presumably knows what the trumpets signify). More significant passages of narrative exposition often occur in speeches at the beginning of plays (as they also do in television and film drama), in order to help the reader/audience understand what is going on. This is the case in Iago's speech in the opening scene of *Othello*:

> RODRIGO   Thou told'st me
>   Thou didst hold [Othello] in thy hate.
> IAGO   Despise me
>   If I do not. Three great ones of the city,
>   In personal suit to make me his lieutenant,
>   Off-capped to him, and by the faith of man
>   I know my price, I am worth no worse a place.
>   But he, as loving his own pride and purposes,
>   Evades them, with a bombast circumstance
>   Horribly stuffed with epithets of war,
>   And in conclusion
>   Nonsuits my mediators. For, 'Certes,' says he,
>   'I have already chose my officer.'
>   And what was he?
>   Forsooth, a great arithmetician,
>   One Michael Cassio, a Florentine
>
>   (*Othello*, I, i, 5–19)

This speech by Iago fills in part of the story concerning what has happened before the opening scene: Iago had attempted to get a position as Othello's lieutenant, but Othello rejected him because he had already chosen Cassio. In telling this to Rodrigo, Iago is also explaining the situation to the audience or reader, and in doing so providing a motive for his hatred of Othello.

24.4.3 The chorus as narrator

Another way that narration is presented by specific techniques in drama is by means of a 'chorus'. In the tragic drama of classical Greece, a chorus of between twelve and fifteen men would deliver speeches that offered a kind of commentary on the action. Since the classical period, such a chorus has largely disappeared from drama, though it has occasionally been revived and used in original and effective ways.

Shakespeare employs a chorus consisting of a single person in *King Henry V* (*c.* 1599), in order to deliver a **prologue** at the beginning of each act and an **epilogue** at the end of the final act. Shakespeare's chorus directly addresses the audience, highlighting that what is being presented is a play, not real life:

> Admit me Chorus to this history
> Who prologue-like your humble patience pray,
> Gently to hear, kindly to judge our play
>
> (*Henry V*, Prologue to Act I, 33–5)

Shakespeare's chorus also serves as a narrative voice for the benefit of the audience/reader, as can be seen in the Prologue to Act II, where he (the chorus) describes England preparing for war with France:

> Now all the youth of England are on fire,
> And silken dalliance in the wardrobe lies.
> Now thrive the armourers, and honour's thought
> Reigns solely in the breast of every man.
>
> (*Henry V*, Prologue to Act II)

As has been suggested above, the chorus device has occasionally been used in plays since Shakespeare, including in Milton's *Samson Agonistes* (1671) and in T.S. Eliot's *Murder in the Cathedral* (1935). Seemingly the chorus underwent something of a revival in the twentieth century precisely because of the way it serves to foreground theatricality, and hence breaks with the naturalistic illusion of the preceding period of nineteenth-century, more naturalistic drama. In *The Three-penny Opera* (1928), for example, Bertolt Brecht employs a chorus-type 'Narrator', who introduces each act and delivers a prologue to the whole play that includes the well-known song 'Mack the Knife'. Brecht used choruses, along with other theatrical devices, to produce what he described as an **alienation effect**. His plays tend to disrupt an audience's uncritical absorption in the theatrical spectacle, because he felt that such dramatic illusion resembled how the people of Europe were being mesmerized by fascism and/or capitalism of the period, each of which used a kind of mass theatre of the public sphere to manipulate populations, viewed merely as 'the masses'.

The way in which a chorus serves to foreground the theatrical process, producing some kind of alienation effect that prevents the audience from consuming the represented events as if they were real, appears to make use of a chorus as an inherently theatrical device, whose effects need to be experienced in live theatre rather than on the page. But for a reader used to the playful fore-grounding of the narrative situation in postmodernist novels, the anti-realist, alienating commentary of choruses such as Brecht's 'Narrator', or Liz Lochhead's La Corbie in *Mary Queen of Scots Got Her Head Chopped Off* (1989), will be appreciated on the page as readily as on the stage.

24.5 Devices written into a dramatic text that only work on stage

Most devices, techniques and conventions that are thought to characterize the dramatic performance of plays are also intelligible to readers of dramatic texts. Such readers draw on whatever experience of seeing live theatre they have (and of watching drama on TV or in films); but they also employ and modify ways of reading used in reading novels and poems. However, there are some dramatic techniques and devices written into dramatic texts that can only be fully effective in dramatic performance.

Like some of the other devices we have looked at above, such devices seek to shatter any illusion that a play is a slice of real life, by foregrounding the techniques of theatrical production themselves. Because of their typical purpose, such devices are predominantly used in anti-realist drama, especially in plays written and performed over the last fifty years or so that critique the naturalism/realism of late nineteenth-century drama and of contemporary popular drama (in mainstream films and TV soaps). The difference between these devices and ones we have already looked at is that, while they are intelligible to the reader (in that they are written into the dramatic text) they only achieve their effect for an audience seeing a stage performance.

24.5.1 Breaking the identity between actor and character

In naturalist or realist drama, practical strategies are adopted to disguise the difference between character and actor, in order to make a play more 'realistic'. The casting process involves choosing actors who appear appropriate for the part, in terms of sex, age, racial identity, and so on; and the acting process involves the actor seeking as far as possible to identify with the character (a process formalized in the techniques of 'method acting' developed by Konstantin Stanislavsky at the turn of the twentieth century and enshrined in Hollywood cinema). But such assumptions have not always held in the history of the theatre.

From ancient Greece through to the Renaissance, for example, there were no female actors. Female roles had to be played by male actors (female actors did not appear on the English stage until after the restoration of the monarchy in 1660). The **cross-dressing** necessitated by this situation was not written into dramatic texts of these periods, but was a recognized social and theatrical convention. In staging *Othello*, it is similarly unlikely that Shakespeare's theatre company would have felt any need to get a Moorish actor to play Othello. (Until quite recently, it was commonplace for white actors to play Othello with blacked faces.) In modern theatrical performance, it has become the norm, without being thought to violate the text, for female actors to play Shakespeare's female characters and for black actors to play Othello. At issue are notions of how far certain characteristics of an actor are needed for that actor to fit a particular role. However, in the 'post-modernist' drama of the last fifty years or so there has been a tendency to include devices and techniques in dramatic texts that serve to expose and even accentuate discrepancies between actors and characters, rather than trying to promote suitability or plausibility.

24.5.2 Role doubling

One technique that breaks identification between actor and character (and between audience and character) is that of **role doubling**. This is the 'practice of using one actor to play more than one part' (Worthen, 2000: 1487). Before nineteenth-century naturalism, it seems to have been quite common for an actor to play two or more parts in a play, for reasons of economy. In productions of the decidedly non-realist *Peter Pan* (first performed in 1904), it was customary for the same actor to play Mr Darling and Captain Hook, a practice that seems to underline oedipal dimensions of the play. Yet such examples of role doubling were production decisions, rather than being written into the script. In Brecht's *The Good Person of Setzuan* (1943), by contrast, the text itself specifies that the same actor should play both the prostitute Shen Teh and her male 'cousin', Shui Ta (a character she has herself invented, out of self defence, to be her alter ego). In this instance, role doubling is not simply a device used to spice up a production, but is written into the structure of the dramatic text (and in this case clearly relates to the play's investigation of gender stereotypes, capitalism and the theatre itself).

Role doubling is now a fairly common technique in contemporary non-realist drama. But it is most interesting when used to dramatize whatever critical issues the play is engaged with. A particularly intriguing example can be found in Athol Fugard's play *Valley Song* (1998), which is set in a small village in South Africa shortly after the end of apartheid. There are three characters in the play: a white South African man simply called 'The Author'; a coloured farmer in his seventies called Abraam Jonkers (also known as Buks); and Buks's seventeen-year-old granddaughter Veronika. Only two actors are required for a performance of the play, however, because the dramatic text specifies that 'The role of the Author and Buks must be played by the same actor' – a use of role doubling that creates many resonances both within the play and in the post-apartheid world that the play addresses. 'The Author' buys a farm and a piece of land, the cultivation of which has sustained Buks's family over several generations. 'The Author' and Buks are in this way potentially in conflict with one another, but the fact that they are played by the same actor suggests that there is some significant kinship between them (including a shared love of the land and of farming). This suggestion of kinship as a kind of overlaid similarity and difference relates in turn to the play's concern with how the apartheid-era separation of people according to racial categories is beginning to break down. At the same time, however, the play suggests that some consequences of apartheid may take longer to disappear. The coloured characters in the play refer to 'The Author' as 'Master'; and when he eventually acquires the farm he will become the 'master' of the coloured family who have lived and worked on the farm for generations. Use of role doubling in *Valley Song*, then, contributes to the play's exploration of complexities associated with the social, economic, interpersonal and inter-racial issues of post-apartheid South Africa. Although role doubling is written into the dramatic text, however (in stage directions such as '*In the course of the song* ['The Author'] *moves into the character of* Buks'), the effects of this device can only be fully experienced by an audience. While a reader of the text of the play may think of 'The Author' and Buks as different characters, the audience at a performance is constantly reminded of how there is a significant connection between them, by witnessing the actor repeatedly switching between the two roles.

24.5.3 Cross-dressing

Another device that serves to disassociate actors from characters is cross-dressing: the practice of having male actors play female roles, or female actors playing male roles. Cross-dressing was an inevitable feature of theatrical production in Britain prior to 1660, since women were not allowed to appear on-stage. More recently, however, since the early part of the twentieth century, cross-dressing has become another alienation device written into many dramatic texts in order to highlight issues that the play is addressing. A pioneering example of use of this device is Brecht's specification that the female actor who plays the prostitute Shen Teh in the play described above, *The Good Person of Setzuan*, should also play her (invented) male cousin, Shui Ta. Like role doubling (with which cross-dressing is combined in this instance), cross-dressing is a device that can be read in a dramatic text, but only fully experienced by watching a play in performance.

24.5.4 Directly addressing the audience

In realist and naturalist drama, a conventional pretence was maintained that the audience looks through a transparent fourth wall into the private lives of the characters on stage. If a character were directly to address the audience, such pretence would inevitably be shattered. If a character soliloquizes, accordingly (that is, if he or she engages in a **soliloquy**, by speaking alone on the stage, directly to the audience), then he or she is taken to be thinking aloud rather than addressing the audience. However, in plays (and films) of the twentieth and early twenty-first century that seek to shatter the realist illusion, direct address to the audience (or to camera in film or television) is often written into the script. Examples of this can also be seen in Fugard's *Valley Song*.

ACTIVITY 24

Caryl Churchill's *Cloud Nine* (1979; published 1996) is divided into two acts. The first 'takes place in a British colony in Africa in Victorian times'; the second 'takes place in London in 1979. But for the characters it is twenty-five years later'. Role doubling occurs because the actors play different parts in Acts I and II. The list of characters for Act I also specifies use of cross-dressing:

CLIVE, a colonial administrator
BETTY, his wife, played by a man
JOSHUA, his black servant, played by a white
EDWARD, his son, played by a woman
VICTORIA, his daughter, a dummy
MAUD, his mother-in-law
ELLEN, Edward's governess
HARRY BAGLEY, an explorer
MRS SAUNDERS, a widow

The first scene of Act I opens as follows:

Low bright sun. Verandah. Flagpole with union jack. The Family – CLIVE, BETTY, EDWARD, VICTORIA, MAUD, ELLEN, JOSHUA

ALL [*sing*]	Come gather, sons of England, come gather in your pride.
	Now meet the world united, now face it side by side;
	Ye who the earth's wide corners, from veldt to prairie, roam.
	From bush and jungle muster all who call old England 'home'.
	Then gather round for England,
	Rally to the flag,
	From North and South and East and West
	Come one and all for England!
CLIVE:	This is my family. Though far from home
	We serve the Queen wherever we may roam

continued

I am a father to the natives here,
And father to my family so dear.

[*He presents* BETTY. *She is played by a man.*]

My wife is all I dreamt a wife should be,
And everything she is she owes to me.

BETTY: I live for Clive. The whole aim of my life
Is to be what he looks for in a wife.
I am a man's creation as you see,
And what men want is what I want to be.

[CLIVE *presents* JOSHUA. *He is played by a white.*]

CLIVE: My boy's a jewel. Really has the knack.
You'd hardly notice that the fellow's black.

JOSHUA: My skin is black but oh my soul is white.
I hate my tribe. My master is my light.
I only live for him. As you can see,
What white men want is what I want to be.

[CLIVE *presents* EDWARD. *He is played by a woman.*]

CLIVE: My son is young. I'm doing all I can
To teach him to grow up to be a man.

EDWARD: What father wants I'd dearly like to be.
I find it rather hard as you can see.

[CLIVE *presents* VICTORIA, *who is a dummy*, MAUD, *and* ELLEN.]

CLIVE: No need for any speeches by the rest.
My daughter, mother-in-law, and governess.

ALL [*sing*]   O'er countless numbers she, our Queen,
Victoria reigns supreme;
O'er Afric's sunny plains, and o'er
Canadian frozen stream;
The forge of war shall weld the chains of brotherhood secure;
So to all time in ev'ry clime our Empire shall endure.
Then gather round for England,
Rally to the flag,
From North and South and East and West
Come one and all for England!

[*All go except* BETTY. CLIVE *comes.*]

BETTY: Clive?
CLIVE: Betty. Joshua!

[JOSHUA *comes with a drink for* CLIVE.]

continued

BETTY:	I thought you would never come. The day's so long without you.
CLIVE:	Long ride in the bush.
BETTY:	Is anything wrong? I heard drums.
CLIVE:	Nothing serious. Beauty is a damned good mare. I must get some new boots sent from home. These ones have never been right. I have a blister.
BETTY:	My poor dear foot.
CLIVE:	It's nothing.
BETTY:	Oh but it's sore.
CLIVE:	We are not in this country to enjoy ourselves. Must have ridden fifty miles. Spoke to three different headmen who would all gladly chop off each other's heads and wear them round their waists.
BETTY:	Clive!
CLIVE:	Don't be squeamish, Betty, let me have my joke. And what has my little dove done today?
BETTY:	I've read a little.
CLIVE:	Good. Is it good?
BETTY:	It's poetry.
CLIVE:	You're so delicate and sensitive.

----

1   What dramatic functions do the opening song and the embedded introduction of the characters seem to perform? Which, if any, of the following terms are helpful in describing those functions: prologue; chorus; narrative exposition; dramatic irony; realism; alienation effect?

2   In order to examine the opening song and introduction of characters in greater detail, consider the following, more specific questions:

2.1   What do the opening song and introduction of characters imply about (a) the colonial situation; and (b) the colonial family?

2.2   What implications or effects of the song and introduction of characters follow from the fact that (a) Betty is played by a man; (b) Joshua is played by a white; (c) Edward is played by a woman; and (d) Victoria is 'played' by a dummy?

3   What does the opening of the prose section (from '*All go except* BETTY' to 'You're so delicate and sensitive') imply about (a) the colonial situation; and (b) gender relations in the colonial family? In particular, what implications or effects of this prose section follow from the fact that Betty is played by a man?

4   Which of the effects identified in your answers to the questions above can be grasped from reading the dramatic text (as we have given it), and which would only be intelligible if watching the play being performed?

5   What relationship is it reasonable to infer, if any, between the play's use of theatrical devices (including cross-dressing) and the play's representation of British colonialism?

continued

Reading

Aristotle (1965) *On the Art of Poetry*, in T.S. Dorsh (ed.) *Aristotle, Horace, Longinus: Classical Literary Criticism*, Harmondsworth and New York: Penguin.

Burton, D. (1980) *Dialogue and Discourse: A Socio-linguistic Approach to Modern Drama Dialogue and Naturally Occurring Conversation*, London: Routledge and Kegan Paul.

Lennard, J. and Luckhurst, M. (2002) *The Drama Handbook: A Guide to Reading Plays*, Oxford: Oxford University Press.

McIntyre, D. (2006) *Point of View in Plays: A Cognitive Stylistic Approach to Viewpoint in Drama and Other Text Types*, Amsterdam: John Benjamins.

Pickering, K. (2003) *Studying Modern Drama*, London: Palgrave Macmillan.

Preminger, A. and Brogan, T. (eds) (1993) *The New Princeton Encyclopedia of Poetry and Poetics*, Princeton, NJ: Princeton University Press.

Wallis, M. and Shepherd, S. (2010) *Studying Plays*, 3rd edn, London: Arnold; New York: Oxford University Press.

Worthen, W. (2000) *The Harcourt Brace Anthology of Drama*, 3rd edn, Boston, MA: Heinle.

UNIT 25

Performance and the page

UNIT 25

This unit:

- reviews the relationship between speech and writing as employed in printed literary works and aspects of dramatic or 'live' performance;

- summarizes practices of spoken performance, briefly tracing traditions of 'oral literature' as well as public readings by published authors and kinds of modern poetic performance;

- considers contrasting attitudes towards published print works and spoken performances that also contain literary features and qualities;

- concludes with discussion of how much the future of literature, and ways of reading literature, will be affected by a rapidly changing electronic media environment.

Ask almost anyone what the main kinds of literature are and they will say novels, poems. . . and plays (see **Unit 4, Recognizing genre** for the derivation of this view ultimately from Aristotle). For many people involved in theatre, however, plays are not literature. Or rather, they are more than literature. Plays, they suggest, combine conventional literary qualities with something more: the performance, spectacle and pleasure of social occasion associated with theatre.

The complicated position of drama in notions of literature, as we saw in **Unit 24, Ways of reading drama**, tends to be responded to in two main ways. Printed versions of plays are merely notation, we might say, for the fuller experience of theatre. Alternatively, drama may be seen as exemplary of the problematic relationship between *all* literature, viewed as a set of books, and literature conceived as something less tangible and more abstract. That less tangible 'something' may be stored in books (including e-books), but its essence lies elsewhere: perhaps in a set of values, in an attitude of mind or in particular ways of reading.

The relation between literature, books and performance begs an important question: how far what we consider to be literature can be found in other media than on the printed page or the stage. This is an especially important question in a period of easily accessible (and culturally massively influential) audio-visual, multimedia and other online forms.

25.1 Medium and performance

An important consideration in relation to questions of literature and performance is 'medium': the distinction, for example, between writing and speech. Most literary works are fixed as printed (written) text; yet one of our deepest habits in reading is to imagine a speaking inner *voice*. Until relatively recently in historical terms, people did in fact mostly read out loud, to children, family and friends – and also to themselves. Many people still do read aloud, for instance to children, and books are serialized and read aloud on radio, as well as being downloadable as audio-books and podcasts. Even considering literature narrowly as a set of books requires us to take into account an interaction between those books and the spoken and performed.

25.1.1 Oral literature

Literature that is spoken, rather than printed in book form, is not new. In many oral societies (that is, societies that do not employ writing as a system of representation), stories and lyricism are presented in memorized and improvised spoken performances. Such **standardized oral forms** are collectively known as **oral literature**. This term can at first seem paradoxical: 'oral' means to do with the spoken; yet the etymology of 'literature' in the Latin word '*litterae*' ('letters') suggests a central preoccupation with, or necessary existence in, the written form.

Composition of oral literature in oral societies generally occurs as part of a communal practice, and as improvisation, linked to specific social occasions or festivals. It is only with a transition to a substantially literate society – especially one with printing and arrangements for the publishing and circulation of books – that the modern categories of the author and the work emerge (see **Unit 14, Authorship and intention**).

Consider the classical Greek culture of Homer, around the eighth century BC. The period in which Homer was 'writing' is usually considered to represent an especially significant historical moment, in some sense the beginning of Western, writing-based literature (see Ong, 2002). Yet the elaborate patterning of poetic language found in Homer's epics, the *Iliad* and the *Odyssey*, appears to have developed cumulatively over many generations as a combination of tradition and improvisation. Writing was not widely used at the time for literary purposes, so bards recited without the aid of a written text. Instead of composing and memorizing fixed works, they used a stock of verbal formulae that allowed them, by altering and recombining elements to suit the performance context, to perform long poems more or less spontaneously. The works now attributed to Homer may in fact be substantially a written record – a transcript – of earlier, spoken productions.

Traditions of oral composition and performance involving improvisation and variation between occasions are not necessarily remote, however, either historically or geographically. Nor are they to be found only in cultures that do not have writing systems. Oral literary traditions also continue in industrialized, especially multicultural, societies. In Britain, some poets (especially poets with Caribbean origins or links, or poets with connections with performance traditions such as stand-up) recite in ways that foreground live performance – as well as publishing collections of their work. **Poetry slams,** and other kinds of performance poetry, form part of a contemporary literary landscape that also includes readings by authors of published poetry and novels in bookshops and at literary festivals. Storytelling maintains its oral traditions in other ways, too, in the form of extended anecdote (on rhetorical occasions as well as in conversation, and in talk-media formats), as well as in the form of stories written for narration on radio, television or to be uploaded to YouTube. Oral storytelling also continues in actively maintained cultural traditions from Africa, the Indian subcontinent and among Native Americans, coexisting in flexible and changing interaction with printed and published editions of 'literary works'.

25.1.2 Public readings

The phenomenon of public reading from a published literary work is not new; and sometimes the scale of public readings from literary works as a form of entertainment in earlier periods is forgotten. Possibly the most celebrated example of a literary performer is Charles Dickens (1812–70).

Dickens had a lifelong enthusiasm for amateur theatricals, and began to read aloud to friends as an extension of his involvement in theatrical performance. He moved on to reading in public first for charity, then gradually developed public readings of his work into a lucrative business, despite initially sharing the reservation of many of his contemporaries that paid public reading undermines the dignity of literature. Even early in his reading career, Dickens performed to audiences of nearly four thousand and went on tours of between fifty and a hundred readings (eighty-eight readings in ninety days during 1858). When Dickens started his farewell tour in 1869, on one occasion at least a thousand people had to be turned away because the auditorium was full.

The example of Dickens's public readings makes clear, in respect of fiction, what is already evident in the example of drama: that the stereotypically lonely creative experience of an author writing is interwoven with far more social conditions of performance and reception. There is no historically fixed boundary between literary writing and kinds of performance, either in terms of composition or in terms of reception.

25.1.3 Literature, lyrics and music

The sorts of interconnection seen above between literature and performance are also found in the cluster of literary concepts and approaches that surround lyrics and **lyricism**. The term 'lyric', for instance, now typically evokes poetic qualities such as individual contemplation of experience. But the word originally indicated connection with the lyre, the musical instrument on which Classical Greek poetry was conventionally accompanied. In medieval France, lyric forms (such as the canzone and rondeau) were developed by troubadours for singing, rather than reciting; and in Germany the early lyricists sang, and were called *Minnesingers*. In Britain during the sixteenth and seventeenth centuries, the term 'lyric' applied to verse that was sung (as in madrigals, and the songs of poet-singers and composers such as Thomas Campion or John Dowland), though increasingly the term was also used of verse that was not sung. In some cases we now read a lyrical poem as a 'poem on the page' when in fact it was composed as a song and originally performed with musical accompaniment.

Lyricism still combines with forms of accompaniment, most notably in popular music. Emerging from earlier traditions of toasters and DJs, rap forms involve highly accented speech based on rhyming couplets. Some established poets, connecting popular traditions with high-cultural literary expectations, have performed from published works but with backing bands; and some singer-songwriters first successful in the music industry have published collections of their lyrics in print. Such performers blur the boundaries between high and popular culture. Less acknowledged but equally significant, they also blur boundaries between verbal and other (audio and audio-visual) arts linked to performance.

25.2 The effect of performance on ways of reading literature

The two illustrations above – of oral literature and lyricism – suggest that our notions of literature and the literary cannot be easily separated off from performance. This seems to be the case whether we are thinking about genre conventions and technique, or history. Interconnection of this kind between literature and performance can in turn affect how we perceive the texts we are 'reading'.

If you 'read' a poem in an audio-book format, you experience a heightened responsiveness to its sound properties (try it: there are many freely available audio files of poets reading online). The text as performed *is* the text: spoken delivery is an integral part of it. Your response to the distinctiveness of the spoken voice may even begin to clash with your sense of words on the page. If you attend a public reading, you will be struck by how differently phrases are grouped together, or particular words given emphasis, as compared with your mental representation of the printed page of the same text. Speech on a public platform or in reproduced form performs aspects of language that are only reflected in simplified form in writing. Spoken delivery also links written language with visual cues given by facial expression, gesture and posture.

Such aspects of literary texts are important in theatre. When written stage dialogue is realized in a performance, the speaking voice extends what is said on the written page, by adding features of sound that were not notated in the written form. At the same time, spoken delivery also narrows down what was written, by tracing a specific, spoken path between multiple possibilities that coexist in silent reading (see **Unit 24, Ways of reading drama**). Features that are added involve the **prosodic and paralinguistic systems** of language, and include accent, tempo, voice quality and pauses. **Intonation** adds things too, but importantly negotiates nuances of meaning that remain unspecified on the printed page, including emphasis and the speaker's attitude towards what is being said. The linguist Roman Jakobson reports how, for example, the Russian theatre director Konstantin Stanislavsky (1863–1938) used intensive training to develop subtlety of performed speech: he is said once to have required an actor at audition to depict forty distinct situations just by saying the Russian words for 'This evening' (Jakobson, 1990, p. 67).

During the evolution of theatre over many centuries, some aspects of dramatic speech have become codified or stylized. For practical reasons, voices in stage drama have to fill an often large auditorium; so specialized, theatrical styles have developed of loud, projected speech. Some of the techniques in question, however, such as the stage whisper, have now become difficult to perform seriously, in an era accustomed to the reproduced, close-up speech of drama in video formats. Even where written dialogue seeks to simulate speech as closely as possible, such written speech never precisely matches naturally occurring spoken discourse. It is always a selective, conventionalized representation. (As we have seen, you can check this by comparing pauses and repetitions in real conversation with dramatic dialogue on the page; for discussion of such differences, see also **Unit 22, Speech and narration**.)

25.3 The influence of medium

As well as interpreting – both extending and narrowing – what is said on the page, the process of turning writing into performed speech can also affect audience perceptions of the achievement and value of a literary work, because of differences between the social status of different media. A written text performed as speech can problematize, for instance, where we draw the boundary between a notion of the work itself, anchored on the page, and somehow less permanent, variable renditions of it.

The process of transformation into a different media form becomes especially complicated if it happens in reverse, from performance to text. A public reading of a printed poem is a performance (and may be perceived as transitory or temporary, a secondary version of the text rather than the text itself). But if a performance is published in recorded form, it clearly becomes a text once again – though now with an audio or audio-visual dimension and associations.

Defining exactly what text it is you are reading can matter, if you feel that the objects of literary enquiry need to be distinguished from related but arguably secondary material that surrounds them. Few people doubt that a TV or film serialization of *Pride and Prejudice* can be an enjoyable and worthwhile version of Jane Austen's novel (1813). But there continues to be vigorous argument about how such an adaptation should be read: whether it should be treated on an equal footing with the novel it is an adaptation of; whether it offers a useful supplement to reading the novel, but is of secondary importance to it; or whether the two texts should be treated as for all practical purposes different works. Another view sees those alternatives as part of the challenge of understanding what literature now is, by suggesting that we can only see Jane Austen's 'original' novel through the lens of all these other, performed versions. If that view is taken, then the other versions are no longer merely incidental, later performances. Instead, they are an addition to or extension of the literary work. (If you think there is a clear-cut answer to such questions, think of all the films and TV drama serializations you know that have either a direct or indirect link to a particular literary work, and for further discussion, see **Unit 13, Allusion and intertextuality**.)

25.3.1 Competing myths of print and live speech

A further consideration makes defining a boundary between literary work and performance more than a question of locating textual versions relative to a historical original. Written and spoken texts are not always treated as equals in matters of textual circulation and influence. The medium of a text can affect that text's perceived value, because of two potentially contradictory myths – or sets of unexamined cultural beliefs – that attach to print and to speech as modes of representation.

First, there is what might be called a 'myth of print'. This myth is created when a piece of language is considered disproportionately important, authoritative, or final and non-negotiable because it appears in print. Mythical attributes follow from both the technological and the social history of **literacy**. Before sound recording, there was no means of replicating spoken performance permanently; and without a permanent record of speech being available, it was often viewed as inconsequential or unreliable, with reports of speech mere hearsay. Anything in a book, on the other hand, could be seen as more serious. Written and printed texts came in many cases to be revered documents, enjoying far higher cultural status than the same words in speech could have achieved. Special authority has been conventionally attached, in many cultures, to legal and religious documents within the broad range of legal and religious practices; and something of the authority associated with religious books in particular is claimed for literature when traditions of literary work are referred to as a **canon**, or specified set of quasi-holy books.

This 'myth of print' collides, however, with another, equally pervasive cluster of beliefs. There is a competing 'myth of orality', which arises when special value is placed on the presumed power of speech (and, with it, live performance in general) to offer immediate expression of physically lived experience. When a speaking self addresses others, a specially valued effect is widely thought to be created: that of direct communication, and potentially a unique kind of communion, between speaker and hearer(s) – even, paradoxically, if they are shouting at each other.

This second myth, of orality, underpins a high value that is often placed on performance by comparison with print. Believing in a special power of speech can encourage us to see uniqueness and 'unrepeatability' in live events (rather than viewing their 'liveness' as an inevitable consequence of performance being a real-time event, which it had to be before audio and audio-visual recording). We may feel inspired to hear an author read, even if we know the published work already, because in presenting in-person the author will give us a more personally authentic version of it. Performance in this sense embodies or breathes life into a literary work (note the vocabulary here of closeness between oral performance, the human body and claimed vitality).

The orality myth also has a wider, cultural dimension. Spoken expression is sometimes treated as if it is the essential channel, or lifeblood, of any organic or fundamentally united community, allowing people to talk directly with one another rather than communicating at a distance. Literature is sometimes viewed as contributing to this social ideal, despite mostly taking a printed form, in that it projects inner thoughts and feelings in the form of public communication. Many modern poets have sought to emphasize links between the personal and the spoken, by viewing themselves as bards of a revived, oral and communal society. Occasionally this bardic perception of literature is presented in exaggerated contrast with the isolation in a garret, or at a screen, associated with the myth of writing (for discussion of language and different media, see Durant and Lambrou, 2009).

25.4 Reading between the myths

How we read performance dimensions of literature is made topical by the scale of recent and current shifts in our textual environment. Over the last hundred years public communication has moved from an environment dominated by the authority of print, through broadcast media such as television and radio, to an environment in which other, new forms dominate: relayed and reproduced forms of speech, interactive messaging, collaborative 'live' documents, still and moving images, and a range of developing forms of online material. The last decade in particular has seen massive expansion in the storage, retrieval and public circulation of spoken, written and audio-visual content, posing a major challenge to established notions of what a text is, and possibly also what 'reading' is.

If many people nowadays consume narrative and drama more in video formats than in books or on the stage (or even on television), and if people experience lyricism more in pop lyrics than in collections of poetry, does it follow that literature of the kind examined in this book is dying? Examples introduced in this unit suggest that literature has always involved a performance dimension, but that the performance dimension has changed and is often neglected. Recent technological developments in modes of performance and reproduction represent growth and change in a continuous process of interaction between written and spoken, rather than fundamental transformation. Warnings of the death of literature, because of its coexistence with other media discourse types, seem unnecessary in this context.

Predicting what mix of text-types, let alone particular texts, will be read in fifty or a hundred years' time would nevertheless be reckless. How much print? How much on-screen text (delivered to devices of many different kinds)? How much streamed audio and audio-visual content? And how much textual material in forms and formats not yet envisaged? It may nevertheless be less the future text-types and delivery systems that determine whether the insights and pleasures associated with literary ways of reading have a future. What may become more important is whether the changing media capabilities are related to the working of creativity at other levels, including in ways we have explored in this book: choice and treatment of topics; adherence to, extension of, and innovation as regards form and conventions; and engagement with changing publishing opportunities and audiences.

ACTIVITY 25

1   Identify, in each of the extracts below, evidence you find in the form of the extract that the text it comes from has been specially composed for performance. At this stage, ignore whatever you may know about any of the texts. In looking for signs of a text being 'written for performance', consider four types of performance:

- reading aloud (e.g. in a public reading);

- musical performance (with the text used as words of a song or other musical composition);

- audio representation (e.g. as a radio drama, audio-book or podcast);

- dramatic representation (including in the theatre, on television, or in an online video format).

Look for any kind of evidence you consider relevant. But pay particular attention to the following: layout, for instance division into lines; repetition of phrases, as in a musical chorus; who, if anyone, is named as speaking; and the naming of speakers as a cast or list of dramatis personae.

2   Are there features in any of the extracts that would make the text resistant to being performed in one or more of the four ways listed above?

[Task continues after the five extracts]

Text A

Can I not sing but 'hoy'
When the jolly shepherd made so much joy?
The shepherd upon a hill he sat;
He had on him his tabard and his hat,
His tar-box, his pipe and his flagat*;
His name was called Jolly, Jolly Wat,
For he was a good herdsboy.
With hoy!
For in his pipe he made so much joy.
[* = *flask*]

Text B

'Bill, Bill, for dear God's sake, for your own, for mine, stop before you spill my blood! I have been true to you, upon my guilty soul I have!'

The man struggled violently to release his arms; but those of the girl were clasped round his, and tear her as he would, he could not tear them away.

continued

'Bill,' cried the girl, striving to lay her head upon his breast, 'the gentleman and that dear lady, told me to-night of a home in some foreign country where I could end my days in solitude and peace. Let me see them again, and beg them, on my knees, to show the same mercy and goodness to you; and this dreadful place, and far apart lead better lives, and forget how we have lived, except in prayers, and never see each other more. It is never too late to repent. They told me so – I feel it now – but we must have time – a little, little time!'

The housebreaker freed one arm, and grasped his pistol. The certainty of immediate detection if he fired, flashed across his mind even in the midst of his fury; and he beat it twice with all the force he could summon, upon the upturned face that almost touched his own.

She staggered and fell: nearly blinded with the blood that rained down from a deep gash in her forehead; but raising herself, with difficulty, on her knees, drew from her bosom a white handkerchief – Rose Maylie's own – and holding it up, in her folded hands, as high towards Heaven as her feeble strength would allow, breathed one prayer for mercy to her Maker.

It was a ghastly figure to look upon. The murderer staggering backward to the wall, and shutting out the sight with his hand, seized a heavy club and struck her down.

Text C

FIRST VOICE
Blind Captain Cat climbs into his bunk. Like a cat, he sees in the dark. Through the voyages of his tears he sails to see the dead.
CAPTAIN CAT
Dancing Williams!
FIRST DROWNED
Still dancing.
CAPTAIN CAT
Jonah Jarvis.
THIRD DROWNED
Still.
FIRST DROWNED
Curly Bevan's skull.
ROSIE PROBERT
Rosie, with God. She has forgotten dying.
FIRST VOICE
The dead come out in their Sunday best.
SECOND VOICE
Listen to the night breaking.

continued

FIRST VOICE

Organ Morgan goes to chapel to play the organ. He sees Bach lying on a tombstone.

ORGAN MORGAN

Johann Sebastian!

CHERRY OWEN *(Drunkenly)*

Who?

ORGAN MORGAN

Johann Sebastian mighty Bach. Oh, Bach fach.

Text D

FIRST VOICE

'But tell me, tell me! speak again,
Thy soft response renewing—
What makes that ship drive on so fast?
What is the ocean doing?'

SECOND VOICE

'Still as a slave before his lord,
The ocean hath no blast;
His great bright eye most silently
Up to the Moon is cast—
If he may know which way to go;
For she guides him smooth or grim.
See, brother, see! how graciously
She looketh down on him.'

FIRST VOICE

'But why drives on that ship so fast,
Without or wave or wind?'

SECOND VOICE

'The air is cut away before,
And closes from behind.
Fly, brother, fly! more high, more high!
Or we shall be belated:
For slow and slow that ship will go,
When the Mariner's trance is abated.'

Text E

And did those feet in ancient time
Walk upon England's mountains green?
And was the holy Lamb of God
On England's pleasant pastures seen?
And did the Countenance Divine
Shine forth upon our clouded hills?
And was Jerusalem builded here

continued

Among these dark Satanic Mills?
Bring me my Bow of burning gold!
Bring me my Arrows of desire!
Bring me my spear! O clouds, unfold!
Bring me my Chariot of fire!
I will not cease from Mental Fight,
Nor shall my Sword sleep in my hand,
Till we have built Jerusalem
In England's green and pleasant land.

3   When you have listed all the evidence you can find in the form of the extracts, consider the following extra information:

Text A: First stanza of an anonymous Medieval poem or song, handed down in a number of slightly different versions. Evidence as to whether this text was sung rather than recited or read is conjectural, based only on what we know about how texts circulated during the period.

Text B: The final passage of Chapter 47 in Charles Dickens's *Oliver Twist* (1837–8), the chapter in which Nancy is murdered by her companion in crime, Bill Sykes; see activity in **Unit 3, Analysing units of structure** (pp. 44–6 and 336) for context. Dickens started to prepare for public reading of this passage (which he in fact began earlier in the chapter than the extract reproduced here) in 1863, but only began performing it, to massive public acclaim, in 1868. So sensational was Dickens's rendering of the passage considered to be that, during his farewell tour in 1869–70, the author included a special reading of the Nancy episode for an assembled audience of professional actors.

Text C: From towards the end of Dylan Thomas's *Under Milk Wood: A Play for Voices*. This work was first broadcast by the BBC, January 1954, then presented on stage at the Edinburgh Festival and in London in 1956, with extracts also shown on television. A film of the play was released in 1972, and it has been produced in many different versions since.

Text D: The beginning of Part VI of Samuel Taylor Coleridge's 'The Rime of the Ancient Mariner', a poem written in a combination of narrative and dramatic modes and included in *Lyrical Ballads* (1798). During the Romantic period, some poets wrote extensively in dramatic dialogue, or in mixed dramatic and non-dramatic modes, even where a work was not intended for the stage.

Text E: The poem 'Jerusalem', from the Preface to William Blake's *Milton: A Poem* (1804–8). This poem is more widely known as a hymn, with music composed in 1916 by Sir Charles Herbert Parry. Together, the words and music also serve as the anthem of the British Women's Institute (since the 1920s), as well as, more recently, of the far-right British National

continued

Party. The musical, hymn version has been released in cover versions by Emerson, Lake and Palmer, Iron Maiden vocalist Bruce Dickinson, The Fall, Billy Bragg and the Pet Shop Boys, among others, as well as in instrumental versions including one by the Grimethorpe Colliery Brass Band.

4   How much does the form in which you have encountered a text before, or what you know about it, affect your view of its suitability for performance in a different medium? And how much is the 'quality as literature' of a text affected if it is translated into a different form of representation?

Reading

Briggs, A. and Burke, P. (2010) *A Social History of the Media*, 3rd edn, Cambridge: Polity.

Durant, A. and Lambrou, M. (2009) *Language and Media: A Resource Book for Students*, London: Routledge.

Finnegan, R. (2002) *Communicating: The Multiple Modes of Human Interconnection*, London: Routledge.

Jakobson, R. (1990) *Language in Literature*, Cambridge, MA: Belknap Press.

Ong, W. (2002) *Orality and Literacy: The Technologizing of the Word*, London: Routledge.

Appendix:
notes on activities

Unit 1 Asking questions as a way into reading

The author, Ee Tiang Hong, is a Malaysian writer, who was born in Malacca in 1933 and educated at Tranquerah English School and High School, Malacca. Until his death in the early 1990s, he lived mostly in Australia.

Tranquerah Road: the road is an extension of Heeren Street, in Malacca.

Kampong Serani: 'Portuguese Village', in the suburb of Ujong Pasir.

Limbongan: a suburb adjacent to Tranquerah. The Dutch used to moor their vessels off the coast here.

Kimigayo: the Japanese national anthem.

Nihon Seishin: 'Japanese Soul'.

Greater East Asia Co-Prosperity Sphere: the Japanese scheme to unify Asia, during the Second World War.

Meliora hic sequamur: the motto of the Malacca High School ('Here let us do better things').

Merdeka: 'Independence'.

Negara-ku: 'My Country'; the Malayan, and then Malaysian, national anthem.

pontianak: a succubus, or evil spirit.

jinn: genie; evil spirit.

Omitohood: a Buddhist benediction ('Om Mane Pudmi Hum'), in the Hokkien Chinese dialect.

Unit 3 Analysing units of structure

The first sentence should read:

Following Nancy's death Sikes tries to escape the hue and cry.

The order of the sentences in the published companion is:

15, 11, 3, 8, 9, 2, 6, 12, 4, 7, 1, 14, 5, 10, 13.

Glossary

Accent The distinctive pattern of pronunciation associated with a place, region or group. In the analysis of poetic rhythm and metre, the term 'accent' means an additional amount of stress on a syllable that makes it relatively prominent compared with surrounding syllables.

Address The means by which a text seems to be 'talking' to a particular reader or group of readers: the text's addressee. See also **Direct address**, **Indirect address** and **Mode of address**.

Addressee Designated or implied recipient of an utterance. A text's addressee needs to be distinguished from its actual reader. Shelley's 'To a Skylark' is addressed, for example, to the skylark (see **apostrophe**), but the poem is read by human beings. Similarly, the mistress addressed in Marvell's 'To his Coy Mistress' is not the reader but an imagined woman who the speaker attempts to seduce. In special circumstances addressee and reader may overlap, for example where the 'author' directly addresses the 'reader'. In *Jane Eyre*, exploiting this device to striking effect, the narrator famously announces, 'Reader, I married him'.

Aesthetics Systematic study of the abstract properties of beauty. In philosophy, aesthetics is a branch of study dealing with what appeals to the senses. In the study of literature, aesthetics is especially concerned with kinds of formal patterning, such as rhyme, rhythm and alliteration, which help to define its distinctive appeal.

Affective fallacy An error or failing in interpreting a text caused by over-attention to our own personal responses at the expense of what the words of the text actually say. The term was first used by two American critics, W.K. Wimsatt and M.C. Beardsley, in 1946. (See also **intentional fallacy**.)

Agent Person (or animal or similar) who makes something happen.

Alienation effect The effect produced in drama when the theatrical illusion is broken in ways that make the audience perceive the drama as a product of theatrical techniques rather than as something 'real'. The technique was developed by Bertolt Brecht, whose purpose was to 'estrange' realist theatrical conventions and the bourgeois ideology he believed such conventions support. The term is also used to describe the equivalent effect in other literary forms.

Allegory (From the Greek for 'speaking otherwise'.) A narrative fiction in which characters and actions, and sometimes also the setting, can be viewed as referring to a parallel (often political, religious or moral) story.

Alliteration A type of sound pattern in which nearby words begin with similar sounds (or have their most strongly stressed syllables beginning with similar sounds).

Allusion Moment in a text when the text makes an implicit or explicit reference to another text, either by directly quoting the second text or by modifying the second text in order to suit the new context.

Ambiguity An effect created when a phrase or statement can be interpreted in more than one way. The capability of being understood in two or more ways sometimes arises from the different meanings of a given word, and sometimes from the possibility of understanding the grammatical relationships between words in a sentence in more than one way. Ambiguity is an inevitable feature of language use and can be accidental or deliberate. But in literary forms of expression (especially poetry) it is generally assumed to be deliberate because of the degree of care typically taken in composition, and may be used to keep more than one meaning in play or to suggest connections between different possible meanings. Ambiguity should be distinguished from ambivalence, which means having conflicting feelings about something.

Anglophone English-speaking.

Anti-language In sociolinguistics and literary stylistics, a mode of expression or linguistic variety adopted by a group of people to mark off their way of speaking or writing from dominant traditions they choose to reject. Anti-language may consist of private words ('jargon', 'cant', 'argot'), or of a more extended code of specialized idioms.

Apostrophe A rhetorical figure in which a speaker addresses either someone who is not there, or even dead, or something that is not normally thought of as able to understand language or reply (e.g. an animal or object).

Archaism Language that would normally be found in an earlier period, and whose usage is therefore unusual or marked.

Archetypal genres Four selected genres (comedy, romance, tragedy and satire), which, according to the literary critic Northrop Frye (in *Anatomy of Criticism: Four Essays*, 1957), correspond emotionally to the four seasons and may be linked to a rich cultural reservoir of myth (related, for instance, to imagined stages in human life). These genres may be considered 'archetypal' in the sense of not being just conventional styles but being expressions of something collective and more profound about us as human beings.

Attitude See **propositional attitude**.

Author Person credited with composing a literary work. This person is not necessarily the same as the **implied author**, who is a presence inferred by the reader as the guiding personality behind the work. A single author may compose texts featuring different implied authors.

Background knowledge Information that it is assumed a reader will know and is likely to activate in understanding a text in the way anticipated. (See also **schema**.)

Ballad A folk ballad or traditional ballad is a narrative song or poem in an oral tradition; its usually dramatic or violent story is told by means of action and dialogue, and the narrator remains impersonal. Such ballads are often told in the **ballad stanza** and use set formulas and incremental or gradually modified repetition (repeated refrains, for example, that gradually change as the story advances). Ballads were often accompanied, in the early history of the form, by music and were danced to. But the form gradually evolved in two different directions: a continuation of folk ballads, performed out loud in spoken form; and the development of urban **broadside ballads**.

Ballad stanza Four-line stanza in alternate four- and three-beat lines, normally rhyming ABCB.

Binary opposition A two-way choice, or dichotomy, between mutually exclusive, alternative options. The two terms need not be simply neutral: one may have a positive, the other a negative value (as in good/evil, life/death, hero/villain). Such oppositions, which were of particular interest in **structuralism**, provide a simple, pervasive mechanism for organizing thought and experience, but have important cultural effects because of the way they distribute value with one term preferred and the other implicitly inferior or rejected.

Blank verse Unrhymed **iambic pentameter**.

Bricolage In art, a technique (used particularly in **modernism** and **postmodernism**) in which works are constructed from various materials available or to hand. In cultural studies, the term describes a wider process by which people assemble objects from across social divisions and use them to project new cultural identities. (See **collage** and **montage**.)

Broadside ballads The **genre** known as **ballads** circulated in printed form on large, single sheets of paper ('broadsheets'), or in what were called chapbooks. Such ballads typically present popular songs, romantic tales and sensational or topical stories, often celebrating or attacking particular people or institutions.

Canon A body of literary works regarded as the most important, significant, long-lasting and worthy of study: literary classics. Earlier, 'canon' was used to describe the collection of books of the Bible accepted by the Christian Church as genuine and divinely inspired. The term was then applied to other sacred books and later extended to writings of a secular **author** who was accepted as being authentic or genuine. In this enlarged definition, 'canonical' means accepted, authoritative or standard.

Catharsis Purification of the spectator's or reader's emotions by a powerful work of art, especially through watching an emotionally powerful play. In Aristotle's *Poetics*, the purging or purification brought about by catharsis is achieved by means of feelings of pity and fear aroused in the audience by the dramatic spectacle involved in tragedy, especially in its **dénouement**.

Chiasmus Type of **parallelism** where the order of elements in the first part is reversed in the second part.

Chorus Originally a grouping of twelve to fifteen men who sang odes and delivered speeches in the tragic drama of classical Greece. The classical chorus typically represented a conservative view of society and so served to contrast with the tragic hero and his society. Use of a chorus fell out of favour after the classical period, but is occasionally used – usually taking the form of a single character, rather than a group – in plays from the Renaissance to the present. In contemporary drama choruses feature mostly to create an **alienation effect**.

Chronicle play A play that presents a historical narrative and topics drawn from the English Chronicles (histories, in prose or verse, from the Anglo-Saxon to the Renaissance period). A number of Elizabethan plays (including some by Shakespeare) are based on the sixteenth-century historian Ralph Holinshed's chronicles or stories from English history.

Classic realism The form of **realism** employed especially by nineteenth-century writers such as George Eliot; the techniques involved in this kind of realism are seen as the standard mode of realist writing.

Clause A full or partial sentence contained inside another sentence. A clause usually contains a verb, but may be missing some of the components of a full sentence such as a subject or tense associated with a verb.

Code-switching Behaviour consisting of (sometimes repeated) changes between different varieties of language – for example, between styles addressed to different audiences or matched to different situations, or between a standard variety and a dialect. (See also **register** and **dialect**.)

Cognitive Associated with mental processes, and so with psychology. The term is commonly used to describe approaches to interpretation that seek to model how the mind tackles tasks of making meaning, using its available, finite resources of memory, attention and processing effort.

Coherence/coherent How parts of a discourse hold together in an intelligible fashion. Coherence may depend as much on the ability of readers to supply connections between parts of the discourse as on explicit connections made within the discourse itself. (See also **schema** and **inference**.)

Collage Composition formed when different pieces of text, or styles or genres, are placed alongside one another. The juxtaposition of such materials forces us to consider the two (or more) things side-by-side; we either unify the contrasting materials into some new, compound form, or else see in them some form of implied comparison. (See **bricolage** and **montage**.)

Collocate Occur next or close to one another (of words in a sentence or text). Words show a variable (but measurable) tendency to co-occur with particular other words, depending sometimes on grammatical or semantic constraints and sometimes on idiomatic and social factors. So, for example 'hot summer' is a more common pairing than 'happy summer', 'horticultural summer' or 'hexagonal summer', even though the 'h' words here are all adjectives.

Comedy A term used primarily to categorize plays and novels that are designed to amuse the audience/reader. Although the characters encounter problems and crises, we anticipate that the main characters will achieve happiness at the end, often through love and marriage, while unsympathetic characters will receive punishment or some other kind of misfortune.

Concordance A list of all the words used in a particular text (or collection of texts, often of a particular author), usually arranged alphabetically and created either in print or electronically. The list shows where particular words are used, and often quotes some surrounding context. (See also **corpus**.)

Conjunction A term from **grammar** used to describe words whose major function is to signal a relationship between one sentence and a previous sentence or sentences. Examples of conjunctions are *and*, *but*, *so*, *then*. In speech, such conjunctions are usually found at the beginning of a new sentence; in writing, equivalent terms include *moreover*, *however*, *therefore*, *afterwards*.

Constituent element Some identified part, or component, of a larger whole that is important in giving the larger whole its overall form; an element that organizes something or makes it what it is (see **form**). If a sentence must contain a noun phrase, for example, then 'noun phrase' is a constituent element of a sentence; or if a refrain is usually found in songs, then 'refrain' might be considered a constituent element of a song.

Content A broad term used to indicate the characters, actions, ideas, thoughts, emotions, etc., that a text contains; usually differentiated from the text's **form**.

Corpus Body or collection of writings; the whole body of written material on a given subject. Also commonly used to mean a body of written or spoken data, collected either from particular texts or from language use more generally, on which a linguistic analysis may be based. Such corpora are mostly electronically stored and searchable, making it possible to find all examples of any particular word (as a 'key word in context', or KWIC).

Cross-dressing Practice used in drama of having male actors play female roles, or female actors playing male roles.

Cultural code A set of terms, references and assumptions drawn on in a text that relate to a recognizable set of cultural values (e.g., Puritanism, Englishness, feminism, etc., but also what people eat, how they view different sorts of holiday destination or types of music, and other kinds of belief or attitude).

Death of the author A theoretical and rhetorical claim made by the French post-structuralist critic Roland Barthes in order to undermine the habit in traditional criticism of invoking authorial intention as a supposition or device to control interpretation.

Decorum Convention or rule, important in the history of **rhetoric** and literary composition, that **style** should be appropriate to subject matter and situation. Following classical authors such as Horace, styles were often categorized as 'grand', 'middle' or 'plain', with each style judged suitable for a different literary genre (e.g. a 'grand' style was considered appropriate to epic composition). In more recent literary work, such fixed style expectations tend to be less important, and mixed styles are far more common, along with deliberate experiments in style-switching.

Defamiliarization The suggestion, introduced by Russian Formalist critics in the early twentieth century, that the characteristic effect of devices and techniques in works of art and literature is to make us see familiar and taken-for granted aspects of our world in new or unusual ways.

Deixis, deictics Devices in language that indicate meaning relative to the location or social status of the speaker, or relative to the particular time of utterance. Such devices include words and phrases such as 'now', 'shortly', 'yesterday', 'here', 'sir', 'come'/'go'.

Deictic shift A practice adopted in some kinds of discourse, including in many fictional works, of communicating relative not to the location or social status of the actual or supposed speaker, or relative to the moment of utterance, but by projecting from this point of utterance and indicating relative distance and time with respect to another deictic centre (i.e. relative to a different speaker, at a different moment of utterance). Examples include expressions such as 'out to the right wing', used in football commentary, or 'shall I come there?', as spoken during a phone conversation.

Demonstrative In linguistics, words whose prime function is to point to something in the immediate context of speaker and hearer. Examples of demonstratives (which are **deictic** in function) are *this*, *that*, *here* or *there.*

Dénouement French term meaning 'unknotting', often used to describe the conclusion of a novel, film or play in which the problems that have driven the action are resolved, either comically or tragically.

Dialect Regional (as well as social class and occupational) variations in grammar, vocabulary and **accent**. Common dialect contrasts include those between urban and rural, or between different rural areas; between classes; or between different social roles and jobs. The term 'dialect' carries no necessary implication that one dialect is better than another, though some speakers do use the word in that way. In many literary texts, regional varieties have been used, especially in dialogue, for comic effect, thereby exploiting and contributing to stereotyping.

Dialect map A map based on linguistic field work which shows the different areas where dialect features such as particular words or forms of pronunciation are used.

Dialogism The usual English version of a term developed by Russian critic Mikhail Bakhtin to refer to the way novels (and some other kinds of discourse) are inhabited by a multiplicity of different and perhaps competing voices: those of narrators and characters, but also potentially including all the voices or registers (of philosophy, of horticulture, etc.) that are available at the time of writing. (See also **hierarchy of voices**.)

Dialogue A conventional way of presenting, in writing, the conversational interaction that takes place between two or more characters in speech. Literary or philosophical dialogue is stylized because many features of real-life verbal interaction (e.g. overlap between speakers, pauses, repetition) are either excluded or tidied up and simplified.

Diction The style of language, usually vocabulary, chosen in a particular literary text or by a particular author (a term now more commonly used in describing poetry than about other literary forms).

Direct address An effect created when a text directly addresses the reader by using questions or commands (such as 'Could you be mortgage-free faster?' or 'Stop smoking'), or by using 'you' or 'we'.

Discourse In linguistics, stretches of language use for which the necessary units of description project beyond the sentence. The term is also used in literary and cultural criticism to mean something like a unified field of statements that construct domains of reality in a particular way (e.g. 'legal discourse', 'the discourse of empire', 'neo-conservative discourse'). In narrative theory, 'discourse' (or **plot**) is sometimes distinguished from 'story': while the story consists of the imaginary events in the order in which they supposedly happened, the 'discourse' is the way that the story is told by means of particular narrative techniques (through a particular narrative point of view, and in a particular non-chronological sequence, etc.).

Dominant reading The interpretation of a text that the text itself seems to encourage, or which is agreed by most literary critics, or which correlates with a dominant ideology at the time of writing or reading.

Dramatic irony An effect created when a character on stage and involved in a dramatic action expresses a belief that the audience knows to be false. Typically, the incorrect belief will be about some crucial component of the plot, and so determines the character's fate. In comedy we are encouraged to feel amused at the character's error; in tragedy we feel sympathy.

Elegy A poem or song lamenting someone's death; a funeral poem. Historically, elegies were associated with a particular metre, so sometimes 'elegy' is used as the term for all poetry written in such 'elegiac' metre, including **pastoral** poems delivered in the voice of shepherds that are not concerned with anyone's death.

Enigma Literally 'a puzzle'. Many narratives are driven by a character's quest to resolve an enigma (e.g. crime or detective fiction is typically organized this way). More generally, textual enigmas stimulate a desire to keep reading.

Epigraph An inscription or quotation at the beginning of a literary work or document (or of a section of one), setting out or highlighting its theme. (See **prologue**.)

Epilogue A speech, often in verse, addressed to the audience at the end of a play. (See **prologue**.)

Epithalamium A wedding song or poem declaimed in praise of a bride and bridegroom.

Exposition A passage or passages in a literary text or play, often early on in the plot, in which a **narrator** or characters provide the reader/audience with necessary information about events that have led up to the events presented in the text or on stage.

Feminine rhyme A rhyme created between two words in which the final syllable of each is not stressed.

Figurative language The general term for a number of non-literal uses of language. (See **metaphor**, **metonymy**, **simile**, **synecdoche**).

Focalizer In theories of narrative, a term used to describe who or what witnesses the events of the **narrative**. There may be more than one focalizer in the course of a narrative. What the focalizer sees or experiences is called the 'focalized'.

Foot In metrical analysis, a group of two or three **syllables**, the first or last of which is more prominent (has more stress) than the others. The four main types of foot in English are: iambic, anapaestic, trochaic and dactylic. (See **metre**.)

Form The form of a text is how it is constructed as a pattern or system of components. Such components include linguistic components (such as grammar and syntax), verbal features (such as rhyme and alliteration), metrical structures (such as feet) and narrative techniques (such as plot structure, contrast between 'hero' and 'villain', etc). Aspects of form also include the division of a text into sections (such as lines, stanzas, narrative episodes, or chapters), and relationships that arise between components or sections (such as juxtaposition or **parallelism**).

Formalism The direction of critical attention onto how components of language, or of a particular text, fit and work together (see **form**). As a branch of linguistics, an emphasis on grammatical structures and the meaning of sentences largely in isolation from their communicative function or the context in which they occur. Russian Formalism was a school of literary criticism and linguistics that emerged in the early twentieth century and focused on the analysis of linguistic form and literary technique (see **defamiliarization**). **New Criticism** also contains elements of formalism.

Formalist theories In historical linguistics, modes of analysis that concentrate on formal features of language such as change in the pronunciation of vowels. Such forms of analysis view these changes as occurring because of fairly autonomous processes intrinsic to language itself. The term is also used to refer to a number of literary theories, including **New Criticism** and Russian Formalism (see **formalism**).

Free indirect speech A term used in **stylistics** to describe a kind of **indirect speech** or reported speech in which the words spoken by (or thoughts of) a particular character are blended with the voice of the reporting narrator, normally with no reporting clause.

Free verse Verse whose lines do not have their length and rhythm regulated by a metrical pattern.

Functionalist theory In historical linguistics, a form of analysis that sees language change as due to (or reflecting) communicative, social or political processes.

Gender specific A description of terms used exclusively for either women or men: for example, 'actress' (now widely considered anachronistic) used to refer only to women actors.

Generic noun A noun, like 'police officer', that refers to both men and women, but which may often be used as if it is referring primarily to men.

Generic pronoun Use of the pronoun 'he' to stand for people in general, including both men and women.

Genre A term used to indicate any particular type or kind of text. Each genre is typically characterized by specific kinds of content, theme, language, structure and conventions. Genres include **allegory**, **ballad**, **chronicle play**, comedy, elegy, epithalamium, haiku, lyric, masque, naturalism, pastiche, pastoral, picaresque, realism, sonnet, tragedy and many others. (Also see archetypal genres.)

Grammar Rules of selection and combination that govern possible relationships between words in a language. Relatedly, the systematic description of a language as we find it in a sample of speech or writing, or by eliciting examples from native speakers. Sometimes 'grammar' is used to refer only to features of structural organization (principally sentence structure or syntax) which can be studied independently of sound or meaning; but sometimes the term is used more widely, to include all aspects of how language is organized.

Great Vowel Shift A set of interrelated changes in pronunciation that occurred across a range of vowels in English during the fifteenth to eighteenth centuries.

Haiku A Japanese genre much imitated in English. Haikus consist of three lines of five, seven and five syllables respectively, usually presenting a natural image to embody a moment of spiritual insight and designed to elicit a similar response in the reader.

Hierarchy of voices A hierarchical relationship that is often found between the various voices and perspectives presented in a complex, layered text such as a novel (which may contain one or more narrators, as well as possibly a large number of major and minor characters). In interpreting such a text, the narrative voice is usually accorded more authority than the voice of characters.

Iambic pentameter A type of metre consisting of lines of ten **syllables** divided into five feet. In each **foot** (pair of syllables), the second syllable is more strongly stressed than the first.

Implied author A critical term used to distinguish between the real author and the impression produced by some texts (especially novels) that there is a designing consciousness or voice within the text itself.

Implied reader An imagined reader implicitly addressed by a text; not to be confused with an actual **reader** (a given person who is reading the text).

Indirect address An effect created when a text 'speaks to' its readers not by using forms of **direct address,** but by presenting them with opinions or attitudes with which they are assumed to agree; in such circumstances, readers are implicitly encouraged to activate the expressed opinions or attitudes in order to make sense of, and so in effect align themselves with, what is being communicated.

Indirect speech A way of reporting the words spoken by a person or character without directly quoting them. The character's words are made subordinate to a reporting clause and introduced with the word 'that' (e.g. 'Tess replied that she already knew' rather than 'Tess replied, "I already know"'); this effect is sometimes also called reported speech. (See also **free indirect speech**.)

Inference The process of a logical or reasonable conclusion from statements or evidence, or the result of carrying out such a cognitive process.

Inferencing The interpretive process based on a reader's or hearer's assumption that a piece of language is a meaningful communication; the process advances by making inferences about the author's likely intentions on the basis of evidence presented in the text and its context.

Intentional fallacy An error or defect in interpreting a text which results from an unwarranted shift from what words appear to mean to what we imagine the author meant by using them. The term was first used by two American critics, W.K. Wimsatt and M.C. Beardsley in 1946. (See also **affective fallacy**.)

Intertextuality A term used to describe a variety of ways in which texts interact with other texts. In particular, the notion of intertextuality stresses the idea that texts are not unique, isolated objects but are made out of recycled voices and registers which to a greater or lesser degree echo other literary texts and the general culture they inhabit.

Intonation The melodic patterning of the voice in speech that serves to place unusual or emphatic stress on particular words. Intonation conveys information, feelings or attitudes that go beyond the meanings of the actual words. Apart from occasional italics or capitals, written texts do not notate intonation; but readers often assign imagined intonational patterns to what they read.

Irony An effect created by use of language in which the speaker or writer covertly indicates disagreement with what is directly expressed by the words. (See also **verbal irony**, **situational irony**, **dramatic irony** and **structural irony**.)

Literacy Skill in using a code of communication, especially ability to read and write. The term can be used to describe individuals, social groups or whole populations. Sometimes the term is also applied to other, non-written forms of communication, as in 'media literacy' and 'computer literacy'.

Lyric poem Usually a short poetic composition devoted to the expression or exploration of the thoughts and emotion of a poetic speaker (who is often distinct from the poet). The term derives from the Greek word for a stringed instrument (the 'lyre' – similar to a harp), which was used to accompany song and recitation in classical Greece.

Lyricism Poetic qualities, especially aesthetically pleasing arrangement or musicality. (See also **lyric poem**.)

Masque A form of courtly dramatic entertainment popular in the sixteenth and seventeenth centuries and containing music, masks over the face, and dancing. Costumes and stage machinery were elaborate, and members of the audience (which was generally aristocratic) were invited to contribute to the action or dancing.

Medium (pl. media) The means (or channel or material) by which something is communicated. The term is typically used to refer to modern electronic media of radio, television and the internet, but also includes film, telegraph, print and other forms of inscription and transmission. In media studies the plural term also includes those agencies and institutions associated with particular means of transmission.

Metafiction A type of narrative fiction that distances itself from the effect of creating a fictional world within the text (a **text world**), by commenting on the processes involved in creating such a world.

Metalanguage Language used to talk about language itself. Metalanguage includes terms such as 'noun', 'sentence' and 'figurative', and extends into terms that are used to talk about language but also other kinds of presentation or behaviour, such as 'witty' and 'truth-claim'.

Metaphor A figure of speech in which one thing or idea or event is spoken of as if it were another (revealingly similar) thing, idea or event: the two fields are blended together by use of the metaphor.

Metonymy A figure of speech in which one thing or idea or event is referred to as if it were another thing, idea or event with which it is normally associated (e.g. a part of the whole, the effect of cause, etc.). So with the common expression 'the kettle has boiled', we are obliged to interpret 'kettle' metonymically: it is the water in the kettle (i.e. the contained, rather than the container) that boils.

Metre Pattern regulating the length and, to some extent, the rhythm of lines of poetry. Metres are often named in terms of a type of **foot** they are held to consist of and how many of those feet there are; e.g. **iambic pentameter**.

Mimesis The attempted faithful representation of the world and human life in literary texts. (See **realism**.)

Mode of address How a text directs its communication towards, or invokes, its audience, whether directly or indirectly; mode of address includes features such as honorifics (e.g. 'thou'/'you', 'madam'/'sir'), choice of register and markers of politeness. Such features signal attitude towards – or how we wish to relate to – the person or people we are communicating with.

Modernism A literary movement most commonly understood as exemplified by writers – such as James Joyce, Gertrude Stein, T.S. Eliot and Ezra Pound who were writing mainly in the first half of the twentieth century, between the

First and Second World Wars. Modernist writings often foreground major kinds of experimentation with form and language.

Montage In film editing, the juxtaposition of seemingly unrelated shots or scenes that, when combined in sequence, produce a meaning that goes beyond what is contained in the isolated shots themselves, typically because of **inferences** drawn from juxtaposition of the shots. (See **bricolage** and **collage**.)

Motif A recurrent thematic element in a literary or musical text or group of texts.

Narrative A story; an account of a series of events, with implied causal connections, and typically a beginning and some kind of ending.

Narrator The voice that tells a story. Not all narratives have narrators: film and theatre, for instance, depict stories but usually do so without a narrator. Other genres and media, however, depend on narrators. The novel as a genre has been particularly inventive in using different types of narrator, ranging from a character within the story (first-person narrator) to an impersonal, anonymous voice speaking from outside the events depicted (third-person narrator). In both cases it is important not to view the narrator as being too directly connected with the author. (See also **implied author**.)

New Criticism A critical theory and practice promoted by a group of critics who taught in British and American universities from the 1930s onwards. New Criticism promoted the idea that students of literature should focus on close analysis of literary texts, rather than on literary history or authorial biography. The New Critics argued that the goal of literary criticism is to discover, through close analysis, an organic unity between a text's **form** and its **content**. (See also **organic form**.)

Non-realist texts Texts that may draw on some elements of realist style but subvert that style in some way.

Non-self-reflexive language Language that seems to be simply delivering information and does not draw attention to itself as an active expression of ideas, rather than simply as ideas that have somehow been expressed; language that is not literary or poetic in any way.

OED The *Oxford English Dictionary*, which not only gives the definition of words and representations of their pronunciation, but also their etymology, their meanings at various historical moments (with extensive illustrative quotation), and, by means of an associated thesaurus, their connection with other words used in a given period to express broadly the same content or meaning.

Oral literature Forms of poetry, storytelling and drama in a tradition or culture in which the spoken word is the chief form of communication. Works of oral literature are memorized and improvised, and handed down from generation to generation.

Organic form The idea, developed in literary criticism by the poet Samuel Taylor Coleridge but extended and adapted subsequently, that the various parts of a literary work are coordinated into a unified whole like a living organism.

Paradox A statement that goes against received opinion or what is generally believed to be the case; the term is more usually used to indicate an absurd or self-contradictory statement. Paradoxes in literary texts often present profound insights or important and unresolved concerns.

Parallelism Similarity of sound sequence, sentence structure or word meaning between two close or adjacent sections of a text, often highlighted in order to convey similarity or contrast between the meanings of two or more parallel expressions.

Paratextual Term used to describe material that surrounds the main body of a text (such as a specially designed cover; a dedication or acknowledgements; the text's typography and formatting; or footnotes and appendices). Such material is often prepared by people other than the author, including editors, publishers or printers, and is subject to their decision rather than the author's. According to literary theorist Gérard Genette, such additional elements frame the main text and affect how it is interpreted, acting as a textual 'fringe' or zone between the text itself and the reading public.

Parts of speech Types of word, classified on the basis of their function in sentences. Common parts of speech include nouns, verbs, adjectives, adverbs, articles and prepositions. (See also **grammar**.)

Pastiche A literary or artistic composition that imitates a distinctive style from the past or from a contemporary genre. Pastiche sometimes exaggerates or makes fun of a particular style by clearly signalling its element of imitation. Conventions from one genre are typically merged with the subject matter from another in a way that is obviously incongruous.

Pastoral A literary style or genre that portrays rural life or the life of shepherds, especially in an idealized or romantic form. Pastoral writing celebrates country life in depictions of simple rural and idyllic scenes, and tends to have a reflective or nostalgic dimension.

Pathetic fallacy An effect created by ascribing emotions and feelings to inanimate objects and processes in the world (such as the weather), then assuming that those objects and processes share our feelings. The technique is often found in paintings and literary texts, but the Victorian critic John Ruskin saw it as a weakness of those painters and writers in whose work it is found.

Persona An invented character or voice assumed by an author in a novel, poem or other work, in order to convey the impression that the writer is writing as a different person, or as a particular character. The views or values of the persona cannot be straightforwardly taken as those of the author. (See also **implied author**.)

Personification A figure of speech in which a thing or idea or event is spoken of as if it were a human being, or had human characteristics.

Picaresque A characteristic of novels that tell the story of a roguish hero or antihero who lives by his (virtually always his) wits in a corrupt society, as exemplified in English by Henry Fielding's novels *Joseph Andrews* (1742) and *Tom Jones* (1749).

Plot In common usage, the 'plot' of a novel, play or film is any form of summary of what happens in the story. More technically, in the field of narrative theory, 'plot' is distinguished from 'story': while the story consists of the imaginary events in the order in which they supposedly happened, the plot is the way that the story is told and rearranged in order to achieve artistic effects. (See **discourse**.)

Poetic speaker The 'speaker' of a poem, reflecting an assumption that a distinction needs to be drawn between the creator of a poem and its fictional speaker (since the fictional speaker is a poetic device or effect, not an origin in an actual person). (See also **persona**.)

Poetry slam (sometimes **poetry jam**) A type of poetry performance event, originating in US clubs during the 1980s as a variation on 'open mike' sessions, often with a competition format and involving audience participation.

Postmodernism A philosophical and cultural condition or response to cultural conditions thought characteristic of the contemporary period in post-industrial societies. Postmodernism, in one interpretation, is a cultural condition or outlook that comes after the supposed failure of modernity (as characterized by the Enlightenment stress on universal reason and science). According to Jean-François Lyotard, the postmodern condition is shaped by the failure and impossibility of 'grand narratives' – historical narratives of human progress based on transcendental truths such as God, or the human spirit, or economic forces. In the postmodern condition, human experience is taken to consist of an endless recycling of cultural texts via technological systems of communication, with the consequence that authentic personal experience is illusory. Rather than striving to represent authentic experience, postmodern texts play with their own constructedness and inauthenticity by being ironic and self-reflexive.

Prologue A prefatory speech delivered by a **narrator**, **chorus** or character introducing a play, or part of a play. The term is also used to refer to the character who delivers such a prefatory speech. (See **epilogue** and **epigraph**.)

Propositional attitude A proposition is a statement about the world, or about some fictional world; attached to each proposition is an attitude (such as belief or doubt) that expresses the speaker's or writer's relation to that proposition.

Prosodic and paralinguistic systems Features of the sound structure of language that go beyond individual sound segments and concern such features as

intonation, tempo, loudness, **rhythm**, pauses and voice quality. Prosodic and paralinguistic systems create meanings by superimposing additional contrasts onto the flow of sound segments.

Protagonist The chief character or 'hero' in a literary text, especially in a play. The term is also used in the plural (since there may be two or more protagonists).

Reader In a basic and general sense, whoever reads a piece of writing. In literary studies, an 'ideal reader' or **implied reader** is a reader who has the requisite literary competence and **background knowledge** to understand a literary text in the ways anticipated by the form of its composition. (See **resisting reader**.)

Readership Idealized group of anticipated **readers** for a text or group of texts.

Reading The process of interpreting or analysing a written text. When used in literary studies as a count noun ('a reading'), the term refers to the interpretive outcome, or product, of the reading process. A text may yield alternative readings and may be designed to do so. (See also **implied reader**; **ambiguity**.)

Realism A literary style or genre of the novel that attempts to represent the social world as convincingly as possible, especially the world of nineteenth-century Europe. Characters are represented as having inner lives, experiences and motives; and they are placed in detailed social and economic settings, and interact with one another in ways that echo real social interactions. Events and actions are represented as occurring because of psychological, social or natural relations of cause and effect. Central characters are shown as developing through time, as a result of the impact of inner and outer experiences. The narrative technique constructs a **hierarchy of voices** in which the characters' failings and mistakes are mediated for the reader by a reliable and often omniscient narrator. (See **classic realism** and **reality effect**.)

Reality effect The effect created by the conventional devices and strategies adopted in realist novels, namely that we are reading about a real world with real people in it (the novel's characters).

Received Pronunciation Often known as RP, the least regional form of British English pronunciation, traditionally considered the most accepted form. RP emerged during the nineteenth century as a non-regional prestige form, but continues to change, including in social status.

Register In linguistics and literary criticism, a term used to describe how the kind of language we choose is affected by the context or setting in which we use it, so that certain kinds of usage become conventionally associated with particular situations.

Repertoire As regards language use generally, the range of styles a speaker is able to speak or write in, or **accents** he or she habitually uses. In dramatic performance and music, the stock of pieces that a performer, group or company is able to perform.

Representation The act of making something present to an audience or reader through description, portrayal, symbolization or some other form of embodiment or enactment.

Resisting reader A reader who resists the representation or interpretation of the world that a text appears to present, or who challenges a dominant reading of a text in order to present an alternative reading that exposes previously unnoticed, and perhaps problematic, features of the text.

Rhetoric The study or use of the art of persuasion; a way of using language in order to persuade. Politicians, advertisers and many others use rhetoric as a matter of course; but literature also uses rhetoric in equivalent and related ways. Literature may also depict the use of rhetoric, as in Mark Antony's well-known speech in Shakespeare's *Julius Caesar* which begins 'Friends, Romans, countrymen, lend me your ears' (III, ii, 73–107).

Rhyme scheme A pattern of line-final rhymes in verse, such as AxAx to indicate that the first and third lines of a passage of your stanza rhyme but that the second and fourth do not, or ABABCC to indicate that the first and third, second and fourth, and fifth and sixth lines rhyme.

Rhythm A regular pattern of relatively strongly and relatively weakly stressed syllables in speech or oral performance of a literary text.

Role doubling The practice of using one actor to play two or more parts in a drama.

Romantic irony An effect created by a mode of writing that gives the impression of representing reality but then shatters that illusion by foregrounding the fact that the author or narrator is an artist who creates this illusion by manipulating conventional techniques and devices. The author–narrator commonly addresses the reader directly, foregrounding the process of creation and even inviting the reader to participate in that process. Pioneering texts in English are Laurence Sterne's *Tristram Shandy* (1759–67) and Byron's *Don Juan* (1819–24). (See **irony**.)

Schema A structured set of assumptions about how things are done (e.g. laying the table, telling a story). Schemas are largely unconscious but nevertheless order our expectations and guide **inferences** we draw as we interpret situations, events and texts. In jokes, literary composition and some kinds of behaviour, schemas are disrupted in order to draw attention to and possibly criticize them, or to create absurdity and humour.

Semantic field A general area of meaning characterized by two or more words that denote some common area of experience or thought. For example, 'uncle, aunt, cousin, son, daughter' belong to the semantic field of 'kinship'; 'rain, drizzle, hail, snow, sleet' belong to the semantic field of 'precipitation'.

Shot The minimal unit in film analysis consisting before digital technologies of a continuous strip of motion picture film, and made up of a series of frames that runs for an uninterrupted period of time. Shots may be classified by closeness to the subject: close, medium or long. When a human figure is involved, a close shot will show head and shoulders, a medium shot will frame the figure from the waist upwards, and a long shot will place the whole figure against a background.

Signified In the linguistic theory of Ferdinand de Saussure, the mental image or concept associated with a **signifier** to make a linguistic sign. The mental image of a 'tree', however, as signified by the word 'tree', is not to be confused with a real tree in the world (which would be the referent of some given use of the word 'tree').

Signifier In Saussure's linguistics, a 'sound image' associated with a mental image or **signified** to form a linguistic sign.

Simile A figure of speech in which one thing or idea or event is said to resemble, or be similar to or be like, another thing, idea or event; an explicit verbal comparison.

Situational irony A **plot** device whose main feature is that the audience/reader knows more than the characters who are victims of the irony. The effect of the irony is produced when the characters speak or act in a way that is contrary to how they would if they knew what the audience/reader knows. The ironic situation may either be comic or tragic, depending on the circumstances, the outcome and our feelings towards the characters. (See also **irony**, **dramatic irony**, **structural irony**.)

Soliloquy A speech delivered by a character in a drama who is usually alone onstage and who speaks to him- or herself and/or to the audience.

Sonnet A kind of **lyric poem** of fourteen lines that conforms to a specific pattern of rhyme and metre. Typical **rhyme schemes** for the sonnet are ABBA ABBA CDE CDE (known as Italian or Petrarchan) and ABAB CDCD EFEF GG (known as English or Shakespearean). Sometimes there is variation from these two patterns. The change indicated in the rhyme scheme at the end of line eight or line twelve is called the volta, and is sometimes accompanied by a change of direction in the poem's tone or argument. The rhythm is typically **iambic pentameter**.

Sound symbolism An effect created when the sounds of words (as distinguished from their definitions) are felt to have conventional meanings or effects (e.g. of gentleness, hardness, etc.). Such meanings or effects are mostly associated with specific word sounds either by convention (because of previous use) or because of context in the text.

Speech event A speech act examined in its social setting. Beyond the form of the utterance itself, we can specify what kind of speaker is making the utterance, who to, when, where and for what purpose.

Speech situation A text's speech situation may be worked out by asking 'who is speaking to whom?' The speech situation identified in this way characteristically differs between genres. In drama, characters speak to one another or, in soliloquy, to themselves and/or the audience. In **narrative**, characters speak to each other, but their speech is reported by a **narrator** (who addresses an **implied reader**). In **lyric** poetry, a poet or poetic speaker speaks to him- or herself or to a silent or absent person (or even an animal or object) who is part of a fictional situation represented in the poem. Working out the speech situation is often the key to understanding a **lyric poem**.

Standardized Oral Form A term used in anthropology to describe stories and lyrics presented in memorized and extensively improvised spoken performances, especially in societies where writing does not exist and so cannot be used to produce a script or text. (See also **oral literature**.)

Structuralism A cluster of literary and cultural insights associated with intellectual work in France during the 1950s and 1960s, often based on Ferdinand de Saussure's linguistics. Individual literary texts were considered to be made possible and meaningful by a pre-existing literary system consisting of conventional techniques and devices, such as conventions of **genre** and the wider symbolic codes of a culture. The goal of **reading** was taken to be not so much to interpret an individual text as to study the underlying literary system on which any individual text depends.

Structural irony An ironic effect produced when a speaker or character says something sincerely but which is made ironic by the situation, usually because he or she lacks a vital piece of knowledge (available to the reader or audience) that would allow him or her to realize that what is said is not a true view of the situation. The gap between what is said and what is the case creates a structure in which the reader or audience sees the irony, while the character or speaker does not. (See also **situational irony** and **dramatic irony**.)

Style In literary studies, the distinctive patterning of language associated with an **author**, movement or period amounting to a 'verbal fingerprint' or 'verbal trademark'.

Stylistics A branch of linguistics devoted to the study of **style**. The term is also used to describe the overall class of techniques used in analysing how language achieves its expressive purposes (mainly in literary works, but also in adverts, jokes and other verbal forms).

Surrealism As typified in visual arts by the work of Salvador Dali and René Magritte, surrealism strips ordinary objects of their usual significance by juxtaposing them in startling ways to create a new image that cuts across ordinary formal organization and assumptions. Surrealist work often has a dreamlike quality and is sometimes seen as an attack on conventional notions of reality.

Syllable In speech, the group of sounds around a single salient sound such as a vowel or diphthong. The most salient sound is called the nucleus; the sounds before the nucleus are the onset, and the sounds after the nucleus are the coda.

Synecdoche A figure of speech in which one thing or idea or event is spoken of by referring to a part of that thing, idea or event (e.g. using the expression 'many feet have passed this way' to mean that many people, rather than just their feet, have travelled in a certain direction).

Tense A grammatical distinction in linguistics used to indicate the potential of verb forms to signal the relative time (past, present or future) of an action (e.g. 'she *smiles*' versus 'she *smiled*').

Tragedy A literary or dramatic genre that represents actions that typically result in the death of the main **protagonist** or protagonists. From Classical Greece up to the eighteenth century, the tragic protagonist was normally a man (sometimes a woman) of high birth in a situation of conflict (with him- or herself, with society, or with God or the gods). The outcome of the tragedy was the protagonist's fall and had serious consequences for the state. From roughly the eighteenth century onwards, more bourgeois or domestic tragedies emerged that focused on the tragic fate of middle-class characters. Since the mid-twentieth century, plays such as Arthur Miller's *The Death of a Salesman* (1949) have explored tragic possibilities in characters drawn from 'ordinary' life.

Transitivity An aspect of the grammatical analysis of sentences concerned with identifying who does what to whom, who acts, and who is acted upon by whom. Analysis of choices about how to represent an event can also be extended throughout a text, so that generalizations can be made about, for example, literary characters or about the representation of political actors in newspapers.

Verb As traditionally understood, the part of speech that encodes action or predication; instances are italicized in the following example: 'She *was* happy. She *smiled*. Then she *turned* and *left*.' A verb can be modified to encode time (i.e. it can carry **tense**).

Verbal irony An effect created by use of language in which we do not mean what we say literally; instead we imply an attitude of disbelief towards the content of our utterance or writing. (See also **irony**; **situational irony**; **dramatic irony**.)

Verse A form of text divided into lines that have one or more of the following features: (1) there is a pause, or major syntactic break at the end of the line; (2) the line is structurally parallel to an adjacent line; (3) the line is of a certain length, counting **syllables** or stressed syllables (in which case it is a metrical line); and (4) when printed on the page, the line does not reach from one side of the page to the other and may be followed by blank space. (See also **rhyme scheme**; **rhythm**; **accent**.)

References

Abrams, M.H. (2011) *A Glossary of Literary Terms*, 10th edn, New York and London: Harcourt Brace Jovanovich.

Aitchison, J. (2004) *Teach Yourself Linguistics*, 6th edn, Teach Yourself Series, London: Hodder.

Aitchison, J. (2007) *The Word Weavers: Newshounds and Wordsmiths*, Cambridge: Cambridge University Press.

Allen, G. (2011) *Intertextuality: The New Critical Idiom*, 2nd edn, London: Routledge.

Aristotle (1965) *On the Art of Poetry*, in T.S. Dorsh (ed.) *Aristotle, Horace, Longinus: Classical Literary Criticism*, Harmondsworth: Penguin.

Attridge, D. (1996) *Poetic Rhythm: An Introduction*, Cambridge: Cambridge University Press.

Attridge, D. (2004) *The Rhythms of English Poetry*, London: Longman.

Auerbach, E. (1953) *Mimesis: The Representation of Reality in Western Literature*, Princeton, NJ: Princeton University Press.

Bakhtin, M. (1981) 'Discourse in the Novel', trans. C. Emerson and M. Holquist, in V.B. Leitch (ed.) (2010) *The Norton Anthology of Theory and Criticism*, 2nd edn, London and New York: Norton, pp. 1190–220.

Bal, M. (2009) *Narratology: Introduction to the Theory of Narrative*, 3rd edn, Toronto: Toronto University Press.

Barber, C. (1997) *Early Modern English*, 2nd edn, London: André Deutsch.

Barthes, R. (1968) 'The Death of the Author', in V.B. Leitch (ed.) (2010) *The Norton Anthology of Theory and Criticism*, 2nd edn, New York and London: Norton, pp. 1466–70.

Barthes, R. (1971) 'From Work to Text', in Vincent B. Leitch (ed.) (2001) *The Norton Anthology of Theory and Criticism*, 2nd edn, New York and London: Norton, pp. 1470–5.

Barthes, R. (1989) *The Rustle of Language*, Oxford: Blackwell.

Bate, J. (1999) *The Burden of the Past and the English Poet*, London: Chatto & Windus.

Bergvall, V., Bing, J. and Freed, A. (eds) (1996) *Rethinking Language and Gender Research: Theory and Practice*, London: Longman.

Berlin, A. (2008) *Dynamics of Biblical Parallelism*, Grand Rapids, MI: Eerdmans Publishing.

Biber, D. and Conrad, S. (2009) *Register, Genre, and Style*, Cambridge: Cambridge University Press.

Biber, D., Conrad S. and Reppen, R. (1998) *Corpus Linguistics: Investigating Language Structure and Use*, Cambridge: Cambridge University Press.

Bloom, H. (1997) *The Anxiety of Influence*, 2nd edn, Oxford: Oxford University Press.

Booth, W. (1975) *A Rhetoric of Irony*, Chicago: University of Chicago Press.

Branigan, E. (1985) *Point of View in the Cinema*, New York: Mouton.

Brecht, B. (1977) 'Against Georg Lukács', in T. Adorno, W. Benjamin, E. Bloch, B. Brecht and G. Lukács (eds) *Aesthetics and Politics*, London: New Left Books, pp. 68–85.

Briggs, A. and Burke, P. (2010) *A Social History of the Media*, 3rd edn, Cambridge: Polity.

Briggs, K. (1970) *A Dictionary of British Folk Tales in the English Language*, London: Routledge.

Burgin, V. (1976) 'Art, Common Sense and Photography', in S. Hall and J. Evans (eds) (1999) *Visual Culture: The Reader*, London: Sage/Open University, pp. 41–50.

Burke, S. (ed.) (2008) *Authorship: From Plato to the Postmodern: A Reader*, Edinburgh: Edinburgh University Press.

Burke, S. (2010) *The Death and Return of the Author: Criticism and Subjectivity in Barthes, Foucault and Derrida*, 3rd edn, Edinburgh: Edinburgh University Press.

Burton, D. (1980) *Dialogue and Discourse: A Socio-linguistic Approach to Modern Drama Dialogue and Naturally Occurring Conversation*, London: Routledge and Kegan Paul.

Burton, D. (1988) 'Through Glass Darkly: Through Dark Glasses', in R. Carter (ed.) *Language and Literature: An Introductory Reader in Stylistics*, London: George Allen & Unwin, pp. 195–214.

Cameron, D. (1992) *Feminism and Linguistic Theory*, 2nd edn, London: Macmillan.

Cameron, D. (ed.) (1998) *The Feminist Critique of Language: A Reader*, 2nd edn, London: Routledge.

Carper, T. and Attridge, D. (2003) *Meter and Meaning: An Introduction to Rhythm in Poetry*, London: Routledge.

Caughie, J. (ed.) (1981) *Theories of Authorship: A Reader*, London: Routledge & Kegan Paul and the British Film Institute.

Colebrook, C. (2003) *Irony: The New Critical Idiom*, London: Routledge.

Coward, R. (1986) 'This Novel Changes Lives: Are Women's Novels Feminist Novels?' in M. Eagleton (ed.) *Feminist Literary Theory: A Reader*, Oxford, Blackwell pp. 155–60.

Coward, R. and Black, M. (1990) 'Linguistic, Social and Sexual Relations: A Review of Dale Spender's *Man Made Language*', reprinted in D. Cameron (ed.) *The Feminist Critique of Language*, London, Routledge, pp. 111–33.

Croft, W. and Cruse, D. (2004) *Cognitive Linguistics*, Cambridge: Cambridge University Press.

Crowther, B. and Leith, D. (1995) 'Feminism, Language and the Rhetoric of Television Wildlife Programmes', in S. Mills (ed.) *Language and Gender: Interdisciplinary Perspectives*, London: Longman, pp. 207–26.

Crystal, D. (2006a) *The Stories of English*, Harmondsworth: Penguin.

Crystal, D. (2006b) *Language and the Internet*, 2nd edn, Cambridge: Cambridge University Press.

Culler, J. (2002) *Structuralist Poetics: Structuralism, Linguistics and the Study of Literature*, 2nd edn, London: Routledge.

Culpeper, J. (2005) *History of English* (Language Workbooks), 2nd edn, London: Routledge.

Duff, D. (ed.) (2000) *Modern Genre Theory*, London: Longman.

Dunant, S. (1994) *The War of the Words: The Political Correctness Debate*, London: Virago.

Durant, A. and Lambrou, M. (2009) *Language and Media: A Resource Book for Students*, London: Routledge.

Eisenstein, S. (1979a) 'The Cinematographic Principle and the Ideogram', in G. Mast and M. Cohen (eds) *Film Theory and Criticism*, Oxford: Oxford University Press, pp. 85–100.

Eisenstein, S. (1979b) 'A Dialectic Approach to Film Form', in G. Mast and M. Cohen (eds) *Film Theory and Criticism*, Oxford: Oxford University Press, pp. 101–22.

Eliot, T.S. (1919) 'Tradition and the Individual Talent', in V.B. Leitch (ed.) (2010) *The Norton Anthology of Theory and Criticism*, 2nd edn, New York and London: Norton, pp. 13–22.

Emmott, C. (1999) *Narrative Comprehension: A Discourse Perspective*, Oxford: Oxford University Press.

Erlich, V. (1981) *Russian Formalism: History – Doctrine*, 3rd edn, The Hague: Mouton.

Fabb, N. (1997) *Linguistics and Literature: Language in the Verbal Arts of the World*, Oxford: Blackwell.

Fabb, N. (2002) *Language and Literary Structure*, Cambridge: Cambridge University Press.

Fabb, N. (2005) *Sentence Structure*, 2nd edn, London: Routledge.

Fabb, N. and Durant, A. (2005) *How to Write Essays and Dissertations: A Guide for English Literature Students*, 2nd edn, Harlow: Pearson.

Fabb, N. and Halle, M. (2008) *The Meter of a Poem: A New Theory*, Cambridge: Cambridge University Press.

Fairclough, N. (1992) *Discourse and Social Change*, London: Polity Press.

Fauconnier, G. and Turner, M. (2003) *The Way We Think: Conceptual Blending and the Mind's Hidden Complexities*, New York: Basic Books.

Feather, J. (1988) *A History of British Publishing*, London: Routledge.

Fetterley, J. (1981) *The Resisting Reader: A Feminist Approach to American Fiction*, Bloomington, IN: Indiana University Press.

Finnegan, R. (1992) *Oral Traditions and the Verbal Arts: A Guide to Research Practices*, London: Routledge.

Finnegan, R. (2002) *Communicating: The Multiple Modes of Human Interconnection*, London: Routledge.

Fludernik, M. (1993) *The Fictions of Language and the Languages of Fiction: Linguistic Representation of Speech and Consciousness*, London: Routledge.

Foucault, M. (1978) *The History of Sexuality*, vol. 1, Harmondsworth: Penguin.

Fowler, R. (1996) *Linguistic Criticism*, 2nd edn, Oxford: Oxford University Press.

Fox, J. (ed.) (1988) *To Speak in Pairs: Essays on the Ritual Languages of Eastern Indonesia*, Cambridge: Cambridge University Press.

Frye, N. (2007) *Anatomy of Criticism*, Princeton, NJ: Princeton University Press.

Fuller, J. (1979) *The Sonnet*. Critical Idiom Series, 2nd edn. London: Routledge.

Furniss, T. and Bath, M. (2007) R*eading Poetry: An Introduction*, 2nd edn, London: Pearson Longman.

Furst, L. (1984) *Fictions of Romantic Irony in European Narrative, 1760–1857*, London: Macmillan.

Fussell, P. (1979) *Poetic Meter and Poetic Form*, New York: McGraw-Hill.

Gavins, J. (2007) *Text World Theory: An Introduction*, Edinburgh: Edinburgh University Press.

Garvin, P. (ed. and trans.) (1964) *A Prague School Reader in Aesthetics, Literary Structure and Style*, Washington, DC: Georgetown University Press.

Genette, G. (1980) *Narrative Discourse: An Essay in Method*, tr. J. Lewin, Ithaca, NY: Cornell University Press.

Gibbs, R. (1999) *Intentions in the Experience of Meaning*, Cambridge: Cambridge University Press.

Gifford, T. (1999) *The Pastoral*, New Critical Idiom Series, London: Routledge.

Gilbert, S. and Gubar, S. (2000) *The Madwoman in the Attic*, 2nd edn, New Haven, CT: Yale University Press.

Glucksberg, S. (with M. McGlone) (2001) *Understanding Figurative Language: From Metaphors to Idioms*, Oxford: Oxford University Press.

Hall, S. (1980) 'Encoding/Decoding', in S. Hall, D. Hobson, A. Lowe and P. Willis (eds) *Culture, Media, Language: Working Papers in Cultural Studies*, 1972–79, London: Hutchinson, pp. 128–39.

Halliday, M.A.K. (1978) *Language as Social Semiotic: The Social Interpretation of Language and Meaning*, London: Arnold.

Halliday, M.A.K. and Hasan, R. (1976) *Cohesion in English*, London: Longman.

Harner, J. (2008) *Literary Research Guide: An Annotated Listing of Reference Sources in English Literary Studies*, 5th edn, New York: MLA Publications.

Hobby, E. and White, C. (eds) (1991) *What Lesbians Do in Books*, London: Women's Press.

Holmes, J. and Meyerhoff, M. (eds) (2005) *Handbook of Language and Gender*, Oxford: Blackwell.

Hutchinson, P. (1983) *Games Authors Play*, London: Methuen.

Irwin, W. (ed.) (2002) *The Death and Resurrection of the Author?*, Westwood, CT and London: Greenwood Press.

Jakobson, R. (1990) 'Linguistics and Poetics', in K. Pomorska and S. Rudy (eds) *Language in Literature*, Cambridge, MA: Harvard University Press, pp. 62–94.

James, H. (1934, 2011) *The Art of the Novel*, Chicago: University of Chicago Press.

Jeffries, L. (2009) *Critical Stylistics: The Power of English*, Basingstoke: Palgrave Macmillan.

Jeffries, L. and McIntyre, D. (2010) *Stylistics*, Cambridge: Cambridge University Press.

Kaplan, C. (1986) 'Keeping the Colour in *The Color Purple*', in C. Kaplan (ed.) *Sea Changes: Culture and Feminism*, London: Verso, pp. 176–87.

Kidd, V. (1971) 'A Study of the Images Produced through the Use of the Male Pronoun as Generic', *Moments in Contemporary Rhetoric and Communication* 1: 25–30.

Kirkham, S. (1990) *How to Find Information in the Humanities*, London: Library Association.

Kövecses, Z. (2010) *Metaphor: A Practical Introduction*, 2nd edn, Oxford: Oxford University Press.

Lakoff, G. and Johnson, M. (2003) *Metaphors We Live By*, 2nd edn, Chicago: University of Chicago Press.

Lambrou, M. and Stockwell, P. (eds) (2007) *Contemporary Stylistics*, London: Continuum.

Laws, S. (1990) *Issues of Blood: the Politics of Menstruation*, Basingstoke: Macmillan.

Leech, G. (1973) *A Linguistic Guide to English Poetry*, London: Longman.

Leech, G. and Short, M. (2007) *Style in Fiction: A Linguistic Introduction to English Fictional Prose*, 2nd edn, London: Longman.

Leitch, V. (ed.) (2010) *The Norton Anthology of Theory and Criticism*, New York and London: Norton. (Contains a number of essays on authorship, including the essays by Barthes, Eliot, Foucault, and Wimsatt and Beardsley mentioned in this unit.)

Leith, D. (1983) *A Social History of English*, London: Routledge.

Leith, D. (1997) *A Social History of English*, 2nd edn, London: Routledge & Kegan Paul.

Lemon, L. and Reis, M. (eds) (1965) *Russian Formalist Criticism: Four Essays*, Lincoln, NE: University of Nebraska Press.

Lennard, J. and Luckhurst, M. (2002) *The Drama Handbook: A Guide to Reading Plays*, Oxford: Oxford University Press.

Lodge, D. (1989) *The Modes of Modern Writing*, London: Edward Arnold.

Lodge, D. (1994) *The Art of Fiction*, Harmondsworth: Penguin.

Lukács, G. (1962) *The Historical Novel*, London: Merlin.

McIntyre, D. (2006) *Point of View in Plays: A Cognitive Stylistic Approach to Viewpoint in Drama and Other Text Types*, Amsterdam: John Benjamins.

Martin, E. (1997) 'The Egg and the Sperm: How Science has Constructed a Romance Based on Stereotypical Male–Female Roles', in L. Lamphere, H. Ragone and P. Zavella (eds) *Situated Lives: Gender and Culture in Everyday Life*, London: Routledge, pp. 85–99.

Maynard, J. (2009) *Literary Intention, Literary Interpretation*, Peterborough, Ontario: Broadview.

Miller, C. and Swift, K. (1979) *Words and Women*, Harmondsworth, Penguin.

Mills, J. (1991) *Womanwords: a Vocabulary of Culture and Patriarchal Society*, London: Virago.

Mills, S. (ed.) (1994) *Gendering the Reader*, Hemel Hempstead: Harvester Wheatsheaf.

Mills, S. (1996) *Feminist Stylistics*, London: Routledge.

Mills, S. (2008) *Language and* Sexism, Cambridge: Cambridge University Press.

Mills, S. and Pearce, L. (1996) *Feminist Readings/Feminists Reading*, 2nd edn, Hemel Hempstead: Harvester.

Montgomery, M. (2008) *An Introduction to Language and Society*, 3rd edn, London: Routledge.

Muecke, D. (1983) *Irony and the Ironic*, London: Methuen.

Mulvey, L. (1981) 'Visual Pleasure and Narrative Cinema', in T. Bennett, S. Boyd-Bowman, C. Mercer and J. Woollacott (eds), *Popular Television and Film*, London: Open University/BFI, pp. 206–16.

Murray, J. (1998) *Hamlet on the Holodeck: The Future of Narrative in Cyberspace*, Cambridge, MA: MIT Press.

Newton-de Molina, D. (ed.) (1976) *On Literary Intention*, Edinburgh: Edinburgh University Press.

O'Keeffe, A, and McCarthy, M. (2010) *The Routledge Handbook of Corpus Linguistics*, Abingdon: Routledge.

Onega J. and Garcia Landa, J. (eds) (1996) *Narratology: An Introduction*, London: Longman.

Ong, W. (2002) *Orality and Literacy: The Technologizing of the Word*, London: Routledge.

Orr, M. (2003) *Intertextuality: Debates and Contexts*, Cambridge: Polity Press.

Pauwels, A. (1998) *Women Changing Language*, London: Longman.

Pickering, K. (2003) *Studying Modern Drama*, London: Palgrave Macmillan.

Preminger, A. and Brogan, T. (eds) (1993) *The New Princeton Encyclopedia of Poetry and Poetics*, Princeton, NJ: Princeton University Press.

Propp, V. (1968) *Morphology of the Folktale*, Austin, TX: University of Texas Press.

Renza, L. (1995) 'Influence', in F. Lentricchia and T. McLaughlin (eds) *Critical Terms for Literary Study*, Chicago: Chicago University Press, pp. 186–202.

Richards, I.A. (1965) *Philosophy of Rhetoric*, Oxford: Oxford University Press.

Rimmon-Kenan, S. (2002) *Narrative Fiction: Contemporary Poetics*, 2nd edn, London: Routledge.

Rivers, I. (1994) *Classical and Christian Ideas in English Renaissance Poetry: A Student's Guide*, 2nd edn, London: Routledge.

St John Butler, L. (1999) *Registering the Difference: Reading Literature through Register*, Manchester: Manchester University Press.

Said, E. (2007) *Culture and Imperialism*, New York: Vintage.

Semino, E. (1999) *Language and World Creation in Poems and Other Texts*, London: Longman.

Semino, E. (2008) *Metaphor in Discourse*, Cambridge: Cambridge University Press.

Semino, E. and Culpeper, J. (2002) *Cognitive Stylistics: Language and Cognition in Text Analysis*, Amsterdam: John Benjamins.

Semino, E. and Short, M. (2004) *Corpus Stylistics: Speech, Writing and Thought Presentation in a Corpus of English Writing*, London: Routledge.

Shklovsky, V. (1917) 'Art as Technique', in D. Lodge (ed.) (1999) *Modern Criticism and Theory: A Reader*, 2nd edn, London: Longman, pp. 16–30.

Shohat, E. and Stam, R. (1994) *Unthinking Eurocentrism: Multiculturalism and the Media*, London: Routledge

Showalter, E. (1982) *A Literature of Their Own: British Women Novelists from Bronte to Lessing*, revised edn, London: Virago Press.

Simpson, P. (1993) *Language, Ideology and Point of View*, London: Routledge.

Simpson, P. (1997) *Language through Literature: An Introduction*, London: Routledge.

Simpson, P. (2003) *On the Discourse of Satire: Towards a Stylistic Model of Satirical Humour*, Amsterdam: John Benjamins.

Spender, D. (1998) *Man Made Language*, 4th edn, London, Routledge and Kegan Paul.

Spiller, M. (1992) *The Development of the Sonnet: An Introduction*, London: Routledge.

Stacey, J. (1994) *Star Gazing: Hollywood Cinema and Female Spectatorship*, London: Routledge.

Tannen D. (1991) *You Just Don't Understand: Women and Men in Conversation*, London: Virago.

Toolan, M. (2001) *Narrative: A Critical Linguistic Introduction*, 2nd edn, London: Routledge.

Van Zoonan, L. (1994) *Feminist Media Studies*, London: Sage.

Voloshinov, V. (1973) *Marxism and the Philosophy of Language*, New York: Seminar Press.

Wallis, M. and Shepherd, S. (2010) *Studying Plays*, 3rd edn, London: Arnold; New York: Oxford University Press.

Watt, I. (2010) *The Rise of the Novel*, revised edn, Harmondsworth: Penguin.

Widdowson, H. (1992) *Practical Stylistics: An Approach to Poetry*, Oxford: Oxford University Press.

Williams, R. (1983) *Keywords: A Vocabulary of Culture and Society*, 2nd edn, London: Fontana.

Williams, R. (1985) *The Country and the City*, London: The Hogarth Press.

Williams, R. (2006) *Modern Tragedy*, 2nd edn, London: Chatto & Windus.

Wimsatt, W. and Beardsley, M. (1946) 'The Intentional Fallacy', in D. Lodge (ed.) (2008) *20th Century Criticism*, 3rd edn, Harlow: Longman, pp. 334–44.

Wimsatt, W. and Beardsley, M. (1949) 'The Affective Fallacy', in D. Lodge (ed.) (2008) *20th Century Criticism*, 3rd edn, Harlow: Longman, pp. 345–58.

Worthen, W. (2000) *The Harcourt Brace Anthology of Drama*, 3rd edn, Boston, MA: Heinle.

Subject index

Italic entries indicate a cross-reference to indexed names and texts discussed.
Bold numbers indicate entry in Glossary.

Index of names and texts discussed